WAITING ON THE BOUNTY

WAITING ON THE

Bounty

THE DUST BOWL DIARY OF

Mary Knackstedt Dyck

EDITED BY PAMELA RINEY-KEHRBERG

UNIVERSITY OF IOWA PRESS

ᴪ IOWA CITY

University of Iowa Press, Iowa City 52242

Printed in the United States of America

Design by Richard Hendel

http://www.uiowa.edu/~uipress

Printed on acid-free paper

Library of Congress Cataloging-in-Publication Data

Dyck, Mary Knackstedt.

Waiting on the bounty: the Dust Bowl diary of Mary
Knackstedt Dyck/edited by Pamela Riney-Kehrberg.

p.   cm.

Includes bibliographical references and index.

ISBN 0-87745-694-1

1. Dyck, Mary Knackstedt Diaries.   2. Women farmers—
Kansas—Hamilton County Diaries.   3. Farmers—
Kansas—Hamilton County Diaries.   4. German American
women—Kansas—Hamilton County Diaries.   5. Dust
storms—Kansas—Hamilton County—History—20th
century.   6. Droughts—Kansas—Hamilton County—
History—20th century.   7. Farm life—Kansas—Hamilton
County—History—20th century.   8. Hamilton County
(Kan.) Biography.   I. Riney-Kehrberg, Pamela.   II. Title.

F687.H3   D93   1999

978.1'415032'092—DC21   99-29217

[B]

99   00   01   02   03   C   5   4   3   2   1

To those who write diaries,

and those who care enough

to preserve their pages

CONTENTS

ACKNOWLEDGMENTS

Editing Mary Dyck's diary has been a labor of love, but a labor nonetheless, and one that could not have been completed without the support and encouragement of a number of people. First and foremost, I wish to thank Mrs. Thelma Dyck Warner and Mrs. Verna Dyck Gragg, who preserved their mother's diary, and so generously allowed me access to it. To them I am profoundly grateful.

A number of other individuals have lent their support to the labor involved in the diary's publication. The following student assistants at Illinois State University gave their time and effort to photocopying and transcription: Lori Mizzuno, Tari Doehring, Gretchen Peters, and Kristine Cooley. I particularly wish to thank Sharon Foiles in the History Department office at Illinois State. Without her tremendous skills, the task of transcription would never have been completed.

Cynthia Miller, former editor-in-chief at the University Press of Kansas, encouraged me first to think about publishing Mary Dyck's journal; Holly Carver, of the University of Iowa Press, saw it to completion. A number of other individuals and groups have encouraged me to seek the publication of this diary: the members of the summer 1993 National Historic Publications and Records Commission historical editing workshop; the wonderfully supportive members of the Rural Women's Studies Association; the rural network of the Social Science History Association; and my many friends and valued colleagues in the History Department at Illinois State University. University Research Grants from Illinois State University made much of my work financially possible.

Portions of the introduction and conclusion have been published previously. I wish to acknowledge the University Press of Kansas, Indiana University Press, *Frontiers: A Journal of Women's Studies*, and *Agricultural History* for allowing me to make use of this material. Full citations for these publications appear in the bibliography.

As always, it has been friends and family who have provided the moral support that I needed to complete this task: the ISU women (you know who you are) who have gathered each month for many semesters to commiserate over lunch or a happy hour; my dear friend, Roberta Trites; and my parents, Norm and Mary Riney, and brother, Scott Riney. But most of all, I thank my husband, friend, and companion, Richard Kehrberg, who continues to believe in me.

I first became acquainted with Mary Knackstedt Dyck's diary in the spring of 1989, when I interviewed her elder daughter, Thelma Warner, of Syracuse, Kansas. I was working on my doctoral dissertation and listening to the oral histories of dozens of residents of southwestern Kansas, asking them about their experiences during the dust bowl era. I also would ask my subject if he or she had saved any materials from that era that might be useful to me, such as letters, photographs, and diaries. At the end of my interview with Thelma Warner, she turned to me and said, "You know, I have my mother's diary." She walked into her living room, pulled out a large potato chip tin, and opened it. Inside were hundreds of pages of lined notebook paper, covered with faded entries, written in pencil. At the conclusion of my visit, Mrs. Warner loaned me several large chunks of the diary dating to the 1930s. It was a very generous act that greatly improved the quality of the dissertation and subsequent book, *Rooted in Dust: Surviving Drought and Depression in Southwestern Kansas*.

When I returned the diary to Mrs. Warner, she commented, "You know, there's more of this." That revelation led to a trip to the basement and a chance to view the more than 3,000 pages of manuscript stored there. I expressed an interest in working with the materials at a later date, once the dissertation was complete. In 1991, on one of my first days on the job as a newly minted Ph.D. and assistant professor, I found a box on my shelf in the office, filled to the brim with Mary Dyck's diary, an enormous manuscript that covered the years from 1936 to 1955. I was to photocopy and return it to its owners, Thelma Warner and her sister, Verna Gragg. Thus began the long process that led to the transcription, editing, and annotation of the dust bowl years of the diary, from October 1936 to May 1941.

Those of you who are familiar with my previous work will be more closely acquainted with the name Martha Schmidt Friesen. This was a pseudonym for Mary Knackstedt Dyck used in a number of previous publications. In the summer of 1997, Mary Dyck's daughters graciously agreed to let me use their mother's real name in further publications based on her diary. The manuscript diary remains in private hands, the property of Thelma Dyck Warner and Verna Dyck Gragg.

I was drawn to the document for a number of reasons. The first is its rarity. In the years that I have researched dust bowl Kansas, I have never found anything quite like it. Manuscript diaries from this era and region are extremely rare, and those written by farm women with minimal educations are even more so. The only similar document I encountered was the transcribed diary of Iman C. Wiatt, which appears in edited form in the *History of Kearny County, Kansas*. Wiatt's diary covered many of the same years and issues, but from the perspective of a male who spent his time in the fields rather than the farmhouse. The same may be said of Lawrence Svobida's 1940 autobiography, *Farming the Dust Bowl*, which describes his short-lived and poorly timed career as a farmer in Meade County, Kansas. While his is an excellent account, Svobida had very little to say about the impact of this disastrous decade on those trying to preserve their homes and family lives. Mary Dyck's diary allows the reader a rare glimpse into life inside the farm home in a time of tremendous environmental and economic stress.

The diary is also remarkable because of the many things that teaches those of us who are too young to remember the Great Depression or life before electricity, the telephone, and indoor toilets. It takes the reader to a time before television, when radio was an enormously important link between isolated farmsteads and the world at large. It reminds us that even in the years immediately before World War II, many remote farm families did not have telephone service; calling actually meant visiting one's friends and neighbors. It introduces modern readers to an era when it was possible to put in long hours cooking three meals from scratch, cleaning a house without the benefit of electricity, and tending to chickens and cows and still believe that one was "playing hookie," or simply attending to one's "daily routeen." Mary Dyck's was a world where the working day started early, and staying in bed until 5:00 A.M. on a summer morning might be considered sleeping "later than usual." Her diary reminds us of the degree to which many modern Americans take good health for granted in an era of antibiotics and sophisticated medical technology. She suffered from numerous ills that proved impervious, in most cases, to both diagnosis and medical treatment. Mary Dyck lived life at a different pace and with a different set of limitations than her modern readers.

Although recognizable from more than half a century away, her world is not, in many ways, our world. Because of the limits of technology and the great distance she lived from a town of any size, Mary Dyck could choose to be quite insulated from the major political and diplomatic events of the time. Although these were turbulent years, the New Deal and the Second World War existed for Mary Dyck only at a very great distance and only to the degree that they had a direct impact on herself and her community. Mary Dyck's life was most importantly defined by family, home, and farm.

I think of this diary as a companion piece to *Rooted in Dust*. It is the story of those who remained in southwestern Kansas through the dust bowl, told from the perspective of one middle-aged farming woman who defined herself as a wife and a mother. In many ways, Mary Dyck and her husband, Henry, were typical of the many moderately prosperous, mature farm couples who rode out hard times on their dusty, windswept acres. They marshaled their resources, drew upon their strengths, and brought their agricultural enterprises into the relative prosperity of the 1940s. Their biggest sorrow was not losing their farm but dealing with the separations forced on them by hard times. They might be rooted firmly in southwestern Kansas, but friends and family would travel as far south as Arizona and as far west as California and Oregon searching for jobs and hope. In 1937, a year of great stress owing to continual dust storms and children's migrations west, Mary Dyck tucked a poem into her diary entitled "Are All the Children In?" The first two stanzas capture her desperate concern for her grown children as circumstances took them farther and farther from her.

> I think ofttimes as the night draws nigh,
> Of an old house on the hill,
> Of a yard all wide, and blossom-starred,
> Where the children played at will.
> And when the night at last came down,
> Hushing the merry din;
> Mother would look all around and ask,
> "Are all the children in?"

'Tis many and many a year since then,
And the old house on the hill
No longer echoes with childish feet,
And the yard is still, so still.
But I see it all as the shadows creep,
And though many years have been
Since then I can hear our mother ask,
"Are all the children in?"

Mary Dyck's diary paints a poignant picture of the mothers and fathers who waved good-bye from the porch as daughters and sons
left the dust bowl, often for good. It is a far different story from that
of the era's migrants and one that is far less well known.

For all these reasons, Mary Dyck's diary is a remarkable historical
document. Her words take the reader to a time and place that most
of us have never visited and can only imagine. It cannot tell the reader
everything that there is to know about the social history of the 1930s,
but it provides an unusually intimate view of the trials and tribula-
tions, as well as the joys, of farm life on the southern plains during
the Great Depression.

WAITING ON THE BOUNTY

1. A WOMAN AND HER WORLD

Wh   hen Mary Knackstedt Dyck died in 1955 at the age
of seventy, she left behind a husband of fifty years,
two surviving adult children, and the family farm she
had lived on for most of her life. She also left behind
a diary. Covering the period from 1936 to 1955, that diary is the
chronicle of a life lived outside of public view. Dyck was a farm
woman, a wife, a mother, and a resident of an extremely isolated
farming community. Hers was a life that would have remained outside
of the realm of historical scrutiny, had she not chosen to record her
days in a journal, and had her family not saved the lengthy manuscript, written in pencil on lined notebook paper.

Mary Knackstedt Dyck grew up in the German ethnic community
in McPherson County, Kansas. Her parents, Wilhelm and Margreta
(Mata) Knackstedt, were German immigrants. Her mother had been
born in Barrien, Germany, and had arrived in the United States with
her family as an eight-year-old child. They settled on a farm in Illinois.
Wilhelm and Mata married in Staunton, Illinois, then emigrated in
1883 to McPherson County, Kansas, settling near Inman. Their farm
was in Little Valley Township, in the southwestern corner of the
county. In 1884, they had 160 acres of land.[1] The Knackstedts raised
a large family. Eight children, four girls and four boys, were born to
the couple. Only one son, Edward, lived to adulthood but all four
daughters, Hannah, Elizabeth, Mary, and Altophena, survived.[2] On
February 17, 1884, twin daughters were born to Wilhelm and Mata,
Mary and Altophena, or Phena.

At the time of the Knackstedts' arrival, McPherson County was an
interesting mix of cultures and nationalities. Swedes congregated in

the north central portion of the county, in the area around Lindsborg. The county was also home to a large German-speaking population. Much of that population belonged to the Evangelical Church, a branch of the Lutherans. Another community in the county consisted of Russian Mennonites, also German speakers, who had found their way to McPherson County from a parent settlement in Jansen, Nebraska. They settled largely in the southern and eastern portions of the county and in 1875 established the Hoffnungsau Mennonite Church near Inman. Many within the Mennonite community had been born in Russia, and emigrated to the United States as adults.[3]

On September 1, 1904, Mary Knackstedt married Henry Dyck. Although Mary was an Evangelical, she married into the Mennonite community of McPherson County, as did her twin sister. The two, in fact, married brothers. For the first year of their marriage, Mary and Henry lived with his parents. Their first child, Clarence, died of "summer complaint" in August 1905.[4] They buried him in the cemetery of the Evangelical Church and soon afterward joined more than ninety other Russian Mennonite households in their trek to Lamont Township, Hamilton County, Kansas.

The early years of the twentieth century were a time of growth and rebuilding for the counties of the southern plains. After the devastation caused by the drought, grasshoppers, and depression of the 1890s, farming families began to settle on lands that had been vacated at the end of the previous century. This burst of development coincided with the creation of a number of Mennonite settlements throughout the West. Beginning in the 1870s, Russian Mennonites had found homes in central Kansas, seeking land and the proper environment for the creation of their distinctive religious and ethnic communities. By the turn of the century, land in central Kansas was becoming scarce and expensive, forcing some members of the community to found daughter settlements farther west. These migrating families, often younger and poorer than those remaining, created fifty-three new congregations between 1892 and 1940. Eight of these new Western District Conference congregations were in western Kansas.[5]

One of these settlements was Menno, Kansas. Mennonite leaders from central Kansas scoured the countryside for appropriate settings for new communities farther to the west, examining land in Stanton County as well as Hamilton County.[6] The lure of cheap land in Hamilton County led migrating families to take up claims in the homestead lands of Lamont Township, in semi-arid sand hills twenty miles south of the Arkansas River Valley. Hamilton County was just beginning its development as a farming county; cattle ranching was actually the leading industry in the area. Those few farmers in the area generally grew milo, broomcorn, kafir corn, and sorghum and were just beginning to grow winter wheat.[7]

The founding of Menno meant change on a revolutionary scale for Lamont Township. The township was located in the far southeastern corner of Hamilton County and had been occupied previously by a few scattered ranching families. The 1905 Kansas state census, taken prior to the Mennonites' arrival, found only nine households, four composed of single men. There were only twenty-four people, in an area encompassing nearly 100,000 acres. The 547 cattle outnumbered the township's human residents by a considerable margin.[8] The agricultural practices of these ranchers conformed with those of the county as a whole. In 1905, there were only 170 acres of winter wheat planted in the entire county, and 659 acres of broomcorn. By contrast, ranchers sold more than 60,000 head of livestock for slaughter.[9]

An article published by the Santa Fe Railroad explained the Mennonites' choice of land in these terms: " These people do not object to the more fertile valley lands; but valley lands were out of their reach on account of high values, and so they choose the free homestead lands, lying far and away above the valleys, where only the scant twenty inches of rainfall may be depended upon for the nourishment of plants, and 'dry farming' must be practiced."[10] The railroad's promotional materials lauded the Mennonites' efforts as acts of courage and faith, guaranteed success because of the "virtue, piety, industry, and thrift" of the young settlers.[11]

The Mennonites' arrival brought a new day to Lamont Township. Between the state census in 1905 and the federal census in 1910, the population achieved previously unknown and never replicated heights, with 495 persons appearing in the decennial census. None of the residents enumerated in the 1905 state census remained in 1910, and the township had become overwhelmingly Mennonite. Only 103 persons, forming twenty-seven households, were outside of the Menno community.[12]

Menno itself was a diverse grouping of individuals and families. As might be expected in a frontier settlement the "average" family making a home there was fairly young and in the early stages of family

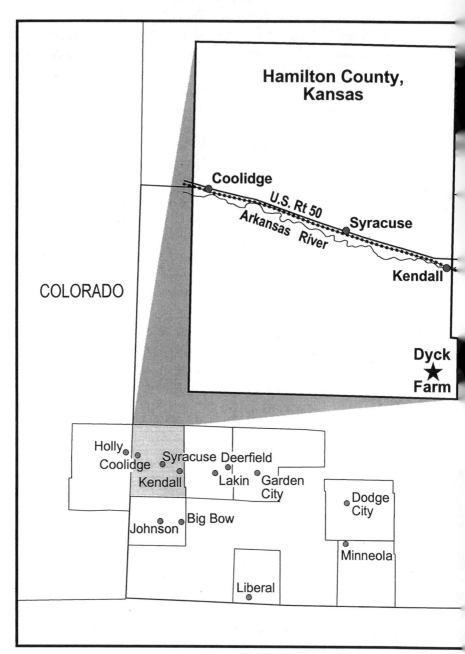

Mary Dyck's Kansas and Colorado.

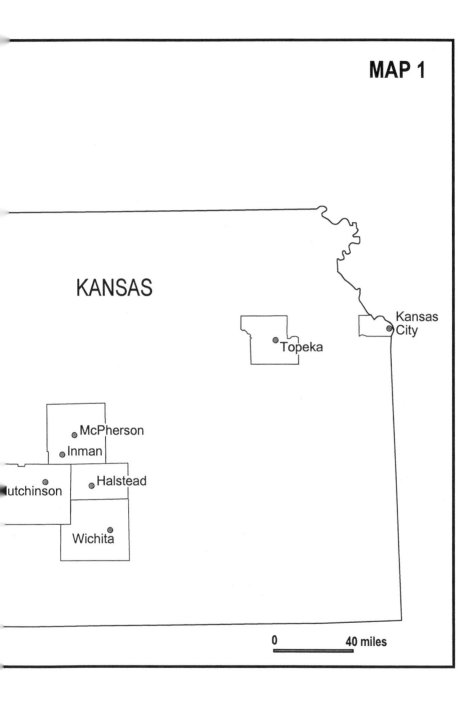

MAP 1

KANSAS

Topeka

Kansas City

McPherson

Inman

Hutchinson

Halstead

Wichita

0   40 miles

formation. The average male head of household was thirty-seven years old, his wife thirty-five, and their family included three children. In fact, the largest group of residents in the township were children, 257 in all. Although this was the average family, there was a wide variety of household structures within the community. Fifteen single adults, settling alone, made their home in Menno, eleven of them men, four women. A widower raised his son alone. At the other extreme was the family of Jacob and Eliza Kaufman and their twelve children, ranging from daughter Eliza, age twenty-eight, to daughter Hilda, age two. The youngest head of a household was a single male, age seventeen, while the oldest was a married man, age seventy-two. Despite the preponderance of young people, it was a community of the young and the old, of children, parents, and grandparents, male and female, with the common goal of establishing a successful Mennonite community.[13]

It was not immediately apparent that the Menno community was destined for failure. Settlers such as Henry and Mary Dyck began developing their farms and putting down roots. Their choice of crops reflected a certain sensitivity to the dry climate in which they lived. Most farmers planted broomcorn, kafir corn, and varieties of sorghum, all of which were drought resistant. Some planted hard winter wheat. Although the Mennonites probably could not be credited with all of the change, the farmers of Hamilton County were becoming involved in the production of crops. Winter wheat acreage increased from a mere 170 acres to 2,464, and the production of broomcorn from 659 acres to 10,878.[14] The Mennonites raised beef cattle, milk cows, swine, and chickens, attempting to create farms that would provide a family self-sufficiency as well as a profit.

The built landscape showed signs of change as well. In the earliest days of the settlement, the first structures families erected were barns that sheltered both them and their animals.[15] Their next homes, sod houses and dugouts, were a logical choice, given the lack of timber in the immediate vicinity. By 1908, visitors from central Kansas were commenting on the building of "new square houses" of frame construction, new windmills and wells, and the planting of trees for windbreaks.[16] The residents conducted church services in the local school until they raised the more than $1,000 needed to build their own church. When the community dedicated the Ebenflur (Prairie) Church in May 1908, the editor of the local paper hailed the event as a sign of the growth and prosperity in the county. "The building of this church is the final notice that the old days are no more. It is more than a prophecy, it is a fulfillment. It means that the 'wide open' days will never return. It means that this part of Kansas is going to steadily advance in the ways of civilization. It means that the people who are changing the cattle ranges into farming lands will stay on the job."[17] The Ebenflur Church was not the only sign of the accomplishments of the young community; there was even talk of establishing a German-language newspaper in Hamilton County.[18]

As this flurry of activity might suggest, the Mennonites' initial response to their new home was largely positive. A steady flow of central Kansas Mennonites trekked to Hamilton County to visit friends and family and reported on the progress of the infant settlement. In fall 1906, Henry Hildebrand, a resident of McPherson County, returned from a visit to the west and reported that the new settlers were busy in their fields, and vigorously pursuing the establishment of their community. To the *Inman Review* he commented, "In the new settlements where all are beginners . . . people don't envy each other or quarrel, but enjoy and help each other."[19] Another visitor, putting the best possible light on the spartan conditions in the new settlement, reported that Menno was much to his liking. Progress was visibly under way, and even those still in dugouts and sod houses were prospering. At the Voth home he found "two of the liveliest, chubbiest little boys I met, who evidently think that to live with mamma in a dugout is the finest lot in the world." The night he spent camped on the floor at settler Lizzie Richert's dugout was no hardship but "snug."[20] Heinrich Janzen, a leader in the settlement, commented to one of the local papers that the Mennonites were successfully adapting to their new environment. Their crops were planted, some of the first profits were in, and the Mennonites were ready to make a commitment to Hamilton County.[21]

It became clear early in the settlement process, however, that there would be tension and difficulties between the Mennonites and their neighbors. Local ranchers evidently felt some resentment at the influx of farming families. "The herds of the stock raisers have been doing some damage to the crops of the new settlers, but some of them have been invited and compelled to pay damages and the good naturedly retreat before the host of homesteaders, who indemnify them liberally by making they [*sic*] lands of the ranches more valuable."[22] Whether the stock growers felt that the increase in land values in the county justified the loss of open rangelands, they did not say. The ranchers were perhaps not the only Hamilton County residents who harbored some prejudice against their new neighbors. Heinrich Janzen believed that a goodly number of those in the county looked "askance at the German settlers." He attempted to justify the Mennonite presence to those elsewhere in the county by asserting that they were hardworking American citizens who were just as willing as their neighbors to work for the good of the county.[23]

Some of the settlement's residents believed that anti-Mennonite prejudice manifested itself in poor provision of services to the southeastern corner of the county. Lamont Township lacked sufficient roads, and farmers found that transporting their products to the rail line at Kendall was a trial. In 1908, in spite of repeated requests, the county commissioners failed to authorize a new road through the sand hills from Syracuse to Kendall.[24] In 1912, proper roads still did not exist. An observer from the central part of the state noted: "It is certainly a fine place to raise cattle, chickens, milo maize, kaffir corn and some broom corn but it is not easy to market anything but cattle. Hogs grow just as fat and fast there as anywhere but there isn't a car load of fat hogs in the county at one time so there is no sale for them."[25]

The loss of a bridge in 1909 seemed a further sign that all was not well between the Menno settlement and the rest of the county. The bridge at Kendall washed out and was not repaired immediately, delaying the mail and other business. The "Menno Happenings" column in the local paper took on a decidedly militant tone. "If things don't move soon now people here are talking of getting up a petition and sending it to headquarters; then we will see if they can keep putting Kendall off. We want our mail and are entitled to it, as much as anyone else."[26]

The biggest problem facing the new settlement, however, was conflict not with neighbors or a hostile county government but with the environment. The southern plains have always been a dry and somewhat difficult land to farm, and the Mennonites had settled on their new lands near the beginning of a short period of drought. As early as 1908, farming families were succumbing to the vagaries of the western Kansas climate. That summer, they discovered two of the common denominators of southwestern Kansas weather, "very hot winds and no rain nowadays." Although some locals were beginning to harvest what they deemed an acceptable crop of wheat, others were arranging with the federal government for leaves of absence from their land or moving back to central Kansas permanently. Two visiting ministers from Russia and California exhorted the Mennonites to remain. "They very much encouraged the people to be in a good humor and hang to the country. Some thirty years ago they had seen worse times than this in their settlement."[27] Despite the encouragement, the exodus continued throughout the fall, and in November shipments of relief supplies from the central portion of the state arrived in Menno. Although the provisions were much needed, the comments from non-Mennonite writers in the local newspaper were not entirely positive; "we rather think that kind of spoils the reputation of this county."[28]

The community's problems continued as the years progressed. In 1909, more settlers returned to their families farther to the east.[29] No doubt this phenomenon troubled those who wished to remain in the community and see it prosper. Heinrich Janzen, as an unofficial spokesman for the settlement, expressed his opinions in one of the local papers. He asserted that the area was not, nor had ever been, "a desert. I believe that this country was intended to feed Man, make him comfortable and in this hardy climate be able to raise up a healthy, vigorous family." He further claimed that the Mennonites were there to stay, and to prosper. Janzen affirmed that he had made a commitment to the Menno community. "I shall invest all the spare money I have in this county, I am here to stay. I have cast my lot here and am for Hamilton county, first, last and all the time."[30]

Despite the opinions of boosters, the news from Hamilton County continued to be less than wholly positive. The following year ended with few crops harvested, although residents asserted that "what little we do raise is good stuff."[31] The conditions remained the same in 1911. There was little rain, and several small children succumbed to illness during the hot, dry summer. Many men went east to work during harvest, "as there is but little work here."[32] As the year progressed, the notices of families leaving for points farther east increased in frequency.

By 1912, the demise of the Menno settlement was more or less assured. "Colonization agents" from other locations had been in the county, and encouraged a number of the Russian Mennonite families to move. Many had relocated to Colorado, Oklahoma, and eastern Kansas.[33] Although there had been "several nice rains," discouragement was overcoming the community, and those resolved to stay anticipated serious problems as their neighbors sold out.

We are . . . sorry that several of those who have left have made it hard on those of us who remained, because most everyone had a good well and they invariably rent their places to some "big bug" who is an owner of lots of stock. The stockman can water his stock there, then let it graze in the same neighborhood, and as we need all the grass there is — it also suffered during the drought — we are inclined to the opinion that they should help us and keep the cattle men out.[34]

The stockmen and their herds seemed to be swallowing up the township. The reports from visitors to the county lacked their previous jaunty tone. A writer for McPherson County's *Inman Review* found conditions dismal. Transportation was terrible, the Russian thistles were on the verge of taking over the township, and the loneliness of the area was oppressive. Poverty seemed to stalk the settlement, with "fewer fine farm houses and smaller barns" than those to be found farther east. He, too, noted that the cattle ranchers were taking over the county. The Mennonites of Hamilton County remained brave despite their hardships, but the maintenance of the settlement, to this observer, seemed hardly worth the trouble.[35]

In the midst of these disappointments, internal dissension was forming, between those who wished to leave Menno, and those who desired to continue their residence in the township. A dispute arose over the rights to the Ebenflur Church, the center of the Menno settlement. In December of 1913, those church members leaving the community, led by Heinrich Janzen, gathered and voted to disband the church and sell the property for approximately $150 to a Methodist congregation at Mitchell, in neighboring Stanton County. Although Janzen had previously been a staunch community booster, he now believed that the congregation had come to the end of its existence. They stripped the Ebenflur Church of its fittings, sold its contents, and prepared the building to be moved.[36]

The Dycks were at the center of this controversy. Within days, those who had elected to remain in Lamont Township expressed their outrage. Henry's father, P. H. Dyck, a merchant and the postmaster for Menno, requested and received a restraining order against those who were selling the church. The use of an injunction in the dispute was a rather extreme example of the degree to which the community had fragmented. Mennonite tradition prohibited community members from resorting to secular authorities to resolve conflicts within the group. Dyck and his fellow complainants alleged that merchants and individuals in Syracuse had donated a considerable portion of the funds to build the church, that they had buried members of their families in the churchyard, and that Janzen and others had no authority to sell the building. Furthermore, they asserted that many former residents of the Menno community would be returning and in need of the spiritual center of the settlement.[37]

Those selling the property believed otherwise. Services were no longer being conducted at the site, and Heinrich Janzen, as the sole remaining trustee, claimed the authority to conduct a vote and sell the property. Janzen argued that of the twenty-three remaining members of the settlement, "some are too far from the church to go, many women and children who are too far away and would have no vote, and some never were members at Ebenflur, and only three of the twenty-three belong and can vote." The Western District Conference, to which the congregation was affiliated, also appeared to have approved the sale.[38]

After much mudslinging and contradictory stories in the two local papers, the *Hamilton County Republican and Syracuse News* and the *Syracuse Journal*, the dispute was settled in favor of the remaining members of the Menno settlement. The Methodists in Mitchell had been unaware of the problems within the Menno community, and had no desire to be a part of the feud. In March, the Western District Conference returned to the Methodist congregation its money, as well as reimbursing the church for court costs. The *Syracuse Journal* reported that "this was done in the interest of peace among the Mennonites who yet remain in that neighborhood, and is the best solution of the whole matter under the circumstances."[39] The building would remain a church until 1923, when the Menno Community Club purchased it. During the 1930s, it would be demolished to make way for a Works Progress Administration–sponsored building project, erecting a new community center on the site, built of native stone.[40] Henry Dyck would take an active role in this project.

With the dispute settled, Menno more or less faded from the history of Hamilton County. In the months that followed, the remaining residents of the township tried to put the best possible face on the situation, claiming that the outward migration was temporary, and that their friends and neighbors would be returning. The *Hamilton County Republican and Syracuse News* was "reliably informed" that the migrants were expected to return, and that "the settlement is here to stay."[41] In March, the paper printed letters from former residents, bemoaning the day they ever left Hamilton County.[42] A month later,

the paper published an advertisement for the community, with a picture of the settlement's members standing in front of their church in earlier, more hopeful days. The caption read "In the German Mennonite [*sic*] settlement. Goed [*sic*] houses, good schools and a fine church make it the best improved settlement in the county."[43] What the ad failed to mention was that very few of those pictured in the photograph remained, and that as an organized unit, Menno no longer truly existed.

In 1915, only ninety-nine persons lived in Lamont Township, in twelve households. The drought had destroyed the farms of Mennonite and non-Mennonite alike; of the twenty-seven non-Mennonite households existing in 1910, only five remained in 1915. Only seven Mennonite households remained. Among the Mennonites, most of those who persisted were relatively old; only two of the heads of households were under forty-five. Most were over fifty-five. Only one young couple remained, Henry and Mary Dyck.[44] Although the Mennonite community had more or less disappeared, a small presence would continue to exist in the county, in the form of a small cluster of related families. In 1979, the county's official history commented, "The only mark left by the Mennonite colony was the change from range land to farm land and their name and example."[45]

It was perhaps not surprising that the Dycks stayed behind, while other families left. The Dycks' marriage was an interfaith union. Although Henry had been born and raised a member of the Hoffnungsau Russian Mennonite community in McPherson County, Mary was not a Mennonite. She had been born and raised an Evangelical. Although Henry and Mary migrated with the Hoffnungsau Mennonites, neither of the Dycks were ever active participants in Lamont Township's Mennonite community. Church records indicate that the family did not attend the Ebenflur Church, and Mary remained a devout Evangelical at the time of her death.[46] The religious convictions and community ties that bound others to migrate with the group did not seem to be shared in the Dyck home.

Although without a supportive community, the young couple set about creating a farm of which they could be proud. In 1915, their family was complete. Henry was twenty-eight, Mary thirty-one, and their three surviving children included Thelma, six, Ervin, two, and Verna, an infant. Their farm was not a large one, consisting of only

160 acres of rented land.[47] Henry had patented a homestead claim in 1911 but had sold it in 1914, probably because of economic hardship. After the departure of the Mennonites, this portion of the county was rather thinly settled, with only thirty-seven farms in the township. Eventually, Henry's brother Pete and Mary's sister Phena would return to farm nearby.

The 1915 agricultural census describes a small but productive and diversified farm. The Dycks grew sorghum, milo, feterita, and pasture grasses. They produced 105 pounds of butter for family use, and sold $285 worth of milk and cream. They also sold $15 worth of poultry and eggs. Their livestock consisted of three horses, four cows, twenty-six cattle, and eight swine.[48] Despite ten years in the county, the Dycks were really still at the beginning stages of developing their farm.

For the next eleven years, their enterprise remained relatively small. Some years the Dycks farmed as much as 240 acres, but just as often they farmed 160 acres or less. While the size of farms in the township moved steadily upward, the Dycks held their ground. Their choice of crops remained relatively conservative as well. They generally planted broomcorn, sorghum, milo, and pasture grasses, and moved very slowly into winter wheat production.[49] Mary was very active in home production, regarding the flock of chickens as her sole responsibility, and sharing responsibility for the milk cows with Henry. Milk and cream sales, as well as sales of poultry and eggs, were an important source of income for the family. The real innovation was the family's purchase of both a tractor and an automobile. Their tractor was one of only four, in a township of fifty-three farmsteads.[50] In 1925, they again became landowners when Henry purchased a quarter section in the far southeastern corner of Lamont Township.[51]

The innovation and growth of the Dyck farm continued at an even greater pace in the years leading up to the Great Depression and drought. In 1927, they began renting a considerable amount of land in addition to the acres they owned, bringing their farm size up to 800 acres; in 1928, they farmed over 1,000 acres. Into the 1950s, they would cultivate 1,000 acres or more most years. Farmers in this part of Kansas regularly rented a large portion of the land they cultivated. In an arid climate, this was a means of managing risk. Henry also began experimenting seriously with the production of wheat, and made further investments in mechanical technology. In 1929, the family was able to purchase two tractors, a Caterpillar and a McCormick Deering, a new truck, and two cars.[52] By 1927, Mary enjoyed the use of a radio, one of only three in the township, and often listened as she went about her daily chores. While the farm homes of the Great Plains were late to receive improvements of any kind, nearly three-quarters of Kansas farm homes had a radio by 1940. Radio made life much easier for women who spent long hours working alone in their farm homes, and Mary Dyck discovered that earlier than most.[53]

Although the 1920s had been a decade of growth and prosperity on the Dyck farm, their experience of the 1930s would be much different. As a decade, it had little to recommend it. In 1931, farmers in the Dycks' corner of Hamilton County harvested a fantastic crop, as much as forty bushels to the acre, just in time for the market to fail.[54] Prices for wheat and other farm products crashed to all-time lows in 1931, the same year as an unprecedented drought and record-setting temperatures began to afflict the region. Terrible dirt storms accompanied the drought. Between 1931 and 1940, the residents of southwestern Kansas, as well as those of other areas of the Great Plains, saw their topsoil and their neighbors scattered to the winds.

The problems of Hamilton County were very much like those of other dust bowl counties, beset by drought and depopulation. Between 1930 and 1940, the population of Hamilton County fell from 3,328 to 2,645, a reduction of 21 percent. The farming population fell even more drastically, from 1,692 in 1930 to 1,160 in 1940, 31 percent fewer farm residents.[55] The same depopulation was occurring in the Dycks' neighborhood. The township's population tumbled from 269 to 159 during the decade. Many of those who left were young people, facing the decade without productive land or jobs, or the opportunity to obtain either.[56] A 1937 description of what a visitor would see in Lamont Township easily explains why so many were leaving. "After two years of practically no production, the area will present a bleak appearance to visitors from the eastern part of the state . . . visitors will drive through sage covered sandhills from the north, along road ditches drifted level with dust. Fields will be as barren as a school playground, and heaped with dust behind each thistle clump. From the south his eye will behold the same desolation and bareness."[57] There was no soil to hold the grass and no prospects to hold the area's young people.

In October 1936, the point at which the preserved portions of her diary began, Mary Knackstedt Dyck was fifty-two and the mother of adult children. She and Henry managed the family farm, while their oldest daughter, Thelma, lived on a nearby farm with her husband,

Cliff Warner, and two children, Patsy and Leroy. Her second daughter, Verna, was often working away from home, and her son, Ervin, found what temporary employment he could in surrounding communities and farther afield. Mary and Henry operated a fairly substantial farm. In 1935, the agricultural census noted that their land amounted to 1,200 acres, with 100 acres in wheat, 80 in broomcorn, 25 in sweet sorghum, 15 in sudan grass, and 400 fallow. They sold $75 worth of milk and $350 worth of poultry, and made 100 pounds of butter. They owned 144 hens, 1 horse, 4 milk cows, 9 other cattle, and an unspecified number of swine. They owned one tractor and one combine. Theirs was a large farm for the community; of the ninety-one farm households in the township, only fifteen ran larger operations.[58]

Although Mary and Henry remained residents of Hamilton County during this difficult period, they watched their community of kin diminish significantly. Mary's mother died in 1924, and the only other sibling with whom she corresponded, her sister Elizabeth, lived half a state away in Hutchinson, Kansas. Lizzie would later migrate to Oregon, as did many from central and western Kansas. In 1931, Mary's sister Altophena, her only sibling living in close proximity, died. Henry's brother, Pete, and his son, Elmer, remained close at hand, spending a great deal of their time in and around the Dyck home. They provided a good bit of paid labor at times when the Dycks' son, Ervin, was away. The Dycks' children were also among those who left the area during the 1930s, unable to make an adequate living. Instead of handing their farm over to the next generation, Mary and Henry watched them leave, unable to support an extended family in their difficult circumstances.

In spite of the departures suffered by rural Lamont Township, the Dyck diary paints a picture of a remarkably active small community. The Bishops, longtime friends and neighbors, came to visit. Between migrations, the Dyck children were constantly in and out of the home, and Mary's daughters shared her work. Mary occasionally went to quilt at a neighboring farm. Mary and Henry went to some community events such as dances together, although Henry sometimes went alone. The automobile, which appreciably shortened the distance between widely scattered farms, allowed more visiting than otherwise might have been possible. One issue does become clear, however, when careful examination is made of the visitors to the Dyck farm: daughters aside, most of the Dycks' visitors were men. The mobility afforded by the automobile was more easily enjoyed by males, who were generally unfettered by the constant round of repetitive daily chores that tied the area's women to the farmhouse. The forces of nature could also conspire to create isolation for all, in spite of modern transportation technology. Dust storms often made it difficult and unpleasant to leave the farm, although it was sometimes necessary to venture out into them. The blizzards of late 1939 and early 1940 filled the roads with impassable drifts and stranded the Dycks in their home for days. The immense spaces and extreme weather that had always defined life in western Kansas continued to exist, although technological change allowed some relief to isolated people. A strong family life was a woman's most important protection against loneliness and isolation. Unfortunately, the circumstances of the thirties threatened Mary Dyck's supportive web of family connections.

Ervin, the couple's only surviving son, probably would have been his parents' choice to inherit the family farm, but he would not live to take on this task. During the middle years of the 1930s, he made regular forays away from the family farm, looking for work. When he was home, he helped his father and brother-in-law with their tasks, but he was absent more often than he was present. In 1936, he picked cotton in Arizona and New Mexico, work that was not always pleasant or easy for a young man accustomed to working in the wheat fields of Kansas. In December 1936, Ervin returned from cotton picking in the Southwest feeling the ill effects of his labors. His mother remarked in her diary, "Ervin's hands have very big soars on them yet, from the Cotton field effects," and "Ervin lunched all day long, for good measure, after being on a cheap diet in the Cotton fields." After Christmas in 1936, Ervin resumed his travels. The early days of 1937 found him working for the Civilian Conservation Corps. This federal program furnished jobs, room, and board to young men whose families were on relief, and sent the larger part of their wages to their parents. Later that year, he and a friend ventured to California to work as migrant farm laborers. In his last move, Ervin made use of family connections in the Northwest, and traveled to Oregon to work as a logger. It was an unfortunate choice, and one that would cost him his life. In May 1941, Ervin died of injuries he received in a sawmill accident. He would never return to his parents' farm in Hamilton County.

The middle years of the decade also found their elder child, Thelma, and her family on the move. She had married Clifford Warner in 1930, and they had attempted to establish their own home. As she commented many years later, "Our marriage was badly timed. The depression, drought and those horrible dirt storms simply found every one unprepared to deal with so many things at once." [59] Thelma had been a schoolteacher, but the law required her to resign upon her marriage. Cliff supported them with odd jobs and jobs with the county, and the couple lived with relatives in order to earn a bare living. In the mid-1930s, they moved to a farm in Stanton County, not too far from the Dycks' home. There, they did what they could to provide a living for themselves and their two small children. The couple took advantage of the federal farm program and accepted commodities from the government. Cliff worked for neighbors, although he often received little in the way of cash wages. Their first radio was a payment from a neighbor for helping to stack feed. It was not cash, but Thelma remarked that it "was our source of entertainment, and we loved it." [60] Thelma did what she could to support her family by canning, keeping a cow and chickens, and sewing. In the end, however, these efforts were insufficient. An endless succession of problems, both small and large, sent the Warner family to Oregon. Her husband's sister and parents were there, and although they could not be guaranteed jobs, the family could promise Thelma and Cliff "a clean country to live in." [61]

Their sojourn in Oregon lasted approximately two years, with Cliff earning a living in the timber industry. Thelma went to Portland to stay with friends, and also earned extra funds by picking strawberries. She loved the state's greenness and beauty. In 1939, however, they were on their way back to Kansas. It was her husband's dreams that brought the family back to the dust bowl. " When we came back to Kansas, oh, it was terrible. I never dreaded anything so bad in my life. But Cliff wanted to come back. Dad had found this land for him, and you know all of our men who farm have this dream of having quite a lot of land and having a big farm and he just wanted that so much, and I wanted him to have what he wanted. So I just didn't say anything, and we came back." [62] They established their farm in Kearny County, just east of Hamilton County. Although they maintained close contact with the elder Dycks, their farm was a separate enterprise, one that Thelma still relies on for part of her income today.

The Dycks' youngest child, Verna, also spent much of the decade away from her parents' farm. Early in the decade, Verna lived in town with Thelma, in order to attend high school in Syracuse. [63] After high

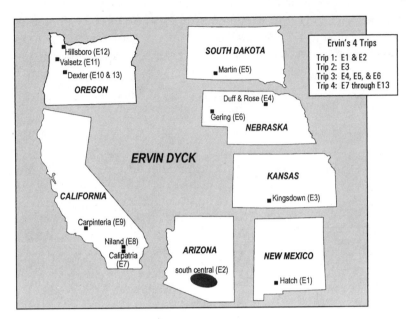

Ervin's 4 Trips

Trip 1: E1 & E2
Trip 2: E3
Trip 3: E4, E5, & E6
Trip 4: E7 through E13

Hillsboro (E12)
Valsetz (E11)
Dexter (E10 & 13)
OREGON

SOUTH DAKOTA
Martin (E5)

Duff & Rose (E4)
Gering (E6)
NEBRASKA

ERVIN DYCK

KANSAS
Kingsdown (E3)

CALIFORNIA

Carpinteria (E9)

Niland (E8)
Calipatria (E7)

ARIZONA
south central (E2)

NEW MEXICO
Hatch (E1)

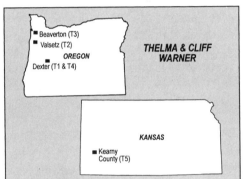

Beaverton (T3)
Valsetz (T2)
OREGON
Dexter (T1 & T4)

THELMA & CLIFF WARNER

KANSAS

Kearny County (T5)

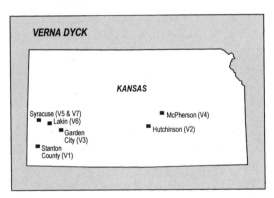

VERNA DYCK

KANSAS

Syracuse (V5 & V7)
Lakin (V6)
Garden City (V3)
Stanton County (V1)

McPherson (V4)
Hutchinson (V2)

Children on the move.

school graduation, she worked on farms in neighboring counties, and also in Hutchinson, occasionally returning to her parents' farm. By the late 1930s, she was working as a beautician and hoping to open her own shop. When Verna was home, she was a great help to her mother, doing much of the family's baking, sewing, and cleaning. Mary commented frequently upon her industry. "Cleaned up dust some in fore-noon. Verna did most all of it." "Verna helps Mo out her misery." When Mary was ill, Verna often came home to help her mother and father. She would continue her pattern of periodic visits home, and longer periods away, until her marriage in the mid-1940s, when she would leave the family farm for good. She and her husband would reside in Syracuse, the county seat, approximately twenty miles distant from her parents' farm.

Ervin, Thelma, and Verna's moves represented a significant challenge in Mary Dyck's life. Although she never complained about this issue specifically in her diary, her work no doubt became more onerous. She lost her daughters' company as she worked her way through her daily chores, and no other woman, neighbor or kin, replaced them. She was much more reliant on friends and neighbors coming to visit than was her husband. Mary's chores tied her to home and hearth, while Henry's work often took him into Syracuse or Kendall. Days spent at home alone were often "very blue & cloudy." Her only companion at work was the radio, which was frequently disrupted by the static electricity generated by dust storms. At times, the dirt storms themselves made Dyck's work almost unbearably difficult, regularly undoing her attempts to keep a tidy house. In the spring of 1937 in particular, her mounting dismay was evident as she worked in vain to rid her house of the persistent dust.

Her daughters' absence became an even greater problem because of Mary's deteriorating health. She often complained of feeling "tuff," which could encompass any number of ills. Rheumatism often left her "cripled up" after a day of washing. She experienced ringing in her ears and dizziness on a regular basis, and suffered from severe pain caused by bad teeth. A local dentist removed all of her teeth in September 1938, but that measure failed to resolve completely her dental problems. Her dentures never fit properly, and she spent a good deal of time nursing a sore mouth and gums. Without her daughters to spell her at her chores, she suffered through her routine as best she could. Eventually the Dycks hired household help.

Most seriously, Mary Dyck suffered emotionally from the forced separation from her children. Their centrality to her thoughts and concerns is easily visible in each day's record. She wrote letters to each of her children three or four times a week, and faithfully noted the letters she had received. With the receipt of each letter, she noted the name and location of the sender, as if by naming and placing each child, she could keep watch over him or her. Naming and placing her children, whether they were in Hutchinson, Kansas, Duff, Nebraska, or Dexter, Oregon, seems to have reassured Mary that they were indeed accounted for and safe.

Despite these comforting rituals, the absence of Thelma, Verna, and Ervin depressed Mary. Their periodic departures were occasions for mourning. The box of Post Toasties sitting on the dining room table reminded Mary of Ervin's departure for Duff, Nebraska. "And another very lonely day to content with since the vacancy of Ervin Our Toastie eater we certenly miss him. All the emptyness is staring Mo in the face ever where she goes. . . . Mo cant keep from sobing." When Mary and Henry took Verna back to Hutchinson after a visit home, she experienced the same emotions. "Ma had a lump in her throat that she couldnt swallow eyes where full of mist that she couldnt see the way ahead. It took her all that day to come out of such state of mind." The Warner family's departure for Oregon was particularly trying. "They packed all fore-noon and at 2 P.M. They where bound for Oregon. And now the junkie Basement and Hydron the little [children's] Battle field where they allways fought their battles, look so very lonesome." Mary and Henry were still feeling their loss two months later when she wrote that "the lonesome couple enduring the Dust Bowl rolled in the Hay at 9:30." The Dyck home was too quiet without the reassuring sights and sounds of children and grandchildren. Much of the period covered by Dyck's diary was one of watchful waiting, and hoping for children to return home to the farm in western Kansas.

The pain of separation was amplified by the economic struggles of the decade. The Dycks kept their farm going, although it was not an easy proposition. The decade was marked by regular crop failures. In 1937, crops on 700 of the farm's 1,040 acres failed. In 1938, 1,000 acres of crops failed, and in 1939, 600 acres failed and another 400 were left fallow. In 1940, the last of the dust bowl years, 400 acres of their crops failed, while they chose to leave another 500 acres fallow. Given the dismal precipitation, high winds, and persistent dust, there was little the Dycks could do to improve their luck. In 1935, at the height of the dust storms, they did invest in a lister, the only agricultural equipment available to fight wind erosion, but it is doubtful that its use substantially improved the family's fortunes.[64]

The Dycks were left to piece together an income from whatever sources they could find. One of these was work relief. Henry Dyck participated in the construction of a community building on the site of the old Ebenflur Church. It was made of native stone, and its construction spanned many months. This was a Works Progress Administration construction project, and Henry worked in a supervisory position. They also received government commodities, particularly meat. During the time that Ervin worked for the Civilian Conservation Corps, Mary and Henry received income from their son's employment, as stipulated by the agency. Ervin earned $25 a month; $5 went to him and the remaining $20 to his parents. The Dycks also participated in the programs of the Agricultural Adjustment Administration. For example, in 1935, the only year for which farm accounts are available, they received an $18 hog allotment, a payment for animals they agreed not to raise.[65] They also participated in the crop reduction program. In 1937, they received $1,941 from the government. This was a substantial payment, based on the large number of acres that the Dycks farmed.[66] The amount of the government grant, however, needs to be put into perspective. The Dycks were farming a thousand acres of land. When the wind blew they sometimes needed to run tractors nearly around the clock to keep the dirt listed and on the ground. Listers dug deep furrows in the land that encouraged dirt to blow into the furrows rather than into the sky. This was an expensive proposition, which required that they purchase gas, tractor repairs, and labor. While this was a large federal payment, the Dycks still had to watch their budget very carefully. Another important element in the federal farm program was the Soil Conservation Service, which provided financial assistance to farmers engaged in conservation work. The Dycks were active participants. Henry regularly attended soil conservation meetings, received seed loans, contoured his land, and cooperated with the local agricultural extension service.

Mary's work around the farm, always a source of income, was extremely important during the thirties. Although the dirt storms foiled attempts at gardening and killed the orchard, she still was active in preserving food for the family. Each year she canned gallons of fruits, vegetables, pickles, jams, and jellies for home consumption, although she often had to purchase the produce for these efforts. She and

Henry also canned meat and rendered lard from home-butchered livestock. Her efforts in 1935 also demonstrate the importance of her poultry flock to the continuation of the farming enterprise. In that year, she sold eggs worth $221.85, and chickens for $42.15. A restaurant purchased most of the chickens she sold, but neighbors also bought them. This, however, was not pure profit. She bought nearly $70 worth of chicken feed, and the chicks themselves cost $15. Her profit, however, was $181.91, nearly enough to cover the family's grocery bill. Cream and milk, which she and Henry cooperatively produced, added another $51.26 to the family income.[67]

The receipts from Henry's enterprises help to put the importance of Mary's contribution in perspective. In 1935, Henry sold two loads of wheat for $134. He also sold livestock worth $141, while purchasing a bull for $50. The expenses involved in maintaining his side of the farming operation were also substantial, $390.60, the largest cost being $274.07 expended on the upkeep and fuel for the family's tractor. The expense of maintaining the crop and livestock operations of the farm was greater than the income produced. Like most of his neighbors, Henry Dyck's operating expenditures exceeded his profits, and the Dyck farm survived only because of an adequate combination of the husband and wife's efforts, plus a generous dollop of federal aid.

Despite their financial concerns, the Dycks kept their farm, rather than migrating to the West. This, however, was not a foregone conclusion. They questioned their ability to keep on farming, particularly in the spring of 1937. That year was one of the worst of the decade in terms of the number and duration of dust storms. In the first six months of that year alone, Dyck recorded nearly 100 days when dust clouds filled the sky. It was also the year in which two of their children left for Oregon. The elder Dycks thought about joining them in the West. They were lonely and frustrated with the problems of home and farm making in the heart of the dust bowl. In May 1937, Mary commented on her poor physical condition, and blamed it on the weather. "I spose she's filled with dust endouring these duststorms 5 days in succession. Then 2 days of piece, and nother 5 days of it in succession with out eny let up." The same day, Henry came in from the fields to announce that the time had come for a change. "Mo pack your Suit Case lets go, and get clear out of the Country. Moving along . . . the River isn't far enough." Eventually, their desire to stay won out, and the Dycks remained during the summer of 1937.

In the spring of 1938, it appeared that the Dycks were again con-templating a move west. On March 30, Mary wrote "When Mo went to get these Eggs to Nite she certenly found the Henhouse lonesome & all empty. She felt like sheding tears. It seems as if she's taring herself up by the roots & is planting them some where else." Whether she was worried about a short trip, or a relocation of longer duration, is unclear. They settled for a visit to their children in Oregon. They returned in April, and resumed their struggles with the dust bowl and the depression. They succeeded, and their farming enterprise lasted until 1956, the year after Mary's death. Henry then retired from farm-ing, sold his land, and moved to Syracuse to live with his younger daughter, Verna. His children did not take over his farm, and the land did not remain in the family. Henry Dyck died in 1963.

The Dycks' farming enterprise survived the dust bowl and Great Depression while many did not. The family had entered hard times in relatively good condition financially. They were well established, and rooted to the area. Their operation was large, and fairly prosperous. They were able to withstand the troubles of the 1930s in spite of their doubts. It is likely that they knew that if they left, they would lose everything for which they had worked. During the depression, land values in Hamilton County fell drastically. They never would have recovered a fair price for their land and years of labor. For them, with a lifetime of work invested in Lamont Township, staying was the only viable option.

For their children, the situation was somewhat different. They had lived their lives in Hamilton County, but they lacked their parents' resources, and their parents' farm did not generate a great enough income to support an extended family. Ervin chose to look for a job, and perhaps a better life, on the West Coast. He would not live to inherit the farm. His sisters followed their husbands away from the family farm as well. Verna moved to town after her marriage, and Thelma lived and worked on her family's own land in Kearny County, moving to town only after her husband's death. After decades of sup-porting the Dycks, the farm passed out of their hands when Henry Dyck retired.

The depopulation of rural communities was a well-established fact well before the 1930s. The drought, depression, and dust bowl, which affected the young of farming families particularly, guaranteed an ac-celerated rate of family farm failure and rural depopulation during the decade. Many of the farms that survived, like that of the Dycks, would succumb in later decades. Children followed a path away from the family farm during the thirties and continued to do so in the decades thereafter. The circumstances of the decade meant the beginning of the end for the Dyck farm, and for many a family farm in southwestern Kansas.

The Dyck farm, although large, was much like others in southwestern Kansas. The problems the family faced, given the drought and dust bowl, were much like the problems of the surrounding region. Poor prospects and family dislocations were common elements in the lives of many of their friends and neighbors. What makes the Dycks uncommon is that Mary Dyck kept a detailed, almost daily diary, and her daughters preserved it. While historians may surmise how the problems of the decade affected families throughout the plains states and may speculate on the impact of these stresses on the interior lives of families, the Dyck diary provides an intimate look at the life of a family under tremendous stress.

Historians know a great deal about the impact of rural depopulation on affected communities. As young people left the farms and rural areas, small towns lost their tax bases, then their schools, and often their identities. Small farms disappeared into larger farming units as families relinquished their holdings. Small towns became ghost towns as their populations and businesses moved on to the next bigger town down the road. The facts about this process are relatively well known. What historians know very little about is the impact of those events on the families who watched their children leave home. There are very few documents recording these events from the perspective of those who were left behind when rural communities disintegrated. Mary Dyck's diary is a record of the impact of trying times, from the perspective of the family.

When scholars contemplate the major historical events of the twentieth century, such as the Great Depression and dust bowl, their tendency is to read history from the outside in. They move from the larger, seemingly all-encompassing event, in to the lives of those experiencing the event. While personal writings such as diaries and letters are extremely useful in such a project, they also challenge the reader to examine these historical phenomena from the inside out — from the perspective of the individual living the moment, and perhaps not perceiving themselves as engulfed in historical cataclysm.[68] Mary Knackstedt Dyck's experience allows the reader a unique opportunity to view rural life in the midst of the dust bowl through the lens of the farm home, and from the perspective of a woman who had lived through droughts, depressions, and rural depopulation previously. Dyck's extensive daily writings allow the reader to explore what was important in her world, and how the continuation of the ordinary and everyday elements in her life may have helped to anchor her in the midst of the decade's troubles.

THE DYCK DIARY

It was during the turbulent years of the Great Depression and dust bowl that Mary Dyck evidently began keeping a detailed diary. Thelma Warner remembered that her mother had kept a diary for a number of years previously, simply noting weather conditions and daily work schedules. The diary had a place of prominence, on the kitchen table, available for consultation by family members. These early writings, however, no longer exist. The preserved portion of the diary, for unknown reasons, begins abruptly in October 1936. At some point prior to this date, the diary became a more elaborate document, not just recording these items, but other information that interested Dyck. She began to write about the programming on the radio, the comings and goings of family members, and her family's reactions to the hard times of the thirties. As the years passed and the trials facing this family accumulated, Mary Dyck's writing became more personal and less detached. Even as the diary became more individual, it remained a fairly simple document, written in simple language. Judy Nolte Lensink's generalized comments about rural women's diaries hold true for Mary Dyck's writing as well: "intensity of experience is usually signalled by quantity of language rather than by metaphor."[69]

The origin of the diary as a family "story" may account for some of its idiosyncracies, such as Dyck's use of the third person in reference to herself. During the 1930s and early 1940s, she generally wrote of herself as "she," "Mo," or "Ma," and her husband as "Po" or "Pa." References to herself as "I" in the early portions of the diary are relatively rare and often appear to be momentary lapses of attention. In one entry, written on June 17, 1937, she referred to the document she was writing as "the family Diary." On another occasion, she wrote that making the family's log was "her duty." The best evidence that she thought of this journal not as a personal document but as a family's or farm's account is found in her writings in the spring of 1937. In late April, she went to Hutchinson, Kansas, to visit family. While she was gone, she did not write about her own experiences in Hutchinson. Instead, when she returned home, she questioned the resident men about what had happened while she was away and wrote about the events that had occurred in her absence. Predictably, these entries are spare.

Mary Dyck's diary has other idiosyncracies as well. Clearly, she wrote throughout the day and often completed the entries for one day the following morning. This is the only way that she could record the time at which each family member retired, particularly when others often went to bed after she did. Her own notations indicate that she wrote during the day whenever the opportunity presented itself, writing early in the morning while she waited for Henry to come in for breakfast, during the day while the bread rose or a meal cooked, or during the evening as the family gathered around the radio. The journal is really a rolling account, developed throughout the course of a day, or often two. Sometimes she revisited a portion of the diary weeks or months later, in order to revise messy or incomplete entries. It is impossible to know what might have been added or deleted in the process.

Dyck's spelling, punctuation, and grammar were quite erratic and consistent with her education and background. She spoke German in the home as a child and had only a third- or fourth-grade education. The eccentricities of her spelling and grammar are reproduced here because they say a good deal about the writer. As Judy Lensink wrote in her introduction to the diary of Emily Hawley Gillespie, the way in which a diarist wrote was most likely the way in which he or she spoke. The preservation of Mary Dyck's own, uncorrected, highly individual writing is part of an attempt to recover and preserve the "voice" of a shy and retiring woman, who seems to have expressed herself freely only in her journal.[70]

Radio drama often occupied a line or more of each day's entry, and Dyck often referred to the characters on dramatic radio serials, otherwise known as soap operas, by their first names, without transitions indicating that they were purely fictional creatures. For example, on October 15, 1936, Dyck moved without punctuation from a discussion of mending her husband's trousers to the announcement that "Bob is making plans to get his Marriage Lisense tomorrow," and back to the day's weather. Since none of the men in her family or her neighborhood were named Bob, it is most likely she was discussing *Betty and Bob*, her favorite soap opera. Although they are not usually reproduced in this edited version of her diary, she often provided detailed descriptions of the plots of her "epesodes," particularly those involving romantic content. Radio provided the spice in her life, and she may very well have agreed with many other Americans in the heart of the depression that her radio was her most valued possession.[71]

The portion of the diary presented here covers the period from October 1936 to May 1941. During these years, Mary Dyck's children left home, and she learned to adapt to their migrations. She and her husband struggled against the environment and the economy, and endured when the same conditions forced many of their neighbors to leave farming for good. Although these were difficult years, they were filled with the small pleasures of visiting grandchildren, soap operas on the radio, jokes shared with Henry, and occasional respites from hard times. Although Dyck's mood was often grim, a ray of hope persisted in her daily writings.

EDITORIAL METHOD

The transcription of this diary is as close to a literal transcription as it can be. Mary Dyck was a German speaker as a child and had a limited education. Consequently, the grammar and spelling within the document are sometimes quite creative. Most of the time, however, the writing is fairly easily understandable, if read phonetically, and has been preserved as it appeared in the diary. Where words require a great deal of creative reading, I have inserted the correct term in brackets. Annotation has been added where necessary in order to clarify points. I have standardized daily headings throughout the diary, the one place where I have departed from a literal transcription. Do note, however, that the dating of entries is occasionally erratic, reflecting Mary Dyck's somewhat loose concern with the calendar.

The voluminous nature of this diary required that I carefully select portions of the diary for publication. What is published here is roughly a third of the writing done from October 1936 to May 1941. Some entries have been omitted entirely. Within entries, I have used ellipses to indicate my editorial omissions. I have presented several complete entries in the appendix, so that readers may have a better idea of the appearance of the larger work. Most unedited entries include a daily summary of the weather, including temperature readings and conditions early in the morning, near the middle of the day, and late in the afternoon. A log of the work done by all resident family members usually also appears. Dyck often recorded the dishes she served at each day's meals. She also noted who visited the farm. Dyck generally concluded a day's entry with the time family members went to bed.

A day's writing might also include the number of eggs the chickens laid, the radio programs to which the family listened, and other entertainment they enjoyed. Dyck would record any correspondence written or received. When any family member left the farm to go to town, that event would be recorded as well. She attempted to make as full a record of the day's events as possible. While hens and cows were producing, Saturday entries would include the number of eggs she sold, the price she received, and the volume, quality, and price she received for cream. The entries might also include a list of the groceries and supplies she had purchased in town.

My selections from this vast amount of writing reflect my own judgments about what in this diary is most important historically and what was most important to the diary's author, Mary Dyck. I have included all references to dust bowl conditions, since drought and blowing dirt so thoroughly shaped the life of the family and the surrounding community. I have also included extensive descriptions of Dyck's work and that of those around her. Family relations were the core of Mary Dyck's world, and I have paid particular attention to her relationship to her husband and her children. Where the Dycks' lives intersected the larger issues of the day, such as the depression, the New Deal, and the Second World War, I have also chosen to include that material. Any selection from a larger document is bound to be subjective, but I have attempted to provide to the reader material that most thoroughly and successfully describes Mary Dyck and her world.

2. WORK, FAMILY, AND "PLAYING HOOKIE"

1936

SUNDAY, OCTOBER 11

. . . Mo & Ervin went to the kids at 8 A.M. to get Verna, came right home & almost noon the kids came & stayed for dinner.[1] We all went to the church at P.M. to see the beautiful building,[2] then at 5 P.M. Thelma took Verna back to Mr. Trostles, where she is working.[3] Ervin tore his Car down & worked on it all afternoon. we took a snapshot of the family groupe this afternoon . . .

MONDAY, OCTOBER 12

. . . Ervin has worked on his Car all day long. . . . Henry is drilling Wheat on the old 80 all day. . . .

TUESDAY, OCTOBER 13

. . . Mo churned. Baked Bread & Caned 6 q Pairs. Mo also cleaned the Cupboard & wrote a letter to sister Elisebeth.[4] . . . Henry is drilling by Kend[all]. Has been cloudy all day, wind is not to strong. Mo had an exciting time to-day. Hens layed 21 Eggs to day. . . .

WEDNESDAY, OCTOBER 14

. . . Henry drilled Wheat A.M. and toped Maze P.M.[5] Mo Baked 3 Lemon Pies at P.M. and washed some Windows cleaned Cupords & Oil Stove . . .

THURSDAY, OCTOBER 15

. . . Mo Fried down some Meat, Baked Bread, washed some windows & cleaned dust, the rest of the day also patched 1 pr. of Trousers for Mr. Henry. . . . Henry headed Maze in after noon. . . . Another caller apeared on the sene, while I was shining the Flour, in middle Bedroom, leaving a Calender & a post Card on the stand, saying it was Rawleigh man ha.[6] Mo thought it was, Mr. Henry. . . . We got a letter from Verna. . . .

FRIDAY, OCTOBER 16
Ervin sowed Wheat all day. Henry sowed while Ervin eat his dinner. Henry toped Maze at A.M. & haweled a load Water to the church at P.M. about 2 Oclock P.M. they moved the Tractor to the Doerr quarter[7] . . . Mo Baked 3 Cream Pies, also churned & mended Ervins green Shirt. In the Evening at 7 both of us took in the first Niter Play o boy was it ever good. . . .

SATURDAY, OCTOBER 17
. . . Henry took a load Cement also Lime to the church at A.M. then he took the Truck to Syracuse, got a load Coal Ervin sowed Wheat till 10 A.M. then he was lared up out of the Wheatfield so at 2 P.M. Mo & Ervin went to Johnson & got Verna got back home at 5 P.M. . . . Thelma & the kiddies came here, and we all went to the Show. Drifting along with the Tumbling Weed. & took in the Owl Show so we got back home at 1-15 not much sleep for this Day. Thelma also kidies where here for Supper also Breakfast . . . Mo got away from work all after noon hookied.

SUNDAY, OCTOBER 18
. . . Mo & E took Verna back at 6 P.M. got home at 8 stoped in, at the Warner family, both ways Henry was sowing his wild oats, all day long ha, so now, I spose its ready to sprout[8] . . .

TUESDAY, OCTOBER 20
. . . Ervin is working at Cliffs helping him put up feed. Henry is drilling Wheat. . . . Wind Whisteled, sad tunes all after-noon, made one think of the dead ones. It got colder from noon on. Wind is blowing very hard at 8 P.M. yet, is sprinkling a little. Mo churned, also strung Beans all after-noon. Static is very bad to-nite. . . .

WEDNESDAY, OCTOBER 21
. . . Ervin Came home this morning, so he Drilled Wheat at P.M. Carl Griswold came down this morning early, so him & Henry took the big old Stove, to the Church to keep the men from freezing stiff while working on the new building.[9] Mo mended some also Baked Bread. . . .

THURSDAY, OCTOBER 22

. . . Thelma & family where here all day also for dinner Ervin & Cliff went to Syracuse at 7,30 got home while we where eating Dinner. Men played hookie, at the present Ervin is at Wayne's.[10] Mo also hookied just Cooked washed Dishes got in Fuel & Swept the Floor. . . .

FRIDAY, OCTOBER 23

. . . Thelma & family where here all day long, she Sewed. Mo churned & Baked Bread. Ervin worked some at his Heater at A.M. Cliff Worked at the Church. Well the time at last arived, that Betty & Bob, became Man, & Wife, Betty wore Bobs mother's Satin Wedding Dress.[11] Hens layed 15 Eggs.

SATURDAY, OCTOBER 24

. . . Ervin & Henry went to Syracuse at 10 got home at 4 P.M. Mo played hookie most of the day. Verna quit Trostles to night. Was very windy, also dust blowing some. . . .

MONDAY, OCTOBER 26

. . . Ervin piteled on his Car & Henry went to the church all afternoon along. Thelma & kids where here all day long. Verna came home from Trostle's this morning. . . .

TUESDAY, OCTOBER 27

. . . Pete & Elmer stopcd in Elmer stayed all Night, so he'd be on hand, to start on his & Ervins, long trip, out west, I spose, or dont know where.[12] Mo & Verna Washed in afternoon, In fore noon Mo churned. also Baked Bread Verna Baked some cinnomon Rools. . . .

WEDNESDAY, OCTOBER 28

. . . Mo Ironed some baked 1 Lemon Pie & Apple Dumplings Verna Ironed & Henry fixed the Gate part of the fore-noon, hawled one Load Water. then the rest of the day he listened to the lectionering. To Night Henry is taking in political talkes, also at the present time he's listing to the gang Busters.[13] Ervin left this morning at 8 oclock . . .

FRIDAY, OCTOBER 30

. . . Wind so strong at 3 P.M. mostly terying the earth up. Verna is reading Cappers Paper.[14] . . .

SATURDAY, OCTOBER 31

. . . Thelma & Cliff went home & did the choars, came back after supper are taking in all sorts of Politicals talks Po & Cliff are puffing their Pipes, also Cigerets. Verna is making fancy work Thelma has helped her some, now around eight oclock she's taking in Rosevelt's Speech, so now this Saturday winds up old October, the fight will soon be gone, now only 3 more days then their Battel's el be fought, Campaning will be over with Tuesday at 12 oclock.[15] . . .

TUESDAY, NOVEMBER 3

. . . We went to the Poles to Vote at 2-45 got home at 3 P.M. about 5 the Warner kids arived, stayed for Supper, all took in the Lection votes, kids stayed till 10 in the Nite, Henry & Mo stayed up till 11-15 then Po & Mo went to roost . . . then at 2 Po got up & listened in on the Lecton Report some then after 15 mi or so he went to Bed, sleeping till 6 A.M. . . . Well Campaning time is over, the Battle is fought, & Rosevelt has won the Chair again. Well Landon was swept away, cause Rosevelt toook his Broom away. ha. . . .

WEDNESDAY, NOVEMBER 4

. . . Henry hawled 1 Load Water for the Church, also Cement a load of it P.M. at A.M. he dug some Post holes. Verna has made fancy Pillow Cases. Mo just Churned A.M. played lazy, took in some plays doing work, that just had to be done. Verna also Washed half of the Kitchen at A.M. . . . Well to-day peace is at hand, Political talks are over. A very nice day at hand just a little wind, so's the Windmill can run. . . . Pete Dyck was here at 7 A.M. to see who was Elected for President Now Landon men, Cheer up get beling Rosevelt rejoice & March on.

THURSDAY, NOVEMBER 5

. . . Verna made fancy work she worked at the Table cover. Mo played lazy. Verna is taking a strole, down in the Pasture through the thistles getting the Cows. . . . to nite about dark the wind went to the north west. Henry is full of mischief to nite, is acting, like a nett wett ha. . . . We got a card from Ervin to day, while hes in Hatch New Mexico picking Cotten.

FRIDAY, NOVEMBER 6

. . . Mos playing lazy most of the day listening to some plays just did a little house work, Baked Bread & took care of the chickens some, she also went to sleep at the Radio ha. Henry has been to the Church fenced A.M. also is fencing at P.M. Verna has backed Thelmas beautiful Birth.Cake this fore-noon, is reading Capers Papers this after-noon she Corled the Cows, also drove the Truck this fore-noon, while Henry was distrubiting some Posts to build the Fence. . . . Well Mr Rosevelt, is beeting us out of the first niter ha. on account of his speech. . . . It misted this morning so after it froze the trees looked like X-mas Trees. Verna frying Eggs this morning for Breakfast, fatt pooped all over her Arm, blistered it, got excited & droped one on the floor.

SATURDAY, NOVEMBER 7
. . . Po & Verna left for Syracuse at 11 A.M. got home at [   ] P.M.[16] Mo is home alone all day long. . . . Today is Thelma's Birthday she's 28 years old I'm sending her Cake home with Cliff to-nite on his way home, from Work. Mo potered around all day, trying to Clean little ods & ends ha Mo took a strole to the Barn, finding one big Egg there, which was layed by some of the lazy Hens that have their head-quarters in the Hog Pen ha . . .

MONDAY, NOVEMBER 9
. . . Cliff & family where here Thelma and kids where here all day long. Leroy smashed his dear little Thumb on his left Hand. Verna made her Blouse Thelma helped her some, the rest of the time she sewed on her Yellow Lounge Cover. Mo played lazy. Po hawled 1 Load Water at A.M. then in after-noon he hawled 1 Load Cement Its Pipe smok-ing time, at the Dyck ranch at the present time, the House is litered with fog ha. . . . Thelma brought us a piece of her birthday Cake.

TUESDAY, NOVEMBER 10
Southwind dust flying considerable. . . . Thelma & all the family where here for dinner. Thelma & Verna went to Syracuse started at 1-30 got home at 3-45 . . . Mo Baked Bread & Churned, was home all alone in after noon Very blue & clowdy day for Mo her heart was busted.[17] We got a Letter, also Card from Ervin to day. . . . wind is singing a sad tune. Po fixed Fence all day long.

WEDNESDAY, NOVEMBER 11
. . . Teakettle is wistling a sad tune ha. Mo is playing lazy to day, with a busted Heart, & shadows all over her. Henry titened up the Rods on his Car to-day. . . .

THURSDAY, NOVEMBER 12

. . . Thelma & family where for dinner. This fore-noon Mr Bishop & son Dean where here on buisness, telling Henry to come to have another little scouble [sociable] to-nite about the church.[18] . . . Henry worked on his Truck all day long. . . .

SATURDAY, NOVEMBER 14

. . . Thelma, the kids, Mo & Verna went to Syracuse 9-30 got home 3-40 on our way back from Syracuse, not far from Kendall we meet Po, giving him Cliffs Shoes, to get half soled in the mean while the Car Door being slamed shut, poor little Patsy got her dear little Thumb mashed in it. . . . at 20 till 4 we went to the Church to get Cliff after his days work was completed. Henry went to the church early in the fore-noon where the men was having a gamberee. he stayed there till 2 P.M. then he came home eat a bite and left for Syracuse. Henry & Mo had an argurment about beeting [betting] on Presidents also liquer.[19] . . .

MONDAY, NOVEMBER 16

. . . Henry went to Syracuse, he started at 10 A.M. got home at 5-10 We Washed Mo also Baked Bread Hens only layed 3 Eggs. Just one caller, Cappers men 2 of them. . . . We got a Card from Ervin to-day. he's in Arizona, at present, has been picking Cotten at Hatch Texas left for Arizona Sunday P.M. . . .

TUESDAY, NOVEMBER 17

. . . Henry unloaded his Coal this fore-noon, then sat at the Church to recuprate then after noon he drilled the Wheat Drills empty, then put Lugs on the Tractor. . . . Was a very plesent day not much wind, at all. We Ironed to-day Washed all the Curtains. Mo also Baked Bread. Verna Washed her Head. Verna also made some fancy work to-day. Mo also churned. Mo was quiet scared this morning, when she went into the Henhouse she spied a Turtle it certenly scared her for one moment.

WEDNESDAY, NOVEMBER 18

. . . Thelma was here all day long, also the kidies . . . Thelma made 1 fancy Apron for X-mas present, she also worked on her Lunchen Cloth. Patsy & Leroy went in the little Henhouse, there where 5 baby Pigs Patsy running them out, stiring up dust that Patsy Leroy & Mo almost coughed our Liver out. little Sunshine laughing all over Patsy.

little Leroy also Mo laughing as hard as we could, quiet a joke ha. We're lisning in at Fred Allen, o say he's a scream. Broaodcasting the Town hall to night. . . .

THURSDAY, NOVEMBER 19
. . . The Boss somewhat unplesent in upper storie ha.[20] . . . Henry is listing to the Coarse voiced mans News ha. Mo & Verna listened to a 15 minute of intertainment of Bob Burns & Bim Crosby's bunk. We got a letter from sister Lizzie, also got one from Ervin to Night. . . . Mo had a lazy day, to content with to day. The lady of the House, also Verna was gossiping, wasn't that refreshing, for a change, while they where having the house, to them selves. then 9-15 the lady of the house goes to Hay for recoupratation, while the Mr. is finishing up with this Papers. . . . sister Lizzie send us a Guny Sack of good Fruit from Oregan how nice of her.

FRIDAY, NOVEMBER 20
. . . very plesent weather just like summer Henry dear moved the Combine down to Cliffs at 10 A.M. before 10 A.M. he went to the church to see how the workers where coming. Then at 10 Henry took part of the Combine Cliff took the other half so they eat Dinner very early & then to the field they went, & cut the rest of the day. Verna took Cliffs Car went to Cliffs & came back home with Henry dear, got home at 4-45 . . . Henry took the A Battery out of the Radio so the lady of the house couldn't take in all the plays that she had been listing to.[21] So she had her first dissapointment, to face for to-day. Dust blowed some wind came up at 5 P.M. . . .

SATURDAY, NOVEMBER 21
. . . Thelma, Mo, kids, also Verna went to Syracuse started at 11-15, got home at 5-30. Henry & Cliff went to the church at 1 P.M. then started to Syracuse, got home at 6 mosing their way very slow through the dark with out eny lites. Cliff had a worn out transmission. We all certenly had a blue dissapointed day, to face Mo came home with the Headache. so did Verna Thelma was very nervous & sick. . . .

SUNDAY, NOVEMBER 22
. . . Wind blew fierce all night long, whistled, howled sang sad tunes. Mo was sick couldnt sleep much also had sick headache, doors gingled banged, also squeeked, most of the Night . . .

MONDAY, NOVEMBER 23

. . . Thelma & family where here P.M. a little while. . . . It was to cold & windy to combine Maze, so Henry just fenced a little while, the rest of the day he played lazy. . . . Mo didnt do nothing just tried my Drees on what Verna was making. Mo hit the Hay at 7 in the evening.

TUESDAY, NOVEMBER 24

. . . it was blowing, was dark from dust setteled in the clowds. very discourening also dissatisfaction all day long, Blue that we couldn't see through the Clowds, & more blues, couldn't find no blues chaser either ha. Verna is working on her Pillow cases. Mo churned after Supper, to Night. . . . Henry & Verna are listing to a detective story its very sad one man that had a 3 day old baby, boy, in the hospital, he was hung for murdring a girl by the name Ruth.

WEDNESDAY, NOVEMBER 25

. . . Henry dear & Cliff Combined Maze to-day. just had very little wind to-day. . . . I say to day at the Breakfast Table, we had quiet a comotion. Found Worms in the Bran Box so Henry took it back, it back to the Store, give it to the manager's Wife, she said o I never new that could get Moldie, Henry says its wormy she took a look at it. then saying O. O. shouting out loud. So they both where tickeled about it.

THURSDAY, NOVEMBER 26

. . . strong wind storm also dust storm came up at 1 oclock so the men couldn't Combine Maze, just chated . . . then eat their Thanksgiving dinner, this is what Thelma had Chicken Dressing cramberry sauce white Cake Lettuce Squash Pumpkin Pie & Mashed Potatoes a swell Dinner, its a wonder that a doctor didn't half to Call after all the eating was done down there ha. . . . Hens played thanksgiving as we all did they just layed one Egg ha. . . . Henry went to the church after we got home from our big dinner. to see how the church is progressing. . . . To-day the lady of the house couldn't listen to much of her plays cause she had to obey her boss for one time ha. . . .

FRIDAY, NOVEMBER 27

. . . it was very windy at 2 P.M. & dust blowed very bad for 3 hours then it got very plesent. Henry & Cliff Combined Maze all day. . . .

SUNDAY, NOVEMBER 29

. . . We all left for the Warners at 9 A.M. Butchered a Hog got home at 3 P.M. Henry is listing to the good Will Court. Now at the present time Eddie Canter is broad casting his program, he said that he's going to kiss all the Audience ha. Verna is trying to snoose ha. Verna went to Bed at 7 Mo hit the Hay at 7-15 Henry at 7-30

TUESDAY, DECEMBER 1

. . . Henry dear made 2 trips to church Mo Baked Bread P.M. Cooked Vegetable soup for Dinner, Cooked a Hog bone for Supper. We got 3 Bullets to-day[22] Pos listing to Husbands & Wives, disgusing each others faults. Verna hit the Hay at 8 then the 2 bosses rolled in 30 mi later. Cold old disagreeable December is rolling in. Mo churned about 2 lbs Butter after Supper.

WEDNESDAY, DECEMBER 2

. . . Henry & Mr Bishop went to Kendall A.M. Henry dear made two trips to church one A.M. another one P.M. Verna sewed her a Dress also Baked 2 Pumpkin Pies Mo just got Dinner all fore-noon. Hens layed 3 Eggs ha. Mo cut out her spotted Ginnie Dress. . . .

FRIDAY, DECEMBER 4

. . . Henry dear & Verna went to Syracuse at 8-30 got home 2-30. Henry dear & Verna both got a Hair cut. At the present time Verna is working on a Organdy Apron a Xmas present. Mo finished cutting out her Dress . . . Henry dear is puffing his Pipe, while listing to the Comedian Jack Pearl that the hole room is satachrated with smoke fumes ha. Verna dear is eating Peanuts at the present time Henry dear is now eating Peanuts these 30 mi while he's listing to Cope Karter giving the news. To-day Mo didn't play so much lazy, she washed the Dishes all meals, also Washed the Seprator . . . Mo worked at her Rug which she started last winter she also Patched a pair of Socks for Po & her self. . . .

SATURDAY, DECEMBER 5

. . . Verna is making a fancy Scarf. This fore-noon she baked a Burned Sugar cake then at P.M. she made the Icing. Mo only rendered some Lard. she just putered around some. Well last Night we changed our menue had just been living off of Spuds & Sowbelly for severel days, so for a change we had Lettuce also Carrots for Supper also Din-

ner. . . . Henry went to church A.M. helped lat the Wall also went &
helped at P.M. . . .

MONDAY, DECEMBER 7
. . . Henry made 2 trips to the church at A.M. worked at his Truck put
rods in at P.M. then at sunset he haweled 1 Load Water to church . . .
Mo & Verna washed to-day this evening Verna was working at her
fine Apron. . . .

TUESDAY, DECEMBER 8
. . . Henry went to the church at A.M. also P.M. Dear Henry haweled
1 Load Water to church Cliff Warner & family called in fore-noon
Cliff went to church, so we all eat dinner here & Cliff & family, also
Verna went to Syracuse Mo went along to Kendall and atened Gertrudes Stork Shower. 34 Women there and most 12 Babies. Gertrude
got a great deal for presents, for the arrival, in the feature [future]. . . .
We did some of our ironing at A.M. at present dear Verna is address-
ing her Xmas Card at present Henry dear is listing to a interview its
very intresting. . . .

THURSDAY, DECEMBER 10
. . . Henry went to Syracuse after 13 dollars of oilcake he started A.M.
8-30 came home P.M. 4 . . . Pete Dyck the trouble maker called P.M.
trying to find faults with the Dycks also start a quarrel. . . .

FRIDAY, DECEMBER 11
. . . Pete was here for dinner stayed all night, also Thelma & kiddies
called at A.M. Henry made 2 trips to Church. . . . The Prince of Walles
made his farewell speech to-day while he's with his beloved sweet
heart whom he's planing on maring in the near-feature.[23] Verna is
getting Supper while Mo is scribbling down her dierie . . . to-day Ervin got back home after his long journey from Mexico Arizona picking cotton for 4 weeks or more. Ervin arrived after midnight.

SATURDAY, DECEMBER 11
. . . Mo played lazy most all day long just Henry also Ervin are looking
at the Arizona Map for entertainment

SUNDAY, DECEMBER 12
. . . Cliff Warner & family where here all day long . . . we all went to
Syracuse except Ervin Verna Thelma Mo Leroy also Patty took in the

picture show Remona. got home at 10-30 P.M. . . . Wayne Henry Pete Elmer also Ervin disgussing their adventures picking Cotton, also living around Mexicans, the boys seem to think its quiet a joke, after it's all over with . . .

MONDAY, DECEMBER 13
. . . Henry hawled 2 Loads Water, also 1 Load Cement to the church, at P.M. he's getting a load of Coal from Kendall. Verna's taking a strole after the Cows at the present time in after noon she's working at her Dresser Scarf. . . . Mr. Bishop. Wayne Rogers called to Night, also Henry sweet, trying to settle up their discourgements about their beautiful church not being satisfactory to all the farmers in this comunity, and at seven to Night these 3 went to the Church, to see if they could make some more plans. Henry sweet got home at 11 P.M.[24] . . .

TUESDAY, DECEMBER 15
. . . Thelma & family Verna Ervin also Mo started to Syracuse at 11 A.M. got home 4-10 Mo did her Xmas shopping Henry dear is listing to Earl May telling about Mexico, Verna is working on her Scarf Ervin the num leged-boy is lying on the Davenport eating Candy. . . . Mo is warming her Bread now & then so she'l get it Baked by 8-30 so she can retire not later then 9 oclock. . . . Windmill is play a squeeking tune at the present time. . . . Mo got her Order from Monkey Ward to-day, her Xmas good.[25]

WEDNESDAY, DECEMBER 16
. . . Verna is listing to Gracies love afairs at present Ervin is filing his fingernails Henry on the Davenport snoozing. . . . Mo cleaned cabinet knife Draws also scoured all Pie Pans also Cake Tins, o say it was a job, I've been putting it off cause it's hard, also dirty. Ervins hands have very big soars on them yet, from the Cotton field effects. Verna finished up the fancy parts of her scarf. Mo listened to these plays Betty & Bob Molly the Movie Star, Bachlors Children, to-days children David Harren. Nancy & Bill. Johns other wife. . . . Just now Ervin is studying his Arizona Map for pass away time. Po is still in piecefull slumber on the Davenport . . . To day son had to cary water to exercise his num Lims, from his long mexico trip.

THURSDAY, DECEMBER 17
. . . This morning Mo cleaned the Coupboard. at P.M. mo churned Verna & Mo Baked a batch o Xmas Cookies Verna trimed up some

Cooks to see how they Cake director [decorator] works Verna finished up her Xmas Scarf in fore-noon. . . . Henry dear is listing to Bob Burns jokes at present. Ervin eat cookies candy and apples for courisity ha. he also had to pump water in the House to dijest his food, he also had to slop & feed the Hogs for exercise. . . . Ervin lunched all day long, for good measure, after being on a cheap diet in the Cotton fields.[26] . . . Trees looked like Xmas trees this morning, where very beautiful

FRIDAY, DECEMBER 18

Northwest wind in morning, it got stronger around ten oclock, blowed very hard till noon so dust blowed considerable for a while then a while after dinner it let up some then around four P.M. it was quiet. . . . Cliff & family called for dinner. also Granpo Warner. after Supper Elmer & Pete called. . . . Mo cleaned Pantry shelves also scrubed cleaned middle Bedroom. Henry dear was home all day long, reading magazines was a good boy, cause there was nothing stirring at the Church. Mo listened to Bob & Betty, Bill & Nancy David Harrem, Mother Marand Lary & Mary, Mary Marline, also the Oniels family also Andy Gump. . . .

SATURDAY, DECEMBER 19

. . . Ervin stayed home, eat Toasties also dried Apples for dinner. Po Mo Verna started to town at 10 A.M. got home 5 P.M. Warners where here for supper, went home at 7 P.M. . . . Mo did some more Xmas shoping to-day Cliff bought Thelmas Xmas present. . . . town was just jamed full cause it was Santa Clause day.

MONDAY, DECEMBER 21

. . . Verna & Mo washed Ervin nursing his sores, also lunshing on Toasties, calatouging, also moping the rest of the day. I spose, he also raidoed some. us two women also did most of our Ironing at P.M. . . . At present Henry dear is listing to a detective story. how sory & cruel it sounds & such terriable cries. . . . Mo Cooked some dried Apples to Night on the Heating Stove, while the room had to be warmed, she also cooked Spuds for breakfast also cooked them on the Heating Stove. Henry dear drove up to the church twice for nothing, just enspected things & finding faults ha. . . . Well to-day's the shortest cheerfull day gone by seems very encouring, to think, that to morrow & in the future, the days grow longer then we all can acomplish more in one day, then we did in the past. This after noon Henry dear drove out west to inspect the blowing soil, also drove up to Clarence Shafer to see the soil in that Country. We washed all our Coushion Slips to-day.

THURSDAY, DECEMBER 24, XMAS EVE

. . . Henry went to Bishops very early this morning so he has been gone all day long its 8 oclock at present & no mr. at home. Ervin has just hit the hay. Verna is snoozing at the present time. So us two women & Ervin batched we just lunched all day long. Candy & Nuts where the most important part, so for Dinner Steak, also for Supper Steak also Carrots for desert Cranberries & Xmas Cookies. Amos & Andy where very interesting to night Ames was showing the Radio set, that he'd got Ruby for Xmas, the boys where playing a Xmas song on it and right before the close our Revern gave a spiritual talk on Xmas. . . .

FRIDAY, DECEMBER 25, XMAS DAY

To day was Xmas every body having a great time with the Xmas Spirit piece on Earth & good will to men. . . . Henry dear is lying on the daven-port snoozing after sowing his wild Oats all night last Night, without eny sleep. at the present time Ervin & Verna took Pete Dyck to Wayne's where they're playing razel dazel.[27] Pete called this morning at 7-30 with Henry when he got back from Holly. Last Night Henry got his Car in the ditch, had to get some one to pull him out in the mean time to get help, he had to walk 5 miles. We all went to Cliffs for a xmas dinner Ethel & Olyan Pete also Grandpa Warner was there,[28] this is what we had for Xmas dinner Chicken dressing Gravy Peas White Cake, fancy Cookies Fruit Salad place Cards Nut Cups also Lettuce Salad, all trimmed, all had merry Xmas, also lots of fun. . . .

SATURDAY, DECEMBER 26

Well to-day xmas is over I spose every one is still tired from the after effects also tired and lac of ambition from the big xmas dinner they ate probely some of them had to see a doctor from the effects of their eats. Well Henry dear is snoozing on the Davenport from the effects of the Holly trip. Verna is Cataloging at present Ervin is filing his fingernails. Mo feels like some one thrashed her one on the Head with a Hammer. . . .

MONDAY, DECEMBER 28

Well old December is purnear gone only 5 more days to wind it up. Well to-day is a very dark clowdy day for all that are in the house. the effects after the razel dazel game one sleeping, one reading, one smoking and the other trying to sew, not getting very far lac of ambition in a murky old day on account of soil a blowing some where in the south and east I spose wind is in the south at present has been a little in the east at A.M. wind has blowed very hard ever since 10 A.M. . . .

TUESDAY, DECEMBER 29

Very quiet this morning till 9-30 then the wind started to houp her up kept it up in the meantime, dust started to blow by spells the lectricity interfeered with Radio lisening to Big Sister, so I didn't get to hear all the play. So then the Sun got dim no Sunshine at all Skies was murky till 4 it was quiet, so then at 5-30 up came the Wind circeled around to the north east again, at A.M. it was southwest . . . Verna & Mo baked 5 galls. Cookies with Raisins, Mo also Churned, while these Cookies where baking, Mo cooked a Stew pot full of Spuds with Jackets for Breakfast, also while the Stove was hot Mo cooked Po some Prunes for New Year Proon Soup . . . Well to night while listing to Dick Tracy, the Battery blowed up so . . . we couldn't hear what Ames & Andy was doing just now & then a couple words. Beings the Battery went haywire to night so to bed at 7 Verna went 1/2 hour later Ervin went so this old dungen is very lonesome to night. Po is reading a Book for entertainment with the Lamp on the Sewing Machine for a change, its usualy place, is on the Radio while Radio is going on, so that makes all things look like Bachlors Life ha. . . .

WEDNESDAY, DECEMBER 30

. . . Henry took a trip to church to day to settle his courisity he's very courious to see whether or not the men are working down there . . . Mo washed the kitchen chairs in the fore-noon at present Verna is sitting with her hands in her lap, Calculating, Ervin reading a newspaper, Henry at a magazine. Mos in mizery since she got home. This morning Mo was nutty in her head after having a headache, the most of the Night. . . . Verna & the men are listing to the Gang Busters they're so fierce . . .

THURSDAY, DECEMBER 31

this last day in year. Well another good old year comes to a close the year of 1936 it's be gone at 12 midnight. It brought us much joy peace chear and comfort. The radio was very entertaining to day, at present they're ringing out the old year & ringing in the New. Well Henry stayed home, with us . . . preceating, his family for once he was very nice to us all. So at P.M. he went to the church so Ervin did all his choars he just got home 4-45 to day Verna Baked a white cake with New Year trimings also poped a dish Pan of Popcorn, so Mo & her made it to Balls. Verna also made some Devenity. Mo cleaned the Pantry her Bedroom, also scared the Oil Stove. Today Verna & Mo listened to these plays Betty & Bob John's other wife, Nancy & Bill, David Harrem, to-days children, Big Sister way down east, Judy & Jane also the Oneals family. . . . Men & Verna are sitting playing cards for pass away time to see the old year out & the new one in, the men are eating Candy Popcorn Balls, also drinking water for fill ups also good measure. it is now 10-45 and no one came to join us to see the old year roll out Well when the time came to eleven fifty, Po had hit for his snoozing quarters, Ervin had hit it at 11-15 so when the Old Year went out. Verna was sitting in her Pajames, at the Radio, hollering. Happy New Year, away to bed she went in her dark room. Mo was sitting by the fire, looking at the Stove thinking. Good-by old year bu,hoo. how I hate to see you go, you been so good to us, but we not being so good to you. So now the New one, we're going to be more cheerfull to you. Go then away to the Hay I went. . . .

3. BLOWING DUST AND DEPARTURES

1937

FRIDAY, JANUARY 1, FIRST DAY OF THE YEAR
Well to-day is the first day of the New Year. It sort of looked like Xmas this morning, was very beautiful. Trees where all decorated with white frost . . . Verna, Po, also Ervin are playing cards at the present time it is after noon this fore-noon they where listening to some plays, eating Pop Corn Balls, also eating Candy for pass away time. . . . This morning it was a job for all of us to come out of the Hay. After the celebration of the Old Year, we all looked like we where half shot. . . .

SATURDAY, JANUARY 2
. . . It was real windy to Bishop's field blowed a great bit. . . . Po dear is running the Radio, also reading at the same time. Ervin is reading, Verna snoozing. . . . Neal Dean, Mr. Bishop came along, with their Truck . . . they loaded 3 of our Pigs sold them got $16.82 cts for them. . . .

SUNDAY, JANUARY 3
. . . Henry & Cliff took Cliffs Broom corn to Syracuse, left at one got home at 3-30.[1] . . . Ervin & Verna went to Wayne Rogers, played cards came home at 2 in the morning. . . .

MONDAY, JANUARY 4
. . . Henry & Ervin hawled 1 Load Water to the Church at P.M. also hawled 1 Load Straw in the Henhouses. This fore-noon they just putered around. . . . at present Ervin is lying on the Davenport sleep-

ing sleeping from the effects of the Sun. Night Card Game. . . . Henry
is sleeping in the Rocking Chair near the Radio Lux play is on at the
present Verna is lying on the floor listening to this play. . . .

TUESDAY, JANUARY 5
. . . At this fore-noon wind started kept on getting worse till noon it
was going 60 miles an hour wind in the Southeast at present, its 4 P.M.
This fore noon awhile it was straight south dust blowing the air is
murky, so one cant see no Sun. . . . At present Ervin is Kalatoguing.
Verna is snoozing on the Davenport, to cover Dust blues . . .

WEDNESDAY, JANUARY 6
Wind was north early this morning, fierce wind all night at P.M. the
wind is northeast still blowing in good hickory. . . . Henry dear nailed
Sacks on the Henhouse, to get some breeze out of it so the Hens
wont freeze their Combs. This after-noon Ervin is cleaning his Bed
Room up in the Basement, Henry sweet is at the church for courisity
walked down there, Verna is fancy working at the present time. . . .
Mo baked Vernas birthday Cake to morrows her birthday. At present
Po, Ervin, also Verna are playing Cards having lots fun. . . .

THURSDAY, JANUARY 7
. . . Men & Verna are playing Cards for pass away time while Mo is
writing her Direy. . . . This is Vernas birthday. Thelma & family came
at 7 P.M. All played cards except the kidies & Mo kidies were playing
with their Dolls also their cards about 8 oclock they all got skuppering
around here drinking coffee eating Cake . . .

FRIDAY, JANUARY 8
. . . Mo just watered Hens 3 times to-day, brought their scraps to them,
got 3 loads full of Coal for good measure between 4 & 5 she darned
Ervins Woll Socks Mr. Henry went to Bishops to settle Church mat-
ters he's lonesome cause he cant run much Radio on account of the
Battry, just about to run out of Juice. Verna made a fancy Pillow Case,
at the present time the men also Verna dear are playing razel dazel.
Henry puffing away his cigar.
. . . Mo just heard todays childrens play, part of Judie & Jane part of
Richmans darling on account of the week Battory. its very lonesome
when we cant have much Radio. . . .

SATURDAY, JANUARY 9

. . . Mo has a little cold she feels like someone thrashed her one on the block, Throat hurts, Sneezing like no ones buisness. Ervin has a cold now for 3 days Verna got one to-day, head feels stuffed . . . The men & Verna are playing Cards with the New Deck of cards, which Ervin bought to-day. the Radio is very beautiful at the present time. . . . Thelma & Cliff set up their Radio to day.[2]

SUNDAY, JANUARY 10

. . . Well to-days Sunday Henry smoking his pipe, Verna on the Davenport tears in her eyes from a cold. Ervin having a headache along with his bad cold. Mo's head giving her fits eyes watering. Windmills squeeking makes one think of good old warm weather, but not to hot ha. . . .

MONDAY, JANUARY 11

. . . some comotion took place in the Pantry in the Night Mouse jumped into a Crock of Milk Mo jumped when she saw this. . . . Mo got up this morning with a terriable cold in the head & nose. Verna is still feeling bad with her cold but her fierce head ache was gone this morning when she got up. . . . Verna & Mo are batching to-day nursing their colds its very lonesome lonesome since Ervin is leaving for severel months I spose . . .

WEDNESDAY, JANUARY 13

This morning was another nice quiet day suddenly at 9 came a breeze at 10 A.M. it got much stormier then at 11 A.M. o boy dust was flying to beet the band then at 11 A.M. no more Radioning lectricity so bad I never heard another think till 3 P.M. at 3 wind let down also dust . . . This after-noon Henry & Cliff drove around to see soil conditions got back at 3 P.M. . . .

FRIDAY, JANUARY 15

This morning trees, grass, weeds where beautiful looked like Xmas. . . . this morning Mo Baked Bread . . . Mr & Mrs. Cross came at 4 P.M. to get Verna to work for them Verna washed & Ironed some, also Baked a Chocolate Cake. Mo finished up her Nightgown, also hemed some Wash cloths. Put the protecter on the Orange Comforter, also sewed a new bottom in the purple Blanket. . . .

SATURDAY, JANUARY 16

... sky looks murky, started to look unsettled at 11 A.M. .... Wind has come up is howling. ... The Warners family where here ... The little Warner kids played out of doors, & got scared of the Pigs, it was comical, they took a long stick & run them away. .... Henry dear ground up the Lard also some meat from the old sow. .... Mo made a night gown also patched stockings, also Socks. ...

SUNDAY, JANUARY 17

... it is 5-20 now the fierce wind came up was blowing some places but not so bad. This forenoon while Mo was all alone ... she was feeling very broken hearted, seeing the lonesome Toastie Box not being touched but once or twice since sonny boy left. tears came in her eyes so she was so lonesome, with a big lump in her throat, to keep Po from seeing her sobing, seeing his clothes here & there & everywhere couldn't keep from thinking he'd never return. Verna dear's clothes in all rooms, to see ever little bit. Mo feel much home-sick, also so very lonesome. Mo feels tough all day long. .... Mo wrote a letter to Verna dear also Ervin dear. ...

MONDAY, JANUARY 18

... At 10 we went to the Warners to butcher ... Mo was so sick that she just sit around with a such headache also sick Stomache, she didn't eat a bite for supper.[3] We got home from the kids at 3 P.M. kids butchered 3 hogs just shoats.

WEDNESDAY, JANUARY 20

... Pete called this morning for breakfast to eat Bachlors cooking, after breakfast the Dyck brothers, disgussed church affairs & some more gossip, its not only women that gossip, men to. Pete says to day he didn't care for show it was just nonsense just love & loving each other & still they just sued each other & getting divorce ha ha nothing but bunk.[4] Well another big blister pooped out on my nose in the nighttime so now that's the third night blisters came out on my mouth & nose I spose about 8 all toll Mo feels some better, after her fever has left her. ...

THURSDAY, JANUARY 21

... Mr. Chasteen called at 8 trying to get Henry dear, to hawl water as cold as it was, Henry just told him that he just wouldn't hawl any in such cold weather, Henry was all mad at him not using no better judjement as all that. . . . Po is rendering Lard to-day which he killed last week Wednesday, also is canning some ribs in the oven. Mo feels better to-day has some cold in her head yet. Mos nose was so painfull, in the night that she just couldn't sleep well, dreamed about, so much, that she forgot what it was. . . . Po dont feel so very good to day still blowing his nose, ever little bit. he just pottered around a little. . . .

SATURDAY, JANUARY 23
. . . at 9-30 a terrific dust storm lectricity up in the air at 9-40 that we couldn't radio in the day time . . . Lectricity quit at 4-45 then we could Radio. But wind didn't quit it still blowed in the Night yet, dust settled at 5-30 P.M. . . .

SUNDAY, JANUARY 24
. . . the two Dyck brothers are at the church looking around to see what the workers have been doing down there since they've not been present for some time. . . . Mos face feels terriable with all the blisters & o how does it look. Mo still feels tough & weak.

MONDAY, JANUARY 25
. . . We got a letter from Ervin. . . . Thelma & kiddies stayed here all day long & sewed Patsy a dress & sewed up her quilt, while Henry & Cliff went to Syracuse & Ma playing lazy just cook a little now & then . . . Pattsy & Leroy are playing with the Coushons, making baby dolls out of them, one Patsy made dressed it with Leroys coat & cap making it look like Leroy, another one dressed it in her Coat & Hat making it look like Patsy. The men got home from Town at 3 P.M. so a little while later, they went home. . . .

TUESDAY, JANUARY 26
This morning early it was very beautiful out of doors. Trees Grass all weedse, where coated with Ice just like Xmas . . . wind came up and at 11 A.M. dust was flying & lectricity in the air. . . . Henry started to Kendall at 10 A.M. he broke a Hub for his car 3 mi. north. . . . This after-noon he's hawling 4 Barrels Water to the church he left home at 2-30 he got back home from church at 4-30. Henry came home from the trip breaking the Hub he was all in a whirl. Then from the church all digusted on account things not going his way. . . .

WEDNESDAY, JANUARY 27

... at 3 P.M. wind came up went northwest dust came up 1 hour and cleared up. Henry hawled a load Water to the church got back at 11 A.M. then he went to Kendall got home at 1 P.M. he eat a cold lunch. . . . the 2 brothers are having a chat about the church as usual its eretating for me. . . .

FRIDAY, JANUARY 29

This morning its very beautiful out of doors ground is full of white frost, Trees are full of Ice ciciles are looking very pretty. . . . Mos real week leged yet dont do much just cook Wash dishes & Sweep the flour her nose & lips still hurt her yet. She also has a very sore tooth. Henry is taking his Truck apart, getting ready, to take Cliffs Sow, also his two little Pigs. Henry seprated to-day for a change its been six days since he seprated. . . .

SATURDAY, JANUARY 30

... Henry went to Cliff at 8-30 to get Cliffs Sow also loaded up his 2 Pigs, started to Syracuse at 9-50 got home at 12-50, got $5.30 cts a piece for the Pigs Cliff got $20. Cliff also sold 4 little Pigs . . . Henry went to Crosses & got Verna at 3-30 got back at 4-30

SUNDAY, JANUARY 31

... Henry dear brought Verna back to Crosses at 4 P.M. they stoped at the Warners & eat ice cream. Leroy Cliff & Patsy went along to Crosses to her working home at the present time. . . .

TUESDAY, FEBRUARY 2

... at 9 A.M. fierce wind came up at 9-45 dust was rolling the air being full of lectricity at 10 A.M. so that blowed up listening to the Radio wind went to the south east then now its 1 P.M. its southwest. . . .

WEDNESDAY, FEBRUARY 3

... the wind came up 10 A.M. dust started to fly so at 10-30 no more radioing lectricy up till 12 noon it quit dust settled some so the sky wasn't very murky sun shone some right along at 3 P.M.

THURSDAY, FEBRUARY 4

... wind came up at 9 dust rooled some, till the sky looked murky just a very little lectricity . . .

FRIDAY, FEBRUARY 5

. . . Henry hawled a load cement to the church this fore noon. This after-noon is the Soil meeting.[5] . . .

SUNDAY, FEBRUARY 7

. . . it was real windy wind also had blowed some all night long, wind is in south west, it is not 9-30 & its very dark, almost dark enough to light a lamp. Terific dust storm started at 9-30 lectricity fierce at the present time. Storm calmed down some at 2 P.M. Po radioed 15 min then at 2-15 it come over with another storm so then we lit the Aladin Lamp so we could see. its dark at 4-30. Stayed dark until 5-45 then it cleared up some, lectricity quit, wind came up harder dust settled considerable at this time . . . Po is calculating about the dust storm, so at the present time hes, devouring an Apple. It blowed all, night long.

MONDAY, FEBRUARY 8

. . . Wind came up at 3 P.M. kicked up a little dust for about 20 mi then quit. . . . Henry cleaned up all dust in 3 rooms, being very contended, cheerfull, just kept on going till it was all done, all Mo done was just brushed dust off the window sills, machine, also phonograph.[6] This afternoon Mo washed some clothes, also fixed the collar of pops shirt. . . .

THURSDAY, FEBRUARY 11

. . . at 10:45 wind came up dust started to roll, lasted 1 hour 1/3 so strong then at 12:50 we could radio wind went to the north. Henry hawled 1 load Water to the church this fore-noon. . . .

FRIDAY, FEBRUARY 12

. . . air is looking dusty at the present time. . . . To day Mos companion was mucky, run over his long Hose with the Tractor, cut it in three pieces. Then another accident broke one of the big Window Lites in the Well House. This fore noon Henry is fixing on his Tractor in fore-noon this after-noon he went to Syracuse at 12-15 got home at 5 P.M.

SATURDAY, FEBRUARY 13

. . . at 10 A.M. wind let up some but it was dusty almost 2 hours after ten it went down. . . . Ervin went to Crosses to get Verna they went on to Syracuse. . . .

SUNDAY, FEBRUARY 14

This morn. South west Ferocious Dust Storm early in full cession when we got up this morning, lectricity fierce till P.M. 2 dust settled also static quit then we could radio wind changed to north west very plesent after 2 P.M. . . . Ervin pulled back to his home at 12-30 taking 5 boyes with him. Cliff & Thelma took Verna back to Crosses to Night after 5 P.M. Thelma brought some Chickens down, roasted them for dinner, also Baked a beautiful decroated Cocoanut Cake all trimed up Cake for Mo's birthday. . . . This morning at one oclock dust storm came a terriable one. We both got up & covered all things up to keep dust out. so in the morning when we got up lectricity had quieted down, also dust . . . Well to-day is Valentine day.

MONDAY, FEBRUARY 15

This morning air was full of dust sky was merky. At seven wind started stronger, kept on 2 hours so at 9 Terific Dust Storm started . . . It never cleared up in the skies till night. O boy Pete just called 1/2 hour ago, these two brothers ha. One in the Rocker the other in another Rocker. O boy how they're arguring. Pete against the President Henry for him, Pete says if these people had to do their voting over again, none of them would have give Rosevelt a change.[7] Pete is getting very noisy & loud at the present time. I think after 3/3 of an hour of this stouff, his jaws would be tired, also short winded too. . . .

TUESDAY, FEBRUARY 16

This morning we got up at 5:15 it was quiet & clowdy & at 9:30 came a terific Dust Storm. . . . The Mail Man didn't venture out in the dust. So no Mail for us. Henry went to the field, & I Listed at 7-30 came home at 9-45 on account of Dust Storm.[8] Dust & wind kept on till 6-15 lectricity let up some . . . To day is the fifth day, that Mo didn't eat a bite of supper. Po has to eat by himself . . . Mo hasent eat eny Supper for 4 weeks at Supper time[9] . . . We just listened to the Radio from 6 in the evening on & off till seven we then retired it never did clear up, nor quit, it just kept on not quiet, so strong, as it was in the after noon but this wind & dust continued all day long didn't even clear up the next morning, we had lamps lit. . . .

WEDNESDAY, FEBRUARY 17

Wind went to the north in the night we got up at 6 this morning, so lamps are still lit yet. It's now 9:30 no sign of letting up, it's dark out side almost as night. . . . in the after-noon sun came out at 4:30 in the after noon, it was all cleared up nice at 5 P.M. wind all let up.[10] The sky was full of dust it was almost dark at 5 O say it certenly takes a lot of Lotion to protect ones hands, so that they can sew or patch. I used up 1/2 bottle of Hand Lotion in a little bit over a week. Henry used a little of it O boy doors all furniture & walls full of dust. Henry is reading papers waiting for it to let up a little so he can milk & do some choars. . . . Washed all the Lamp globes, but it never did no good at all. Also washed the door Glass didn't look nice & clean just a few hours.

THURSDAY, FEBRUARY 18
. . . Wind came up at 11 this fore-noon, then at 12:30 dust was blowing static was so bad that we couldn't radio for a while. Wind went to the south late in the after-noon. We had a firce dust storm in the night it came at midnight, from the north east. Air didn't look very merky 6 A.M. I just missed out on the Oneals, Mirt & Marge, also Judie & Jane, on account the lectricity. I heard 10 of the plays that I listen to quiet often. I cleaned dust all fore noon & churned this after-noon. . . . Po went to the field just at 4 P.M. He listed on the Doerr quarter this fore-noon. At 4 P.M. he went to the field one mile east of here. after the dust quit, so he could see. . . . O boy to day, eating was a temptation for Mo, she'd like to eat but no not at all. . . .

FRIDAY, FEBRUARY 19
. . . A nice chilly day to list. It just kept on being clowdy no chance clowds looked like Rain clowds but we was fooled so much that we dont think we'll get it. Henry has listed all day long. . . . Mo cleaned dust most of the day. . . . So to day we got a Bu. of Mail. Didn't get it for 5 days. Henry cleaned dust in the Basement, before the kids came to go to town.

SATURDAY, FEBRUARY 20
This morning when we get up at 6 A.M. O boy Ground is white with Snow. O what a consolation for all of us for a change. . . .

SUNDAY, FEBRUARY 21
. . . O say it certeanly seems like Paridise yesterday, & to day it seems, as if we're in a different world. . . .

MONDAY, FEBRUARY 22
. . . never even had enough wind to turn the Mill so it'd pump water.
To day a very beautiful day. . . . Roosters are crowing seems like
Springtime. . . .

THURSDAY, FEBRUARY 25
. . . Henry didn't work to-day on account of the frost in the ground.
. . . Mo Patches Pos Overalls & still's working at her dress. We seper-
ater the Milk to day its 5 days ago since we went through the machine. . . . Well this is the 7th day now that we're enjoying wonderfull piece. . . .

FRIDAY, FEBRUARY 26
. . . This morning when we got up at six we had an inch of Snow. Its
been snowing very fine on & off all day long it was cold. . . . Henry
dear has been reading the magazine most of the day, when he wasn't
listing to the Radio. In the fore-noon he cleaned up the south bedroom. Mos Baking Bread this after-noon. This forenoon she churned.
And in the after-noon she cleaned the Pantry cupboard Cabinet &
the middle Bedroom. . . .

SATURDAY, FEBRUARY 27
. . . Thelma & Cliff came at 1-30 Cliff went on to town Thelma &
kidies stayed here Cliff went to Croses & got Verna about 12 at noon
by our time. Verna stayed all night with us. . . .

SATURDAY, FEBRUARY 28
. . . Henry took Verna to Crosses got back at 5 P.M. we certenly had
a fine time time lots fun, also & fine dinner Pumpkin Pie, Lettuce
Salad Carrots Mashed Potatoes Gravy also Pumpkin Pie with Whip
Cream. . . . The two old folks hit the Hay at 8-15 both where very
lonesome after Verna left us again for a week or so. . . .

TUESDAY, MARCH 2
. . . Its been a little clowdy also murky looking. . . . Henry went to the
Tractor this fore noon for several hours fixed on it. This after-noon
he's Listing. . . . Mo Baked 3 Lemon Pies to-day. Washed some &
made 1 pr. Bloomers. . . .

WEDNESDAY, MARCH 3

. . . we had a terific Dust Storm at 9 it hasn't enterfeered with the Radio till 9-30 just a very little then at 9 it let up considerable. But soil is blowing it is now 2 P.M. . . . It sprinkels at 8 p.M. Wind is still blowing dust is all vanished now. . . . it sprinkeled on & off for about 3 hours so the dust settled for the next day. . . . Mo Ironed a little the forenoon in the after noon she sewed some on a pair of Bloomers also cut out her dress. Mo also churned this fore-noon. . . .

THURSDAY, MARCH 4

. . . Mo Baked Bread to day. . . . Rosevelt made a speech at 2-30.[11]

FRIDAY, MARCH 5

. . . Mo wrote a letter to Ervin to day. Mo wrote a letter to Verna to day. Adressing it to Mr. Verna Dyck instead Miss ha. . . . The junk man Wrights called just before dinner wanting to buy some junk. Henry sold them over $3.15 Dollars worth Henry Listed this fore-noon got in from the field 12-25. In the after-noon till 4:30 they hunted up the junk. . . . Mo washed & cleaned dust. Baked 3 Mince Pies in the after-noon This fore-noon she sewed a little, also scrubed the Pantry Mo washed the Cabinet doors Cupboard doors also the Merrior [mirror]. . . . After Midnight some time it blowed like sixty. But at day break wind had went down. Mo had 5 Dresses 1 Shirt & several pr. Socks out on the Clothes line through it all. . . .

SATURDAY, MARCH 6

. . . We got Ervin's check to-day.[12]

SUNDAY, MARCH 7

. . . at 6 A.M. at 8 dust started to blow then at 10 A.M. We had a terific Dust Storm. Sun not shining much now & then it peeps. . . . dust kept on till 6 P.M. Then it let up Mo lost out on her 2 plays Grand hotel & Tale of today. o gosh on account of the Dust Storm. Kids stayed all night went home at 8 this morning. . . .

MONDAY, MARCH 8

. . . Henry is Listing this after-noon. . . . Mo churned this afternoon cleaned dust most all fore-noon she washed the Lamp globes in fore-noon. . . .

TUESDAY, MARCH 9

Southwest breeze at A.M. this after noon its straight north. This morning the sky looked sorta murky, north west & south east of here. Sky is not very clear at noon. . . . Henry went to the field at 8 this morning work all fore-noon without trouble. Hes Listing this after-noon. Mo Baked Bread & Churned to day. . . .

THURSDAY, MARCH 11

. . . Dust started at 7-30 lasted 3 hours then it let up that the dust, had a little wind all the rest of the day. . . . We got a Card from Verna to day also got Todays children Book.[13] Po got tired of having wiskers under his nose so to-day he shave it off & did he ever look like himself again. His upper lip is all healed up again. O boy I'm glad. Henry enjoyed reading stories. . . .

FRIDAY, MARCH 12

. . . Mos Baking bread, chearning. Also Ironing some. Po read his story in the Pictorial Review. . . . This fore-noon Henry boy cleaned up in the seller. This after-noon he went to the church to see how things are progressing. . . . Mo baked 3 Lemon Pies this after-noon. Listened to her usual plays. To-night static was drownding things out. . . . Mo run onto a Yellow Cat in the hens nest last night while gathering Eggs. She certenly jumped. Ervin came home at 10-30 from Kingsdown last night.

SUNDAY, MARCH 14

. . . We took Verna back to Croses this after noon at 3:30. . . . Ervin started back to Kingsdown at 12 noon to-day. . . .

TUESDAY, MARCH 16

. . . Charlie brought Verna home from Croses this fore-noon. Got here at 10 A.M. They got stranded several times on their way over. He had to scoop their way out. . . .

WEDNESDAY, MARCH 17

Northwind came up hard at 9 A.M. Cecil Buyers field blowing ter-riable.[14] . . . Wind is howling fierce. At 2 P.M. Cecils Field camed down. . . . Verna Waxed the flour this fore-noon Scrubed & made her a pair of Pajamas. At present she's lying on the Davenport, reading the Morand Book. Henry boy is at the church medling in on the Relief workers . . .

THURSDAY, MARCH 18

. . . A Terific duststorm aproaching at 11:30 A.M. Lectricity aproaching that we couldn't Radio. At 2:30 P.M. Lectricity it had let up then at 4 some more interferred with the Radio . . . It sprinkeled some at 8 so the dust quit. but wind kept on pacing allnite. Verna Baked a Prune Cake. We washed the bigest lot of clothes that we washed this year. We couldn't hang it out. Mother ironed pa a shirt in evening. . . . Mo Patched some socks in the evening.[15]

FRIDAY, MARCH 19

Wind blowed through all the night. . . . At 8 A.M. Dust started in so at 9 A.M. a Terific Dust Storm aproaching. . . . To day we're drying the remains of our clothes in the house & some of them ought to be washed over & will half to be . . .

SUNDAY, MARCH 21

. . . Mo Washed Ervins Clothes over this morning. . . .

MONDAY, MARCH 22

. . . At 10 A.M. wind came up went to the southwest at 1 P.M. dust started to roll. So at 2 P.M. it kept on getting worse no sign of letting up. Wind kept on raving till Midnight but the sky didn't clear up. . . .

TUESDAY, MARCH 23

Wind southwest. It was blowing at 5:15 this morning it never had let up all to gether all night long. . . . Static was fierce at 8 A.M. while I listened to Betty & Bob. Terific Dust storm came up at 8:15 While Mo listened to Bachlors children. The Radio blew up with Lectricity so that was enough no more Radio on for a while. It gets dark ever now & then that we cant see without a Lamp lit. It raged all night long We never blowed the Lamp. Ever little it got dark till dusk. Henry radioed a very little around 7 & 8 oclock on account of Lectricity. So Mo never got to hear all of Betty & Bob. Never got to hear nothing of Bachlors children. Henry went to the church. To see how the work is progressing. . . . Wind is still raging 120 miles an hour. First Mexico rolls by. Then Idaho & then how many more I don't know. And we all cuddle around in this Dust Bowl. Henry started home at 3 P.M.

when it cleared up a little while he couldn't get the Car started he cranked for one hour. The men pushed it & still it wouldn't start.[16] So Po walked in just a long walk in such Dust storm. . . .

WEDNESDAY, MARCH 24
. . . We still have the Aladin Lamp lit. Its 11 oclock A.M. Its now 4 P.M. Wind still raging dark. So we have to have the Lamp lit. It gets light on & off. Then it gets dark again. . . . Verna is fancing working at her Pillow Case. Po's reading magazines for entertainment. & Mo is playing lazy. Entertaining her self Reading Mother Morand Book of todays children. . . . Verna moved her beding on the DavenPort while the Storm & Dust was raging. That was 2 Nights. To day all day the Car was at the church all day long not getting bothered nor touched. . . . Vernas Powder Puff got drowend in dust all her Close Closet & Bed room.

THURSDAY, MARCH 25
. . . Mo Baked Bread & Ironed this afternoon. Cleaned up dust some in fore-noon. Verna did most all of it. I also Ironed Ervins clothes packed them up & send them to him, with the Mail Man. I was only a shadow most all fore-noon & some of the after-noon that's why I couldn't get all our Bedroom cleaned up. . . . We got a letter from Sonny boy to day. Mo wrote a card to Son. . . . Po a reading Papers. Verna a reading the Liberty Magazine. & Mo surounded with dark Clowd trying to get them away. Tomorrow I hope she'l see the Ray of Sunshine. . . .

FRIDAY, MARCH 26
. . . Verna is Mop[p]ing. Mo has started to churn & will finish it as soon as I get this direy completed. This after-noon Henry is inspecting how much ground people have listed. He must get the report in tomorrow.[17] . . .

SATURDAY, MARCH 27
. . . Its very peacefull now for the third day. . . . No wind just a little breeze & cold. . . .

SUNDAY, MARCH 28, EASTER
Southwest wind this morning. Clowdy that we couldn't see the sunrise. Then at 9 A.M. Cecil's field started to fog 1/2 hour later all

ground was blowing some it blow by spirts. The wind is stronger now as it was 2 hours ago. . . . Wind let up at 12 noon. It started to snow for one hour till the ground was all white. Snow was very wet. Sun shone a little while. Then it got clowdy again. Wind came up strong at 7 is still blowing. This is a disagreable Easter Sunday. Henry reading Newpapers. Verna's studying her Cook Book. Mo is cooking Proon Soup for Easter Sunday. . . . The folks all went to see the church. Mo stayed at home. Its now 4 P.M. The folks all played cards now for 2 hours. Excepting the kidies are playing with their Easter Eggs. Also Easter Baskets & Bunnies. . . . Mo had the Stomache after her Easter dinner. . . .

WEDNESDAY, MARCH 31
. . . Big Black dust storm came up at six blowed 2 hours, then dust quit. but wind blowed part of the night. . . . Henry & Cliff took the Motor out of the Car this afternoon. They went to Syracuse at 9:45 Verna stayed & Cliff & Henry got home at 4 P.M. With lots of bunk in their Cocoanut. Henry got his Soil Monday. Mo listened to her usual plays. Warners started home about 15 till 6. Dust storm was almost aproaching, when they left here. . . . Well to day comes another wind up for this old Dusty March month. Another month of eretation in the Dust Bowl. . . .

THURSDAY, APRIL 1
. . . Wind came up this after-noon dust blowed till 5:30 sky looked murky. . . . Thelma & Mo went to the Sewing Circle started at 10 A.M. got home at 4:30 P.M. . . . They had all kinds of good eats enything you could want for your Menue All had a swell time. . . .

FRIDAY, APRIL 2
. . . dust started to blow some at 9:30 so Mo couldn't get the Weather forcast. . . . Sky looks hazy on & off was delayed some on account of Lectricity dust is still at it Its 3:30 now. Dust & wind let up at 5 afternoon. . . . Verna is home again. . . . Mother, Sisters, Patsy & Leroy went to the picture show. "Love is News" starring Don Ameche Loretta Young and Tyronne Power.[18]

SATURDAY, APRIL 3
. . . Dust blowed hard after midnight when we got up this morning house was all sifted full of dust. Couldn't see that Mo had it all cleaned

up yesterday. . . . Storm started bad at 7 A.M. dust blowed so hard that it just Shadowed the Sun. It blowed for 3 hours like that, then it let up considerable. Dust also wind. At 1 P.M. Sun came out. It still blowed dust, but not half as bad as in the forenoon. Its 6 P.M. wind has mostly let up. . . .

SUNDAY, APRIL 4
. . . Dust started in rolling it's now 10 A.M. It has let up some. . . . Sky seems a little murky dust quit blowing. & Sun shines off & on. . . . Well to day is Ervin's birthday he's 25 years old. He dosent have a beautiful birthday. Po is snoozing on the Davenport. Verna is reading some of her Letters, from times ago. Well to day is the fifth day of dust ereta-tion, One has to take a Broom along with him to sweep his way out. When he goes to see Mrs. Northwest.[19] In the Dust Bowl. . . .

MONDAY, APRIL 5
To day is a nice quiet day for a change. Its quiet apreceation for all of us. . . .

TUESDAY, APRIL 6
This morning was a beautiful day for a few hours. Then the wind came up . . . In the after-noon sky looked unsettled on account of the dust. Dust blowed about 6 hours all tole. . . . Us women Lunched when ever we pleased. The men was in Syracuse . . . Mo baked Bread & Verna baked Oatmeal Cookies. This was a runaround day for Henry & Cliff. Henry hawled one load of water to the church late in the evening. After a day of lazyness and some jokes of entertainment. Mo tries to patch up what she neglected she now gets buizy. Mending some garments also severel pairs of Socks. . . . Mo writes a card to Sonny boy to day. We get Ervins check from the CCC Camp.

WEDNESDAY, APRIL 7
. . . This morning wind gets stronger. At 8 We have a Terific Dust Storm. It keeps this up till between 12 noon & 1 P.M. It sprinkles on & off for one hour. So the Dust clears up. But the wind keeps up so strong that after the P.M. it blows dust worse as ever. Windows are plastered up with Mud on the North, that the Pantry is dark Kitchen's not quiet so bad. The North side of the house is Black as Coal. Also other buildings are to. Thermotimetr was so black that you couldn't see the Tempture for Mud. After 3 it has sprinkeled on & off it's now

4 P.M. Dust is still in cession. Dust let up at 5 Wind kept on some all nite long. It warmed up some around 6 P.M. & Mrs. Southwest, got her side all plastered up with Mud. . . . Work To day at the Ranch it's not much just filling the Tank with Water & all the bbl for the church workers. Women just cooked Breakfast & Dinner for a little exercise. They sat & looked at the Dust go by. . . . Verna helps Mo our her misery, She sweeps the way going out to see Mrs. Southwest. . . .

THURSDAY, APRIL 8

. . . Mo listens to her usual plays to day. Bachlors Children she dosent get to-day on account of the Battry being low. . . . Po hawls two loads Water to-day. Mo & Verna to clean on Dust after the dust explosion in the Dust Bowl. Mo works button & buttonholes in two of her dust Caps also Washes 4 garment hangs them on the dirty line so they're all dirty. . . .

FRIDAY, APRIL 9

. . . This after-noon at 3. Dust started to blow. Wind blew hard enough to get the Soil rolling. . . . Henry & Cliff put the head on the Car. Old Tin Lizzy. Women. Washed a very big Washing to day. . . . Mo didn't listen to all of her usual plays on account of the Washing she leaves Harem Bachlors children Betty & Bob Way down East out. Ervin came rooling in at 2:20 after midnight he brought a boy along home from Camp. Ervin and his CCC Pale are working at his Car.

SATURDAY, APRIL 10

. . . Mo gets weighed to day. After being on her Supper diet she has lost 2 1/2 lbs. the last 4 or 5 weeks. That's fine. . . . Women washed Ervins CCC clothes after we got home from Syracuse. . . .

SUNDAY, APRIL 11

. . . Wind came up harder at 9 A.M. Dust bowl in cession dust is still blowing at 11:30 A.M. Dust got worse so in the after noon Terfic Dust Storm aproching. Its now 8 oclock P.M. Dust is in full cession. . . . Ervin & his Pal started on their way home back to the CCC Camps. This fore-noon Mo Ironed all Ervins CCC Clothes also sewed Buttons & packed some of them. . . . Ervin enjoyed his birthday Cake which Verna Baked & Thelma trimed it all up.

MONDAY, APRIL 12

. . . Little Warners where making Mud Pies. Where riding their Cyckles. Leroy took a nap. That while Patsy cut out funies, When Leroy woke up he helped her cut. Then for something new to do. They eat butered crackers also Apples for good measure.

TUESDAY, APRIL 13

. . . Po Verna & Mo finaly got started . . . The first Scene on our way up was big banks of dust pilled up under the fences fence high. Next, big heaps of dust pilled in the fields. Next we scened some Wheat needing rain very bad. . . . After all this we saw some more Wheat fields that had been damaged by the Dust Storms. Where very much in need of Rain. . . . on our way home . . . We seen more Dust piled up. Then we kept on going so finally we reached the Clifford Ranch [Warner farm]. . . . Then on our way home from there, we seen green pastures that was something new. . . . After a bit we reached the lonely School House right in the middle of the bigest heaps of Dust. . . .

WEDNESDAY, APRIL 14

. . . We all went to Dodge. . . . Dust blowed a little around 6 A.M. we soon left for Dodge so we dont know how much it blowed. We couldn't see much dust had got in the house so it must not have blown much. . . .

THURSDAY, APRIL 15

. . . A dust storm came from the north east at 6 P.M.[20] . . . Mo went to the quilting party to Mrs. Bishop. In the after-noon. There were 12 Ladies there. . . .

SATURDAY, APRIL 17

Northeast dust storm. I dont know no temp. I spose it was cold cause that is what it was in Hutchinson Kansas. That's where Mo is for a weeks time. Dont know nothing. It was nice at P.M. Dont know return time. Nor their Menue. But by the looks of things they had plenty of it.[21]

MONDAY, APRIL 19

Dust Storm from the South. It rained till the Water stood & that setteled the dust . . .

. . . We had a Terific dust Storm at 6 P.M.

FRIDAY, APRIL 23

Northwest wind to day. It blowed till 1 P.M. . . . There was no lectric-ity in this terific Dust Storm for once it just blowed dust till 1 P.M. Then dust quit. But was clowdy. . . . Today is the first day that Mos on the job for a hole week. She certenly had to work all day to clean-ing Dust, also getting things back to their places. Mo listens to her usualy plays no interference conceted up with the dust Storm. . . .

SATURDAY, APRIL 24

. . . Wind was terriable. . . . It started to blow Dust terriable when we got to Town. it was 11:30. at 3 P.M. when we where a few miles from Syracuse. It blowed that we couldn't hardly see our way sometimes. . . . in the night time before mid night Ervin arrived from Kingsdown. . . . Henry worked at the Truck till we started to Syracuse at 10:45. Mo hunted Vernas clothes up, Packed them & send them to her. After home arivel from Syracuse. Mo washed Ervins CC Clothes. also some of our clothes. . . .

SUNDAY, APRIL 25

Northwest wind again. Terific Dust Storm started at 9 A.M. Let up at 4 P.M. considerable about 6 P.M. it was all let up. . . . Mo Ironed Ervin's clothes A.M. In the after-noon she churnes 2 batches of Cream. One batch for baking purpuses The other for a spread. Ervin about go back to Camp to-day. . . .

MONDAY, APRIL 26

. . . Henry worked at the Truck this fore noon. On the car in the after-noon. Mo Baked Bread also cleaned Dust & more Dust and try to find some of her usual plays that she has listened to on & off. . . . Ervin boy goes back to C Camps this morning. . . . Mo listened to the Lux Play. O boy was it ever good. Robert Taylor & Irene Dun played the leading. Irene sang after they got through with their play. . . .

TUESDAY, APRIL 27

Southeast Wind this morning, It's dusty ever since 8:30. . . . It got worse & worse so now ever since 11 A.M. we haven't been able to hear nothing over the Radio on account of the Lectricity. Its now 6:30 P.M. Lectricity is still in full force. Wind blows till mostly midnight then lets up. It was 7 P.M. when electricity quit so we could hear a few things over the Radio. . . . Mos Eyes are full of Dust that they smart, to beet the band. . . .

WEDNESDAY, APRIL 28

. . . Dust blows on & off all day long some after 9 A.M. sky looked murkey till a little while before Sunset. the Sun shone a little very dim. . . . Henry cleaned out the driveway in the Barn this after-noon. This fore-noon he tore the Tractor down. Mo Cleaned Dust all fore-noon. After noon she cleaned Cupboard also Pantry shelves, and other articles. . . . Po & Mo Moter down to the kids, no body home . . . Mo help herself at the Radio, it was just time for the Oneals. . . .

THURSDAY, APRIL 29

. . . Dust blowed from 10:30 on some but gets worse it lets up at 3 P.M. after that it blowed a very little. Wind is blowing in good hickory at 7:30 P.M. . . . Thelma baked Po a Birthday Cake & Mo looked on while she was dacorating it. All Mo did was Cook the Icing. Mo & the kids licked out the icing kettle, also the mixing bowl. Mo just played hookie most of the time she ironed a few pieces also Peeled Apples & got Dinner. Thats all she did till it was time to get something to chew for her Husband. . . .

FRIDAY, APRIL 30

. . . Dust takes a few whirls through the pasture. At 4:30 We get a Dust Storm from the Northeast. It sprinkles so it dont last 1/2 hour. . . . Mo cleans House, also cleanes the Oilstove all up. . . . Mo home batching, cleaning Dust is she, ever having a time. . . .

SATURDAY, MAY 1

. . . We're starting to Mr. Carber at 7 A.M. Got back to Thelmas at 12 their time.[22] So it took us 4 hours to make the round trip. We eat Dinner down there & got back home at 1:50 got the mail, and in about 20 minutes a Dust Storm apeared on the scene. So after it was in full cession for almost 10 minutes, it sprinkeled enough to clear up the dust. Then we started on our way to Kendall, when we got as far as Bill Gambles place it struck, was very dark. . . . It just lasted mostly 1 hour & then it cleared up. . . . we landed back to the old dust piled Farm at seven with choars to do of all description. . . .

SUNDAY, MAY 2

. . . At 12 dust started a little was some lectricity. So at 1 P.M. it got bad that you couldn't see the church at times. At 5:15 it lets up & the Sky clears up & breeze is a little more north. . . . To day Mo churns & Po works on the Truck all fore-noon Mo also cleanes house. She breaks the Sabath, & Po does to. The Dust Bowl becomes a determent after all these storms. People work when ever the dust dont blow. Even if they break the Sabath.

MONDAY, MAY 3

Northwest wind at 5 A.M. It was clowdy & air filled full of Dust. So after 20 minutes it got worse. But it sprinkled a little in the mean time so dust didn't get so terriable bad . . . Dust kept on blowing some all day till 4 P.M. . . . Mo Baked Bread to-day that's all she did except read & Radio.

TUESDAY, MAY 4

. . . Dust starts in full blast at 7 this morning, blowed on and off all day long it sprinkeled a little two different times, it settled the dust so it wasn't so terriable bad. It kept this up till 5 P.M. Then it all settled down. . . .

THURSDAY, MAY 6

South east Wind Dust blowed all day long statac is terriable wind is very strong. . . . Dust was a hole lot worse at 4:45 it mostly got dark, it was very clowdy Lectricity interfered when I listened to Girl alone. . . . We get Sons CC check to day. We also got a letter from Verna to day.

FRIDAY, MAY 7

Southwest wind now & then a little dust would make the sky look merky. . . . Henry has worked at the Tractor mostly a long day to-day. Mo Bakes Bread & Churns to day. We went to the Warners this morning was gone 1 hour all tole including our trip. The kids where eating breakfast when we got there. Leroy was playing with their Doll Bugy full of Cats & Patsy was just coming out of the Hay, just as we left. Grandma swipes a couple kisses, from the kidies. . . .

SUNDAY, MAY 9, MOTHER'S DAY

. . . We had a Dust Storm in the Night some time, which we didn't hear. I spose we all was to deep in Slumber. We could see it this

morning when we got up by the way the house was full of Dust. Mo
has a dark clowd hanging over her this after-noon, a while this morning. The Warners where here all day long. Thelma Baked a Cake also
brought 2 boxes of Strawberries. . . .

MONDAY, MAY 10
Southeast wind and plenty of it this morning. Dust is flying southeast
of here. to beat the band. . . . Po & Mr. Bishop goes to Syracuse in
this Terific Dust Storm. Mo has had seen a Blue monday all day long
so far. She feels like a Black Thunder Clowd looks. First thing after
breakfast she cleans dust then she gets bluer & bluer cries & cries
some more. Then when this Terific Dust Storm aproaches, She thinks
things are as worse, as they can get. Then she upsets the Phonograph.
Then the worst is yet to come it breaks and just keeps on running.
Then Mo cries, and cries, more brokenheart more & more & more.
She then churns all that while she churns she cries. And all these Tears
that she's shed hasn't mended the machine. And all it takes, to mend
it, will be Money. . . .

TUESDAY, MAY 11
. . . it was clowdy all day long not much Sunshine all day. Till 6:30 a
Terific Dust Storm. . . . It just lasted 1 1/2 hour. Wind settled down
before midnight. . . . Henry hawled 1 Load Water to the Community
Building. Then Po goes to Syracuse to prepare for Seed Loan. Mo
goes to Iva Clossen to help quilt.[23] Mo takes 1 qt Sweet Pickles with
her for her Menue. . . . Iva bring me home while dust is in full blast
when Mo gets home. Door stands open House is all full of Dust. . . .

WEDNESDAY, MAY 12
. . . Very plesent, Till 9:30 oclock A.M. After that we had a little street
of wind & Dust. Then at 1:30 Wind had come up till Dust was blowing in a steady Stream also Eectricity aproaching on & off. . . . Terific
Dust storm at 2 P.M. . . .

THURSDAY, MAY 13
. . . We just had a little dust for 15 or 20 mi. Also had a little
Lectricity . . . Henry & Cliff worked a little on the Tractor from
11:15 till 2 P.M. While eating their dinner, they where away from the
Tractor work. After reading some of Papers, Cliff gets awful sick so
Thelma takes him home at 2:45. . . . This was a gloomy day, Cliff in

the Car rolling for pains. Mo having the sick headache & Po being so sleepy. . . .

FRIDAY, MAY 14
. . . Po hawled one Load of Water to the Church this fore-noon. Mo Washed a big washing Po dear also worked a little on the Tractor. He Cleaned out the Well House, also cleaned the Granary. . . . Mo & Po went to the Warners to see how the sick and Eflected was. . . . On our way home . . . seen a number of Rabits.[24] And not much Green stuff to break the menoty [monotony], just big piles of dirt Banked up as high as the Fences. also so much of it piled up on the fields. . . .

SATURDAY, MAY 15
. . . Terific Duststorm from 7 A.M. till 10 A.M. it let up a little at 12 noon it was fine had let up. . . . Mo Washed Ervins CC clothes also some things for all of us. Mo also Baked 2 Apricot pies and 2 Raisins Pies. Mo also baked Bread from her new starter from Iva. And baked Biscuits for Dinner. The men all went to Syracuse Ervin & his Pals started at 2 P.M. . . .

SUNDAY, MAY 16
. . . At 2:30 we get a Terific Duststorm still is going 30 miles an hour. . . . Wind and Dust still blows when we hit the Hay, it was 8:30 I spose it kept on till Midnight. . . . Po also Waters the Trees ataches the Hose to the Hydran and puts the Water to them. Ervin & his pall go back to their Peacefull Valley again at 12:30. . . . Breaking the Sabath. . . . Mo in the Kitchen, Ironing, Cleaning House. . . .

MONDAY, MAY 17
Southeast breeze this morning, It kept on getting a little stronger, So at 1:P.M. the Dust started to blow. It's now 3 P.M. We can't see Bishops plain, nor the Community House. . . . it kept this up till 7 P.M. . . . Henry hawls a load of Cement to the church right over noon. At A.M. He works on the Doerr quarter. Mo Cleans Dust for some time after having a Terific Storm all after-noon yesterday. . . . Po comes home from the field at 3 P.M. Its so dark & Dusty again. . . . The Radio goes mad with static. We couldn't hear the Lux Play for Static so Henry read a Liberty magazine. . . .

TUESDAY, MAY 18

. . . Wind comes up at 12:15 dust starts to blow hard by spells. Static is in full blast ever since 8 this morning. . . . Po Works on the Doerr quarter. And Mo Washes the black sut out of the Rug, also Irones in the after-noon. Its now 1:30 Henry is still at work Henry comes home from the field at 2 P.M. dust is terriable by spells. . . . Mo washes her Hair right in the midst of a Duster. But never the lest it has to be washed she'l wear her Cap.

WEDNESDAY, MAY 19

. . . At 5 A.M. The sky looked murky. So at 5:15 It came didn't last but 20 minutes till it setteled down. But still was some clowdy yet. It stayed nice for 1 1/2 hours. . . . Its a Terific storm from 8:30 on Now at 4 P.M. it sprinkeled some Its very dark. . . . Henry works on the Doerr quarter till 9 A.M. then comes home on account of the Duststorm Mo churns also Bakes Bread. Mo gets up this morning at 4:15 with Backache also side ache. I spose she's filled with dust endouring these duststorms 5 days in succession. Then 2 days of piece, and nother 5 days of it in succession with out eny let up. . . . Po comes from out of the Field this fore-noon at 8:45 And says Mo pack your Suit Case lets go, and get clear out of the Country. Moving along some where the River isn't far enough. . . . Po's reading the Country Gentleman for pass a way time, while Dust is raging. Well after Mo reading, the lastyear Diery, it sorta, put a Sunny side on life for her. It Thunders to day but seems as if it can't Rain. . . .

THURSDAY, MAY 20

. . . Henry listed east of the Church to-day also some on Coils. Mo Washed some Dresses for herself a pair of Socks & Irones them. She also sweep off the Walls in the Kitchen, also Pantry. . . . Cliff says o boy when I see such beautiful evening as all this I just think, I'm never leaving this Country. . . .

FRIDAY, MAY 21

Terific Duststorm, mostly all through the Nite. It comes from the northeast. . . . And Static was so fierce, that you couldn't hear yourself think. At 10: A.M. it had let up considerable. And at 10:30 A.M. Dust Storm had completely let up. . . . And at 4 P.M. we got another Terific Dust Storm from the Northeast it's now 5:30 P.M. Storm is raging in full blast. It lets up at 11 in the Night its cleared up then. . . . Mo Churns, also bakes 4 Raisin Pies. And cleans her hole house, so when she had got her Bedroom swept, here it comes good & proper. . . . Lewis Laymeyer Eats Supper with us, also stays allnite.[25] I spose his Wife wouldn't venture out on account of the Dust Storm. I spose it kept on some till almost Midnight.

SATURDAY, MAY 22

. . . Henry lists on the 80 close to the Comunity house this morning . . . Mo cleans Dust also scrubs this morning till 10 A.M. Takes her Bath gets ready to go to Town. . . . Po & Cliff got to Holly in our Car. Of coarse they get their selves some Wine for the Carnation day tomorrow.[26] Thelma is sick with Tonselitious. It gets worse & worse. So when the men came home with the Wine, she takes a drink of it, so her Throat feels so much better. . . .

SUNDAY, MAY 23

. . . Dust was blowing, had blowed some I spose since Midnight. At 8: 90 It was a Terific Dust Storm. . . . Po gets up at 4 this morning while Mo still in Bed, snoozing he finds his Cows milks them . . . Po comes home at 7:30 Mo having his Breakfast made He eats, And goes to the Church, and lists some ground, strips it, so it wont blow so bad. Its now 10:30 A.M. He's still there. Storm is still raging. . . .

MONDAY, MAY 24

Wind in the southwest. Storm is still raging. that we cant even see the Tamarecks up north. Its so Dusty. It let up some before Midnight. At 4:45 it was starting in again when Mo came out of Bed It just kept on getting worse, till 6 A.M. . . . Storm hasn't been so bad since 2 oclock. . . .

TUESDAY, MAY 25

. . . Henry & Mr. Laymeyer, are giving the suitcase Farmers fits, cause they don't work their Ground.[27] . . . We came out of the Hay at 6:30 this morning, after celebrating, at the Hall till one oclock. We both are sleepy, also all faged out. . . .

WEDNESDAY, MAY 26

. . . Terific Duststorm came up at 5:15 it just lasted 55 minutes. It sprinkeled enough to settle the dust. Duststorm came from the southwest. . . . Henry swept the dining room flour, also the Poarch. Henry also swept the Kitchen for me to-day. Henry longest pass time to-day was Sleeping, & read some Papers for almost 1 hour. Mos Work to day was churn 2 different times. One Bach of Cream was not to sweet. Henry buys Mo a pt of Ice cream. Ervin writes us a Card to day. Today is sleepy time a Henry Dyck's Ranch in the Dustbowl. We all go to Bed at 7. . . .

THURSDAY, MAY 27
. . . Mo Washes in the after-noon. Has good results. Duststorm stayes away. . . .

FRIDAY, MAY 28
. . . Wind came up. At 10 A.M. it was very strong & a Duststorm, aproaching.[28] . . . Henry worked south on Doors till 10:30 A.M. Listed. Mo Churned, also Ironed. Also writes a letter to Verna & a Card to Ervin. Henry reads his Liberty Magazine. To settle the strain, from the efects of the Duststorm. . . .

SUNDAY, MAY 30
. . . We had a Duststorm at 3:40 It just lasted 2 hours or a little more.

MONDAY, MAY 31
Southeast wind early this morning, also a little dust storm from the same direction for 1 1/2 hours. . . . Winds howling around 6 P.M. as if it might rain. Dust blowed real bad for 2 hours or more. . . . Ervin went back this noon, to his headquarters at the CC Camp after a 8 day stay at home. While Mo did some washing, also some Ironing for him. We had a Duststorm, just lasted mostly 20 minutes or 1/2 hour. . . . Dust dry old May comes to a close . . .

TUESDAY, JUNE 1
This morning things look very encourgening, holes are all full of Water. . . . We go to Town to day, to Sign up the Papers for Seedloan. . . . Its the second time to sign the Seed loan papers. . . . Frogs are Croking. Its wonderfull to hear the Frogs holler. But the Thunder out of doors is not very interesting nor the Lightning. But the Rain is wonderfull. . . .

WEDNESDAY, JUNE 2
. . . Po & the County Agent staked off the Ground this fore-noon before 10 ready to Contouer.[29] . . . Mo just cleaned up Dust. . . .

THURSDAY, JUNE 3

. . . Wind goes to the southwest P.M. and at 6 its straight west. Wind came up very strong just for about 15 minutes. It sprinkled a little dust blowed for a few mi. . . .

FRIDAY, JUNE 4

. . . We get a Terific Black duststorm at 4 P.M. It lasts 1 hour 5 mi. then it sprinkled enough to settle the dust. Wind stays 60 mi an hour. . . . The sprinkle on top of all the Dust Coates We got a nice long letter from Ervin to day. He's in the CC Camps at the present time. . . . Po comes in from work at 4 P.M. At the present time he's reading, the Liberty Magazine. To Cam his nerves from the effects of the Duststorm. Flies just crawl over one that it just makes one nervous. . . .

SATURDAY, JUNE 5

. . . Windows are coated thick with dust, from the Sprinkle on top of the coating of Dust. . . . Mo's been making Soap this fore-noon, also has cleaned Dust a great deal of the fore-noon . . .

SUNDAY, JUNE 6

. . . Wind was in all directions, expecting the East. Soil blows some east by the Church. Also south of here. Henry said it blowed hard around Kendall. . . . Henry rolled out of Bed at 4:45. And you see, he's much more Ambitious since we've had our Rain as Mo has. . . .

FRIDAY, JUNE 11

. . . Wind got so strong that dust is blowing, till no sunlight can be seen. It started at 8 A.M. It blowed till 7 P.M. and then it cleared up & In the nite we had a Black one from the Southwest. . . . It was a Terific Duststorm from 9 A.M. till 7 P.M. . . .

SATURDAY, JUNE 12

Wind in the South very strong, at 9:30 A.M. Dust is raging 70 miles an hour. . . . A Terific duststorm from 2 P.M. up till 5:30 it let up some. And in the night, we had another Terific one from the northeast. In the after-noon after it had let up some . . . Radiator is cloged up so they [Henry and Elmer] fix it while the storm is raging . . . Mo Bakes Bread. Bakes two Plum Pies. Also churns gets Butter in 15 mi. And cleans dust, also Scrubs the Pantry. . . .

MONDAY, JUNE 14

. . . Dust has blowed now for 1 1/2 hour in good hickry. Wind goes
to the East in after-noon at 1. It quits blowing late in the after-noon,
but not much sunshine just a little now & then. . . .

TUESDAY, JUNE 15

. . . The men get the Tractor back to-gether at 9 A.M. . . . The men
are planting 1 mile East of here. . . . Mo Bakes 2 Plum Pies Writes a
letter to Verna & a Card to Ervin. . . . We got a nice long letter from
Ervin to-day. While being in the CC Camp. . . .

WEDNESDAY, JUNE 16

. . . Wind howled to-day it sounded very sad. Mo Milkes the Cows to-
day also, feeds the Calf. It was very cool & plesent to take a strole
down the Pasture. And see the beautiful Green Grass also Water in
the Ponds. Henry went to Syracuse at 8 A.M. To see about getting
some dough. . . . Mo cleans dust to day Bakes Bread & Churns. Also
Scrubs. Po buys 1/2 Bu. Tobacco. ha. So he wont run out. . . . Po
worked till 12 something got wrong with the Lister. He came home,
eat a bite & went to Bed. . . .

THURSDAY, JUNE 17

. . . We couldn't see the Community Hall. It kept on getting worse.
And at 4 P.M. Dust let up some. It's now 5 P.M. It's still kept on
blowing . . . At 9 the men took a bath & got ready to got to the
dedication [of the Community Building]. We got there at 9:45. At ten
the Masons layed the Corner Stone. Mo fixed some fruit Salad & Pota
Salad & made some Pies. Thelma came alone & the kids. She brought
a Cake. A Meat Loaf Potato Salad & one Buterscotch Pie. So We
Elmer & the Warner family eat Dinner here at our place. . . . Mo
comes home with the Warners. While Henry atends the Ball game . . .
Flies are sting me to beat the Band. I'm kicking like a hor[s]e, while
writing the family Diary.

FRIDAY, JUNE 18

. . . It was hot this morning when we came out of the Hay. Dust was
blowing that the floors where all covered with it. It blowed for 2 1/2
hours then it let up & was very beautiful. But hot. . . . Today it was
103 degrees. . . . Po went to Kendall at 3:30 P.M. to get the Lites fixed.
He got home at 6 eat his Supper in a hurry went to the field to work,

while Elmer eat his Supper. It was blowing so bad it was to dark to work without Lights. Moon didn't make enough light. so he went to sleep on the Flour on a Coushin while Mo finished reading her story . . .

SATURDAY, JUNE 19
. . . Dust started to blow at 6 got worse, at 9:45 lots Lectricity and at time there was some. After 2 P.M. it got so bad it was a Terific Storm it got mostly Dark at 3:15 P.M. . . . . Henry starts back to the field at 6 P.M. when dust has let up some. We eat Supper at 5:45. Mo Bakes 3 Cream Pies. Bread. also Cleans the Oil Stove. We get a letter from Verna. She also sends her pictures and Po a Doller Bill, two Handkerchiefs, also a card for Father's day. . . .

SUNDAY, JUNE 20
. . . Dust started to blow at 7:30. Sometimes dust was terriable. It let up on & off some lectricity. . . . Today it was 110 hot. . . . Ervin & his Pal David Kopeland came home this morning at 3 A.M. . . . Mo churned to day, also cleaned dust. & she broke the Sabbath. . . .

MONDAY, JUNE 21, THE LONGEST DAY AT HAND[30]
. . . Mo cleanes dust & scrubs to-day. Mo listens to her usual plays to day exepcting Mary Marline. Po listens to some talks that while. . . . The longest day of June Mo goes after the Cows they are way down at Bishops field. She drives them way around the road & Meets Carl Griswold & Van Trussel on the way carying her slat Bonnet in her Hand.[31] & Hair flying all directions. . . .

TUESDAY, JUNE 22
. . . Wind started to blow so then 1 hour later dust was fogging. . . . Today 100 degrees. . . . this day was not near as hot, as it was yesterday . . . Po discovers Snake tracts in the Celler, but don't find it. Po also killed a big Bull Snake by the Mens toilet to-day. . . .

WEDNESDAY, JUNE 23
. . . Southwest wind this morning early came up very strong at 6 A.M. Dust was just forming at 6:30. Lectricity started at 7:45. . . . Today it was 105 degrees. . . . At 9 A.M. its a Terific Duststorm. . . . Henry worked till 12 oclock midnight.[32] Mo just don't do much to-day just what has to be done. She reads part of her story also the one weeks

issue in the Star Week End make believe. The dust is sifting everywhere it don't do no good to clean House. Mo has to travel 2 1/2
miles after the Cows before Breakfast it takes her 1 full hour to make
this trip milk & feed the Calf.

THURSDAY, JUNE 24

. . . We hat one dust storm at 5 P.M. It settled down. & at 7 P.M. we
have another one it lasts just about 1/2 hour Then the wind soon
quits . . . Today they move the outfit north of the Community Hall.
. . . Henry moves it while Elmer eats his dinner. Henry got up at 3
this morning goes to the field and workes till 5:15 they both eat breakfast at the same time. Dinner they eat in diferent chifts. Supper they
eat at 6:30 Henry didn't work after Supper on account of the Dust
Storm. . . . Mo Washed this after-noon and right in the middle of the
act the Dust starts in blowing. This fore-noon Mo cleans dust.

FRIDAY, JUNE 25

. . . We had a Terific Black duststorm at 7:45 lasted till Midnight &
then it turned very cold. . . . Henry got up at 2 and went to the field
Elmer eat at 6 & went to the field Henry eat at 7:15. 7:45 he starts to
Syracuse. They men where both home & sodered the Gasline Henry
took Elmer to the field on his way to Syracuse. Henry gets home from
Town at 4 P.M. The Lister is Idle while Elmer eats his Dinner. . . . Mo
has to run some of her Clothes through some water & give them
another drying starch some. She also Ironed some this fore-noon. . . .

SATURDAY, JUNE 26

. . . Dust blowed about 2 hours this forenoon so I couldn't wash. . . .
Henry got up at 3 this morning & went to the field come home at
6:45 and eat his Breakfast. I got up at 4:15 Ervin got the Cows Milked
them & fed the Calf. While Mo cleaned dust o how I did apricate that
for once after doing all that before getting Breakfast. . . .

SUNDAY, JUNE 27

. . . This was the Sabath. But makes no deeference. One as bad as
the other. . . . Mo Bakes Cup Raisin cookies. And Irones Ervins CC
Clothes, also some of his shirts, And some other garments. Mo also
gets up at 5:30 Cleanes Dust 1/3 hour before she gets breakfast she
very hungry when she gets through. . . . Ervin goes back to his old
CC home at 12:30. . . .

TUESDAY, JUNE 29
. . . Its been nice & cool weather ever since the 17 of this month. . . .

WEDNESDAY, JUNE 30
. . . Well good old June has brought a number of Duststorms hartships and sorrows, but now in good old hot July we must see the sunny side of life & be cheerfull. . . .

THURSDAY, JULY 1
. . . Henry gets up at 2 A.M. . . . Mo Milks and feeds the Calf. And Mixes the bread before breakfast. she rools out at 4 this morning. Mo Cleans the Oilstove all over. Cleans the Cupboard Washes the windows and all glass Doors. She dont get the Cows cause they're so far. . . . Mocking birds are very lively to day are singing the most beautiful Songs this morning. they seem to enjoy this clowdy weather. There seem to be mostly a dozen of them. How enjoyable they are. Flies are a big pest are stinging like pins sticking. While Birds are singing Meerily. . . .

FRIDAY, JULY 2
. . . Its beautiful to-day up till 10 A.M., haven't had no dust storms for one week. . . . The past week, Pastures greened up so nicely. And it sorta makes one feel like he's on the Sunny side of life. For a change. The Duststorms struck at 7 P.M. and had most quieted down at 8 the themotor had droped 18 points in one hours time. . . . this was a Terific Storm. Windows also all white buildings on the north are all peppered all blown. . . .

SATURDAY, JULY 3
. . . Henry goes to the field at 5:30 He milkes for me this morning and feeds the Calf. So Mo's sorta lazy for a change. She's been milking real promp for some time. I only got up 20 till five thats way later as she usualy gets up. I got breakfast and washed the Dishes went right to cleaning dust. . . .

SUNDAY, JULY 4
Well a very hot fourth to content with this year. but makes no difference, its better hot and quiet as having the Dust whirling. . . . Today at the warmest it was 109 degrees. . . . Work is still in cecession on the good old Sabath day. Po fixes on his Weeder this morning 3 hours after he gets up before he gets eny Breakfast. While Mo is in Bed a

snoozing. Po gets up at 4 and milks & feeds the Calf. Mo gets up at 6:30 old lazy. And the reason she got out of her slumber at that particular time. Po musta sorta got a hollow Belley. He came in the House and turned on the Radio. And that woke her up, ha. After Breakfast at 7 Mo Churns. Before gets so awful hot. And the reason she churned this particular day, so the Cream wont get so sour in this heat. I spose people got to wicked here at this place, after such long endourance in the Everlasting Dust Bowl. And seems as if no end is to come. . . .

MONDAY, JULY 5
. . . Dust started to blow at 9 A.M. It just blows some by spells, that we cant see the church. . . .

TUESDAY, JULY 6
. . . Southwest wind also south the later part of P.M. dust blowed very bad at times. That you couldn't see the Hall and Bishops from 9 A.M. till 3 P.M. it let up considerable at 4 P.M. it started to blow at 6 A.M. kept on getting worse till 8 A.M. . . . Mo just played hooky. And never got to hear no plays cause the Battry was blowed up yesterday. Po put the full charged Battry in the Radio. So Mo still heard the Guiding Light. That is better then nothing at all. . . .

WEDNESDAY, JULY 7
Southeast wind the dust blowed a little in the fore-noon. . . . Mo got up at 4:15 Scrubed the Kitchen also Pantry before Breakfast. . . . And this was a day of mischief. The Hydron was flowing most all day long Patsy made a mud puddle for Curley [Leroy] to cool his karkes in and decorated it with greens, to make it look beautiful and attractive. The kids where nudest most of the day taking their shower under the fosset & part of the day, they wore just a panse with the water flowing out of them. . . .

FRIDAY, JULY 9
. . . The dust started to blow at 9 . . . Wind blowd hard almost till 7 P.M. . . .

SATURDAY, JULY 10
. . . just to much dust for a washday, at least a good one. . . . Henry got up at 4:15. Mo got up at 4:30 with sick headach she took an aspirin at 3 in the morning. . . . Pete & Mr. Dyck calls. So they all sit on the

shady side of the Wellhouse. Chat about the big blow piles, also the way the soil is getting treated out here. Elda and Mo haveing some time to gossip instead of cleaning dust in the way as we have had to all week along. . . .

SUNDAY, JULY 11
. . . the dust is blowing now for the 7th day. . . . We had a terific Duststorm from 2 P.M. till 5 P.M. The rest of the day dust blowed a great deal. It still blowed some when we hit the Hay at 8. After breakfast he again breaks the Sabath, goes out & fixes fence for 1 1/2 hour I believe. . . . And Mo cleans up, dusts and does other things that need to be done Even if its Sunday. She even cleans out the Toilet on Sunday. . . .

MONDAY, JULY 12
. . . Henry goes to Syracuse at 6 this fore-noon on Soil Concervation buisness. He gets home at 9:40 P.M. Work around here to day. Ervin cleans the Gasline before mo starts to wash. He also tinkers on his car some early A.M. He fixes the Windmill he also keeps the washer filled with Gas. . . . Po brings home 1 qt. of Icecream Walnut. Mo was in Bed & Ervin was writing. Mo gets up In her Night Clothes and helps eat it. We all retire at 9:45. Today Mo washed 6 pair Trousers for Ervin 7 shirts for Son. And 3 pair Overalls for Po and 4 shirts for Po. Thats the most trousers that Mo ever washed at one time. And one pair for Elmer. Ervin was on the Davenport Slumbering when Mo had finished her washing Ervin is writing a letter to one of his pals in the CC Camps. . . . Po comes after Mos retiring, he wants some supper by Mo dont make him eny after being in Bed she tells him to fry himself some Bacon, no was the answer. He then finds some government Beef in a dish he fills his cavatie with the greatest pleasure.[33]

TUESDAY, JULY 13
. . . We got a dust storm at 4:30 just a small one at P.M. At 8:30 we got another one from the northwest at P.M. . . . Mo Baked Bread. And Ironed All Ervin's Trousers She'd never in her life ironed and washed all white ones so at this age she ought to have a metel for making a go of it. . . . We go to the Warners at 3:30 to see if they're going to Butcher their Hog. Running right into a duststorm we get back home at 4:15 and no one home there . . .

WEDNESDAY, JULY 14

. . . a little dust storm came at 3 P.M. from the northeast, And only lasted 20 mi. but it cooled the atmosphere. . . .

FRIDAY, JULY 16

. . . Po got up at 4:15. Had to get the Cows from the Pasture & Mo had almost finished churning, that while. When Po had finished milking. He finished the churning. While Mo got Breakfast. And that was very sweet of him. He told me he hadnt churned for so long. . . . At 2:30 P.M. he went to Cecils north of us to stop it, from blowing on our ground.[34] . . . An another very lonely day to content with since the vacency of Ervin. Our Toastie eater we certenly miss him. All the emptyness is staring Mo in the face, ever where she goes. So while being all alone, And Po off at work. Mo cant keep from sobing. . . .

SATURDAY, JULY 17

. . . The wind foged all night along. At 4:15 we got up the dust was just foging at 7 it got considerable worse at 9 A.M. it again let up a great deal. At P.M. it didn't blow dust. . . .

SUNDAY, JULY 18

. . . It was 7:30 P.M. when we got a triple west duststorm. Lasted 3/3 of and hour. But still blowed some till Midnight. Henry got up at 4:30. And so did Mo he milked and Mo churned before breakfast. it was 6:30 when we eat. Henry worked at his Lister while Mo cleaned up the House, and washed the Seprator. So this is another Sunday while the Sabath was broken. We just had enough sprinkle with the dustorm that the west side of the white buildings where chaterated [saturated] with black dust. . . . While Mo and Po where out on the Poarch, lying on a quilt having a chat about not caring about the Icecream party at the Church a Car drives by. This was before dark just at Sunset. So the both of us had to jump up.

MONDAY, JULY 19

. . . Henry crawls out of Bed at 4:30. And has to walk after the cows, that while Mo tends to the chickens & puters around. . . . So at 4:15 P.M. we started to the kids . . . And we got home before the Rain and dust struck. Mo Makes 3 Mince pies cleans dust. . . . To day while going to the Barn, to look for Eggs. Mo happens to spy the Pet Snake which has been there all summer. There set the Spade And while it was Crawling into its den Mo spaded it in several pieces. The head part and 1/2 had went down in its den. And so good bye pet Snake. And then Mo stood looking at it, Thinking to herself, now! I dont need to fear that snake no more.

TUESDAY, JULY 20

. . . At 8 P.M. We had a little dust. And some rain just enough to wet the ground that it run off the Ruff. There wasn't much work done at our house to-day. Mo churned before breakfast while Po was taking a strole after the Cows milked them, and while Po seprated Mo got breakfast. And all Mo did was cook 3 Meals and swept 4 Rooms made the Bed. In the after-noon Po is fixing the Wellhouse Door. . . . This fore-noon Pete called at 7:45 Henry had went to the field to look over the Cituation over about working the Ground and Crop He got home at 8:30 A.M. Him and Pete sat in the Car disguessing the Soil and blowing conditions. . . . Po & Mo was realy playing hookie. We two where reading and disguessing this Dust Bowl. And how things would be, when we pulled ourselves up, by the Roots, and planted them on some different place. Henry told all about Oren Joureys Machinery, was all by its only self all blowed full of Dust. And he says that's the way ours e'l be when we're gone. And such mornfull look as he had on his face.[35] And to much of these clowds to day! And, not enough Sunshine. This again is a very lonely day for Mo. And after getting a letter from Verna we can sorta feel more encouraged again. . . .

THURSDAY, JULY 22

. . . At 2 after Midnight we had a terific dust storm. . . . Henry gets up at 4:30 and Milks the Cows out in the Pasture. That while Mo churns. And we dont seprate eny more for the time being. We eat at 5:30 — Po goes out to the field at 7 A.M. And Mo goes on awashing the Walls where she left off yesterday. She started in to day again P.M. . . . We got a card from Ervin to day.

FRIDAY, JULY 23

. . . Po pulles out to the field at 6. He takes Cecils Rodweeder but it does no good east of here. Its to dry. He comes in at 11:30 from work. . . . Mo cleans the Cupboard Pantry shelves, washes Ice Box and cleans dust out of Verna's Bedroom and oils and waxes the Pantry floor. . . .

SATURDAY, JULY 24

. . . Mo was so tired and worn out after spending the hot nite with a spell of Rhumetism when she got up. So she took a ride along to the Warners, while Po was seeing them on buisness. She sorta had rekuperated while being out driving for one hour. Henry had to walk after his cows this morning. While Mo churned at 5:30 . . . Mo Ironed some this fore noon, and again the same old work dust and clean flours, and udlens [oodles] of other work till she's so tired she cant hardly sit up. At P.M. she bakes some Raisin cupcakes. Mo waxed 3 flours. And gets her Saturdays work done up in tip top shape. It was 8 P.M. when she got through with all the work including her bath. . . .

SUNDAY, JULY 25

. . . Dust started to blow hard at 6 A.M. And was let up at 10 A.M. . . . Well this is a pieceful Sunday for once no work done by the Boss. Mo dusted a few things this morning, which she didn't get done up yesterday.

MONDAY, JULY 26

. . . Today it was 92 degrees. It was exceptenly cool to-day. . . . Henry didn't half to walk after the cows to-day. They came home. We eat at 5:45. Henry listened to the news, cleaned up some oil buckets and then he tore his Tractor up some. . . . Mo caned 24 qts Apricots out of one bu.[36] We eat 1 qt. She got all through with them at 3:30. She coldpacket'em. . . .

TUESDAY, JULY 27

. . . We had one duststorm at 3:30. It cleared up. And at 4:30. We had another one it just lasted 1/2 hour. We got a little shower a havy sprinkle at 4:45. . . .

THURSDAY, JULY 29

. . . We got out of the Hay at 4:30. And Henry boy had to get the Cows o boy he did hate to. He milked and that while Mo waiting on him for breakfast, she read part of the Story After April. . . . We got a letter from Ervin to-day. He's at Duff Nebraska. . . .

FRIDAY, JULY 30

. . . Mr. Lameyer proceeded to work on his blowpiles to-day for a change.[37]

SATURDAY, JULY 30

And good bye to the beautiful cool 30th day of July. . . . To-day it was 102 degrees . . . Henry had his Truck all serviced till 4:45 he milked. The cows had come home for once again. And at 5 We eat breakfast. At 6 he was on his way to work on the piles of blow dirt north of Big Bow.[38] . . .

SUNDAY, AUGUST 1

Well to day the first day of August rolls in, the hotest old month. . . . It started to blow about 9. A.M. was very dusty at the Warners who we went to see starting from home at 7.A.M. . . .

MONDAY, AUGUST 2

. . . At 7:30 we had a dust storm P.M. . . . Mo just played hooky to-day. She felt terriable all day yesterday and to-day. She took several doces of Painrelief to make her self come out of it I spose, it was to much Icewater for her. . . . Mr Lameyer proceeded to work on the piled up dirt some more to-day. . . .

THURSDAY, AUGUST 5

Southeast dust storm arived at 7:A.M. And let up at 11.A.M. some. And it blowed on and off all after noon. The sky was mostly clowdy, before the dust storm struck It was very nice and cool in the morning. . . . Mo just putered around this day. Got Water so mo could Churn He just hookied. Mo Ironed some at P.M. Po read Liberty Magazines and Papers. He visited with the Road graders. And Listened to the news severel times to day. At present he's puffing a Cigar. And later in the after-noon he's puffing his bu. Pipe for good measure.[39] . . .

SATURDAY, AUGUST 7

. . . at 1 in the night it was 87 degrees. It certenly was a hot Nite. We got a little dust storm at 7:30 P.M. We slept out in the yard till 4:30 Sunday morning. . . . We got the Sears Catalogue. . . .

MONDAY, AUGUST 9

. . . It got windy by spirts that a little dust blowed, just enough to pepper the clothes after washing it. A little static in the fore-noon And terific in the after-noon from 12 noon on. Mo couldn't hear the Luxplay. Mo missed out on Mary Marline Youngs Oneals and Betty & Bob. . . .

TUESDAY, AUGUST 10
... Two local dust storms one at 4:30 another at 5:45. They just lasted
40 mi and 1/2 hour. Dust blowed some till 1:30 in the night. ... Po
fixed some on the Tractor. ... Him and Mr Brothers pulled out for
Hutchinson ... Mo went to sleep at seven.

WEDNESDAY, AUGUST 11
... Its a very gloomy day and lonesome Wind sounds so mournfull
And Windmill squeeks. ... Mo's all by her lonely selves. ... The kids
came at 5:30 and took Mo along to their place it was dark when we
got there.

THURSDAY, AUGUST 12
... dust blowed a very little, to-day. Mo stayed with the Warners ever
since Wednesday 7 P.M. We all went to Syracuse to-day. Started at
2:15 got home to our place at 6:45 milked the Cow, fed the Calf gathered the Eggs watered the Hens and went back to the kids again and
stayed down there all Nite. ...

FRIDAY, AUGUST 13
... Terific dust storm from 5 A.M. till 10 A.M. it let up it was just
very breeze at P.M. dust blowed in the night from 12 oclock on, and
got worse, up till 11.A.M. and then it had let up a little. ... We got a
letter from Ervin to day from Rose Nebraska while he's haying, for
Mr. Knortzel.

SATURDAY, AUGUST 14
... dust blowed terriable, started in at 7 A.M. Had let up some at
9 A.M. ... At 12:30 a terific duststorm aproached and continued in
full blast till 7:P.M. It let up some. But the wind continued real strong.
Dust settled at 7:P.M. on account being damp. ... Po's reading his
papers after 3 1/2 days vacation he had lost out on them, so he's
making up for lost time ...

SUNDAY, AUGUST 15
Southwest terific duststorm started at 6:30 A.M. ...

MONDAY, AUGUST 16
... Wind blowed some to-day a little dust to. We got up very late to-
day it was 5:30. ... We started down to the kids at 10 A.M. Was there
for dinner loaded up some of our junk, which was there. We had to

drive slow, beings we was trailing the Lister. We where on our way
1 1/2 hour. . . . We slept in the house ever since Friday 13 we've had

some warm nights in August.

TUESDAY, AUGUST 17
. . . had a little duststorm at 5 P.M. We got up at 4:30 And Henry went
to the Pasture to milk while Mo mixed the Bread and cleaned up some
We eat breakfast at 5:30 and then Henry took the Truck and went to
Cecils place.[40] And 15 mi later we started on our to Warners to get a
Truck load of their dishes Washmine [washing machine] and other
articles, which they are going to ship to Oregon.

WEDNESDAY, AUGUST 18
. . . In 1937 Ervin was in Duff Nebraska in the faul working in the
Hay field for Robert Knoetzel he worked there 6 weeks. Sep 5 he was
in Martin Dakota. Today the kids had their sale and after it was over
we all came to the Dyckranch. With a Truck load of junk. Mo baked
5 Cherry Pies for the Sale.

THURSDAY, AUGUST 19
. . . Dust is blowing at 4:15 It was cool and comfortable. . . . We got
up at 4:45 Henry went to the pasture to milk, While Mo churned. And
at 7 we got through with Breakfast And then we went to the Warners
to get another Truckload of stuff and the kids got their Car full of it,
including the Radio. . . .

FRIDAY, AUGUST 20
. . . At 3:45 we had a little duststorm . . .

SATURDAY, AUGUST 21
. . . The men started to Syracuse at 7:15 to have Cliffs Car reboared
they got home at 7:45 P.M. Well this was a lazy day for Mo she just
hookied most all day. she didn't even earn her food that we lunched
on. . . . We just lunched on scraps for our dinner. Didn't have no men
at home just us two Women and the little kiddies. Thelma Ironed
from 3:30 oclock and kept on till 5:30. Then Mo Ironed 4 Dreeses for
herself.

SUNDAY, AUGUST 22
. . . We got up at 4:45. All of the family even the kidies. We had some
fresh stake for breakfast Thelma and Ma got breakfast, while Henry

was going to the pasture to milk the Cow. We eat at 6. And then the men went out to work some at the Car while Mo and Thelma got the House work done up & after it was all done. Thelma bathed the kidies and her self Mo took her bath and then she churned and at 11 A.M. we where ready to start. And another day of breaking the Sabath at the Dyck Ranch.

TUESDAY, AUGUST 24
. . . At 9 am sky was murky and dusty and wind sounds mournfull. . . . The men had sneeked out of bed this morning at 5. when Mo awoke Cliff was working at the Car, and Po was bringing the Milk from the Pasture. It was 6:30 When we got through breakfasting. At 2 P.M. the men where pulling our Car with the Truck, trying to get it started, and kept on with it till 5:30. It worked fine.

WEDNESDAY, AUGUST 25
. . . Tonite at 11 P.M. very much Thunder and Lightning a dust storm before hand. . . .

THURSDAY, AUGUST 26
. . . Pete & Elmer returned to Dusty Kansas where working in harvest for 4 weeks at Nebraska. . . . Mo and Po taking Verna in to meet the Train, back to her home, where she had worked for 4 months . . . Pete gets a job listing for us and to morrow he goes to work . . .

FRIDAY, AUGUST 27
. . . Dust storm from the southwest at 6:30 it just lasted 2 1/2 hours and then let up. . . .

SATURDAY, AUGUST 28
Southwest duststorm started at 6 A.M. and continued till at 7 P.M. Wind blew till in the night some . . . We got a Card from Verna, saying, I got home fine and am feeling O.K. She's still works for Mr. Farley. . . .

SUNDAY, AUGUST 29
Southwest duststorm from 7 A.M. Continued till 9:30. A.M. Then it let up, and at noon 12 there wasn't eny wind, not enough to run the Mill. . . . At 6:30 a light duststorm from northeast just lasted 3/3 hour. . . . Mo also along with the men breakes the Sabath. She Bakes Bread and churns. Mo also Cleans house in the fore-noon. . . .

MONDAY, AUGUST 30

. . . Mo just hookied to-day. She just cooked 3 Meals, washed the dishes and did some sweeping. . . .

TUESDAY, AUGUST 31

. . . The wind sounds very mournfull. . . . Cliff and family went to Olyan Warners to stay all night with them for their departure before leaving for Oregan.

SUNDAY, SEPTEMBER 5

. . . Mo Caned 1 bu. Peaches and 9 Baskets of Grapes. Po helped Mo peel most of the Peaches and helped pick of all the Grapes. I got 8 Cans Grapes and 10 1/2 gals Peaches. We certinly did break the Sabath. Po fixed the generator on the Car in the after-noon. After getting home from Olyans Cliff starts in painting his Traylor. While Thelma eats Grapes and the little Warners are playing around the hydron fighting a battle sperting water on each other, that the water runs out of their clothes.

TUESDAY, SEPTEMBER 7

. . . The Warners packed all fore-noon and at 2 P.M. They where bond for Oregon. And now the junkie Basement and Hydron, the little Warners Battle field where they allways fought their battles, look so very lonesome.[41] . . .

THURSDAY, SEPTEMBER 9

. . . Mo baked Bread had it finished up at 5:30 and baked 2 Raisins Pies, and one Grape. Mo wrote a Letter to Verna Churned to-day also got the Cows. And swept her hole house. She also carried some junk out of the yard. And she's still burning junk in the old Range Pos running the Tractor till 12 oclock Midnight Pete hits the Hay at 8:45 Mo at 10 Po at 12:15 . . .

FRIDAY, SEPTEMBER 10

. . . Henry went to the field 3:45 Pete worked all day long Henry helped out while Pete eat his meals. Mo milked to-night and Po was so sweet he got the Cow from the pasture. Mo caned 20 qts Peaches to-day. . . . Henry comes in from the field at Midnight. . . . We got a Card from the Warners saying they had got to Peoblo [Pueblo, Colorado] and would visit 2 days, and then on their journey to Oregon.

SATURDAY, SEPTEMBER 11

. . . Mo caned 20 qts peaches to day and cleaned her house while prosessing them. . . . Po bought 1 bu. Cucumbers to day . . . We got a card from the Warners from Laramie WYO. while they're on their way to good old Oregon.

SUNDAY, SEPTEMBER 12

. . . It was clear to-day very beautiful and cool. . . . It seems as if we're living in a new world now for 2 weeks havent had eny dust. Po got up at sun up this morning. Mo the lazy creature slept till 7 oclock she didn't get no cow nor milk she salted her pickels down, and cleaned up. Henry and potered around on the Tractor some. At 6 PM Henry went to the field and worked till 12:30 Midnight We got a letter from Soneyboy to-day. while he's at Gearing Nebraska. Haying for Mr Knoetzel.

MONDAY, SEPTEMBER 13

. . . Mo caned 10 canes of dill Pickels and made 1 gal Peach butter. She washed and Ironed Pos Shirt. . . . and got the Cows at 6. . . .

TUESDAY, SEPTEMBER 14

. . . We got a Card from the Warners at Glens Ferry Idaho on their way to Oregon. . . . Henry went to the field at 5:30 and worked till 8. They got through with the sixeth quarter including the 160 he worked in Stanton Co. Mo caned 16 qts Tomatoes, and 16 qts plumbs. . . . We get a Card from Cliff and a Letter from Soneboy.

WEDNESDAY, SEPTEMBER 15

. . . Henry washes up and shaves, then away to Syracuse they [Henry and Pete] go at 8:45 and forgets the letters that Mo wrote to Ervin and Verna The two men get back from Syracuse at Midnight. This is another day of hooky for Mo. all she did just churned and made pickels and listened to the Radio . . . Well Men certenly sowed their wild oats to day stayed up Town all day and waited for the Tomatoes so they brought 2 bu. This morning at the breakfast table they certenly where hungry The eat a stack of cakes enough for 4 men. They cut shines, at the breakfast . . .

THURSDAY, SEPTEMBER 16

. . . This fore-noon the sky was murky on account of dustblowing. At P.M. it stoped and considerable clowdyness. . . . No Work to day just

run around. . . . The men drove around to look at conditions. . . . Mo
Cleaned up the house. Took her bath. Dusted it all. And caned 6 qts
Bread and Butter pickels 8 1/2 gals Tomatoes, and 10 qts of them. Mo
gets the cow from the pasture and milks her she cold packs her
Tomatoes. . . .

SUNDAY, SEPTEMBER 19
. . . Mo broke the Sabath to day. Baked Bread had it baked at 12:15,
3 Apricot Pies And churned 1 Lb. Butter, she just churned 15 minutes.

MONDAY, SEPTEMBER 20
Southwest duststorm from 10 am till 4:45 P.M. . . . We didn't get just
a very little dust cause I had doors and window open. Mo caned 4 qts
Peaches and 10 qts Tomatoes. The lectricity started in 11:45 it inter-
uped in ever play Mo listened to . . . Tonite Henry isn't in the field, so
he's runing the Radio and almost driving me nuts. While Mo's Ears
are in full blast again. A little while to day P.M. They was peacefull.[42]

TUESDAY, SEPTEMBER 21
Southwest Terific duststorm started at 9 A.M. . . . Sky has been murky
ever since 9 A.M. on account of the duststorm. . . . Henry and Adolph
Clossen go out to inspect the conditions at 9:45 A.M. Get back at 6 P.M.
. . . Mo caned 20 qts Peaches to-day. And 6 pts Peachbutter. . . .

WEDNESDAY, SEPTEMBER 22
Southwest wind at 6 A.M. kept on getting worse at 9 dust was blowing
some by spirts. It kept on getting worse at noon . . . Dust let up at
7:30. . . . Po left for work at 7:15 A.M. gets home at 7:30 P.M. Mo has
another day of hooky, she made Po dear his lunch so no cooking at
all just breakfast and Sup. for Po dear . . . And for supper Po came
home so late that Mo fried him 2 Eggs Tomatoes and Peaches for
desert. Henry boy brings Mo 1 pt of Ice cream to eat by herself. . . .
Well Mo caned 12 more qts Peaches so Good that's all for a week
or so. She cold packed everything execpting 4 qts peaches and the
Plummes of coarse the Pickels to. Well now the poor Washboiler will
rest for a spell, till Mo washes. Mo got the cow and milked her to-day.
It took her 35 mi. to get her and milk her. Flies where bad to-day. . . .

THURSDAY, SEPTEMBER 23
Southwest terific local duststorm started in at 8:30 kept on getting
worse from noon on and let up some at 5 P.M. . . . Hat at blackdust-

storm at 9 P.M. Continued till after Midnight. . . . Mo swept the flour cause it was very dusty. At 8:45 Henry and Adolph started on their way to work at the soil conditions. . . . Mo caned and cooked 7 pts Grape jam. 2 pts and 10 jelly glasses of Grape jelly 3 masionase jars of Plum jelly and 2 Apricots Mo got the Cow. And Po dear milked her. . . . Mo just plays hookie for another day. . . .

FRIDAY, SEPTEMBER 24
. . . Early this morning at 2 duststorm was ragging it had quit at 5 A.M. when we awoke . . . To-day it was peaceable and much enjouyable, after 4 days of dust. Mo had another day of hooky and its the final for a while. Mo cleaned dust baked Bread had it all finished up at 1 P.M. And Churned after supper. She got the Cow and milked. . . .

SUNDAY, SEPTEMBER 26
South west wind a duster south and west of here but we didn't get eny of it, It started in at 8 A.M. let up at 12 noon. . . . Mo Ironed some and even if it was Sunday. She broke the Sabath while Henry boy, was reading papers, and radioing. also puffing away at his Sigar, and part of the time, his bu. Pipe. . . . Mo done up the Doilies for the Cupboard shelves to-day. . . .

MONDAY, SEPTEMBER 27
Southwest wind all day long. . . . a duster started in at 9: A.M. Let up at 3 P.M. . . .

WEDNESDAY, SEPTEMBER 29
Southwest duststorm P.M. A.M. It just was mostly clowdy and merky. Dust was bad at times in the afternoon. This dust kept on till 5:30 P.M. . . .

THURSDAY, SEPTEMBER 30
Goodbye old September good bye. . . . We got a wind blowing over a duster at 2:30. Just lasted 10 mi. With a little sprinkle. . . . Henry's read papers ever since 2:30 till Mo lost out on 4 of her plays Kitty Keen. Mary Marline & the guiding Light. Lindas Love she didn't get in on it yesterday either. Cause Radio was used to get the News. The static and Thunder was so bad that we had to disconnect the Radio we couldn't hear but just about ever 5th word . . .

FRIDAY, OCTOBER 1

. . . Henry cleaned the dust off of the Barnloft A.M. also the driveway at 9:40 he was through. . . . he came home at 11:30 eat his Dinner. and went to the field to cut broom corn 12:45. . . .

SATURDAY, OCTOBER 2

. . . No work all just Town day. We got up at 5:30. Mo did up her mornings work took her bath. At 9 A.M. we started to Syracuse and got home at 5 P.M. Mo bought herself a new Spring Coat for 10 dollars & ninety cents. And bought 1 bu. Apples. . . . She got weighed to day. and weighs 155 lbs. . . .

SUNDAY, OCTOBER 3

. . . Dust started to blow at 8 A.M. and let up completly at 4 P.M. . . . We rooled out of the hay at 5:30 While Po milked and feed the baby calf Mo cleaned up and got breakfast Where through breakfasting at 6:45. And Po shaved got ready to go to the Ball Tournement, and got home at sunset. Mo cleaned up the hole house and even shined up all the caster cups. . . . Well this was another day of hooky for Mo didn't half to cook no dinner. . . .

MONDAY, OCTOBER 4

Southwest wind to-day and dust started to blow at 8 A.M. let up at 3:30. P.M. . . . No work. We rolled out of bed at 5:20. After breakfast it was 6:15. While Mo skimed the milk and did some of her house Henry tried to find the news at Koa but it wasn't there[43] he then at 7 A.M. left for Syracuse. So Mo played hooky again for a change not needing to Cook no dinner she certenly had a time. . . . Mo didn't get eny dust in the house to-day. . . . Mo cleanes the seprator to day so to-morrow we'll seprate. Henry is eating Apples, and listening to Fiber Megee. . . .

WEDNESDAY, OCTOBER 6

Northeast wind this morning at 5 dust was blowing. . . . This dust only lasted hour. The sky was clean all day. . . . Work to day We got up at 4:45. Got through breakfasting at 6. Henry seprated listened to the news at 6:30 7 A.M. He went to the field. He stacked Broomcorn got home for dinner at 1:45. listened to the world Series till 1:30 then went back to the field. . . . Mo churned at 11:30. got Butter in 15 minutes. This was our first day to seprate for a long while. . . .

THURSDAY, OCTOBER 7
. . . Work Mo got up at 4:45 While Po dear was snoozing some more ha. He stayed there till 6 A.M. he then got up to see how chilly it was. Then he went to pump the Cowds. This morning while Po slept I finished Verna letter and wrote the dyrie which is my ever days duty. . . .

FRIDAY, OCTOBER 8
Wind in all directions. And duststormed started at 9:30 kept on real bad at 4:30 it was terriable. . . . Static is so bad at P.M. It mostly kicks you over, when you get close to the Radio. . . .

SATURDAY, OCTOBER 9
. . . No Work just a loafin and playing hooky Mo just did her morning work, and got the Eggs ready. Took her bath & Po loaded his Calves. . . . We started to Syracuse at 11 A.M. And got home at 7 P.M. . . . Po out in the pasture hunting the Cows with a flashlight ha. It was 7:30 when we eat our bite after getting home from Town. We played the new Records Henry Radioed a while. And at 20 minutes till 9 hes out after the Cows ha. Po got a bu. Blue Plumbs 1/2 bu. sweet Spuds and got himself a bottle a bear. And Mo 15 cts worth of Candy.

SUNDAY, OCTOBER 10
. . . I had to clean my house cause I went to Town yesterday, and didn't much of it done Bread was mostly gone. And Elmer & Pete being here I had to bake Biscuits, and they where good, even if I say it my self ha. . . .

TUESDAY, OCTOBER 12
. . . dust started to blow bad at 7:30 just lasted 1/2 hour. . . . Po is sitting by the Stove with his feet in the Oven getting them warmed up. While Rosevelt is making a speech.[44] Mo caned 10 qts Blue Plumbs. . . . To day the Mr takes off his B.V.D. and puts on his long Underwear ha. But the Mrs dont ha. We got a letter from Verna to-day.

WEDNESDAY, OCTOBER 13
. . . We got out of the hay 5:45 Po dear stacked Broomcorn A.M. also P.M. after recuperating 1:15. He comes out of the field at 5:30. Po caned 15 qts sweetspuds P.M. Po seprated to-day. And Mo blowed up a qt jar. We only got 8 Eggs to-day & Mo washed the Lamp globes again to-day. . . .

FRIDAY, OCTOBER 15
... We had 7 hours of dustblowing to day let up at 4 P.M. Work. Not just about hookie, most of the day ha. We got up at 5:45 Mo mixed her Bread while Henry boy milked the Cows. We got through breakfasting 6:30. Mo finished her Bread. at 4 P.M. But just the same it was exelent. And again Mo cleanes up. Washes Lampglobes and sews on her undies. . . .

MONDAY, OCTOBER 18
Northwest wind early 6 A.M. 2 hours later dust blowed Terific scandles wind just raged till 2: P.M. And it let up considerable dust let up at noon. All fore-noon it was dark . . . We got a lot of dust in the north part of the house. . . . It sprinkeled A.M. while dust blew so it spotted the Windows up. . . .

TUESDAY, OCTOBER 19
... Puffs of dust came ever little bit A.M. at noon the Radio had a fit with lectricity. . . . We get up at 5:50 Get through breakfasting at 6:45. Po listens to the news at 7. at 6:45 he takes a shave goes to the field after the news is over and heads Maze . . . So We got a letter from the 2 girls and none from Sonneyboy. And Thelma sends the pictures. Po dear reads Thelmas letter, & Mo Vernas at first then, we each read the other. . . .

FRIDAY, OCTOBER 22
... Late at 6:45 Pete came along for a chat with his only brother in the Dustbowl. He helped us listen to the tale end of Death Valley about the Gold Mines it was a swell play.

SATURDAY, OCTOBER 23
... We got a letter from Sonneyboy to day saying he'd had one cold on top another. Work none at all for Po he just hookied all day long. After working 6 days in sucession he had to have a lay off ha. And Mo goody no dinner astering her in the face to make she certenly always apricates it when she dont need to cook ha. She did a lot of Saturdays work after all. And the worst thing of all she had the Cappers man to content with for An hour and 1/3 till she took his offer that he had to sell and away he went. She went out of doors and shouted after his departure ha. . . .

MONDAY, OCTOBER 25

Well this was another beautiful day. This morning early 1 1/2 hours the wind blew, a little strong as if it'd get bad but it didn't. . . .

WEDNESDAY, OCTOBER 27

. . . After breakfasting Henry seprated. . . . And then Henry cut a pile of wood stayed with it one hour. At 11:15 we went to Syracuse Mo played hooky and Po took in the Soil concervation. We got home at 5:15. Mo blowed herself for a new Dress for 2.98 cts a black one. We took the little Cream to town and got 1.28 cts for it. . . . We seen the most beautiful yellow Trees they just looked as if the Cottenwoods, where painted yellow. . . . We got weighed to day & she has lost 1/3 lb. more. Mr. Bishop's he cow was here to day, & made a two days visit, with our cows.

SATURDAY, OCTOBER 30

. . . Mo Henry and Pete went to Meade Co. left home at 12:25. . . . We got a letter from Verna from Hutch at the residents of J.C. Crump. Thelma from Dexter Oregon Living with Ed. Warners. . . . We also got a Letter from Mrs. Lameyer. Meeting for those who are intrested in temperance cause.

SUNDAY, OCTOBER 31

. . . We got back to home sweet home after our adventure at 6:30. . . . We seened some beautifull Wheat on this side of Plains also near Meade. . . . Lizzie's & Edds Wheat looks fine at this time. Ed. told us that they raised 1000 bu. this last year 1937.[45] Well this is the last day of this beautifull month. It has rolled around to and end for this year & never more will come back to this year of 1937.

MONDAY, NOVEMBER 1

. . . November started in like the bad Wolf. With a dust storm starting at 6:30 A.M. Continued till 10 A.M. . . . Men went to the field at 7 A.M. . . . Henry and Fillip finished cutting Feed & came in at dusk. Pete bought 1 doz eggs, at 25 cts a dozen. Mo just had the luck finding one Penny while going to the Hydron to get a bucket of Water. . . .

WEDNESDAY, NOVEMBER 3

. . . Today while bringing in the cream after seprating Henry stubed his toe on the top step and cream flew all over the poarch and his pant legs.

Mo was standing with the doors wide open. He says dont stand there & laugh at me if you'd helped me with the door it'd never happened.

SATURDAY, NOVEMBER 6

. . . We got a letter from Thelma to day. They're still staying with Warners. Have no steady job. Also got a Card from Ben Osborn from California, saying that Ervin can get a job there. . . . Mo washed the north Window also south Window on the outside & cleaned the Puddy off it took her 1 1/2 hour to do this it was Paint instead putdy and o boy did I ever work hard at it. And polished the Stove Pipes by Lamp light and scrubed the kitchen after 6 P.M. Mo Ears are thumping and throbbing in full blast. . . . Mo got up this morning with a sick headache. She took 2 Asprins and at 10 A.M. she felt better. She had the Ruemetism in her Arms and her Toes where so sore while standing on them when she scared the Paint & Pudy of the window. She didn't now where to laye them down to comfort them, & ease the pain. Henry put on his Clip Clap Slippers after Super. To ease his feet. After a rough day of Maze toping.

SUNDAY, NOVEMBER 7

. . . At 11 dust started continued till 1 P.M. . . . Dust let up at 5:30. sky was a little murky yet at dusk. . . . After breakfasting Henry went to see about his Cow. to milk lastnight also this morning. So we could not seprate, the Calf again had the pleasure of getting hole milk. . . . Henry & Pete went to Kendall at 11 A.M. To mail the letter I wrote to Ervin, with the Card that Mr Osborn wrote to Ervin. . . . There was no dinner at our house beings it was the Sabath & the Mails wheren't home. So Mo played hooky with a big doce of Belly ache the effects of to many Pairs ha. . . .

TUESDAY, NOVEMBER 9

. . . Arose at 6 A.M. & went to the field at 7:30. Eat at 12 noon. And waited for the Mail. And again to the Maze field he went at 2:45. . . . Henry Comes in for Supper at 5. Mo washes some & Irones & does the house work. . . . We bout the lonesome couple enduring the Dust Bowl rolled in the Hay at 9:30

WEDNESDAY, NOVEMBER 10

. . . We arose at 5:45. And got through breakfasting. While Henry had spide that the Cows where gone. It then was 6:30. He went on a cearch for them. And found they where at Wane Rogers. The Red

one was sucked, and the Rone one had scraped her Teat. So when
Henry took a hold to milk She fired him one and spilled 2/3 of the
Milk he had in the Bucket. And after feeding the Calf he only had
3 Pints to strain. And the bucket was kicked up till it was not round
eneymore. He starts to Syracuse at 9:45 He took a shave after milking
the Cow, got himself dressed and away he goes and gets back home
at 5:45 P.M. . . . And to day the absence of the Mister. There's no
cooking that needs to be done. Execpting Breakfast it was only Eggs
and Bran. & supper fried Eggs. . . . And to night while Po being
absent Mo gets the pleasure, milking in the battered up Bucket that
the Rone Cow demolished this morning while my dear Husband,
milks her skined Tet. . . .

FRIDAY, NOVEMBER 12
. . . At 10 A.M. The wind starts in so Mo cant wash to-day. Dust starts
in at 11 A.M. . . . The sky was merky till it was dusk. But the dust
stoped at 4:30 P.M. . . . Elmer, being very sweet, and brings our Mail
to see whether or not Ervin has wrote. At 8 P.M. Elmer again calls to
see wheather Aunt Mary has some Brillen time to help his Hair look
nice & shiney. To be presentable for the Oyster Supper. He being very
polite, and thanking me to be a helpout to him. . . . the Mr. comes
along to go to slumberland at 11 P.M. He started to the Oyster Supper
at 7: and gets home at 11. after looking on at the dance at the Hall.

SATURDAY, NOVEMBER 13
. . . No Work for Dad to-day. Just arose out of Bed Milk 2 bossies,
feed one Calf Seperate the Milk. Took a shave put the Cream Can &
Egg Case, in the Car fill up with Water & Gas & give his wife a kiss.
And away he went to the City for piece & Contment. Getting away
from the old ugly Maze Patch. Heading for another day of Idleness.
And leaves home at 8 A.M. And gets back at 6:30 P.M. bringing Verna
along & 1 P.K. Candy. Mo at home in piece & comfort . . . Mo Plays
hooky. O happy day. No Dinner to be cooked. she eats a cold piece
of Bacon. Bread & Butter & 2 Cinnamon Rools for her desert. And
good measure. Mo finishes her Saturdays work which she left undone
lastnight. And in the fresh Air She takes a strole. Down to the Tam-
meracks and finds a huge big Armfull of Wood on her way back. . . .

MONDAY, NOVEMBER 15
. . . We rolled out at 5:45. Henry listened to the news while breakfasting. At 7:30 he pulled out for the Maze field. He came in for his chow

at 11:30 Went back to the Maze field at 1:25 & got home for Supper at 5 P.M. Bringing in a big load. . . . Elmer called at 1:P.M. With a letter from Ervin at Gearing Nebraska. Telling that he received his clothes & send a Dollarbill to help pay his life Insurance. Mo patches the Mr Blue & white stripes. Cuts out her speckeled Apron & sews part of it. She churns after supper. Patches Overalls for her Mr. And patches & darns Socks for herself & her companion. . . . While seprating this morning Henry kills the Crock and o the pieces where scattered all over the Well House. But lucky he was it happend before he had it full of cream.

TUESDAY, NOVEMBER 16
. . . Ervin drives in at 9:30. After being away for 4 1/2 Months. . . . So we retired at 1 after midnight.

WEDNESDAY, NOVEMBER 17
. . . We got up at 6:30 10 mi. later Ervin came out the Hay & 20 mi. later Verna rolled out. Henry only milked the Roan Cow this morning. Didn't seprate either. He listened to the Radio some. And chatted with Ervin. . . . Verna & Ervin went to Syracuse at 1:10. P.M. And got home after Po had finished his supper. . . .

THURSDAY, NOVEMBER 18
. . . The Mr. & Mrs. rolled out at 6 15 mi. later came Sonneboy. And Verna 10 minutes later. So there was no seprating done at our house to day. Henry spend the day reading. Chating about Ervins adventures at Gearing Nebrasks . . . The 3 men Ervin Elmer & Pete packed up their luggage, and at 1:45 they pulled out for California. And now us three lonely birds are all alone again. Verna is writing a letter to the Warners and the little ones. Mo is going to write to them too. Po is enjoying himself in slumberland, while he's sitting in the Leather Rocking chair for the last half hour. . . .

SATURDAY, NOVEMBER 20
. . . We started to Syracuse at 11:15 took 8 doz Eggs to town 25 cts a doz and $1.19 cts worth of Cream at 33 cts 1 lb. Butterfat. We got a Card from Ervin wrote from Thacher Arizona he wrote this Card the 19 yesterday. And got a letter from the Warners. . . .

SUNDAY, NOVEMBER 21
. . . Sky also looked murky on account of a little dust was blowing. . . . Well I dont spose no one broke the Sabath to-day Only Henry helped

Wayne load Cattle . . . For our breakfast we just had Eggs and one piece of Bacon for the Mr. Verna took a notion to bake some Cream Puffs. So for 2 hours in the fore-noon Henry & Mo where sampling some the rest of the fore noon. Some of them had whiped Cream, and some of them had a chocolate filling and o where they ever lusious. . . . Mo & Verna are writing the Warners a letter for Thanskiving Where they are now living in puddle jumpers land in the rainy season of Autum. . . .

MONDAY, NOVEMBER 22
. . . Verna made her big flowered dress to-day. Mo patched some & had the Hens to take care of the Fuel to carry in all day & to night she milked also feed the Calf. And after dark Po seprated Menue. . . . Mo churned & baked Bread. and got it all baked at 3.P.M. a slow poke. We listened to the Grand Hotel play to night for the first time this faul. . . .

TUESDAY, NOVEMBER 23
. . . We rolled out at 5:10 to-day. And no work was done at our house, just the choars. We started on our way to Dodge City at 7:10 and got back home at 5 P.M. The Trees looked like Xmas morning. . . . When we got to Doge we explored the ten cent store Verna bought 2 scarfs a dimes worth of candy. . . . We got a Card from Sonneyboy from Thaches Arizona Hes on his way to California. . . .

WEDNESDAY, NOVEMBER 24
. . . We got a Letter from Ervin to day from Phoenix Arizona They're on their way to California. . . . Mo had the milking all done she walked till the draw east of here and milked the red Cow. She sunk down in the blow piles 1 foot deep in the draw, while milking the Cow. After getting this Cow milked the Rone one had walked home, so then she had the pleasure milking the Rone one while she could sit on a stool, instead sitting on her shins. After coming in the house she had to pour the dirt, out of her shoes . . .

THURSDAY, NOVEMBER 25, THANKSGIVING
Well this was a beautiful day, no wind, just breeze. This day was certenly beautiful without enything else to be thankful for. . . . We got a letter from Thelma from Dexter Oregon They're still living in a suitcase. And one from Ervin saying they reached Calipatria California the 22 Monday. He says it was just as hot down there, as it was in the

Dustbowl. and the flies are very bad down there. . . . Mo had to dress her Hen before breakfast. So she got it on to cook at 7. Po running around on the farm with a shotgun trying to shoot this animal. It took him longer to get it shot, as it did Mo to get it ready to cook. Henry went to the Maze field at 8:15 got in at 11:45. The Hen hadn't got through cooking it had to keep on cooking till 1 P.M. Till it was tender. He went back to the field at 2:15 and got home at dusk it was 5.P.M. . . . Dinner Chicken gravy fruitsalad mashed spuds Cranberries Pumpkin Pie and Cake for desert. Supper a plenty left over from Dinner. To fill their hollowbelly. The after noon entertainment Bluegrass Roy and a number of plays expressing their Thanksgiving Spirit and the beautiful weather at this time of this year. At this presentime time Henry is listning to Thanksgiving programs puffing away with his pipe. Verna eating Candy while typing a letter to the kids. Mo eating peanut Candy while she's writing the family Diary. . . . And while writing a letter to the Warners and Ervin. The big pink Candy dish of candy stears one in the face every time that they look up.[46] . . .

FRIDAY, NOVEMBER 26

. . . a duststorm from northwest & snow to cover the ground. . . . At 6 we got up and at 7:30 Henry pulled out to the Maze field, and got in for chow at 12:15. And 2:30 he went back to the mazefield, and got home at 5 P.M. Mo walked out to the east field and milked the red Cow. She drove the Rone one home & milked her. Henry seprated the milk this morning. And for once Mo washed the Seprator by her self ha. Mo washed some clothes & ironed some and Verna washed a great bit also ironed them, and washed her pink Blouse & pressed it. . . .

SATURDAY, NOVEMBER 27

. . . We rolled out at 6:30. Where very slow. Seprating was done after breakfasting at 8 A.M. Seprator was washed 8 P.M. after our coming home from town. Henry took the Machine a part A.M. We lunched at 12 noon. At 12:30 we headed for town. We got home at 5:30. No Eggs where gathered, and no Cows where milked. The poor little Calf had to go to roost with a hollow belly. . . .

SUNDAY, NOVEMBER 28

. . . We arose at 6:30. While Mo was getting breakfast & doing some cleaning Po out in the east draw milking the cows. with full bags. that wheren't milked yesterday. . . . Po drove around to his fields to enspect them, and find how much damage had been done, by the Wind Friday night when the duststorm aproached . . .

WEDNESDAY, DECEMBER 1

. . . We arose at 6.P. & Mo. Verna 1/2 hour later. While breakfasting the Denver Man, was entertaining us with the news. At 7:30 the seprating was done. Ant at 8:30 the Mr. went to the Caffer patch [kafir corn] and finished up by noon.[47] He went back to the Maze patch at 1:30. Came in for supper at 4:30. While Mo was out on her journey with a milk stule & milk bucket, to milk the red Cow Po drove in with his load of Maze. Mo milked the Rone one in the Correl. She had fed the Calf before taking her spree. When Mo entered the house Po says well Milk Made? . . . Mo Washed Po dear's Overalls and some other things in a Dish pan. And I never faced such big job. . . .

THURSDAY, DECEMBER 2

. . . Dust from 10 A.M. till 4 P.M. it let up. Sky continued merky all day. . . . Po went to the field of Tricky at 8:30 and got in at 11 A.M. on account of the dust blowing. The dust efected the Radio some around 12 noon till about 1 P.M. . . . We got two letters to-day from Thelma & family. & are still living with Cliffs folks. The little ones wrote to. Mo Ironed some & Po was the milkboy to-day instead Mo . . . Mo packed the Eggs in the crate after supper. She ground up some lard A.M. also ground up some fresh meat. to make sausage for dinner. And to night she renered [rendered] it. . . .

SUNDAY, DECEMBER 5

. . . We got a letter from Ervin yesterday Dec. 4. from Cal where he's working at the present time & is making up to a dollar & 1/2 a day picking Peas. . . .

TUESDAY, DECEMBER 7

. . . Po just played hookie mostly all day long he put in the Moter in the Washer. He read Radioed & read the Mail for 1 1/2 hour or more Hens where very buisy they layed 27 Eggs. They came off of their strike. Mo wrote a letter to Ervin at Calapatria California & Mo & Verna wrote one to the Pudlejumpers at Dexter Oregon. . . .

THURSDAY, DECEMBER 9

. . . Henry went to Kendall A.M. got 10 dollars worth of Coal got home at 12:30. P.M. He bought 1 lb. Red Coffee . . . Mo hookied all day long didn't earn her two meals. Verna made . . . part of Mos. Clown dress as po calls it. Po also played hookie he just did the choars & seprated. So Mo got up this morning Couldn't hear much, and mostly being dum. So she was under the clowds all fore noon. At 12:30 she came out of some of this could hear better not being so dum. And all she did do this fore-noon. Sit in the dumps. After supper o boy. Po & Mo just created saurcasum in stead being lively and rejoicing. . . . We got a letter from the Warners to-day in the puddle-jumping land of beauty.

FRIDAY, DECEMBER 10

. . . Po didn't do no work hookied out side choaring time. Didn't even seprate. Mo mixed her Bread before breakfast and got it baked at 12:30 so Mo had fresh Bread for dinner. Po read a storie paper and radioed he also took in the plays that we usualy listen to. Verna finished my dress to day. And mo packed the Eggs in the Case [13] doz. Mo & Verna started a letter to the Warners. In the garden of Eden. . . .

WEDNESDAY, DECEMBER 15

. . . Po got the Seeder from Bullocs P.M. also got a load of Feed.[48] He seprated this morning and did the milking & Verna got the Cows She pressed some dresses also ironed some. And mended her Pejames. Mo washed and ironed some. . . . Po went to see if she could get some men to seed Broom Corn to-morrow.

THURSDAY, DECEMBER 16

. . . Henry went to Mr. Bishop to see if he'd help seed Broomcorn. They started at 10 A.M. got through at 4:15. We got 9 Bails of it. Mr. Bishop Adolph Klossen Mr. Bulloc & son Walter helped. Where here for dinner. The men went home at sunset. Adolph stayed for Supper and left at 8:10. Mo strowled through the Snow milked the red Cow in the draw east of here. The rone one she milked in the barn. Mo feed the Calf cold milk he drank it & thought it was fine. . . . Henry and Adolph are chating about duststorm rainy weather and taxing all things. farming. And government matters. . . .

FRIDAY, DECEMBER 17

. . . Henry seprated at 8 to-day then he went to bring back the Seeder on the way home he brought back a bad of Feed & got home at 11:30 This after noon he cleaned out some Broomcornseed. Verna Washed & ironed her Blue Pokydot dress. Mo ironed her green Dress to-night at 6 Henry went to the Soil meeting. Verna took her bath while Mo wrote a letter to Ervin in Calpatchia California.

TUESDAY, DECEMBER 21. THE SHORTEST DAY.

. . . Mo & Verna wrote & send off their letter to the Puddlejumpers in piecefull Oregon. Well this particular day a number of the Radio entertainers was preaching Piece On Earth And Good Will to Men. . . . Henry sold his Broomcorn to day to Mr. Blane. Had 1 1/2 Ton. at 45.00 Ton. He's very happy rejoicing of the selling of his Corn. He brought home a bottle of Wine a Pk. of Grape Fruit a bottle of Catsup. also a big Mess of nice Steak, now he's planning on some chicken fried Steak. Henry bought a very fine xmas tree to-day. . . .

WEDNESDAY, DECEMBER 22

. . . Henry took his corn to Kendall at 10 A.M. & got home at 3:15 P.M. And being very happy, after the deliverage. So now he has piece on his mind and contment. Ervin writes us a letter to day from Calapatria California telling us that he's still picking blackeyed Peas . . .

FRIDAY, DECEMBER 24

. . . Henry hawled loads A.M. And P.M. he came in at 3:45 from the field all faged out. We rolled out at 6:30 to-day. No seprating done. Mo baked some Raisin Sugar Cookies. A flop they where. Verna Baked a White Cake with nuts and fixed some Cranberries. And made some Fruitsalad. Verna cleaned up her Bedroom . . . All plays that I've been listining to celebrated xmas program execpting Ketty Kelly also Allen Jones the Widow. . . .

SATURDAY, DECEMBER 25

. . . We went to Edgers & Gertrude at 7:20. And got home at 6:30 P.M. We got a xmas Package consisting of 7 Dishtowls for Mo very fancy a dresser scarf 1 dishcloth from Patsy a Dutch windmill souvenior for Po & Mo. Po a blacksateen Pillow fancy made. . . . Verna a silk perfume silkchatet a very fancy Lunchcloth Mo also got a Purple flower with greenleaves from the kidies. And Verna got a dishcloth from Patsy. . . .

SUNDAY, DECEMBER 26

. . . Ice froze to the peach trees also grass and weeds. It looks like xmas at 2 P.M. . . . We rolled out at 6:30 & got through breakfasting at 7:30. Henry finally got the milking done at 8 A.M. after noon he went to the field to look at the Maze field he went to Kendall to get the Mail & got home 6 P.M.

MONDAY, DECEMBER 27
. . . We took Verna to Dodge. She took the Buss. And left for Hutch-inson at 3:15. The House is very quiet and empty again after our day of departure yesterday. . . .

TUESDAY, DECEMBER 28
. . . We rolled out at 6:15 Got through breakfasting at 7:30. Po sep-rated at 7:45. . . . He listened to a play. Then went to the field and hawled one load of Feed, got in for chow at 11:50. After dinner he unloaded his Feed & waited for the Mail. Again he went to the field at 2:50. And hawled another load of Feed. He came in at 4 P.M. and got this load unloaded at 4:30. Then at 4:30 he listened to the News about War. Po had to eat his Supper all by his lonely self to day for 6 weeks. Mo cleaned the Lampglobes and cleaned the House. She wrote a Card to Soneyboy to Calapatria California. . . . Mo patched and darned socks this eve. . . .

FRIDAY, DECEMBER 31
And 1937 comes to and end with a beautiful day. While the Bells ring out the Old Year ticks out to its doom. The bells ring and welcome the Newone in. . . . We both rolled out at 5:15. And got through breakfasting at 6:45. Henry milked while Mo did the Housework. He hawled a load of Feed to Mr Bishop at 8:30 And got home at 11 A.M. at 12 we eat Dinner and 12:20 Po started to Syracuse to see the Turky race. He came home at 6:45 P.M. after sowing some more Wildoats I spose. . . . Mo went after the Cows at 4:25 to the southwest field she jumped over some lister furrows Sit in a big blow pile, and dipped her slippers about 1/6 full of the loose dirt ha. Mo arrived with the Cows at 5:10 I had them milked. Ha. ha. . . .

The Knackstedt family, circa 1900. Standing, left to right, Hannah, Mary, Altophena, and Elizabeth; sitting, left to right, Wilhelm (father), Edward, Wilhelm, and Mata (mother). Courtesy of Thelma Dyck Warner and Verna Dyck Gragg.

Henry Dyck and Mary Knackstedt, wedding photo, 1904.
Courtesy of Thelma Dyck Warner and Verna Dyck Gragg.

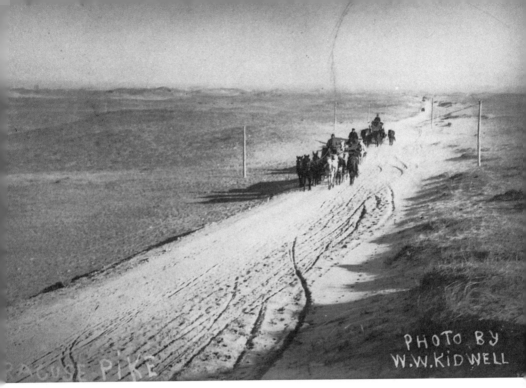

The sand hills south of Syracuse, Kansas, early twentieth century.
Permission of the Kansas State Historical Society, Topeka, Kansas.

A turn-of-the-century dwelling in rural Hamilton County, Kansas.
Permission of the Kansas State Historical Society, Topeka, Kansas.

The Dyck family home, Hamilton County, circa 1920. Standing, left to right, Thelma, Ervin, Verna, and Henry. Courtesy of Thelma Dyck Warner and Verna Dyck Gragg.

The Earl Ross Grocery Store, Kendall, Kansas, late 1920s, where the Dycks often traded. Permission of the Kansas State Historical Society, Topeka, Kansas.

The last family portrait, 1936. Standing, left to right, Thelma and Verna. Sitting, left to right, Henry, Mary, and Ervin. Courtesy of Thelma Dyck Warner and Verna Dyck Gragg.

The Menno Community Building, built by the Works Progress Administration and dedicated in 1937. From the Syracuse Journal, *June 11, 1937, permission of the Kansas State Historical Society, Topeka, Kansas.*

The results of southwestern Kansas dirt storms, 1936. Photo by Arthur Rothstein, FSA/OWI Photo Collection, Library of Congress.

An abandoned Hamilton County farm, 1939. Photo by Russell Lee, FSA/OWI Photo Collection, Library of Congress.

An abandoned farm near Syracuse, 1939. Photo by Russell Lee, FSA/OWI Photo Collection, Library of Congress.

Farm machinery abandoned to blowing dirt, circa 1935.
Permission of the Kansas State Historical Society, Topeka, Kansas.

The return of prosperity. The Dyck home under renovation, early 1940s.
Courtesy of Thelma Dyck Warner and Verna Dyck Gragg.

The Dyck home under renovation, early 1940s.
Courtesy of Thelma Dyck Warner and Verna Dyck Gragg.

4. A LITTLE SNOW, A LITTLE RAIN, AND HOPE

1938

SATURDAY, JANUARY 1

The Bells ring and welcome the Newone in. Starting & Welcoming the Year of 1938. . . . We rolled out at 7:30 this morning. And was 8:30 when we where through breakfasting. Henry seprated and it was 10:30 A.M. When Mo had the work done up. Henry listened to the Football game about 4 howars all tole. Texas Boys lost the game. We got a letter from Ervin from Calapatria Calif. He send 4 smackers to pay his Life Ensurance, which is due the 15 of Jan. Mo also wrote a letter to the Warners at Dexter, Oregon. . . .

SUNDAY, JANUARY 2

. . . We rolled out at 6:45 didn't do nothing to day just choar, and eat which seems as though it's very importend, to eat 3 times a day. Henry radioed all day long & Mo cooked 3 Meals, also did her housework. . . . Po got fed up on the Radio stuff and rolled in at 7. & Mo 15 minutes later.

MONDAY, JANUARY 3

This morning very strong North wind later P.M. It was northeast it let up some afternoon. The dust blowed a little on the Roads. . . . Today was last Episode of Todays Children They discontinued it, cause the story has been completed. So Erna Fillips writes this one instead. The Women In White.[1] Mo didn't hear these Epesodes to-day on account of the President's speech.[2] Arnold Grimms daughter Lindas first love also Betty & Bob. . . .

THURSDAY, JANUARY 6

. . . [Po] got in at 12:10 for his Dinner. At P.M. he read the Mail till 3 P.M. Then he put the Pipes in the House. so now Mo dont halfto

Cary no Water in Its right o how I apricate it, I'm glad. Cause its so very handy.[3] Mo washed all the Windows this fore-noon Cupboards Doors Merrior Glassdoors and Cabinet doors Merriors on the dressers and the Dressingtable. . . .

FRIDAY, JANUARY 7

. . . We rolled out at 6:40 And breakfast at 7:30 at 8 Henry had seprated. . . . He decided to go to Syracuse, to the Meeting at 10.15 he was on his way. Before breakfast he shaved his face to improve his apearance. So Mo had another hookie day. She made out an order for Pops Shirt and 3 Records and curtains for her Kitchen Windows & Pantry. At 4:15 Mo took a strole over the Contured ground Mo took a big piece of Peanut Candy to passify herself while driving home the Cows, she returned with them at 4:50 and had them milked at 5. While milking the Rone one the red one just happened to move so away she went but no damage was done. . . .

TUESDAY, JANUARY 11

. . . Wind grew very strong at noon. Dust started to blow at 1:15 P.M. Sky looked very murky. At sunset dust camed down. . . . We got a letter from the Warners to-day from Dexter Oregon. And a Card from Verna at Lewis Commons at Hutchinson Kans, where she's been a week at work to-day. They run a laundry. . . . Henry hookied all after noon read the Mail & letters while Mo was hard at Work. Mo got her book from Mary Souther in the Mail to day.[4] The Machine stoped twice to day while rinsing the big Ziper Jacket through it. It never had much power. Po came along with saurcasum while Mo called him, saying o say the old Motor stoped. Will you please Crank It.

WEDNESDAY, JANUARY 12

. . . Dust blowed from 2 P.M. and continued till 5 P.M. It was murky till sunset. . . .

THURSDAY, JANUARY 13

Northwest Terific Dust storm from 7 A.M. It kept on getting worse . . . Dust mostly had let up at dusk. But it stayed murky for severel hours. . . . Mo rolled out at 6:15 And Po stayed there in slumber or else he just pretended till Mo set the Table he got up for chow. It was then 7 after breakfasting Po milked & seprated at 9 A.M. He started on his way to Syracuse but didn't get there while the duststorm stirring him in the face he stayed at Kendall . . . Mo had correled the Cows so that she didn't need to walk after them. Mo played the Phonograph to drown her sorrows, while dust was ragging Such mournful sounding wind mostly made her get out of sorts, while being all alone at home. Its been plenty hard on Mos Glicerin also hand Lotin since she's got so much dust to handle.

FRIDAY, JANUARY 14

. . . Afternoon it continued murky till dusk we had a local duststorm. . . .

SATURDAY, JANUARY 15

. . . Local dust started at 1:30 before that it was very nice & warm. This dust just lasted a few hours. The sky is very murky P.M. . . . Mo cleaned house till 2 P.M. And when the dust came it blowed full again. At 4 P.M. Mo started after the Cows, they where 1/2 miles from home the return trip. I had them milked at 5. She drank some coffee while playing the Fonograph she awaited supper for Pop. I strained the milk closed the Henhouse. By this time it was dusk. . . . Bryen Hickson told Pop to-day While he was in Oregon he could fill his belly on fruit & vegetables. And out in the dustbowl. It was dirt instead ha.

SUNDAY, JANUARY 16

. . . At 10 A.M. Terific Dust storm . . . it let up considerable at 2:30. The sky is still murky. At 4:30 it blowed up more dust at 5 P.M. remained murky till dusk. . . . Well this is Sundy and all we have to do is sit and look like a dummy ha. after this dust had raged for 3 hours Pop got the last years Dairy to see how many storms we had, and just what time of the year they started in. He's getting some kick out of the book. It sorta gets his mind away from the dust, for the time being. To look in the past to see what we where doing all the time last year.[5] When lectricity quits buzzing he radioes for pastime. Mo Scrubs and cleans dust after the dust stops. . . . From Mon 9 till Sunday 16 We where expercincing the 1938 Duststorms. Today we make way for a reajustment to endure the duststorm while we're waiting on the Bounty.

MONDAY, JANUARY 17

. . . We got a very nice letter from Ervin From Calipatria California. . . . The three are picking Cotton. . . .

TUESDAY, JANUARY 18

. . . In the fore-noon just a little puffs of dust on and off P.M. from 2 we had a local duststorm. . . . At 8:30 Mr. Bishop arived they fixed on the Combine at 10 A.M. . . . all the rest of the fore-noon they fixed. They went to fixen at 12:30 after dinner they fixed and thrashed a little after Dinner.[6] Dust & wind blowed so at 4 P.M. Mr Bishop went home & Henry radioed 3/3 on an hour then he got the Cows & milked them. . . .

WEDNESDAY, JANUARY 19

. . . Mr. Bishop arived at 8 A.M. The two men went right to Thrashing They didn't stay with it very long at 9 A.M. They went to Bishops. They fixed canvas most of the day. They made the three trips to Bishop got the StrawCarrier Canves and something else and still didn't finish on account of the strong wind and dust.[7] Br [Brother] Bishop went home at 3:45. Henry then comforted himself in his big Leather Chair ha. And listened to the Radio. Being as dirty and black as a Negro. . . .

THURSDAY, JANUARY 20

. . . Po shaved his face and cut a gash in his cheek. He said his face was harsh and dry, he put some of Mos Mary Janes Hand lotion on his face to soften it. He then dressed up and went to Town at 9. This wasn't our seprating day. Po gets home from Town at 5:10 P.M. Mo washes 9 or 10 pieces of clothes which she needs the worst. . . . Mo goes after the Cows at 4:30 east and north of the Hogpen, she hangs her bucket and a shirt on the post which she's putting on her lap while milking. So just as these crithers see this away they run way back in the Hogpen and over the fence & into the pasture just scared out of their withs & Mo after them, so while adventuring all this she was gone 50 minutes. . . . We got a letter from both of the Girls. Thelma's from Dexter Oregon, and Verna's from Louise Commons. Po read Thelma's on the way and Verna's after he got home. Well ha ha. Just the same if Po did take the Mail on his way up to Town Mo still got some. Which he didnt know. The Seprator Rings and 2 Farm Journels.

SATURDAY, JANUARY 22

. . . We got a letter from Ervin to day saying to Address his letters to Niland Cali. It was his closest Post office. That's where they're working now moved their tents under a Pam Tree. . . . Pop is so dirty after 3 day of fooling with the Combine he also sticks fast to the chair

where he sits on. And he's so tired he cant hardly exercise his hands
& legs. And Static just growls as if it where August month the hotest
kinda weather. Mo did all her Saturdays work to day but never took
her Bath and washed her head ither.

SUNDAY, JANUARY 23
... Duststorm at 11:30 A.M. Advance of another Terific Duststorm
& ragged till dusk P.M. . . . Cows didn't get milked tonight on account
of the storm. . . .

MONDAY, JANUARY 24
Northwest Terific Duststorm. It continued through all Sun. Night It
wasn't so terriable at 7 A.M. at 9 she got terriable. . . . A lazy day, on
hand just an endurance of dust enhalence all day long. . . . it blowed
a while by 8 P.M. and camed down in the night. . . . Po's very
buisy playing the Phonograph to pasify himself. He's continued for
4 hours. . . .

TUESDAY, JANUARY 25
Still northwest Terific duststorm from 9 A.M. Mon. . . . about 8 A.M.
Wind came up and dirt rolled by in heaps. from New Mexico and
Idaho I spose.[8] . . . lectricity started at 9:15 A.M. and continued most
of the time we can hear a little over the Radio a few minutes at one
time. Dust let up at 4:30. It still continued murky and cloudy. . . . Pop
went to milk at 6:30. He seprated at 8. And choared. He read a while
and at 11 A.M. He's again playing the Phonograph to pasify himself
with his pipe for his consoler. This after noon before mail time he
sawed up a Tie and after 2 P.M. Po read the Mail. He had something
to keep his mind on till it was 5 P.M. and milking time. . . .

WEDNESDAY, JANUARY 25
... At P.M. local duststorm from 2 on. At 12:15 we had some lectricity
so Po couldn't hear the News 12:15 after 3 P.M. it let up some. . . . It
still stayes murky. till dusk. . . . Mo had a double header the Snifels
and a gloomy Companionship beside. Mo rided the two big rooms
from dust. Henry sawed up 3 ties to day. Mo packed the Eggs in the
Case to have them, ready for action.

THURSDAY, JANUARY 26
... It's a very plesent day once for a change again. . . . We rolled out
at 7 and again played very lazy now 3 days in sucession. We break-

fasted at 7:30 Pop had completed seprating at 8:15. He finished crating the Warners Radio.[9] And the rest of the fore-noon he repiled his feed. . . . at 3:30 P.M. He drove around to see how much damage had been done with the Terific storm . . .

FRIDAY, JANUARY 27

. . . We rolled out of the Hay at 6:30. Where not so polky to day. We didn't seprate breakfasted at 7:20 Po milked before show. He put the radio on the Car. Eggs & Cream in. Took a shave and at 8:45 we was on our way to Kendall. We drove around by Wane's Rectors and Bredock's to see how the dirt had piled up. . . .

SATURDAY, JANUARY 29

. . . It was a little dusty out. . . .

MONDAY, JANUARY 31

January and all it's days wind up to-day. . . . Henry Cut up 3 Ties up A.M. And P.M. He burned the Tameracs way north of the House & torn the Garden Fence down dug away the dirt and burned up the weeds & trash. Mo washed some clothes. Washed the Lampglobes And churned in 20 mi Time. . . . The little baby Calf caused a Comotion He's been growling since Friday was his last day to get milk. so he sneeked to the Cows bag and milked her. He jumped over his stawl paraded around on the Tank, on top of the ice not breaking through either. . . .

THURSDAY, FEBRUARY 1

. . . Henry went right to work at the box Correl got it all tore up at A.M. And also dug out the Locous trees east of the House under the Clothesline the dead ones. At P.M. He's rolling up the southside Hogfence and also digging the Thistels out, and some dirt that is banked up. He read the Mail for one hour and then he went to work again. Mo Washed some to day. . . .

WEDNESDAY, FEBRUARY 2

. . . Westbreeze at 7 and hour later it was northwest and blowing up a little dust. It got merky for about one hour between 9:10 A.M. . . . We had a local duster at 1:25 only lasted 3/3 of an hour. It continued a little murky all day long. . . . Work at the Dyck ranch to day. They wherent very enthusticac. Mo rolled out at 6:50. And radioed some while Po was out in piecefull slumberland till 20 mi till eight. Mo had breakfast ready and was at the table eating when Pop came out of the Hay ha. Hes been fixing some tires. Henry boy shaved his face to day after getting away with some saurcasum, he takes more pride in his aparence. We went to Kendall at 2 P.M. . . .

THURSDAY, FEBRUARY 3
. . . at 12:15 a duster aproached and from 12:30 till 1:45 P.M. Lectricity then dust let up considerable. It continued merky. . . . I forgot to do my ironing on account of the duster a local one only. . . . We got a Card from Ervin at Niland Calif. A letter from the kids at Dexter Oregon and the little kidies pictures & o boy are they ever sweet. And after all this long absence. . . . Pop is listening to We the People a prisoner gave a long speech this was on to day at 5:45. This man was warning the people to try and keep their freedom after birth & not to get into enything so that they'd halfto serve a life long term in Prison. He said he'd be an old man when he's served his term. . . .

FRIDAY, FEBRUARY 4
. . . Not a bit of dust for this great 4th day of Feb. . . .

SATURDAY, FEBRUARY 5
Southwest wind slightly cloudy Local duster aproached at 9: A.M. . . . We had a nother spell of dust right over noon in Town. I dont know how long it lasted at our place. We only got home at 6 P.M. It continued merky and clowdy. Wind kept on all day long blowed real strong at 7 P.M. We rolled out at 7 after our trip to Kendall to the Mock Wedding. A sorta Wed. Shour for George Tope.[10] We breakfasted at 7:30 after pumping the Cows. Mo just cleaned up the Eggs finished up the Cream. Washed the dishes swept & took her bath, and got ready to start to town. Henry took a shave . . . The old nancys where home when we got home from Syracuse at 6:45. Pop milked them. We didn't seprate to-day. . . . We also bought some tape to stick up the House, to keep the dust out some.[11] . . . On our way home we seen the Prairie fire that had taken place, after we went to Town. Which burned 3 big Haystacks, and a big space of Prairie grass. . . .

MONDAY, FEBRUARY 7
. . . The sky was merky at 6:40 at 15 till 8 it had started to blow a little bit lectricty at 9:15 a Terific duster was in full blast The sun could be

seen after it had rose 1 hour. In a little while it couldn't be seen. . . . Henry sawed 3 Ties while Mo listened to these special plays. The widow Jones. The women in White Nancy & Bill and Lindas first love. At P.M. Po churned for Mo, then he went and dug out some banks of drifted dirt the great big one north and the garden fence drift. Po glued up the west bedroom window that's the middle one & the Pantry window. . . . Pop in the House creating some jokes, which he learned Saturday in town. To pass the time, while the dust was in full cession. . . . Lewis Lameyer Listed in all that terific dust till about 2 P.M. He pulled out for home.

TUESDAY, FEBRUARY 8
. . . The Sun didn't rize in a clear sky this morning in the southeast was real merky. . . . A local duster started at 1 P.M. . . . Merky sky continued till dusk . . . Mo send the little Warners a heart of Valentine Candy. The big ones a box of chocolates to Dexter Oregon. Ervin a box of chocolates to Niland California. And Verna a Red Heart of chocolates to Hutch at Louise Commons. She also wrote each one of the children a letter. . . . Pop dug up some fences A.M. . . . He then dug out fences till 2 P.M. till the Mail came. At 2:45 P.M. He dug out some more till 3:45 P.M. he quit. To day the gloomy companion again comeback After the duster Mo had a lot of cleaning to do this day. She also washed the Lampglobes. Packed 9 1/2 doz Eggs in the Case & cleaned them and next she washed the glass doors. . . .

WEDNESDAY, FEBRUARY 9
. . . a local duster at 9 A.M. At 11:15 it had let up . . . Mo washed a little Washed her head. And cleaned up her pantry spic & span. . . .

THURSDAY, FEBRUARY 10
. . . We got a letter from Sonny boy to-day while he still is in Niland California picking Peas at the present time. . . .

SATURDAY, FEBRUARY 12
Well this has been a wonderfull plesent day till 10 A.M. The wind started a Terific duster and let up at 4:45 so that lectricty quit murky sky still continued. . . . Wind's still blowing at dusk from southwest. . . . Henry went to the field and started to list at 8 A.M. He worked north of the Tamarecks and listed east up till the middle fence. Which he rolled up Thursday. Pop started in to list up the Hog-

pen at 10 A.M. When this duster struck. Today beings Lincoln's birthday was, the programs on the radio where much more intresting.

SUNDAY, FEBRUARY 13
For a change the wind's in the northeast. We had a local duster started
in at 8:30 . . . another Sabath broke. Mo bakes 2 Apple Pies while Pop
out at work to. . . . Mo also cleans up the floors and does her Saturdays
work. Cause it blowed yesterday. And it hadn't did much good. Well
to day the gloomyness has left Mo for one day at least. . . .

MONDAY, FEBRUARY 14
. . . We arose at 6:30. While Pop being very embitous to go to the field
and harrow Thistels. We breakfasted at 7:30 He got through seprating
at 6 A.M. He then had changed his mind about harrowing the Thistels. He cut wood Fixed Tires and chated awhile, with Mr. Englert
about the Conditions of the Land & Laws. . . .

TUESDAY, FEBRUARY 15
. . . Everything was covered with ice and very slippy out of doors. It
continued clowdy all day long not a bit we seen of the Sun. The wind
blows 40 mi an hour. It continued icy all day trees didn't thow at
all. . . . We just arose at 7:15 eat choared and red magazines also radioed, some and had some letters to read. To passify ourselves. Mo got
her Dion Quints Hankies from Pamolive today.[12] . . . A very nice long
letter from Sonneyboy, while picking Peas at Niland California. And
the Sears Roebuck Catalogue. . . . part of the day [Po's] been the
Messenger boy. He's been afraid, that Mo would fall on the Ice ha and
crack her craneam. . . .

THURSDAY, FEBRUARY 17
Northeast cold breeze to day. Its clowdy to day but isn't dark as it was
yesterday. you can see a long distance. It snowed very lightly in the
fore-noon snow is deep enough so it covers the ground some places.
some places its mostly 1 inch deep a little yesterday a little Tuesday
night. Ice is still covered over all trees roads fences also in the Wind
mill. . . . Well one feels like singing this song now for severel days.
What the farmers are getting now is a farm relief since dust has not
blowed for 4 days and clowdy snowy & Icy weather. It looks very
cheerfull one can rejoice. One has a new lease on life. . . .

FRIDAY, FEBRUARY 18

... Icycles are still on everthing just as it has been two days ago. This morning we have 4 inches of Snow on level & on some places it banked up some considerable large banks. . . . This was another lazy day. When we rolled out of Bed at 7 and didn't seprate we breakfasted before the Mr milker. While breakfasting we were presented with the News Cast. Also while we were at our coarse at Noon We where presented by the News Cast. Henry says we hear of News till he was black in the face. At p.m. Mo cleaned out the Clothes Closet thourly [thoroughly] and Pop down in the Basement giving it a good cleaning.

SATURDAY, FEBRUARY 19

... Pop milked before breakfast it was seprating day this morning, cause he wanted the Cream to take with him to town. After choaring was all done up. He shaved his stubble off he must have wanted to be more atractive I see. He started on his way to Town at 10 A.M. . . . got home at 6:30 P.M. This morning while Mo was starting to the Hen-house with one bucket of Water, another with clabber Milk. Down she rolled on the ice spilled water on her arm and some clabber milk on the ground. The cat was present to lap it up. . . . . We got a card from Ervin at Niland California while he's just picking peas on & off. . . .

MONDAY, FEBRUARY 21

... We rolled out at 7 A.M. & while Pop was trying to fix the fire, away went the Cows Mail & all. He tried to stop them, but couldn't they kept right on going. So for once in eight days Mo had a chance to build the fire. So Pop didn't have enything to do just eat and shave and away to Town he went at 9 A.M. & got home at 6:15 P.M. . . .

TUESDAY, FEBRUARY 22

This is Washingtons Birthday and all programs where good where basted on it. . . . Mo served all day long cut out her brown tweed Apron and finished the two dresses & sewed at her slip. . . . Mr. Gayler wrote a letter to day saying he wanted to go along to Oregon with us.[13] . . .

WEDNESDAY, FEBRUARY 23

... We rolled out a little earlier at 6:30. Pop milked before breakfast. We got through breakfasting at 7:15 & didn't seprate. Pop cleaned out the Barn had started and worked at it 1 hour at 9 A.M. . . . Mo Baked

2 Cherrie Pies. and churned 15 mi. and P.M. Mo ironed some, washed Lampglobes the door glasses took a bath got ready packed the Eggs up & went to Town P.M. Pop was working at his barn . . . After this work he sawed some ties for fuel. Mo jelled some Jello after 9:30 when we had returned from the Show. Every Day A Holiday. Played by Mae West. . . . Bishops Papa Cow is again acomponing our Cows to night. We didn't milk the Cows to-day cause we could start to town earlier. . . .

THURSDAY, FEBRUARY 24
. . . We got up at 6:30 to-day. Pop had been chaced out by nature some time at 3 or 4 after midnight. We got through breakfasting at 7:30. Pop seprated and fixed some Pop also put fresh battry in the Radio. When this snow apeared at 1:45. A little while of lectricity took place. Mom sewed & washed some A.M. Well we're still enjoying piece and Comfort ever since Feb 16. We're really having Farm relief. Mo sewed on her dust Cap also on her brown dress trimed in red braid. And cleaned house to-day. . . .

FRIDAY, FEBRUARY 25
. . . Pop puttered around some till 9 A.M. a few hours before noon, he dug up some posts on the north hogfence. 1:15 P.M. he went to the field east of the Community Hall and dug up 1/2 mile of fence which he's wanting to do, for 4 years he said.[14] He got home at 5 P.M. Then he shaves his face gets himself ready to go to the Community Meeting. . . . Mom at P.M. did her Saturdays work, Cleaned and packed up the Eggs. Put the Cream in the Bucket & sewd at her slip. She got her bread backed at 4 P.M. It was exelent. And Mo sewed at her dust Cap and finished her brown dress trimed in the red braid. . . .

SATURDAY, FEBRUARY 27
. . . we got our selves ready to go to Syracuse at 10:15. And got home at 8:25. Mo eat a little supper cause she hadn't eat a bit of dinner and a very little breakfast. Mo got her Cawlewells Syrup of Pepsin sampell also her goods for aprons & a bonnet 5 pieces. . . . We got a card from Ervin while picking peas at Niland Calif saying he's moving. . . .

MONDAY, FEBRUARY 28
. . . Mo got up at 5 Pop at 5:45. We breakfasted at 5:30. Mo was eating when Pop got up. We started on our way at 9 A.M. stoped in

Kendall Mo wrote a Card to the Warners at Dexter Oregon. also bought $1.35 gals of Gas. At Hutch he bought 1.45 cts Gas. We eat

our lunch at Spearville We stoped in Hutch got $1.oo Gas [15]

WEDNESDAY, MARCH 2
. . . We got home at 8:25 Stores where closed at Kendall. We stoped at Garden Pop bought a suitcase for 1.98 some bolts. Verna got a Suit Case for 98 cts. Pop a Lock Pop bought 2 qt Oil at 43 cts 11 gals. gas at $2.oo We got to Garden 15 till 6 P.M. 1 qt oil at Garden 20 cts. Mo got a Cup Coffee Verna got a bowl of Chilly. Pop a big meal a hole platter full & o did he ever eat. While Pop & Verna where doing their shopping Mo listened to the One Mans family. . . .

THURSDAY, MARCH 3
Southeast Terific duster for 2 hours. Then it just came by spurts it started in at 10 A.M. and let up considerable. . . . We got up at 6 in the morning Henry went to Bishops and helped him milk his cows. got back when Mo & Verna where at the breakfast at 7:30. . . . Mo wrote a Card to Ervin at Carpinteria Calif. while they're picking Olives. . . . Mo retires at 11 oclock P.M. Pop at 12:30 after midnight when he had the Hens cooped up ready to go to Town.[16] Mo had been in slumberland.

FRIDAY, MARCH 3
Southeast terific duststorm started in at 9: A.M. kept on till 2:30. And let up some. Mo couldn't hear these programs The youngs Guiding Light Mary Marline Arnold Grims daughter on account lectricity. It was clowdy & merky before the dust started. . . . Adolph hawled the Hens to Syracuse at 9 A.M. Mr Bishop got 3 doz. These 3 Dozen layed 23 Eggs to-day. Pop found a nest of 19 Eggs under the Coops this morning, in the little Henhouse. When Mo went to get these Eggs to Nite she certenly found the Henhouse lonesome & all empty. She felt like sheding tears. It seems as if she's taring herself up by the roots, & is planting them some where else. . . . We rolled out at 6 today & breakfasted at 6:30. No milking to do and just 3 doz Hens to take care of. Now this is the fifth day we didn't see the Cows here on the place.[17]

Between March 3 and April 23, the diary would sit idle in the Dyck home,
while Mary, Henry, and Verna visited the Warners in Dexter, Oregon. Dur-

ing this time, Ervin moved north to Dexter to look for work, joining his sister and brother-in-law.

SATURDAY, APRIL 23

. . . Dust blowed just local from early till 3. . . . We rolled out of the Hay 5:30. Pop & Ma Verna came out 1/2 hour later. Pop dug the dirt out of 1/2 of the Tank A.M. Some of it before breakfast. We breakfasted at 6:30. Ma & Verna cleaned dirt all forenoon. . . . Verna & Ma washed some clothes A.M. so they'l be ready to pull out for Hutch to Morrow. Verna pressed Pops trousers her clothes. Mo ironed such wet clothes that it took her 1 1/2 hour on one hours ironing. Mo cleaned her bedroom cleaned the Pantry scoured the oilstove washed her head took a bath P.M. & mended her socks & later she made some Carmel Cocoanut Candy.

WEDNESDAY, APRIL 27

. . . Ma cleaned up dust while Pop went to Mr. Bishops to help milk & got 1 qt milk for breakfast. . . . We got Photas from Eugene.

THURSDAY, APRIL 28

. . . Till noon air was murky & local Duster. At 5 P.M. It had camed down considerable. . . . Henry then went to Mr. Bishop and got the Cows. Pop went to Adolph at 9 A.M. And drove the tractor home arrived at 12 noon 1/2 hour Adolph & Son came and drove the Car home. Pop took him home & at 2 P.M. he was home with the Car.[18] At 2:30 he went to the Dorr Harrowed it & harrowed the south Orchard also garden. And I felt very touf after all days work on my feet. . . . A caller arrived A.M. while Mo was blue & was sobbing, so she wasn't there to answer the door. . . .

FRIDAY, APRIL 29

. . . the wind came up & went to the northwest while another local duster was in full cession. This took place after dark and continued till way late. . . . before breakfast Pop went to Mr. Bishop to get the Cows. He came out of the house with his Pajamas just had come out of the Hay. . . . Mo cleaned dust 1/3 of the day. Aired all her bedding . . . While gathering Eggs to night Mo looked in the bble. thinking of snakes, and spied a nest of young cats half grown. She was very week in the nees her heart in her throat she wound up very scared it was real dark to so she couldn't hardly see. . . . During our

abscence the mother Cats had taken advantage using our out buildings for a breeding place. Mo remained nerveous & very week all
day long. . . .

SATURDAY, APRIL 30
. . . a local duster from 9 A.M. on continued as ordarandly P.M. it got
worse. . . . Mo had toothache & very weak all day long. She patched
her Nightgown. She baked 2 Pies one dried Apple & one a comba-
nation of dried Apples & Cherries. . . . Well this is the end of the
glorious month which we spend part of it beautiful States far away.

SUNDAY, MAY 1
Southeast also southwest local dusters It growed dark at noon & got
worse. . . . Well this is Sunday Pop broke the Sabath fixing fence &
Mo a churning its the first one since her return. . . . Pop has taken a
nap from 12:30 till 2:30 Mo had got ready to go to Olyan Warners on
accound the darkness & such duster we didn't tackel it. . . . the rest of
the time she slept she couldn't read much on account being so sleepy.
She got in on 3 hours sleep. Pop spend the rest of the after-noon
reading the Oregon Papers and American Magazine. . . .

MONDAY, MAY 2
. . . a local dust storm all day from 9 A.M. till dark the wind was harder
then ever after dark. . . . We rolled out at 15 till 5. Pop got up at 4:30
Pop worked with the Curler A.M.[19] He brought the tractor home &
pudered around on it P.M. Cause the storm was to fierce to work. . . .

THURSDAY, MAY 3
. . . Terific duststorm all day long at 5 P.M. It got so dark that we had
to lite the Lamp. . . . Pop curlered the quarter east 1·1/2 miles A.M.
P.M. duststorm was so bad he couldn't work. Pop studied his Oregon
trip while pasifying himself smoking cigars. While letting his supper
digest. . . . Mo made Bloomers Sewed up one Bonnet & made another
New one Blue & Brown with little yellow specks. She also did a little
washing. . . .

WEDNESDAY, MAY 4
. . . At 9 A.M. a local duster let up at 3:30 P.M. It rained some early
this morning just by the house east on our ground we just got a very
little. . . . It certenly looks like living once more instead smothering

in dust. One feels as if they have a new less on life. Mo wrote a card
to both of the girls Verna at Hutch & Thelma & family also Ervin
at Dexter. Mo cleaned up the dust P.M. after her return back home
from Town.

FRIDAY, MAY 6
. . . Pop started out of bed at 4:15 It was raining he then went back
to bed. He cleaned the Basement A.M. at P.M. the drive way and
Wellhouse. Mo made Soap A.M. And pasted up the windows in the
southwest bedrooms. We had a Coal fire in the Heatrola. It was very
comfortable. . . .

MONDAY, MAY 8
. . . Mo had the Toothache all P.M. Her Ears mostly roared herself
insayen. . . . Mo sewed up one bonnet patched washed some clothes
wrapped up the dresses Hat & some more junk and Photo to go to
Dexter Oregon Wrapped up the Photo to go to Verna to Hutch. . . .

TUESDAY, MAY 9
. . . Mo started after the Cows they where away with the Bishop Cows.
She chated a little better then an hour with Nina Griswold who was
washing she returned home at 10:45 A.M. And the old red cow didn't
get her bag pumped. Mo still has her sores hanging on from the effects of making the Soap.[20] Mo's Ears gest kept on roaring all the way
to Bishops & Back. She spied a small gray Snake it looked as if it
where a Bullsnake. . . . Pop & Ma Drove to Bishops after the
Cows. . . . Him & Pop chated a while about the blowing condition
working the ground . . .

WEDNESDAY, MAY 11
. . . Mo washed lampglobes washed her head took a bath aired all
her bedding & completely cleaned House. She milked the Cows this
morning & drove them down to the draw. and milked them to night
again. . . .

THURSDAY, MAY 12
. . . We got a letter from Verna from Hutchinson Kans. Sending
4 dollars to save up for her.[21] We also got one from Dexter from the
Warners. . . .

FRIDAY, MAY 13

... At 5 we got a terific Duststorm Temp dropped 4 points in 20 minutes. Henry got home from the field at 5 P.M. And went to reading papers while dust was in full seccion. He fixed Fence till 8:15 A.M. Then came home afoot he cranked the Truck till his hand was num but it wouldn't start so he left it there. We started to Syracuse 8:40 A.M. Pop took a Shave put on his clean underwear dressed up & away we went I cleaned up the Eggs packed them polished my shoes so I then was ready to start when Pop was. . . . Then made 5 batches Soap after getting home from Town. . . .

126
——
Snow,
Rain,
and
Hope

SATURDAY, MAY 14

... Pop moved to the section 14 southwest quarter. He didn't eat eny dinner at noon he come home at 4:45 he eat & left for Garden at 5 & bought the Radio. Mo went way to the Bishop draw to milk the Cows. She did all her Saturdays work at 2:30 she was through with it. She Baked 3 Lemon Pies & baked an exelent batch of Bread had it finished at 2 P.M. I also scrubed the Pantry & kitchen and washed some clothes We got home from Garden at 8:45 with the Radio & Charger. Mo had the Rumatism in Arms & legs that she set some lunch on the table for Pop & rolled in. While Pop was setting up the machine red some & radioed a while he retired at 10. . . . Ma bought two bunches Invelopes, 1 Jar Cold Cream one Bottle Brillentine & Pop drank a glass of Bear.

SUNDAY, MAY 15

Southwest early Terific Duststorm at 6 A.M. It looked merky at 5 when we rolled. It let up at 1 P.M. was merky & warm started another on arolling at 6 it just lasted from 1 to 2 hours P.M. . . . Went to Kendall at 9 drove around 2 miles east of our place to inspect the soil conditions. . . . We got a letter from Verna from Hutch sending 2 dollars one from Thelma from Dexter saying she's a lone the news saying she's a lone the men went to Valsetz.[22] . . .

MONDAY, MAY 16

. . . Terific Duststorm at 7:30 continued. Thunder & Considerable Clowdyness. . . .

TUESDAY, MAY 17

... at 8 am Local duststorm was in full ceccion kept on till 1 P.M. let up some It was clowdy and dark. The air is nothing but lectricity has been for 3 1/2 hours still kept on at 1 P.M. . . . It quieted down some after 4 P.M. at 6 P.M. It got worse & continued as long as we could see. . . . [Pop] took the Lister to the Doerr quarter & Came home at 6 P.M. when the terific storm struck Pop eat at 7 P.M. again. . . . We rolled in at 7:30 while the Wind was raving Mo did up her work this morning and the longer she kept on going the tuffer she felt. She finally layed down about 1 1/2 hour after having fallen asleep she felt a little better. This morning Glories have started to Bloom to day just a few Blossoms.

WEDNESDAY, MAY 18
. . . Its very dark. Southwest & southeast wind P.M. It blowed terific over noon & again at 3 P.M. It was terific from that time on it blowed some dust. . . . from 4 till 6 it blowed considerable. . . . Mo walked after the Cows twice to-day And milked them twice once she milked them in the Pasture that was this morning. Mo sewed some bloomers & washed some. She felt very tuff today. The Radio was so statice that you couldn't hear yourself think. I only heard Bachlors children. Pop was so tired tonite that he couldn't even read. . . .

THURSDAY, MAY 19
. . . At 6:30 Pop dear came home with the Cows he had run out of Gas so Ma didn't half to get them she only had them to milk. . . . She sewed one Apron Churned & Cleaned house. And sewed some on her bloomers. . . . Well this beautiful day certenly brought piece & ecouragement to me. And I'm so thankfull to think that we had the chance to endure such quiet & piecefull day. After having four of those wild ones it certainly is apricated. . . .

FRIDAY, MAY 20
. . . At 5 A.M. local duster came up and bloded [blowed] as long as you could see. . . . Pop started to the field 15 till 6 worked till 11:30 his clock was a little fast so he came a little early Ma still got his dinner ready at 15 till 12. He got in at 6 P.M. for supper on account the dust came from the East he couldn't see. He moved 1 1/2 mile east of hear at 4 P.M. Took a shave before suppering while Mo got the Cows. . . . She had the Rhumetiz today that she can't hardly get around and the toothache included. . . .

SATURDAY, MAY 21
. . . 1:30 to Town we went . . . We took 106 Eggs to Syracuse and got 15 for them toteled $1.15. Mo sent off for the Salad set for Old Dutch

from Bachlors Children. It was chilly enough to day that Henry was glad to put on his long undersuit. He started to the Community Hall at 8 While Ma retired to her piecefull Slumberland it was 1.40 the next morning when [he] got home with a Raisin Pie, eating most of it before retiring

TUESDAY, MAY 24

. . . Mo washed a greatbig Washing to-day. The machine stoped at 10 A.M. Beings Pop was not here she had the clothes most of it, to ring by hand. . . .

WEDNESDAY, MAY 25

. . . A northwest duster apeared at 6:45 . . . only lasted 20 minutes . . . Pop started to plant to-day at 10 A.M. And came in for dinner at 11:45 He left for work at 12:15 and got home at 7 a while after the duster occured. . . . Mo washed a great deal of Bedding and some other clothes. She baked Bread to-day & got it baked at 12:20 it'ed been through sooner but one of the burners went out. She cooked the old cream that wouldn't got to Butter. And she churned another batch of Cream it was good butter for spread. . . .

FRIDAY, MAY 27

. . . The wind was so mornfull to day it made one lonely & feel gloomy. Po started to the field not so early as usual & is still planting mile east of here he moved P.M. today. Pop got his Car stranded . . . He had so much grief lost two Discs . . . so he came in early . . . While Pop got hungup on the way home for dinner, he was entagnising over dinner couldn't smile period. But when he heard Mr. Rosevelts speech he woke up and had a smile on his face a mile wide.[23] . . .

SATURDAY, MAY 28

. . . A southwest duster apeared from the southwest & continued only for 3 hours P.M. Weather was quiet & hot. . . . Pop started to the field at 4:30 to day and moved to the 160 east of here 1 mile. . . . He came in from the field at 8. It was 9 when he got his bath taken. . . . Mo got the Cows & had them milked at 7:20 she felt so tuff when she retired she didn't know where to lie down to Comfort herself. She took her bath after have had finished with Saturdays work.

SUNDAY, MAY 29

. . . went to Kendall [and] got the Mail. Took Edger & family to Syracuse while Henry transacted buisness Mo got up feeling tuff for

2 hours and then felt better. We got our selves each a Hamburger
at Honey Baums. Henry got a cold Sandwich beside Edger a piece
of Gooseberry Pie. Mo & Gertrude each a pt of Black Walnut Ice
Cream. This recalls memorys of my hamburger days while being on
our trip last March & April. . . .

MONDAY, MAY 30, MEMORIAL DAY
Early at 3 A.M. a north west duststorm. I spose it was a black one it
blowed 60 miles an hour but lasted just a little time maybe 1 hour.
And had 1/4 inch rain wind blowed hard till 3 P.M. It then let up was
very cool all after-noon . . . The wind was very mournfull all day
long. . . . Mo baked Bread and had it all completed by noon. It was
exelent. She baked a plain Cake for the Rhubarb and only put 2 tablespoons of Shugar in it. She tasted it and it wasn't sweet enough she
put in 2 tablespoons sugar in it yet. And seened the Cup Shugar setting on the table instead in the cake. . . . She milked the Cow in the
Rain while Pop suppered. The old Red run away when seeing a black
Tomcat coming along the Pasture and left me sitting on the milkstool.

WEDNESDAY, JUNE 1
. . . Mo went after the Cows with her dust cap. A big clowd in the
West covered the Sunshine. Mo cleaned up the House shined the
flouers churned patched and sewed and washed a little. Washed lampglobes. And got in with the Cows at 7:15 & had old Red milked. she
sewed while the Supper was cooking & waiting on Pop.

THURSDAY, JUNE 2
A terific June Duster from 9 A.M. and continued till 4 P.M. Couldn't
see the sun from 9 A.M. till 4 P.M. . . . Mo sewed patched socks also
other articles. washed Windows & Killed a Snake in the Barn while
looking for Eggs she killed the snake with her heart beating in her
Throat. . . .

FRIDAY, JUNE 3
Wind very strong in all directions. . . . Local duststorm from A.M.
till most noon. P.M. merkyness disapeared. Wind camed considerable. . . .

SUNDAY, JUNE 5
Southwest local duster entered at 6 A.M. kept on till 3:30 A.M. . . .
Winds blowing 60 miles an hour again at 1 P.M. dust continued till

3:30 . . . We drove around east 6 miles of here looking at our crop and at the conditions of Land and weedy fields. And saw a few patches of Wheat not bound to make much just a few bu. to an acker. . . . At 3 P.M. [Po] went to the Ballgame and got home at 5 P.M. Found Ma in slumber land . . . Henry retired at 11. Mo had went there at 9 her usual bed time. She hant got no speed to day her legs are week and won't take her places. She had the stomache ache. . . .

MONDAY, JUNE 6

. . . Henry went to the field worked on our 160 finished P.M. he finished planting there. He came home at 15 till 7 for Supper. He had forgot his Goggles his eyes hurted him cause they had been out in the dust all after noon without eny protection. . . . Mo lost her apron getting the Cows terific wind blowed it off the next day she found it.

THURSDAY, JUNE 9

. . . [Pop] came home at 5 P.M. When the duster and terific wind occured. He went back at 6 P.M. And worked till 8:10 He came in for Supper. Ma drove along to the field with Pop and drove the Cows home. Ma ironed another batch of quilt pieces this A.M. and tor apart the small charm quilt. Ma did a big washing. 4 Sheets two Comforter tops and a lotta Clothes. . . .

FRIDAY, [JUNE] 10

. . . At 4:30 a Terific duststorm struck this one lasted 1 1/2 hours It thundered terriable and only sprinkeled. It Camed down at 6 P.M. . . . Well Ma is stiff and cant get around very good the after effects of using her Arms for a girator after the [washing] machine stopped. She cleaned House this fore-noon after the duster struck.

SATURDAY, JUNE 11

. . . Well after the Terific storm Ma had the hole House to go over to day again. She Baked Bread & had it completed at 12 P.M. She packed the Eggs ready to go to Town. . . . Ma had her crowned Tooth pulled to day also 2 others on the lower jaw on her left side. She couldn't talk for 3 hours on account of the dope couldn't swallow till 7 three hours later and couldn't spit either. She had to take her Hankie to wipe the blood out of her Mouth. Her Tongue was swollen so that she couldn't hardly find room in there so she could wipe it out with her Handkie.

SUNDAY, JUNE 12

. . . After dinner we had a real duster. A.M. it was to damp to blow dust. It let up at 5:30 P.M. . . . Pop went to Adolph and took him all over to see the soil conditions he left at 8:30 and got home 10:30 . . .

MONDAY, JUNE 13

. . . a terific duststorm took place got worse at 5 P.M. it was dark enough to light a lamp. . . . Pop took a sleep while the storm ragged on. Mo washed the dishes. The Cows had come home at 5 and she turned them in.

TUESDAY, JUNE 14

Southwest wind early A.M. Later at 10 A.M. It started to blow. it had rained some late yesterday so it was damp and didn't blow in the forenoon. It kept this up till 15 till 2 P.M. . . . Mo fixed up the little charm block comforter with the light lining. also the one with a green checkered bottom washed Lampglobes and cleaned dirt after the terific duststorm yesterday. Ma milked while Henry eat his supper. Henry was so sleepy hungry & tired. He fought the mud so much while working so we retired at 7:45 With the Chickens. She wrote to Warners at Valsetz also to Cliff. We got a letter from Verna. And sending some more dough $ home to save. Mas left jaw hurts terriable. . . .

WEDNESDAY, JUNE 15

. . . Henry went to the field right after eating but couldn't work on account being to wet. So he come back and shaved his wiskers. And went back about 8 and worked till 12 noon he went back to the field at 12:20. And got back at 3:40 cause it looked so bad and thundered terriable. Mo hemmed dishtowls washclothes cleaned house shined things up washed some clothes patched and washed lampglobes. Pops smoking reading some and watching the terriable clowdy weather and thunder, he's got a path walked from the rocker to the bedroom Window. The cows didn't come home nor get milked. Ma jaws still ache terriable from the effects of her teeth. We retired at 7 with the Chickens. We lit the Lamp at 5 P.M. so we could see to read and Ma sewed some till seven came along.

FRIDAY, JUNE 17

. . . Henry went to the field a little bit brought the tractor home and tightened up the Rods. It was to muddy to work. He got through at 5 cleaned up and worked some more at it someplace. He went after the Cows with the Car milked the Cow. While Mo had went to slumberland being in such misry she had snoozed 1 hour on the Davenport before supper. . . . Ma had ironed a couple hours. And got in such agony, she decided she lye down instead going after the Cows if they'd never get got nor milked to-day. Henry retired at 9 and Mo at 8. The wind sounded so mornfull to day while the Mocking birds where so Merrily singing.

SATURDAY, JUNE 18

. . . a terific duster . . . dust blowed from 8 A.M. Continued till 5 P.M. Then the Murk cleared away some. . . . Ma took her bath cleaned up the Eggs started to Town at 9 A.M. And got back at 15 till 2 P.M. . . . Mo just hookied after her trip back home from Town. We got a Letter from Cliff from Valsetz a Fathers day Card from Thelma at Dexter A card for Father from Verna at Hutch Kans. Ma got him a lb Cocoanut Carmels and Butternut candy. Pop got me a pt of Ice Cream I eat it with a piece of Card board using it as a Spoon made from the container which had the Cream in it. The while Pop was looking at his Crop. . . . The mocking Birds are very happy to-day.

MONDAY, JUNE 20

. . . My Teeth feels some better today for the first day since I had them taken out.

THURSDAY, JUNE 21

. . . Pop tore the Celloglass off the frontroom Door and Mo dug the dust out. Well today was the longest day a beautifull one no dust blowing just interference unsettled on the radio. . . . Mo finished up some of her Aprons finished, and put slats in her Bonnets. And put the Fetherbed slip back on also cleaned the House again It was all blowed full of dust. Which seems to be and everdays routeene. . . . Mo washed lampglobes washed her head which she didn't get done on Sat on account of her jaw being so painfull.

WEDNESDAY, JUNE 22

. . . Henry went to the 70 ackers and planted Broom Corn. finished up by noon. He fixed the Tractor rims on and filed the discs. At 7 P.M. He drove the Car out and tryed to listen to the fight.[24] That radio didn't suit him, so he listened to the one in the House. The fight only lasted 2 Minutes and 2 seconds Louise wiped Max hit him in his kidneys and parilized him at 2 the next morning they took him to the Hospital. When his wife heard this she burst into tears she had never seen her Husband fight.[25]

THURSDAY, JUNE 23

. . . dust blowed considerable and in the southeast it was merky. . . . Mo has a stomach ache today and ever bit she went visiating she's week and her jaw still aches from the effects of her teeth. Ma got the Cows and milked old Red. . . . I felt so tuff and week to. . . .

FRIDAY, JUNE 24

. . . Ma did a little patching some sewing and a little Washing. In the after noon she put up the new Curtains. At 6 I got the cow milked her got Pops Supper took a bath, got ready at 7:15 we started to the Comunity Meeting meeting and they didn't get their Ice cream on account some misunderstanding, and the little folks where very much disapointed. Ruth Bishop a musical number Even tap danced the little Rogers sang I only want a Buddy not a Sweetheart the McMikel boys gave Harmonia Juise Harp and a Mandalin Treao. We chated a while and got home at 10:30. They only started the program at 9:30.

SUNDAY, JUNE 26

. . . we all went to the Ballgame and seen the Country north and east of Kendall we went 8 miles seen some very nice Wheat and nice Houses nice Country and got back home at Seven. . . . the good old Sunday Came and is gone again for this week. This was a beautiful enjoyable and a comfortable day and will never more return. . . . Henry and Adolph chated out on the poarch till Mo retired at 20 till 9 and Po at 9:20 he was as cold as Ice and she had to hover around him & warm him up ha.

MONDAY, JUNE 27

Northeast terific wind later in the after noon it went to the south & camed down after 5 P.M. . . . a local duster Wind camed at 6 P.M. . . . Today Mo got Elmers Rubberboots put them on for protection so the Thistels would smart and make her legs so sore.[26] They made her very tired but O what a relief it was for her. . . .

WEDNESDAY, JUNE 29

Well another June day beside to day old June'el be gone 1938 will never more return. Another terific windy day and murky to, so the

country cant be seen a long distence frome here Considerable clowdyness continued. Wind let up considerable of coarse dust goes with it
also lectricity static on the Radio has been just terific from early on
this morning. . . . It was so terriable dusty, that the men couldn't
hardly stand it He took the Tractor to the Oneway to the field and
onewayed on our old 160 ackers. Well this terific day robes me from
some of the programs the ones I usualy listen to if possiable I cant
wash so I'm writing a letter to Ervin to Hillsboro Oregon to Thelma
at Beaverton Oregon. And try to going on smilling and rolling with
cheer. Mo cut out some pieces for the quilt Wayes of the world
cleaned the Cabinet and Cupboard [27] . . .

THURSDAY, JUNE 30
. . . it was so wonderfull a day that this day really was enjoyable. &
such a contrast yesterday it was just like a Wolf. . . . We also got a
letter from Thelma she finished up picking Strawberries saying she
made $21.[28] We took a comforter out on the Poarch and slept there
for one hour Ma Went to her good soft Bed in the House. Pop came
in 20 minutes later. It was very hot. . . .

FRIDAY, JULY 1
. . . Ma had to take an Asprin so she could get a little something
done. . . . sewed up runners in Pops Shorts. She churned 3/3 of an
hour to-day, before washing breakfast dishes. & cleaned the Eggs
washed Lampglobes doing Saturdays work so she'l be ready to go to
Town at P.M. sometime Well tonite Mo dont need to get the Cows
and the old Rubbers's el'rest. . . . Pop drug the Springs on the Poarch
and made a Bed.

SATURDAY, JULY 2
. . . Today it was 102 degrees at dusk it was 80 and I say it was hot.
even if the breeze was rather strong. . . . at 2:10 P.M. We started to
Town. We drove around by Wane and Louise Lameyer, to see how
the Country looks . . . She didn't stay out on the Poarch very long she
marched to her Bed in the House. Pop slept there until Sunup the
next morning. . . . I felt so bummy this fore-noon I almost washed
1/2 hour at our few dishes had the sniffels and legache. She did a
goodsized ironing A.M. Ironed the Curtains and put them up in the
front room. . . .

SUNDAY, JULY 3

. . . The Radio blowed up again. He put a full Battery in it but didn't do no good. He put the empty Battery on the charger. Po naped another little while on the flour he got up and shaved, while Mo naped on the Daven Port she was no good for nothing. week and had legache and snifels. . . .

MONDAY, JULY 4 ANOTHER NEW DAY.

. . . dust quit at 4 P.M. . . . Mo churned 2/3 of an hour before washing Breakfast Dishes. With a temp of 82 degrees The Butter was real good not so terriable soft either. She patched and as the Radio blowed up yesterday. she goes out to the Car and still hears the most importent ones, which she enjoys so very much. He also listened to the News in the Car Radio. He left it setting in the Car so it was handy. He made the old soft Rocker very usefull while the wind was ragging the Sky was murky in the south east from the efects of dust. . . .

TUESDAY, JULY 5

. . . very hot. Flies mostly drive a man nuts Pm at 3 a local duster & sprinkle occured Considerable clowdyness. This duster came from the southeast. . . . I Baked a nice batch of Bread had it baked at 11 A.M. So I got some fresh hot Bread for dinner. I cleaned up the dusty House from the effects of the duster yesterday. Washed a little. Pop milked old Boss after chow. At 8 he rolled in. I had sleep while he milked. . . .

WEDNESDAY, JULY 6

. . . A terific Wind and duster occured. . . . at 5:45 when the duster occured it cooled down to 80 degrees. It blowed and wind ragged till almost morning. . . . We went in the House 4 hours after retiring. . . . The Flies are so bad just dive their stingers into your Arms & Legs and stay there stinging till you swat them even while coming from outdoors into the House. An embarising moment for Mo. While cleaning off a Brick and singing Just one mile, to the end of the Way. When Mr Baker & little Son appeared on the scene.

THURSDAY, JULY 7

. . . We got a Letter from Ervin at Hillsboro Oregon. One from Verna at Hutch Kans. sending 4 smackers. Thats 20 now in her Bank. . . . She has to give her House a thour Cleaning after the Terific Wind.

Pop went to the Car to listen to two News Cast and the Youngs. Mo Lindas first Love Big Sister Arnold Grims daughter. Bachlors Children and the Guiding Lite. She washed Lampglobes cleaned her lamps and washed a little. . . .

SATURDAY, JULY 9
. . . Today it was 106 At dusk 80 degrees. We rolled out at 4:15 and fried our cottentail had gravy and Apple Pie for desert. Where through at 5 ready to go to Garden at 7.²⁹ Pop washed and shined the car all up while Mo was getting her work done. She had the Letter return that she wrote to Thelma at Beaverton Oregon. We took 6 doz Eggs along to Mr. Ross and only got 11 cts a doz toteled to 66 cts. . . . Pop got the Cows at 6:30 we drove to Kendall. He got her some Ice cream. . . .

SUNDAY, JULY 10
. . . Today it was 105 degrees. At dusk it was 80 degrees. Pop rolled out at 4:30. Ma remained in slumber till 6:30. Pop was frying 2 young Jacks which he'd shot around milking time or after. . . . At 5 P.M. Wane & family came along. We all had a chocial chat at 8:30 These two family's left. The little ones the four youngest where lying out on the Bed on the Poarch jumping on it yelling and having a big time.

MONDAY, JULY 11
. . . It was a little dusty in the fore-noon, P.M. Murkyness left the sky about noon. . . .

TUESDAY, JULY 12
. . . At 5 P.M. we had a local duster a little murky yet at 7 P.M. . . . Pop listened to the Presedents Speech from 9 A.M. Till 9:45.³⁰ . . . The Live Stock Sanitary Commissioner Dr. Van Sickle visit our home at 8:15 A.M. to test the Cattle for Tuberclous. Ma Baked Bread had it all baked at 10:15 A.M. She unrolled 3 lbs. Cotton. And noted [knotted] at the redish brown Comforter. Po took his first shower at 6 P.M. before eating his supper. He walked around with his House Slippers as if he where real comfortable. Out in the Car he radioed after Supper while easing his clean feet out in the Cool air for 1 hour.

WEDNESDAY, JULY 13
. . . We rolled out at 4:15. Pop drove the Cows home with the Car. While Mo made Breakfast. He worked on the Tractor awhile after

chow. He went to Adolph Klossen at 7 A.M. returned home at 8. Took a shave and away to Syracuse he went. It was 8:10 A.M. He got home from Town at 1:30 P.M. . . . And here was my hooky day for a change she was so weak & felt so tuff. That she just radioed most of A.M. She eat her bite alone. While her better half had not yet returned. At 1 P.M. She cut out her Apron. Let the Cows into Water did just barly what she had to. Up till 1:30 P.M. She felt better. She seeded some cherries & baked two Cherry Pies. From equil parts Butter & Lard. It's the second time she made Pie Dough that way. . . . Ma gave the House a thour going over. after 3 dusty days of indurance . . .

THURSDAY, JULY 14
Northeast breeze very mournfull and Birds singing Gaily out in the Trees. . . . Henry walked after the Cows before breakfast. After chow he played a time on the Radio. And went to working at his Tractor. He ground the Valves at 9 A.M. he came in and told me about the Tradig shock of Mr Bradocks death killed by Lighting . . . Dick Spencer & Mr. [] where here early A.M. taking up collection to buy Flowers for Mr Bredoc.[31] . . .

FRIDAY, JULY 15
. . . Ma rolled out at 4:30. While her better half remained in slumberland for 1/2 hour. The cows had came home in the night. So he milked before chow. it was 5:30 when we where through breakfasting. Po went to look at the Crop. While Ma was doing up the work taking a bath. . . . 8:30 the Inspector Called. Henry had got all ready to start on our way to the Furnerel. He had to drive up the Cows to take a blood test. It was 8:45 when we started on our way to Mr Bradocs Furnerel we got to the church and everything was taken up. We had to stand up. All we heard was the one Song The last Mile of the Way. . . .

SATURDAY, JULY 16
. . . duster accured at 6:30 just lasted about 15 minutes. . . .

SUNDAY, JULY 17
. . . Pop rolled out at 5:15. I stayed there till 7:15. If that's not breaking the Record. Henry had walked way on the other side of the draw and milked he read the last nights Hutch Paper. Then he came in the Bedroom talked some to me Then he turned the Radio in full force. I still remained there 1/2 hour longer. Then came out and got his

breakfast cooked. Consisting of 2 fried Eggs Breakfast Cereal and Cherry Pie for desert At noon the same. Henry had snoozed on the Rug a while. While she was cleaning up the House which she had some of it left undone Saturday Cause of Washing. Henry went to the Ball game at 2 P.M. while she had been wore out, ever since dinner and had snoozed for mostly one hour. She snoozed another hour & more while Henry was at the Ball game at the Comunity Hall. She also read the True Story about the Sailor. . . .

MONDAY, JULY 18

. . . Ma just felt week nerveous and good for nothing hers Ears where the worst. yesterday they also raised Cane. She patched Towls Henrys Shirt and did some more patching. And wrote a Letter to Verna. . . .

THURSDAY, JULY 21

. . . We rolled out very late 5:15. The Cows where close by Pop got the red one pumped, while Mo got breakfast. The Radio got so week, that Po fooled around trying to fix it but didn't do eny good. He drove around up by George Prise Freeces looked at the crops found they where no better as ours. So he came back at 10 A.M. hiched to the Harrow and went to the mile east Land and Harrowed it. . . . At 2:15 she washed her Dress one Apron and 2:20 she went along with Mrs. Bishop Nina and Ruth to Ivas Klossen to quilt the rain scared us home at 4:30. . . .

FRIDAY, JULY 22

. . . Mo had ironed some at A.M. At 1 P.M. He took me to Iva Clossen to quilt. he came after me on his way home from Kendall. . . .

SUNDAY, JULY 24

. . . Pop rolled out at 6 and Ma at 7 He radioed all the forenoon till we started to Olins Warners at 11 A.M. Henry made his breakfast had it all over with when I got up. I never had heard a bit while he cooked. we got home at Sunset. Some one was here and snooped around in the Barn while we where away. Could tell by their footsteps.

MONDAY, JULY 25

. . . Pop had rolled out when I awoke this morning. It was then 4:40. I jumped out as quick as possible to get at churning. But he came back from the Pasture at 5 till 5 A.M. So I hurried and made Breakfast. It was 5:15 while Breakfasting. The Radio quiet purcelating. He got a full charged Battery, but nothing adoing. It again happened to be the Tube. That was only 2 weeks of Service. . . . [Po] gets home for Supper at 7:20 eats & takes the Radio to Griswold. . . . Mr Freece calles at sunset wanting to see him about Running Mrs. Bradoc for Co Comissinor[32] . . . This was blue Monday for her the day was sorta shadowed for her. She went out in the Car to listen to Bachlors children at 15 till Seven. Linda's first Love Sunday my Gal. big Sister Arnold Grims Daughter and the Guiding Light. She drove the clowds away while Listning to these plays. . . . I read the Story Everthing's Ducky. While being in a gloom mood. It sorta chased my gloomyness away. I felt so tuff most all day that I just did what needed to be. Looked over a stack of Letters and burned them. Looked over the newspapers. Wrote a letter to Thelma in Dexter Oregon and sent it off the 26. . . .

TUESDAY, JULY 26
. . . Mo had another day that she felt tuff and didn't acomplish much she washed her Head fixed Henrys dress Socks did a little patching. Cleaned up the House which is the order of each day. And washed out some pieces of clothes . . . She cleaned the southwest Bedroom all over washed Windows in it kitchen windows All Glass doors in side of House.

WEDNESDAY, JULY 27
. . . Well I went to the car again to listen to my usual Epesodes yesterday. I included the Youngs whom she haven't so long listened to.

THURSDAY, JULY 28
. . . At 7 A.M. He started on his Way to Griswolds returned at 9:30 with the Radio. He turned it on and it wouldn't budge. He cursed that fumes cented the room. He went to the field on the old 160 at 10 A.M. at 11:50 he returned for Dinner at 12:30 He again on his way to Mr Griswold. And returned home at 5 minutes till 1 P.M. . . . at 8 it clowd up again wind rather strong. At 8:30 it was raining. Ma had pulled in 8:30 Po at 9 at 8:30 after being in Bed for about 20 minutes he gets up & says I'm preparing to go in the Celler. it hails. Its roaring very bad. I got up but stayed in my gown. Just put on my House slippers. When ariveing at Griswolds Nina says I'm begining to believe you're a Radio Salesman. He laughed she said I bet you felt like cursing. Answer I've already did that. Jon had ought to have heard me. . . . I felt very good yesterday. Work steady all after-noon.

FRIDAY, JULY 29

... At 7 Henry went to the Church to inspect the Rain. Learned that the East end of the fields didn't have as much rain as we had down here. ... Mo had to go to the Car in the Barn to listen to Bachlors children. the Car was out in the yard to listen to the rest. She ads Kitty Kelly to her colection for a change she hasn't got in on her all week since Radio got sick and fadded away. She did little ods of work to help complete things. And feels real good in fore-noon. ...

SUNDAY, JULY 31

... Henry had risin from his slumber at six when I heard a ster in the House. I said have you done milked old Red. He said already it's 6 oclock. So I remained there 1 hour and 15 minutes when I heard some one shut door. I had got up and soon heard a voice. It was Mr Bishop had called. Wanting Pop to come and help him raise a fresh Cow up she was down. He returned at 11:15 with Mr Griswold the Radio also Mr Pete Dyck. The Machine went right off to work after putting a Battery in it and connecting it up to the wires. He took Carl Griswold back home at 12:10 P.M. after a little chat about the Radio ... This day is a happy one and hope it'l be happy ever after all the way through life ech day is being a sweet one to live no matter what has come and interfeered. it's been happy. and real. ... Well I had a real hooky day. No man to get dinner for just a bite for myself. ...

THURSDAY, AUGUST 2

Southwest terific duststorm started in at 7:30. At 8:30 lectricity was so bad that the Radio couldn't be usefull for 3 hours. At 7:15 it had let up a little lectricity terific wind still ragged at 3 P.M. still murky at sky. It was clowdy to. At 5 P.M. Murkey had gone ... All I did to-day was to clean up the house and write letters. Patch my nightgown and did what had to be done. We got our Monkey Ward Catalogue to-day. A great deal of Flies cling to the outside of the Door to-day. ... the cows came in at sunset to they'l be here early in the morning.

WEDNESDAY, AUGUST 3

Northwest terific wind while breakfasting 2 hours later it went to the north east. So the dust stopped blowing at 9:30 it had let up some. ... Well I had to give the House a going over this fore-noon on account of the duststorm. ... She felt so tuff after fixing up her Dress she read stories. Her Ears have throbed and roared now for 4 this week the first one in August.

FRIDAY, AUGUST 5

. . . In fore noon it was murky in the south from dust. P.M. It had cleared away. . . . [Pop] build the newborn [calf] a Pen out in the Box Correl. So old Roan wouldn't tear up her teets jumping the Barbs. Today is another week and tuff feeling all day. I baked Bread and had it baked by 10:15 A.M. It was exelent And gave the House a thur going over after all the dusters. and cleaned all the throw rugs. . . .

SUNDAY, AUGUST 7

. . . Henry arose 15 mi. till 5. Mo stayed in slumberland till 6:15 having a Nightmare. Po read papers before I arose. From 7 A.M. till 1 P.M. He had the radio going constently puffing away at his Pipe reading and having enough Volume turned on to make the static growl that much worse. I snoozed one hour from 11 till 12 noon. I felt so week & tuff that I couldn't hardly go. Henry started to the Ball game to the church at 2:45 P.M.

MONDAY, AUGUST 8

. . . At 8 we had a local duster. This duster came from northeast had banked up for a few hours. . . . We rolled out at 5 not very embisous [ambitious] to day Po had the Cows milked at 5:30 where through breakfasting at 5:45. Henry got out to the field at 6. he had been working east of the church Sat A.M. So this morning he moved to the old 80 ackers. Is killing weeds on the Elotement ground.[33] He got in for dinner at 12:10. . . . Pete called at 2 so the two had a chat about Canidates Goverment President and other buisness afairs he came home at 6 wanted to milk early to go to Wane Rogers for Icecream. We went at 7:15 and came home at 10 mi. till 10. . . .

TUESDAY, AUGUST 9

. . . Today it was 110 degrees. at dusk it was 85 degrees. . . . Mo Irones P.M. cleanes her oil stove and gave the House a thour going over after the duster. . . .

WEDNESDAY, AUGUST 10

. . . Today the heat broke. It was chilly so we had to cover up after midnight. Today it only was 90 degrees at dusk it was 65 degrees. . . . He left for Ulyses at 9:45 to see about selling some Maze they only paid 50 cts a 100 so he refused to sell. He got home at 11:45 he read a magazine a while after noon. He washed the car and eregated the Trees. after 4:30 he read some more. . . .

THURSDAY, AUGUST 11
. . . We rolled out at 5 to-day. And Cows where at home even it they warent pend up. Were through breakfasting at 5:50 Pop shot a Cottentail and o boy was it good. A change for our Menue. At P.M. I ironed the Curtains Pop started to town at 7:45 A.M. and got home at 5:45 he then eat his dinner & supper combine. . . .

FRIDAY, AUGUST 12
. . . Pop radioed some A. M. read Papers and part of the time he worked on the Drill. And some in the afternoon to severel hours of work. And came in the House at 5:45 with a hollow belly. His cows tore loose for the pasture twice after they had come home. At 7 he had to get them for the last time. I scrubbed the floors washed Lampglobes in the after-noon A.M. I baked Bread had it all baked at 11 A.M. was very good. And a tiresome forenoon was spent churning I worked at it for 1:20 minutes at 1:30 I had butter P.M. I watered 3 Trees carried 10 buckets water to them. . . . While going out west to day between sunset & dusk Mo spided a Bullsnake. Which she put to death with a fork handle.

SATURDAY, AUGUST 13
Southwest terific wind with a terific duster it occured at 8 A.M. and kept on didn't let up much till 7 P.M. . . . Pop was shaved all dressed up & ready to pull out for Town at 7 and got home at 5:20. Ma amused herself clearing away papers and took Care of the Chickens and doing all things this day which she has to do every day of the week liminating cooking dinner, washing, ironing, or doing eny dusting. Cause its no use to clean tomorrow will bring the day that this dusting will be done. . . .

SUNDAY, AUGUST 14
. . . Ma had to give the house a thour going over. Since yesterday the terific duster. . . .

MONDAY, AUGUST 15
. . . O boy this is a wonderfull enjoyable piecefull day Its so beautiful cool and so comfortable, the beginning of a nother week, which we'll

never again see nor live through There was a double beautifull Rainbow in the sky after the heavy sprinkle. I had went to slumber at
10:20. Pete Elmer and his Pall called and stayed one hour. They left
at 12:20. Pop then had to juice his Roan Cow, this time of a night. He
thought was a hard task.

TUESDAY, AUGUST 16
. . . We rolled out at 5 A.M. We breakfasted an hour later. The Cows
had pulled out so it was 7 when they had got pumped. He had to
spray them cause flies are very bad. Henry went to see the Crop at
3 P.M. And found the hail had it pecked up real bad yesterday. . . .
A joke on Mr. Bishop Sunday night, after the rain. While hearing a
raddle de bang He Jumped in his car, and drove east 1 mile to see if
it was Dean stranded in the mud. It was Henry & Pete out in the Old
Battle ax driving to Wane after 8:45 to take a mellon down there, With
the exaust off the Car. Waynes answer, if you ever come here again,
in that raddle trap. I'll run you off, with a shot Gun. . . .

THURSDAY, AUGUST 18
Southwest and south wind terific started at 8 A.M. At 10 you could
only see the outlind of Bishop buildings. We didn't have no dust here.
Sky is murky all day till at 6 it let up some along with the wind. . . .

FRIDAY, AUGUST 19
. . . We started to Syracuse at 2 and got home almost sunset. We drove
around by the church to look at the crop after getting 1/3 mile east
we turned around and went back, we nowed we couldn't get through
the soft dirt. In the church yard he shot two young jacks. . . . In
Kendall on our way home Pop bought me a Pt Ice cream 15 cts. . . .

TUESDAY, AUGUST 23
Southwest duster from 8 A.M. It let up at 1 P.M. It had cleared away
a clear day for sunrise. . . . I felt tuff all day long. Didn't accomplish
enything . . .

MONDAY, AUGUST 29
. . . Pop went to Big Bow at 8 A.M. to get his seed Wheat. And got
home at 10:45 A.M. . . . Pop took the Wheat drills to the field Came
back to the 60 ackers and cut Broom Corn 1 hour one round then at
5 P.M. he went to see his crops. And got home at Sunset 7:15. Ma
churned 1/2 hour and had fine Butter. It was a little soft. She pealed

Pairs P.M. and put them to set with shugar. And washed some of her Dresses hankies and Henrys socks. she cleaned little ods & ends. A nest of 23 Eggs where found in the grangry so that made 8 doz last week. This is the beginning of a new week and hope to-morrow and later it'l be more enjoyable to endure as windy Monday. The Mistress of the House had a coleasun [collision] with the Seprator it tipping off his rack the hole Bowl and all its belongings it worked good just the same.

TUESDAY, AUGUST 30
. . . At 7 Pop went to the Broom corn field at the 70 ackers. Thats the only field for this year. He got home 25 minutes till 12 noon. Red the mail at 3 P.M. he went back to the field and got home at 7 for chow. . . . Ma washed a doz pieces Caned 4 qts Pairs. . . .

WEDNESDAY, AUGUST 31
. . . Well dear old August the year 1938 rolles out to its doom to day. Much happiness peace it has given us and some darkness to. But this month of August is gone forever and never more to return. My ears are throbing and tearing me almost down to the ground to day. . . .

THURSDAY, SEPTEMBER 1
. . . We drove to Syracuse at 2:30 P.M. . . . We stoped at Kendall got the Mail. . . . Pop bought himself some Bear & 1 pt Ice cream for Ma . . . Po bought 10 cts Candy Cocoanut bars. This is our Wedding Aniservie the 1 of Sept. . . .

SATURDAY, SEPTEMBER 3
. . . We rolled out at 5:10 Pop eat breakfast before pumping the Cows. at 6:30 he seprated. Went tomcatten around from 8 till 12:45 he returned home. . . . Ma churned 15 minutes till butter was made. She mixed her Bread before breakfast had it baked at 10:30. . . . We started on our way to town at 1 A.M. & got home at 6:30. We stoped at Edgers. Pop took him 6 bottles bear. And after devouring this the two men had a social arguement about conditions of Labor men & farmers. . . .

SUNDAY, SEPTEMBER 4
. . . Pop rolled out at 5 cooked his chow, while Ma remained in slumberland till 20 minn. till 7. Pop had fried all the Eggs for himself I

only got 1 slice of Bacon had no milk for cereal nor coffee. Pop never had eny cereal for his breakfast either. ha the fault was all his own he could have milked. . . . This was Henrys funny day. He cut shines all day long. Walked barefoot part of the day and wore his coat A.M. to be comfortable. . . .

MONDAY, SEPTEMBER 5 AND LABOR DAY.
. . . Po seprated 6:15 after chow. Then he went to the field to cut broomcorn it was 7 A.M. when he left. It was 12:15 when he got home for chow. While at dinner President Roosevelt made a speech 1/2 hour period of time.[34] . . . She cleaned Lamps scoured teakettles Oilstove also cleaned house again. And did some other ods & ends. My Ears are throbbing and tongue has been mostly petrified for 5 days its mostly num. . . .

TUESDAY SEPTEMBER 6
. . . We rolled out at 5. Henry fixed fence while Mo milked the Cows & fed the Calf. Then she got breakfast. So we made more progress at the Dyck farm to-day. As we've been for some time. We breakfasted at 6:10. Then Mo seprated while Pop being in the field Cutting Corn. . . . After noon he started to drill Wheat. At 5:30 he came in from the field and fixed fence. While Ma milked & fed the Calf. . . . I didn't do much but clean up the house Went to the Barn to see about the eggs and did I get a good scear it was all covered with snake tracks. . . .

WEDNESDAY, SEPTEMBER 7
southwest wind was terific at times late in the evening its south. . . . Mo caned 14 qts Tomatoes and 2 qts tomato juice. she gave the House a thour going over after the dust had settled some. . . .

THURSDAY, SEPTEMBER 8
. . . At 6:15 Mo had the seprating done. She went out to help Pop unload his load of Corn at 9 A.M. His sack automatily unloaded it so my help was all in vain.[35] Pop drove to the field at 7:15 stacked two Loads of Corn. at 12:15 he eat. at 1:15 he went back to the field to sow Wheat he came in for supper at 6:25 it was just dark. I washed started in at 12 noon & had finished at 2 P.M. . . . I got the Cows I transfored myself to a man. The Cows looked at me as if they thought A funny man, with a bonnet on. . . .

FRIDAY, SEPTEMBER 9

. . . Pop milked before breakfast while Mo mixed her Bread Pop cut Broom corn A.M. He took a shave I a bath at 1:15 we where on our way to town, after Peaches. We bought 2 Bu. at the IGA at 1.15 cts a bu. 1/2 bu. blue Plumbs from Mrs. Jantz at 1.25 cts a 1/2 bu . . .

SATURDAY, SEPTEMBER 10

. . . We rolled out 15 minutes till 5 Mo got breakfast while Pop milked, after chow at 7 he went to the Broomcorn patch and I churned. had it all finished in 20 minutes. He cut corn from 1 P.M. till 4:30 came home cause he was plade out. Tonite he went to the dance at 7:30 and came home at 10. . . . I'm so tired after caning 56 qts Peaches & 3 blue Plumbs took my bath scrubed the kitchen cleaned up some & retired at 9:20. . . .

MONDAY, SEPTEMBER 12

. . . I caned 6 qts tomatoes 9 qts blue Plumbs and 8 qts Peaches I was so tired then I retired at 8 A.M. . . .

FRIDAY, SEPTEMBER 13

. . . At 6 Sun the sun was just setting when I went after the Cows not wearing the Overalls at this special time. Cows where just east of the draw. I milked old Roan also fed the Calf. And as he tried to get out of the Barn. I poured Milk over my Shoes dress also left Stocking and was I disgusted. While I was having this complicated afair Po was in the House Radioing. He had a cold not feeling well. And not having much of an apetite. We retired at 7:30 early for a change.

THURSDAY, SEPTEMBER 15

. . . We rolled out at 5 good daybreak at that time Pop seprated after breakfast it was then 5:20 when he finished. he pulled out for the field at 6:35 dinnered at 11:50. he took the New Car to drive out to see how the Wheat was whether or not the Hoppers where working at it at 15 till 1 P.M. he had to display the Chivie to the Broomcorn Patch.[36] . . . After two weeks of waiting. Soney wrote us a letter from Hillsboro Oregon. This is the third time waiting that long since he's been away from home. To my rotine again to-day I added getting Cows milking also feeding the Calf now for 4 days in succession . . .

FRIDAY, SEPTEMBER 16

. . . We rolled out at 5:15. And this day again Henry seprated, while Mo finished eating her breakfast. She got to listen to Bachlors Children before washing Dishes also Seprator Henry went to Cut Corn at 6:45 A.M. at 1:45 we dinnered. he again, went back to the Field at 1 P.M. He listened to the Youngs. Also the Guiding Lite. While recouperating from the strain of work. He brought home a Load of Broomcorn at sunset and stacked it before he suppered. . . .

SATURDAY, SEPTEMBER 17

. . . at 1 P.M. We where on our way meeting the Mail Man . . . he was a little early at 15 minutes we started to Holly. about 5 he had my teeth all out. he broke one Dr. Lemord pulled them the double one on the upper jaw had a puss pocket on it. The one that I've had trouble with for 2 years. We got home at seven oclock. . . . Po . . . bought . . . a bottle Wine. for 50 cts at Coolige to drown the sorrows of the lost of my teeth ha.[37] he said, tonight o boy I'm glad that I still have mine in my mouth yet. . . .

SUNDAY, SEPTEMBER 18

. . . Pop rolled out at 5:15 Ma at 6. Pop restacked some Broom while Mo remained in slumber. She didn't feel much like herself, she was feeling the effects of being with out teeth and gums where all swollen, not knowing how to get adjusted to eat and what to eat.

TUESDAY, SEPTEMBER 20

A quiet day of piece and contment. . . . Pop rolled out before 5 I slept 20 more minutes got up at 5 milked fed the Calf puttered around some. Then got my breakfast. I then heard the old car belloring on its way back from scattering grashopper poison he had left for the field at 5 A.M. to scatter the stouff.[38] It was then time at 15 till 7 while Po was breakfasting to listen, to Bachlors children. Henry serviced the Car to be ready for town at 8:15. He was on his way to Syracuse and got home at 5:20 P.M. . . .

WEDNESDAY, SEPTEMBER 21

. . . Well this was my lunch day. When ever Henry goes away and dosent return for dinner. I just eat scraps & drink Coffee ha. I was home all day long a quiet piecefull day. I churned 2 batches cream. One I had finished in a 20 minute period The other one the sweet cream took me a 30 minute period of time. I patched Pops Overalls and started some letters. And listened to plays from 7 A.M. leaving out the 15 minutes period 15 after 12. and continued to 1:30. I added a new one today Violent Lady. And went back to the old feeling, of hearing the old sounds of noise which I heard before Xmas 1937. and the biggest joke of the day, was to discover the lone tooth in my mouth. I laughed and laughed some more, about it. . . . We retired after Amos & Andy went off the air 15 after 8. . . .

THURSDAY, SEPTEMBER 22
. . . Got a letter from Thelma & family from Dexter, telling the sad news about Cliff breaking 2 ribs and getting his hip hit bad. also Leroy falling with the Rocker bunging his lips all up, and knocking 2 teeth loose. And later his fever being 105 temp. They had the Doctor from Eugene. & cost was 5 Dollars.[39] at present hes getting better. . . .

SATURDAY, SEPTEMBER 24
. . . We did our shopping. at 3 P.M. we went to Holly to get the lone left tooth pulled. It din't feel so good around 6 & 7 oclock. I took three asprins to num the pains at 7:30 we started to the dance. We stoped in Kendall Henry bought a pt. chocolate Ice cream. . . .

MONDAY, SEPTEMBER 26
. . . Mr. Hitler gave a speech in Jerman & Mr. [] in English about War.[40] they continued with this speech from 12 noon till 1:45 We still got to hear the guiding Light Youngs Maryline Arnold Grims daughter, some which where on at 12 noon. . . .

TUESDAY, SEPTEMBER 27
. . . [Pop] Came in for chow at 11:30 listened to the street report at Nebraska Also 15 mi to the War news and after dinnering again the news Cast 12:45. he went to the field to work at 1:45 he was home reading the Mail he stayed 1/2 hour & again went to the field at 5:30 he came home to chow. . . .

WEDNESDAY, SEPTEMBER 28
. . . A continuation of terific Wind. at 3 P.M. a duster occured, and continued till rain fell. The purtest rainbow in the sky I ever saw. A double one Wind sounds mornfull . . . We arose much later to-day. Where through breakfasting at 6:10. Henry then went to cut Broom-

corn. Came in at 11 to hear the talk on War, and went back to the field & stayed till 12:10 and then came in for chow. At one he went back at 3:20 he came home on account the rain. . . .

THURSDAY, SEPTEMBER 29

. . . I put on Elmers boots & after the Cows I went slid through the Draw, as if I where on skeas I got home with the Cows at sunset milked & fed little baby calf. I certanly did endure piece and joy through the return trip. At first they felt a little stiff but a little while of it I had them limbered up & they seemed very limber. Pop in the house when I got in the House Henry said Hello Boots ha. I answered boots is just fine. . . . Henry was all tired out from the effects of a hard day of work at broom corn cutting.

SATURDAY, OCTOBER 1

And here comes good October staring us in the face for another month of endurance. Terific wind from southwest sky is murky southeast of here from the efects of a duster some dircation out southwest also south. . . .

WEDNESDAY, OCTOBER 5

. . . We rolled out at 5:14. Henry milked before breakfast. where through breakfasting at 6 seprating was all done at 6:30 the men went to the field Elmer called 1 hour later to cut Broomcorn. . . . Henry went to Kendall 12:15 to mail the Card I wrote to the Warners also a letter, which I wrote to Ervin dear at Hillsboro Oregon. Henry got home from Syracuse with 3 bu Tomatoes at 2:45. . . . I got the Cows Milked Roan, and feed the little Calfie. . . . They finished up the Broomcorn cutting. today the World series started in at 12:15.

FRIDAY, OCTOBER 7

. . . Ma caned 64 qts tomatoes to-day & yesterday. I only got 1 boiler full caned yesterday. . . .

SATURDAY, OCTOBER 8

. . . Men went to the field at 7 to cut at Aults place broom corn where in doors 1 1/2 hour for relaxazatation from the effects of hard work.[41] While listning to the Ballgame they finished up stacking at 3 P.M. stacked from 1:30 P.M. till 3 P.M. We started to Kendall at 4:50 after Pop had patched his Tire and taken a bath from 3 P.M. till 4 he read

papers we got home from Kendall at 6:30. At 8 we started to the
dance. Got home at 11:30. . . . No Cow was milked nor was the calf
fed. Ma baked 2 cherry Pies stove went out she only got one baked
fit to serve. didn't do much Sat. Work.

SUNDAY, OCTOBER 9
. . . had to do her Sat. work to day. Cause I didn't hardly get eny done
yesterday. Had to do all dusting washing lamp globes. cleaned and
shined the floors. Also carried the Tomatoes all down in the celler. At
5 P.M. Henry washed the Hopper dope off the Car. A.M. the 2 men
went to the field got the Calf some feed. . . . Henry run a rod through
the oil stove pipes it had been backing on me for some time so to day
it completly layed down on the job. So he had to pump the dirt out
of it. and again breaking the Sabath this Sunday again. and me scrubing, and working, all day long. . . .

WEDNESDAY, OCTOBER 12
. . . Mo made 3 Pumpkin Pies washed Lampglobes and cleaned house.
She got the Cows milked & feed the Calf also took care of the Hens
which is her everday. Bob kissed his Betty dear while being in her sell
in Jail On account of the murder of Winfred Vantz.[42]

THURSDAY, OCTOBER 13
. . . We arose at 5:15 not early enough for work. But made more
progress as yesterday by noon. Men went to the field at 6:15. Pop
milked before breakfast didn't feed the Calf just seprated, and away
to the field they went. . . . We got a letter from the Warners from
Dexter One from Ervin at Hillsboro Oregon. It was rit with very
much entagnisum. . . .[43]

SATURDAY, OCTOBER 15
. . . Ma rolled out at 5 the men stayed in Bed till 5:30 till breakfast was
ready Pop milked after chow. at 6:30 he had seprated. Shaved but not
in a hurry to get to the field at 7 they went to cut Broomcorn at
Adolph [Klassen's] Got home at 11:50. relaxed in the rockers till 1:30
then went to the field. In the mean while they where smoking away
patiently, spilling tobacco while listning, to the Radio. Came in for
chow at 5:20. Ma had got the Cows milked & feed the calf. At 12:30
she started to wash and finished at 2:15. But never hung out the
Clothes on account of the terific wind. While relaxing she pealed 1 gal

Apples and churned completed it in 15 minutes. A.M. She baked a exelent pink cake & iced it after supper. . . .

SUNDAY, OCTOBER 16
. . . the men went out hunting didn't get eny Ducks & brought the Cows home, on their way back. . . .

MONDAY, OCTOBER 17
Well a beginning of another new week & a terrific wind to start it off right I spose. Southwest wind terific from 9 A.M. and kept up . . . The men started to the Klossen Broom corn field at 7 got home for chow right on noon. relaxed in the Rockers till 1:15 away for the field, they went. Returned home from the Broom cornfield for chow at 15 to six. . . . Lamp globes where washed A.M. The House got a thour cleaning A.M. I got the Cows, fed the calf & milked it took me 1/2 hour Milk & to bring them home. . . .

SATURDAY, OCTOBER 22
. . . a killing frost. . . . we started to Syracuse and got home at 6:15 P.M. . . . I came home sick with Headache was very hungry never had eny dinner just a pt pink ice cream. . . . Pop went to the dance & returned at midnight Ma had retired at 10:20 & had looked over a bunch of the kids letters in far away lands, while Pop was away.

THURSDAY, OCTOBER 27
. . . at 9 A.M. we started on our way to Syracuse. Banker wasn't home so we started on our way to Holly. to have the empression taken for my teeth we got back to Town at 11:45 we picked up a hitchhiker for a drive of 22 miles. We returned home at 4:30. Pop bought himself a bottle of Wine to setisfy his longings, while the dentist was at work. . . . And the funniest things of all I let my groceries set at Maricals cause when I took it to the Car Pop had gone with it so I had forgot it there later ha. when my thoughts had stayed away, on sending my leters off also finishing them. And I made such blunder. Henry dear kidded me a lot. I got weighed and learned that I had went down to 140 lbs.[44] . . .

FRIDAY, OCTOBER 28
. . . Henry had snoosed a while in his pieceful rockers where he is when hes being away from work. We listened to 2 plays. Ma washed

the Windows in the Kitchen also glass doors & lamp globes and gave the House a good cleaning. A.M. she churned & completed it after 10 minutes period. she fed the little calf.

SATURDAY, OCTOBER 29
. . . We also got a Card from the Warners, saying Ervin had got a job. . . .

MONDAY, OCTOBER 31
southwest terific wind 8 hours. . . . We rolled out at 5:15 Pop went to milk the milk boy com skipping up 15 till 6. Mo was setting the table he got 3 qts.[45] We where breakfasting at 6. 15 mi later Henry was at his combine. He stayed there till 11:30 when dinner, was anounced. 12:15 he went back to work at it 15 till 1 he listened to the news After chow he listened to Pick & Pat the Lux Play and went to the Hollow ween Party at the Hall 6:15 he returned at 9 P.M.

THURSDAY, NOVEMBER 3
. . . It snowed soon after Aucopens [occupants] where up. At 10 A.M. it snowed more some stayed on the ground a while. Most of it thowed as soon as it hit the ground. . . .

FRIDAY, NOVEMBER 4
. . . It whitefrosted in the night, so it was to damp to start in Combining A.M. Mr. Wots came at 8 A.M. P.M. they started to the field at 1:30 he stayed till 8. . . . I gave the House a thour going over cause it had got all dusty I planed on going to Holly tomorrow & wouldn't get it done.

SATURDAY, NOVEMBER 5
. . . Started to Holly at 11:15 Got Mas teeth. They where all ready for action we returned back to Syracuse at 2 P.M. to Kendall at 3 P.M. & home at 4:30 Henry build the fire while Mo was gagging which took place 8 times . . . Pop listened to Policital talks went to sleep in the midst of one Canaditas speech he continued to stay by the Radio listened to the Canadites speech for a period of 2 hours. We retired at 7:15 Mo sleep all night with her teeth, in her mouth. . . .

SUNDAY, NOVEMBER 6
. . . We had a slumber party P.M. Ma had to remain most of all day in silence for fear she'd gag if she'd talk so after a while I got very sleepy lye on the davenport during her nap. . . .

MONDAY, NOVEMBER 7

. . . wheather was so cold. Pop enjoyed Political broadcasts all day long didn't work just milked fed the Calf at 15 till noon. . . . Ma patched Pops shirts & sewed buttons on his Cipper Jacket also worked button holes in it I wore my teeth all day. But did not eat with them she never went to sleep with them. Po suppered at 6. Mo drank coffee having the teeth in her mouth. . . .

TUESDAY, NOVEMBER 8

. . . Pop went to the Poles to Vote at 8:30 and returned at 9:40. He pottered around A.M. . . . Pop suppered at 5:45 later he listened to the Election Presents & to some more Commidents [comments] retired at 8:30. Mo had another sick spell with her teeth she learned how to eat some with them at P.M. . . .

WEDNESDAY, NOVEMBER 9

Southwest terific wind from 10 A.M. till 5 P.M. . . . Murky skies on account of the dust in the air. . . . Mr. Wots the hired man arived at 7 A.M. The men started to the field to Combine at 8 and home for chow at straight 12. and away to the field at 1 after unloading the Truck of Caffir in for chow at 4 P.M. . . . Mo baked a Cake it was good but a little ragid looking cause the icing got hard it was a one egg cake. Washed Lamp globes give the floors a good shining got the Cows. wittled on her teeth. they made her gums so soar that she couldn't eat for hurts. she went to sleep with them all night long. . . .

THURSDAY, NOVEMBER 10

. . . the men vacated to the field run all day. Mo patched Pops gray shirt also his overalls the Hens only layed 3 Eggs to-day Pop said to many sweet spuds blow me up in the air like a ziplen. We had sweet Spuds Steak & gravy for dinner Orenge Cake for desert Prunes Tomatoes for vegetable. . . .

SATURDAY, NOVEMBER 12

. . . It was 8 when the men pulled out to Combine. They fixed canves, for one hour. Dinnered at 12:20 Men started to the field at 1 Came in at 5:20 for chow. after supper they sat at the table till 6:30 smoking away. . . . She only wore her upper teeth to-day had them in all night, and all day. she's slept with the upper teeth evernight except 2 nights since a week ago . . .

... Mr. Wots arived at 7 when Pop was unloading the Truck of grain

they got started at 8 after the dew, had dried away so it was thrashable Came in for chow at 12:10 went out at 1 P.M. again in for supper at 5:30 complete eating at 6. the two where having a table side chat till 8:15 Mo retired she went to snooze on the Davenport while the Lux Play was on. The Buckeroo. Mo churned A.M. finished at 1 P.M. Baked a fine Jellyroll mixed her Bread at 8 A.M. and completed it at 7:45 P.M. slow poke it was exelent This is the 4th night, that I didn't get the Cows. But added feeding the calf also watering it to my routine to-day. ...

TUESDAY, NOVEMBER 15

... Men went to the east field at 8 A.M. got in for dinner at 12 noon with the Combine eat and went to the Doerr Land. at 1 P.M. Brought the outfit home at 3 P.M. for quits for the year of 1938. Mr.Wots left for home at 4 P.M. ...

THURSDAY, NOVEMBER 17

... [Pop] hawled 3 loads till 10 A.M. He choped some kindling wood. Read a magazine and the papers. The Houselady lost out on the Gill-mans family Arnold Grimms daughter Betty & Bob Mary Marlin on account of lectricity. static was terific from 4 P.M. and got worse. We only got one Egg to-day. ...

FRIDAY, NOVEMBER 18

... Pop hawled in 3 loads of feed A.M. went back to hawlin at 1 P.M. and hawled in 3 loads. He got in at 4:45 with the last one & suppered at 5:30. At 6 we listened to the First Niter, Grandma gives, a helping Hand. It was a very good one. O such terific static like summer heat interfeering with the Radio. Pop started the fire for his wife, to be good. I spose. ... Man with a red Pickup, wanting to buy some maze A.M. Mr. Bishop at 4:40 P.M., wanted the Combine. Ma ironed some & washed her brown Dress, & socks And cleaned house.

SATURDAY, NOVEMBER 19

... At 10 we where in Kendall. started to Holly at 12:30. returned to Syracuse at 2:30. I had my teeth rebalenced. We returned home at 4:30. ...

SUNDAY, NOVEMBER 20

. . . Well Sunday Pete Caught us in Bed. We overslept. The day after
the night before. He brought us some spareribs for good measure.
Henry went to Bishops after listning to Leo Danials a Minister at
8:30.[46] . . . Henry sold 100 bu. grain to some man.

MONDAY, NOVEMBER 21

Northeast terific duststorm started in at 4 A.M. kept on got worse at
7:30 Lectricity occured remained till 10 A.M. it let up so we could
listen to the Radio some after that . . . I lost out on all plays Widow
Jones Lorenzo Jones Women in White Aunt Jenny Bachlors Children.
I just got to listen in the Kissing and love scene at Kitty Kelly also
Damie's kissing scene while having her in his Arms the last scene. We
retired at 8.

WEDNESDAY, NOVEMBER 23

. . . Pop had went to Bishop at 7 . . . Henry dear returned home at
8:30. Went to Iva to buy Turkey. she wanted 19 cts a lb. Said No &
came home right on noon. Again P.M. he went to Wayne 2 P.M. after
chow to get some infermation about Thanskiving. At 4 P.M. Wayne
called after 1 qt milk & some Eggs. But didn't get the Eggs I had
to few to sell. Pete stayed for supper all night we went to Edgers &
stayed till 7:30 returned at 10 min till nine We warmed up & turned in
the Hay Pete 10 till 10. Mo & Po At 10. had both snoozed in a chair
Pop near the Radio Ma near the fire No Egg to-day.[47]

THURSDAY, NOVEMBER 24

. . . we dinnered 12:15. Dinner consist of Cramb. Gravy roast Cellry
Lettuce Bananas & Pumpkin Pie for desert. We retired at 8:15 This
morning while Henry sat down to lace his shoes some of the rounds
gave out down in the flour he slid, saying Mo why in the world dont
you take a broken chair out of this room. fumes where flying in all
directions. ha.

SATURDAY, NOVEMBER 26

. . . Men set the seeder up at 7 Mr. Bishop Dana & Herman sat around
in the House 1/2 hour scattered chaft [chaff] all over . . . Had 16 men
for dinner, Elda Iva also Ivas children.

MONDAY, NOVEMBER 28

. . . Pop listened to Leo McDonal a few more love scenes then got saurcastic at so much love and went to rolling his Broom Corn Bails, around. Ma give the house, a thour going over wash lampglobes

TUESDAY, NOVEMBER 29

. . . Pop had hawled in one load of feed. He hawled in 2 loads feed A.M. P.M. 3 He brought the Cows to the Wheat pasture Cows came in at 2:15 so Mo pend them up. Pop drove to the field at 15 till 12 to see how the cows where progressing. He came home at 4 with the last one. He went to the field 7:30 A.M. at noon 1 P.M. Mr Bishops outfit came after, the Combine . . . We dinnered while listning to the epesode Big Sister at 1 P.M. when the duster ocurred we missed out on all. Pop blinked his eyes while consetrating on this ertiable country later in the day he read old papers . . .

THURSDAY, DECEMBER 1

. . . I went to Bishops at 1 P.M. to help quilt. He came after me at sunset. . . .

FRIDAY, DECEMBER 2

. . . We rolled out at 6:30. at 7 Henry went to work. He cleaned out the Broom corn seed A.M. P.M. He cleaned out the granarys also pulled up and renailed flour in the granary. He suppered at 5:15 pumped the old cows later Pete came after the milk at 6:30 left at 8:30. Mo mixed the Bread at 8 A.M. completed baking at 4:15 P.M. She baked a softassilk cake it was a flop so she dont apraise cake flour. She cleaned all lamp cleaned house, A.M. and ironed P.M.

SUNDAY, DECEMBER 4

Northwest duststorm terific started in at 5 A.M. continued till 3:30 it camed down. . . .

MONDAY, DECEMBER 5

. . . We rolled out at 6:30 where through with breakfast at 7:30 Pop went to work at 7 A.M. fixed his lister from 12:30 to 1:15 some maze buyers bought 100 bu. . . . Ma give the hole house a thour cleaning cellar steps churned made the complesion in 20 mi also washed all lampglobes made a washcloth. Also put her bonnet together. & wrote her diry which hadn't been rit for 6 days & what a job. she gaged so much of the after-noon trying to get use to her lower teeth. Pop had to put a full battry in to keep the radio purlacating. Mo run a sliver in her second finger, on left hand while cleaning up the pantry flour. O she just got sick, from all pain. put it in hotwater, to ease the pains some. Pop went to the meeting at 6:45 . . . Mo snoozed on the Davenport from 9:30 till 10:15 Pop returned home from the meeting he was listning to a Murder Black Nite story when I awoke.

WEDNESDAY, DECEMBER 7
. . . Henry went to the field to burn thistels at 8. later A.M. he listed up the feedyard and north of here. . . . P.M. He went to look over his fields to see how the ground was progressing. The cows got a way went to Bakers Mr had to help him seprate our Cows from his. The both Cows where seeking for a Mail, to pass away some time ha. Henry then came driving in the Cows with the Car at 4. While Mo was in the midst of washing all Windows also all glass doors also Mirrors. He said o gee you certainly are cleaning up ha. Mo rolled out with the Headache & had to take asprin later she washed all lampglobes also lamps also the Cabinet and severel ods & ends which has been neglected for some time. My upper gums was so soar that I had to take my teeth out most of P.M. . . .

SUNDAY, DECEMBER 11
. . . We rolled out at 7:30 to get in on the Leo Danials program. . . . Mo snoozed while Part of chace & Sanborn hour was on the air. Pop snoozed part of P.M. read the longstory in pictorial review. Mo coughed all nite with the throat ache had nightmares dreamed all nite long.

MONDAY, DECEMBER 12
. . . Mo cleaned cupboard coughed all night with a terific throad ache had to take out her teeth to keep from coughing them out . . .

THURSDAY, DECEMBER 15
. . . We rolled out at 7 where through breakfasting at 7:30. I listened to Betty & Bob. Pop went to Kendall at 9:15 to learn whether Mr. Yingling had some hogs for sale. At 12:15 he took the Truck full of Caffir to Kendall. And bought 2 hogs for 26 dollars. he returned at 4:40 with the hogs. he suppered at 5:15. Ma ironed all curtains, & put them up ironed some more clothes. . . . I'm still coughing like no-

bodys buisness. I was much shocket while finding one big Egg, while
looking around in the Henhouse. . . .

——

FRIDAY, DECEMBER 16

North also northeast terific wind. It was real damp so no dust
rolled. . . . We rolled out at 6:45 had breakfasted at 7:45. Pop cleaned
up his table in the basement for butchering purpose stayed in the
house listened to some epesodes read papers P.M. He went after the
Cows at sunset he also cleaned up the Basement. Radio had a lota
static from 4 on P.M. Mo ironed P.M. cleaned up also scared up
the oilstove & did some other scouring To night while listning to the
First Niter she sewed buttons on Pops clothes. and washed 2 suits
underwear.

SATURDAY, DECEMBER 17

. . . We rolled out at 7 Retired at 12 midnight. we went to the dance
at 9 before going to the dance we went to see Wayne & Eldas made a
2 hour stay. At 9 we started to Syracuse went to Holly at 10:30 A.M.
and got back to Syracuse at noon. I did my xmas shopping before
going to Holly. We got a long letter to-day from the Warners also
Ervin a X-mas card from grandpa. . . .

MONDAY, DECEMBER 19

. . . we rolled out at 5:30 made more progress as usual. had breakfasted
at 6:10. Pop went to Waynes to get Pete at 9 A.M. They started to
butcher. Mo baked 2 current pies. A.M. The men cut up the hogs at
11:15 they went to Syracuse . . . returned home at 2. Mo had dinner
awaiting she had cooked spuds fried liver made gravy. Well I'll now
continue with the mens work. they read the Mail at 3 P.M. they went
to work on the hogs till 4:30 they quit. suppered at 5:30. after chow,
they went to Wayne's to get the stuffer return trip 15 minutes while
Mo listened to the Lux Play. Mo stuffed 3 sauseges by hand while Pop
& Pete where in laxation at 7:45 we retired Pete stayed all nite. I got
my teeth witteled down so I've now worn them 5 days succission
except 3 nights I took them out to heal up the gums, with Men-
tholetum. . . . Pop wittled my teeth down some to-day.

TUESDAY, DECEMBER 20

. . . We rolled out at 5:30 had breakfasted at 6:15. Pop went to Waynes
to take Pete home. took them one liver sausage some spareribs, also

some tender Loin returned after 1/2 hour stay he then went to cutting up the meat . . . caned 12 qts meat big jars 9 all cooked in the oven also 2 qts. rendered 3 gals Lard the intestines lard made 2 big liver sausages A.M. sewed 2 sacks for them. . . .

WEDNESDAY, DECEMBER 21

. . . Pop milked after chow. at 7:45 He went to grinding Lard. He completed it at 9. Then went to Kendall, after 50 lbs Salt 50 cts. he bought 50 cts Pecans 50 cts Peanuts Wallnuts 50 mixed 46 cts Salt 65 cts Salt Peter 10 tax 3 toteled 4.17. Gas 1.43. gas & xmas junk toteled 4.17. returned home at 1 P.M. eat a cold dinner consisted of cheese Spareribs sausage Liver Pie. After his lunch he salted the meat also made the dope to cure it. Then for the rest of the day. He was pasified by reading the Mail. He suppered on cheese ribs sausage. . . . We got a Card from Klossens from Dinuba . . . A letter from Lizzie Hildebrand at Dinuba where they've lived ever since Oct. and are planning on staying there till Spring.[48] Pop again witteled my teeth down. I haven't wore them for 3 nights cause they where so sore, had to heal up the sore places. . . .

FRIDAY, DECEMBER 23

. . . went along to the depot to meet Verna she arrived in Syracuse at 5. Train was 40 min. late. Mo took her bath cleaned House got cream in bucket at 2 P.M. We left for Syracuse. . . .

SATURDAY, DECEMBER 24

. . . We left for the xmas tree amedietly Elexender came to the House to bring our presents from Thelma Cliff also Ervin.[49] Ma got a brown Apron trimed with red Braid Vernas Apron trimmed with yellow braid. Mos Bedspread Candlewick yellow & Brown. Verna pink & Verna baked a white cake with Nuts in. Ma baked 2 mince Pies 2 Cranberry Pies. We never had to get no dinner. We just lunched and played hooky. Verna wrapped all presents . . . We rolled in at 11:15. . . .

SUNDAY, DECEMBER 25

. . . Pop rolled out at 15 till 5 Mo 5:30 Verna about 15 minutes later. To unwrap and see all her xmas presents. Where late with breakfast eat at 8 had to get the Turkey in the stove Pop got it right in the Oven after getting the fire made in the Heatrola Pop milked after chow

went to Elmers & took them a treat brought Pete home with him. . . .
Well xmas has again come & gone for the year of 1938. Thanks for
the memory Bob Hope sings.

TUESDAY, DECEMBER 27
Southeast terific dust storm occured at 10:15 continued till 2:30. Then
camed down wind camed down . . . Mo washed some. Verna snoozed
on the Davenport P.M. Also after supper. All Pop did was to carry
fuel & milked the Cow twice. Read the Mail also got the Cows they
had pulled out on him. All I did was to cook 3 meals such as they
where. Mixed the Bread at 8 A.M. Made the completion at 7:30 P.M.
it was good. . . .

THURSDAY, DECEMBER 29
. . . Henry worked some at his broomcorn seed. also puttered around
some. . . . Us three where all where sleepy heads we all slumbered
some while listning to the Radio.

SATURDAY, DECEMBER 31
. . . We rolled out at 7 and didn't retire to-day. Pop shaved dolled up
ready for town Ma & Verna did likewise started to the dance at 7:30
didn't get home till 3 hours after midnight. We returned from Town
at 4:30 & didn't get no work done, just seprating done breakfasted at
7:30 washed dishes swept also seprator washed. And now yon old
year ticked to its doome. Goodbye old year. Good bye.

1939

SUNDAY, JANUARY 1

Begging of New Year. Sunday, January 1, 1939 Hello New Year. . . .
We sleepy heads where all snoozing some part of the day. Ma in the
Rocker Verna on the Davenport Pop in the Rocker. Callers. Elmer
& Wife called at 4 P.M. Left for home at 8:30. . . . Mo showed Zelda
her also Vernas & Henry our xmas presents.[1] The four played cards
while myself and Zelda where intrested in the gifts. . . .

MONDAY, JANUARY 2

. . . Well our way home was very gloomy House was all empty Lonly-
ness & sadness was all over the house. All way home Ma had a lump
in her throat that she couldn't swallow eyes where full of mist that she
couldn't see the way ahead. all to see was black clowds moving over
head. It took her all that day to come out of such state of mind.[2] The
next day she seen more sunlight. . . .

WEDNESDAY, JANUARY 4

Northwest terific wind . . . a terific duststorm occured A.M. kept on
raging till 4 P.M. . . . the Windcharger came down but not hurt. . . .

SATURDAY, JANUARY 7

. . . Pop rolled out at 5. Mo 20 minutes latter she was very sleepy. We
had breakfast over at 6. Henry started to Kendall got home at 9:10
with the Mail & a spool of black thread . . . next load at 10:45. Loaded
the second load he returned home at 11:15, had the third load on at
20 min till 12 eat dinner. At 1:30 P.M. he started with the 4th load.
and returned at 5:15 a little over 5 Ton. $206. . . . So Mo had a lone-
some day at home by herself. . . .

SUNDAY, JANUARY 8

Northeast wind was raining some at 6 when we awoke kept the good work going sprinkled on & of it rained 2/3 inch . . . Pop rolled out at 7:40. Mo remained in slumber till 8:20 suddenly she heard a streak of lectricity on the Radio she jumped out of Bed to shut it off. found Pa eating a cold breakfast. He then milked while Ma eat. He took care of the Hens carried in Coal left the cows correled all day. Milked at 5:45 right after returning home from Zelda & Elmer. Mo snoozed on the Davenport after 7 till 9 when Po retired It was straight up 9 Pop had got the weather forcast so he was ready to retire.

TUESDAY, JANUARY 10

. . . Mo cleaned the hole dusty house give it a thour going over baked Bread made the completion at 2:30. mixed it at 8 A.M. We rolled in at 8:30. . . .

SUNDAY, JANUARY 15

. . . Waynes Cow had come to call on us. . . . While he was asleep the cow was hanging over the board fence, he had to take off a board to get her loose. . . . Elmer & Pete called at 3 P.M. to borrow a fork also to see if they had left their iron skillet. I gave them 1/2 gal milk. They stayed till dust O boy the 3 men certenly had the house turned into a smoker ha.[3] Mo snoozed on the floor 2/3 hour covering herself up with Pops jacket. . . .

WEDNESDAY, JANUARY 18

. . . Ma patched socks red cleaned House and called it a day. After chow she washed the seprator sat by the stove to warm herself. She'd been very icey all evening. Pop had snoozed in the Rocker Ma on the Davenport. So we rolled in while Fred Allen had got on Pops nerve.

FRIDAY, JANUARY 20

Northwest wind dust blowed some A.M. . . . We rolled out at 10 min till 7 Pop milked before chow we where through with breakfast at 7:45 Pop burned thistels by tank also on the north pasture fence A.M. P.M. He cut wood also cut off the south end tamaracks near the drive way. Ma churned A.M. & give the House a thour going over. Including cellersteps also washed all lampglobes. A.M. I patched socks. . . .

SUNDAY, JANUARY 22

. . . A quiet & piecefull house while Ma was cleaning up sut while the Stove had blowed up & scattered sut all over the two rooms. Pop ra[d]ioed P.M. severel hours read in the mean while, while the Radio was running. He had to look over all his Saturdays Mail. also had the Radio a going till 8 it then was very piecefull & quite . . .

MONDAY, JANUARY 23

. . . duster occured at 1:45 some lectricity sky was very murky. it camed down at 4 P.M. . . . I rendered all the old Meatrines ground them & feed them to the Chickens. She then cleaned lampglobes. Mixed her Bread at 9 A.M. & made the completion at 5 P.M. was exelent . . . All Snow thowed excepting on north sides of the buildings.

WEDNESDAY, JANUARY 25

. . . northeast wind duster local occured at 1:30 and camed down at 4 P.M. . . . Ma rolled out at 25 till 7 clock had died out. Pop remained in slumber till I had build the fire & breakfast was ready on the Table. At 7 he rolled out & listened in on the Newscast at KOA. where through with breakfast at 7:30 Henry went to milk at 8 he started in on the 10:20 tractor worked there mostly all A.M. came in at 15 min. till 12 while Gillman family was on. Puttered 1/2 hour P.M. wind was mostly to strong to work. We got 11 Eggs to day. The most this year.

FRIDAY, JANUARY 27

Terific wind after midnight sky was all murky when I rolled out wind took a new holt and blowed hard till 4:30 P.M. . . . We where through with breakfast at 7:30. Pop milked the cow at 7:45. after chow he cut a pile of kindling wood old trees 1 year old which were piled under dirt most of them. The rest of the day he just corelled up the cows at 3:30 P.M. and read and radioed put the battry in the Car, which had been in the radio. . . . Ma baked Bread mixed it at 8 made the completion at 3:30. was exelent she also baked 2 pans oatmeal cookies P.M. & did some ironing. A.M. she patched 2 pr socks cleaned house. . . .

TUESDAY, JANUARY 31

Terific dust storm occured at 1:15 P.M. kept raging till 9 . . . Henry listened to the Newscast before chow at 15 min till 8 he milked after chow he seprated & planed on cleaning the Well House but changed his notion after a while of constration. Probly had a strange Preminition and decided not cause all looked confusing. We endured the most confusing day no Radoing from 1:30 on till no enjoyable evening just howling wind dust blowing lectricity howling so after all saurcasem we rolled in at 9. letting the wind rage & dust scift. Pop was very much engrost in magazines and old papers that had been discarded Well this was the last day of old Jan which brought piece & contment some parts of it was dreary some gloomy some rosy & enjoyable but this last day of the month was some what complated also confusing. After all it was almost thorny ha.

WEDNESDAY, FEBRUARY 1

. . . murky also slightly dusty more so A.M. . . . Pop warmed himself at 7:45 he went out to milk old red. After a while reading & Radeoing He cleaned up the Well house P.M. also broke & did away with a batch of bottels A.M. he took the salt off the meat. Mo mixed her Bread at 8 made the completion at 4 P.M. It was exelent churned & made the completion in 15 min. In the meanwhile she give the House a theour cleaning after the terific duststorm yesterday. . . . And you dear old February brought us a beautifull day to start you month off right & make you sweet & real all the way through . . .

SATURDAY, FEBRUARY 11

. . . We rolled out at 20 min. till 7 next the news cast was entertaining the ockupents next breakfast was served at 8 old Roan was milked in the mean while the milk was getting warmed to seprate which had been saved for 5 days 9:30 Pop had seprated that while Ma was taking her bath then she rushed around getting her dishes done seprater also clean up the House. that while Pop was servicing his Car at 10:30 he was all dolled up Ma had the cream in the can also Eggs packed in the mean while Elmer & Pete arived Pete wanted to go along to Syracuse at 11 we was on our way to town returned at 6:40. . . . We couldn't find Pete so we run off & left him ha. Pop started to the dance at 8 returned at the next morning Mo rolled in at 10:10 with her legs all cold.

MONDAY, FEBRUARY 13

. . . At 8 30 terific wind occured also a duststorm & let up at 10:30 . . . Ma patched one towl cleaned the House all over. Washed a little she got dinner on the Cookstove burning junk the while was cooking. . . .

WEDNESDAY, FEBRUARY 15

... at 9 A.M. terific wind also duststorm occured at that period ... at 4 dust had camed ... This P.M. he was in the House & looked at the dustroll. ...

THURSDAY, FEBRUARY 16

Wind from northeast raged all after midnight damp so no dust was stired up it snowed a very little bit. At 8 A.M. dust accured mixed up with snow. . . . 4 P.M. it managed to shine some wind still raged but dust had let up. . . . Pop pumped old Red at 7:30. all he did to-day was his everday activities read the Mail & old Wimens world that had been here for mostly one year . . . Mo baked 3 custerd Pies A.M. in the evening she read Cappers Weekly and cut out pomes [poems].

SATURDAY, FEBRUARY 18

Southeast wind A.M. till 10 then a southwest terific duststorm occured and continued till 5:15 let up & at six P.M. . . . at 8 a terific duster occured . . . duster which occured at 8 ragged through all till 12 had let up some at 4 A.M. next morn. where so slow at the ranch rolled out at 7:10 Pop grabed the milk Pail and made things fly after the fire was made we where breakfasting at 7:45 when the news was broadcasted. Pop made himself aquainted with the Ax cut down all tamerecks that where left from 4 weeks ago, excepting the ones up north way on the east end A.M. . . . Mo cleaned till 8:45 when she had got dishes washed she baked her Bread at 2:45 was exelent baked 3 Lemon 3 Cream Pies retired at 9. she had cleaned the hole house also all that was in it & at 7:45 P.M. storm was ragging . . .

SUNDAY, FEBRUARY 19

Northwest early terific dust storm occured at 7:15 . . . at 9:30 it camed dust also wind clowds and Sun fought each other wind went to the east & a little north at P.M. again almost dusk dust started in rolling again at 6:15 also 7 P.M. . . . this duster ragged through most of the night we rolled in at 8 it was in full blast. . . .

TUESDAY, FEBRUARY 21

... Ma give the House a theour going over after all dust settled on it next she cleaned all lamps. cooked her dinner on the Heatrol[a] breakfast on the Cook stove while burning brush supper on the Heatrold Supper was warmed over from left overs which we had for dinner.

... Ma sewed a nightgown after supper and sewed some at her bloomers. We rolled in at 9:25. . . .

THURSDAY, FEBRUARY 23
... We rolled out 15 till 7. We breakfasted 7:20 Pop pumped the Cow 15 till 8. after David Harum had played their epesode he put the liquid smoke on the meat. cut some wood 10:15 he went to the field to see how damage had been done on the fields returned at 11: A.M. we dinnered straight up noon. he cut some more wood at 2 . . . at 4:15 then went out to shoot a Cyote. . . . Mo churned A.M. made the completion in 15 min. mixed her Bread at 7:40 completed it at 2:30 P.M. it was very good. Next she baked 2 Cherry Pies Then she gave the House a theour going over & cleaned all lamps. next she gathered 12 Eggs. She cooked dinner on the Heatrola. We retired 9:20.

FRIDAY, FEBRUARY 24
... at 10:45 Wayne called him & Pop chated about the Elotment being so late.[4] . . . All Mo did was her everday activities and patched underwear. . . . Ma froze so much this special day that she had goosepimps on her Arms. Pop whiled away some of his time sitting by the stove to warm his hannces [haunches]. I'm writing this old diary at 4:45 P.M. & my hands are stiff while being on the job. . . .

SATURDAY, FEBRUARY 25
... All A.M. Radio went in full blast excepting while Henry swept the poarch a path to the Well House to the toilet. later he filled a 10 gal. jar full of Snow for Battery water. . . . Static was a billering & growling A.M. an after 6 it was terific. Ma washed some A.M. and wrote a letter to Verna at Hutch. . . . Mr. Bishop called at 12:20 P.M. to see about some soil which should be reported while blowing.[5]

MONDAY, FEBRUARY 27
Northeast terific snow blizzard continued 6 to 7 inch. . . . this Snow blizzard raged till we retired at 9:15 it hadent let up Wind whisteled very mornfull static was terific from 10 A.M. & continued lectricity most all day. . . . Henry read part of the Book of Europe & the Presidents for some new entertainment. P.M. He snoozed for 15 minutes. All Ma did this terific day her everday ecitivites patched some read the Book the Guilding Light. We retired at 9:15 cause the radio was of no good terific static all day long

TUESDAY, FEBRUARY 28

. . . We rolled out 6 to day for once in a long time. Pop went right out
& skooped Snow at 6:30 he came in. Then he turned in news also
shaved & dolled all up . . . At 8:30 he was on his way to town. Returned at 5:15 P.M. his first day of experience being in the Joury box
Henry soon after his return home he went to feed the Cows milked
and close the Henhouse. . . . Ma had this last day of February all to
herself didn't need to cook dinner But she had to be the messenger
boy She wrote a letter to Ervin & the Warners. Henry had run off
with the Mail on his way up to the jourey So she consoled herself
looking over the 1937 & 1938 Diary She got the chance to listen to
Dr. Susen all through the epesode, for the first time. She's been on
the air 2 weeks to day she listened to all her usual epesodes. . . . Well
old February has come to its doom. . . .

WEDNESDAY, MARCH 1

. . . We rolled out at 6 made quick progrees at this camp to-day. we
where breakfasting at 6:30 Pop when to milk before chow shaved at
7:30 he had seprated watered & fed the cows dolled up at 5 till 8 he
left for town to serve on the Joury. cut a gash on his cheek while
shaving to-day, also yesterday he return home at 9 . . . Ma mixed Bread
at 9:15 made the completion 3 P.M. was exelent cleaned up the House
washed all lampglobes had to be the messenger boy while traveling
through Snowbanks to grain the Hens she scratched her fingers on
the broken door of the grainery till bled hurt badly she cleaned all
disks thouroly on the seprator. Her leisure time was spent writing
letters to the Warners also Verna at Hutch Well this lonely and piecefull quiet day it sorta went fast didn't last very long While lisntning to
the usual epesode it sorta whiled it away fast, and well spend by these
entertainments. This day was not so lonely after all.

THURSDAY, MARCH 2

. . . This is pops first day home after serving on the Joury 2 days in
succession. . . . We received a letter from Verna telling us all about her
ailments being dignosed by a Caropractor at $2 1/2 wanting to know,
whether to get 20 treatments to clear her up. Poor kid. One from
Thelma & Ervin telling about his Wisdom Tooth pulled poor kid. . . .
Ma cleaned up the House put the finish to her letters for the kids
patching socks I have another goosepimps day. seems as if I cant get
warm P.M. The Road grader cleared away the Snow on roads much
static late in evening.

SATURDAY, MARCH 4

. . . Henry pottered around all A.M. till 10 he shaved & dolled up got the car ready to start to Town. started at 15 till 11 A.M. Mo went along to Gertrude. took her the Book the Guiding Light to read we certenly had a fine time. Pop returned from Town 3:15 waited for the Mail Train . . . We got a card from Thelma saying they where getting ready to be on their way back to Kans.[6] Mo wrote a card to Verna telling her to go ahead with the treatments . . .

SUNDAY, MARCH 5

. . . We rolled out at 6:30 to day listened to Leo Danals while breakfasting at 7:30 9 A.M. Pop seprated dinnered at 10 till 12 at 1 we was on our way to Elmer & Zelda we took the can of Seprated milk and almost 1 1/2 gal hole milk. At 3:45 we started to Olins to talk it over about their return to Kans. We returned home at 6 P.M. Pop suppered at 6:30 milked 6:15 at 7:30 he's listning to the Negro Holienest Serman. . . . we rolled in at 8 Henry thought it was a little early

TUESDAY, MARCH 7

The beginning of a new beautifull day just like spring. . . . the Sheruf called released him from the Joury. . . . Ma washed her hair cleaned up the house. Washed out serverel pieces of clothes. . . .

WEDNESDAY, MARCH 8

. . . Northwest wind early at 8:30 it was terific a local duster occured about 9 camed at 12. . . . We rolled out 6:20. Henry marched right out to milk. we breakfasted at 10 till 7. at 8 A.M. Henry had went to work on his truck stayed there till 10 till noon We dinnered Pop went back to work at 1:15. . . . Ma started to Wash at 15 till 3 finished up 5 P.M. Forenoon she baked one Custard Pie one cream. At noon Pop seprated during his leisuretime I washed one Bedspread and a lots other clothes. . . . The evening was well spend radoing by Henry Ma had a freezing acking back. Just the same she true storied for 1/2 hour . . .

THURSDAY, MARCH 9

. . . Ma rolled out with a sick headache not taking no asprin So this sick continued all day she churned just did her every day activities. . . . Pete called to buy some Eggs I sold him 2 1/2 doz and 3 that's all I had gave him 1/2 gal milk. Well another beginning of a new chilly day. I read some in a True story. This farm is cented by the oder of burning Cottenwoods. I'd rather smell them then Coal order. Waynes cow called to-day. I spose she gets tired of eating home products so she ventures away to try something new ha. . . .

FRIDAY, MARCH 10
. . . Pop grabed the milk pail to milk. Where breakfasting at 15 till 7 when first news cast was on. I warmed the milk in the mean time Pop seprated. He took a shave powered his face changed the oil in the Car dolled up & at 9 A.M. he started to Syracuse. and returned at 6:45 . . . got his Elotment check I send the cream along with him . . . Well this is a hooky day for Ma again that's what I enjoy. . . . The Cows arived at 2: P.M. They jumped out of the Correl got at the feed stack. & o Ma certenly had to do running after them, to get them to behave. I gave the house a thour going over.

SATURDAY, MARCH 11
. . . terific duststorm just lasted one hour but o how did the dust come in it rained a very little then at 11 A.M. it was snowing . . . it was a terific blizzard for about 2 hours great big snowflakes . . . Henry got out his suit and both pr. trousers planed to go to town to get them cleaned. Ma was huring around fixing up her clothes taking a bath combed her hair Pop got in the car started to drive to Mr Aults when he got there north of his place Dust was so thick he had to turn on the lights, to find his way after 20 min. he returned thinking o my such terific storm. Said I'm staying home glad I got here O boy he said no town for me. . . . we retired at 8 thinking the bed was more comforting as the cold dancehall. He decided it was to confusing to go to the dance. . . .

TUESDAY, MARCH 14
Northwest terific wind early at 10 and continued all day terific dust-storm from north continued after 10. till 6 it camed some at dusk it still blowed . . . Mo ironed P.M. also washed lampglobes. Our Menue was something new cakes for breakfast Cakes eggs fruit for desert. Dinner vegetable soup. . . . Men only worked about 1 hour on the Car. Till terific duster occured. . . .

WEDNESDAY, MARCH 15
. . . We rolled out at 6:15 had started breakfasting while the first news real was broadcasted Pop milked at 7:45 seprated then at 8:45 they

where on their way to the Sale . . . returned at after midnight . . . Pete's now been here the third day Ma had to give the house a theour going over washed both doors made Bread mixed it at 9: AM made the completion at 3: P.M. Ma had a piece & quiet day No dinner to get. . . . I had to run after old Roanie she thought she'd take a strole. I washed my hair to-day also gathered up some brush. And cooked on the Cookstove. My teeth where so confusing and pinched me P.M. So I took the lowers out. . . .

FRIDAY, MARCH 17
. . . She cleaned House churned made the completion did lotta ods & ends. She made cheese fritters for dinner peaches & cake for desert supper scraps including seconhand spuds breakfast the mountain oysters Ma had Spuds & eggs for her breakfast. We both rolled in the same time at 9. Pop washed his feet she took her bath, so she'd be ready for her trip bright & early.

SATURDAY, MARCH 18
. . . We started on our way at 15 till 7 got to Hutch at 1:30. Waited on Verna till 5 started on our way to Hillsboro. Pop & Verna eat their supper in McPherson town . . . We bought Gertrudes Purceolar [percolator] in McPherson. We got to Hillsboro at 7 oclock. P.M. . . . We went to slumber at 12 midnight.

SUNDAY, MARCH 19
. . . We rolled out at 6 breakfasted at 7. helped the lady wash the dishes at 9 we went to Grandpas. Stayed there for dinner . . . at 4:30 P.M. Gertrude was tied up [married] sermonia [ceremony] only lasted 1/2 hour next supper we then left for Inman . . .

MONDAY, MARCH 20
. . . We started for Hutch at 9. stayed all night at Freds rolled out about 6 breakfasted at 7 didn't help her with the dishes we messed around in Hutch till 15 till 12 we got our selves some chow. . . . at 12 we was on our way back home. got to Dodge at 2:15 stoped there 2/3 on an hour Pop bought 10 dollars repairs, for the Combine drove on to a grocery store he got some cocoanut Cookies 25 cts next drove to a vegetable store bought 100 lbs. Spuds 1.65 Oranges 50 cts Where hungry so we started in devouring some of the Cookies next Ma had to peel Pop an Orange. stoped at Kendall at 5. . . .

TUESDAY, MARCH 21

spring begins with local a duster at 8:30. . . . A very mild spring day it wasn't to calm, cause a little spirt of dust several times.

WEDNESDAY, MARCH 22

Southwest wind at 9:30 dust started to roll ever now & then local duster. it camed at 2 P.M. . . . Ma just did her ever day activities. churned two batches Butter made the completion over all 1/2 hour. Baked 2 egg Pies and 2 Current. She milked the old cow just as the men drove up. . . . Ma had a ache in her back also a stiff neck and another cancer [canker] sore to-day, in her lower jaw. . . . No one to cook for just old Ma her self. She just eat a snak at noon.

THURSDAY, MARCH 23

Southwest strong wind a little dusty clowdyness had occured, before rolling out. . . . Ma rolled out at 15 till 6 Pop 20 min. later Pete 15 min. later. Where through with chow at 7:10 Pop milked while I got breakfast they both shaved dolled up at 15 till 8 away they went, to town returned 15 till 12 noon. . . . P.M. at 1 the men went to work at the combine. . . . Radio banged like thunder so we didn't listen to nothing at 8 Ma rolled in Pete 8:15 and Pop followed they where both so tired couldn't hardly see straight . . .

SATURDAY, MARCH 25

. . . men chated about the Country conditions trip to Calif smoked, till House was full of smoke fumes . . . men went to work at 1 P.M. Pop smoked the meat, & Pete worked on the traylor or should I say howler. Pop soon joined after completion with meat was made. . . . I made Bread it was excelent. Completion was made at 2:30. I did a very little on account of Rhumatics its a nucience let me work its so painfull. . . . I cleaned sut out Cookstove also all ashes. Washed lampglobes. Waynes cow came to snout around her to-day. . . . Pop greased my shoulder, it releaved my rhum rhumatism some but still aches yet.

SUNDAY, MARCH 26

. . . Terific wind but to damp soil to blow much. . . .

MONDAY, MARCH 26

. . . We rolled out at 6:10 where at breakfast 10 mi till 7. Pop had milked before chow. Men in the House spreading smoke fumes A.M.

and chating dinnered at usual schuedel again the same routine at 3 P.M. The men cleaned out the driveway in the Barn and went to the Hay mowe cleaned dirt out of the Maze and drug it in the south end. . . . All Mo did was her everday ecitivities added to it churned 2 batches cream. . . .

TUESDAY, MARCH 27

. . . We rolled out at 6:20. where breakfasting at 7 no progress was made cow was milked at 8 smokers where puffing their pipes, for pass away time to quiet their nerves . . . at 2 P.M. the Mail arived so for 2 hours of pass away time they where buisy reading with the House filled with silence and littered with smoke clowds. So today Pop got equainted with the Hens also with the Egg production. . . . Ma just wrote a card to Verna at Hutch also to the left alone dearboy in the far away land . . . And Ma had to write the dairy which had been neglected yesterday on account of rhumatics paines and discontment being down in the darkness not being able to come out of the clowds. . . .

WEDNESDAY, MARCH 29

. . . at 8:30 Men where shaved dolled up at 15 min till 9 they where ready to start for town. Returned at 3:40 while Ma was correling the Cows she had to cary in some fuel, & tend to the chickens I just had a hooky day away from all cooking all I did was to wash lampglobes beside all activities which are du to each day. Men worked a trifle bit after their return home from town and Sale . . .

THURSDAY, MARCH 30

. . . got a card from Verna saying I'm coming home. . . .

FRIDAY, MARCH 31

. . . We rolled out at 6:15 Pop milked, next Pete came along when chow was ready at 7 Pop then unloaded the load of coal at 8 they where at work puttering at the Combine at 10 A.M. they started to thrash 11:15 Olin apeared on the scene & gave them a chance, for 1 hour of relaxation at 12:10 they came for chow at 1 they where thrashing Olin had started once but started in on another conversation & then stayed mostly another hour. I spose he wanted to play some more hooky to get out of work. . . . Ma churned made the completion in 15 min P.M. she patched some underwear. Well this is the last day of March mild and goes out like a lamb. Men had old Waynes Cow to fite three different times while thrashing. I had to iron a shirt for Pop to-day, so he can go dollen up. . . .

SATURDAY, APRIL 1 AND A FOOL DAY
. . . Pop & Pete went to take down the broken parts of the Windmill early after chow Pow had to fix up the fence, which he had torn up yesterday to drive the Combine in. . . . We left at 10.A.M. returned at 6:30 from Syracuse went to see if Verna came home on the fast train she didn't arive We got 2 cards from the kids saying that they started on their way back to Kans. . . . they'd started on their way back Mon. March 27. . . .

SUNDAY, APRIL 2
. . . At 6 P.M. Thelma & Cliff drove in from Oregon all sound but very tired and played out we grownups retired 15 after 11 children had gone to roost at 9.

MONDAY, APRIL 3
. . . Thelma rolled out first we came out the hay at 15 till 7 Cliff 7:15 also children. Had got through with chow at 8 Cliff Henry & Leroy went to see their feature [future] home returned at 10 A.M. Patsy Cut out paper dolls Thelma & Mo chated about old times Men fixed on the windmill at 3 they went to Olins to chat. . . .

TUESDAY, APRIL 4
. . . At 2:10 P.M. We started to Syracuse Verna arived at 3:40. . . . Ervin has a birthday to day. I just send him a little money for his gift all chated till way late 10 before retiring a new get together.

FRIDAY, APRIL 7
. . . Men went to Syracuse at 15 min. till 9 . . . While men where transacting buisness up town. Wimen around this camp eat all hours of the day. eat a snack when ever we felt like it. All household where broke up to-day while Iva Klossen entered House all untidy all where blue about conditions Little Pigy kicked the bucket kids cried, and was all tore up. Iva invited us to come & help her quilt. I was feeling tuff and didn't get to go . . .

SATURDAY, APRIL 8
. . . kids went to town. returned at 5 P.M. Pop Thelma went to the dance Cliff also went the first Saturday he returned to Kans. Patsy & Leroy Ma & Verna stayed home. she went to the Hay at 10:15. Verna had gone sooner and had snoozed a while on the Davenport. Dancers returned home at 1 the next day, and rolled in. The little ones had gone to the Hay around 8. And didn't become aware about the dance going.

SUNDAY, APRIL 9
. . . This is Easter Sunday. . . . While taking the little ones to Sunday school terific Duster occured at 7 P.M. And ragged way down in the night. . . .

MONDAY, APRIL 10
. . . Local dust occured . . .

WEDNESDAY, APRIL 12
Terifit wind most all the day and local duster continued most all day. . . .

THURSDAY, APRIL 13
. . . Local duster occured A.M. Camed at 6 P.M. Pop Libertied while dust was raggin. . . . Pop Cliff and Leroy had went to Springfield, to see about some Barley returned home at 2 P.M. Us wimen had us a picnic lunched when we got hungry. Iva called A.M. 10. While House was untidy and wind was ragging on. . . .

SUNDAY, APRIL 16
Wooly and dusty . . . Wind continued most all day. . . .

THURSDAY, APRIL 20
. . . Terific wind and duster early A.M. Next it sprinkled heavy. Two hours later terific dust occured again, and continued till 4:30 P.M. . . . Pop went to the field 6:15. Came in for dinner at 12 he worked east of the Hall. Came in for chow at 6:45. In the meanwhile Mr Doerr called on Mr Dyck. Verna pieced on her quilt. And Thelma ironed. Schoolman called a few minutes while bringing Patsy home. We had fire all day it was so very chilly. Ma did the milking and seprating to-day.

FRIDAY, APRIL 21

Northwest local duster . . . Pop went to the north field at 6 stayed till 12. Verna had to fix dinner for him. While Thelma Ma and the little Warners where at the last day school. Cliff didn't go . . . Thelma & Cliff took our Car to Syracuse to get the groceries for the last day dinner. We returned home at 2 P.M. . . . Had a very nice time all school Patrents where present. Had a very nice dinner. With all kind of good things to eat. After dinner was served we took snapshots of the school. And all that where present.

SUNDAY, APRIL 23

Slightly clowdyness a terific duster. Wind southwest first Murky sky clowded over. . . . Pop shot a wild Goose & O it was lousios [luscious]. Pop fixed at the Lister at 8 A.M. At 9 he shaved & dolled up took the little Warners and went to Kendall returned home at 10 min. Till one P.M. Had this lusious Goose for dinner In the mean while us Wimen cleaned up the House. We didn't need no fire to-day to keep warm. When Leroy came home he said my belly is hollow I need something to eat ha. Told Pat. You was home & could eat when ever the spirit moved you ha. . . .

MONDAY, APRIL 24

. . . Duster occured at 10 Local A.M. Camed at 5 P.M. . . .

TUESDAY, APRIL 25

. . . Pop went to the field east of hall at 5:15. Listed came in for dinner at 12:10. Thelma got Cliff for his dinner all went back to the same field. Ma got so sleepy snoozed in the Rocker. And Verna on the Davenport. This was mail day. We got a letter from Ervin. Telling us Mrs. Warner baked him a birthday cake how nice of her to do that.

WEDNESDAY, APRIL 26

. . . terific dust storm occured over 1/2 hour period dark clowdyness occured at 3 P.M. . . . Verna wrote a letter Ma a card to Ervin Thelma ironed some yesterday & some to-day both the girls snoozed also little Leroy while Ma cleaned Bed room also pantry she escaped milking old Roan this special day. Pos presence being home on acount of the rain. Static was so bad tonite also to day static just banged I couldn't hear One Mans Family on account of Rain.

THURSDAY, APRIL 27

. . . Ma washed some dresses A.M. baked 3 custerd pies and Cinnamon rolls also Bread completed cinnamon rolls & raisen Bread 2 P.M. . . . Ma run after the Cows while grasing on Mr. Hofmans Wheat, wheat was wet with dew as if it'd rained heavy I was sopen wet after returning to the house. Warner kids found a nest of 17 Eggs on the Hay mow & Barn.

FRIDAY, APRIL 28

. . . We rolled out at 4:15 by lamplight the rest of the Household remained in slumber a while We where through breakfast at 5:15 Pop soon left for the field. . . . Pop moved to the northfield P.M. and harrowed also burned thistels he came in for chow at 12: noon left for the field at 12:45. Came in for supper 7:20 Ma made two trips to Laymers field to drive the cows of the Wheat. she milked 2 times to-day . . .

TUESDAY, MAY 2

. . . Cliff milked at 6 they started to the field came in for chow . . . They worked north of here listed and burned some weedse. I took a bath A.M. played hooky P.M. and did usual ectivities. Thelma & Verna Truestoried P.M. Thelma took a nap A.M. went east to the draw to get some greens. Ma also snoozed. After supper Pop reed papers. All the household was in slumber at 8 including Ma . . .

THURSDAY, MAY 4

. . . We rolled out 4:30 at 5:15 we where at breakfast when the rest of the Household rolled out at about 6 A.M. Men went to work Pop burned some weeds close by up north listed . . . Thelma truestoried & Verna read some to at P.M. Thelma baked some muffins. Ma washed her head baked raisen bread coffee Cake & bread. Had it completed for dinner not to hot so we had fresh for chow. The raisen bread wasn't bake for dinner. She also did some ironing Pops trousers and severel dresses and one apron. while relaxing she snoosed on the davenport to do away with some of her leg-ache at 6 she milked old Roan. she kicked cause the rip in her teet bled. . . .

FRIDAY, MAY 5

South terific wind and duster from 9. A.M. ragged till about 4 P.M. . . . We rolled out at 4:30 breakfasted at 5:25. Pop went to work at 6.

On the Doerr land. to list. Came in for dinner at 12:10. came in for supper. Cliff went to the Willes Farm to disk took his lunch. came in for chow at 6:30. With eyes all full of dust & all in after induring all that dust. . . . Olin Called at 2. P.M. stayed over 100 period so Henry and him had a chat about conditions. That shortened Henrys afternoons work hours. . . .

SATURDAY, MAY 6
. . . A.M. about 10 a duster occured. lasted an hour. At P.M. a terific one occured raged on for severel hours. Pop shaved took a bath at 1:30 we started for town, went around to meet the Mail man. Pop Verna Patsy & myself at 3:30 P.M. a terific duster occured we all went to the dance at 20 min till 9. returned home at midnight. . . .

SUNDAY, MAY 7
. . . terific wind & local dust A.M. P.M. just a very little camed at 5:30 P.M. . . . every one in the Household was grochy blue some entagnestic I spose on account lose of sleep ha. Pop went to Syracuse at 9 A.M. . . . Pop returned from his trip with the rubber tires on front wheels of tractors . . . Verna & Ma had piece quiet & contment. Which was a Wonderfull Sunday.

MONDAY, MAY 8
Southwest terific wind a local duster from 7 A.M. to 4:30 P.M. then dust had camed. . . . All I did to-day was everday ecetivities and washed lamp globes also Verna felt sick after eating some asperges. a new vegetable for our menue . . .

WEDNESDAY, MAY 10
Southeast terific duststorm occured at 5:30 A.M. Camed considerable at 10 A.M. . . . at noon the wind had camed and most dust had settled . . . Pop & Cliff worked on the lister dinnered at 11:30 Henry drove the tractor to the Kendall place to list. . . . I cleaned the kitchen & frontroom after dust camed.

THURSDAY, MAY 11
. . . terific wind ever now & then local dust. . . . Pop went to the field at 6:15 at the north Kendall field came in for chow at 12:10. They shaved up at 1:30 the men & the little Warners went to Syracuse returned at 4:45. went to work came in for chow at 7:15 the two men

went to the field in the same car. All the household was tired & sleepy & retired at 8. Thelma & myself cleaned up the middle Bedroom. The two girls washed their heads later P.M. They both put mudpacks on their faces In fore-noon We did a big washing started in at 8 A.M. and finished . . . up about 11 A.M. some of the clothes got sprinkled with dust. . . .

FRIDAY MAY 12

. . . A great deal of thunder heavy sprinkle ever now and then. . . . We rolled out at 6 enjoyed ourselves in the good old bed while lightning & thundering occured. . . . Thelma & Verna ironed Verna and Ma did some washing and ironing. Also washed my hair. in the evening we all took our bath . . . she washed some windows also the lampglobes. While Thelma cleaned up the Cupboard.

SATURDAY, MAY 13

. . . We rolled out 40 min till 5 breakfasted at 5:30. Got ready to start to Hutchinson & started on our way 20 min. till seven. Got the mail & started on our way. Got to Hutch at 12:30 . . . Verna place all loacated at 2:30. . . . Verna & Ma went to the Kress store & bought the little Warners a Lamar Dairy Car. Thelma & Cliff 2 blue Cearel bowls also Ma one. Went to another store. exchange some pants in on a Uniform paying 50 cts difference. . . . Henry started to Hillsboro at 4 P.M. to see his dad. . . .

SUNDAY, MAY 14

. . . Got ourselves cleaned up and fixed our hair Got the apartment dressed up at 9 A.M. later Verna sewed up her uniforms while Ma wrote her dairy & eat a slice of Bread & butter drank a cup of coffee at 12:45 we started on our way home. Got 5 gals. some Gas at Charleston in Dodge he got me a box of chocolates for Mothers day also 1 pt ice cream he eat dinner while I awaited in the Car and got me a drink. we returned home at 5 P.M. Warners where gone, had went to the Willet place to the Tractor. . . .

MONDAY, MAY 15

. . . Ma wrote a letter to Verna at her new apartment 608 West second St. hunted up the stough to send to her. She had the trots so bad she & Leroy took some Mountain hurb linement to get relief. . . .

TUESDAY, MAY 16

. . . a duststorm localy. . . . No wimen folks home had gone to Syracuse with Olin & Ethel at 11 A.M. returned at 6 P.M. Pop burned weedse P.M. had such pains in his feet that he had to greese them with white Linement. The men where both home when we returned home from town we fixed scrameled Eggs fried some sow belly. Tomatoes & Apples for desert. . . . And o what a blue day for Ma she shed enough tears to make up for a long time. Couldn't find no sunshine no where. Just sit with her head up in the clowds.

WEDNESDAY, MAY 17

. . . Ever now & then a duster occuring. . . . Wind is very mournfull makes one feel all the bluer. Static was so bad yesterday, also today that we couldn't hear nothing. Not even hear yourself think. Pop went to the field and fenced all A.M. . . . at 4 P.M. He dug the straw & dirt out of the tank in the pasture then went to the east pasture fence and fixed more fence. . . .

FRIDAY, MAY 19

. . . We rolled out at 15 till 5. breakfasted at 5:45 both men worked at the tractor dinnered at 12 went back to work 15 till 1. worked there till 6:45 suppered at 7. No cow to milk she had pulled out for Bishops to see herself some companionship. . . . Mo felt to tuff to clean all rooms.

SATURDAY, MAY 20

Northeast terific duststorm howling wind and dark clowdyness at 5 A.M. it camed down at 9:30. . . .

SUNDAY, MAY 21

. . . We both cross bears and all the rest excepting Pop where entagnistic I spose cause we had all house full of dust to clean. . . .

MONDAY, MAY 22

. . . local duster camed at 6 . . . Pop rolled out at 4:15 while Ma & all grownups stayed in bed till 5, little ones slept till 7 We breakfasted at 6. Pop milked before chow, the men went to work at 6:30 for the second time. . . . static was terific in the evening. Just the same Pop listened to Rosevelts speech Mo patched some overalls washed some stockings wrote a letter to Verna & send it off . . . Little Warners just lived in the tank most of the day. . . .

TUESDAY, MAY 23

. . . terific duster P.M. . . . Pop took off all the grease & cleaned up to stay for a few days. . . . Thelma put a facial pack on her face. A.M. P.M. she sewed and quilted her quilt. Ma made soap 2 boxes lye into soap out of scraps of butter, and old grease. She had to grain the hens added to her acativities made a batch of not to awful good Bread. . . .

WEDNESDAY, MAY 24

Southeast terific duststorm not so strong A.M. But o it was a Wolf all P.M. By spells we couldn't hardly see. . . . In the night it was the hottest night on record. . . . Pop puttered at the Lister A.M. . . . Dust-blowed so hard that they couldn't lay off their land. . . . Thelma & Cliff drove to Olin Warners and took Mr Mail [male] hog home after a long stay at the Dyck Ranch to entertain the female shoats. Olin gave the little ones some more ground maze to feed their baby chicks. . . .

THURSDAY, MAY 25

. . . terific wind occured at 3:30 P.M. A terific black duster At 4 it was raining came with a terific splash rain continued for about 1/2 hour . . . Pop went to the field about 7:30 it looked to rainy to trust at 10:30 they came back after the harrow. . . . 12:10 went to work west of Awlts at 12:45, worked till 4:30 P.M. this terific weather occured Pop drove in at 4:30 Cliff 15 minutes later he never got the glass rolled down on account of the terific black duster. Thelma & Ma washed but never got it completed. We had to shut the Motor off when this incedent occured kept it up so all close just sat in the Machine all Night. The next day it had to go through the motion again. Had to heat a batch of new water and put it all through so it was clean twice & fresh. And ready for ironing. Patsy crying with fear thinking, her daddy would perish in the storm.

FRIDAY, MAY 26

. . . Pop put in some time to replace some shingles up on the House-roof, where the wind had torn them off. Some time was spend at the Radio by Pop. . . . After chow Pop Cliff & the little Warners went to see the Water at Bearcreek.[7] . . . Mas poor comforter featherbed sheet spred her 2 Lawn dress all full of mud & water where the roof had leaked. . . . Thelma & family went to the Willet Place to take the measurements of the Windows to make her curtains also to measure the flowers [floors]. To see how big the Leloulnems must be to fit the floures All Household was tired from wading in mud The hole family where very enthusastic about all the rain falls . . .

SATURDAY, MAY 27
. . . dust local P.M. for severel hours murky sky till late in the evening. All Household was up. Ma stayed in the Hay till 6. She arose mostly looking like a pitchfork. . . . All where sitting down to breakfast when Ma rolled out ha. They gave me a good laugh seeing me so sleepy headed. Pop & Cliff went as far as Bear Creek & Cliff waded in the mud. soon returned, looking like Mudhooks. . . . Pop cleaned up all boards and made just an emprovement toard the place. He works at this till 2 P.M. made his own dinner. At 2 when the Mail arived he looked it over at 3:30 he went to harrow the same ground where him & Cliff worked . . . Thelma & Cliff bought one green and one blue Lenoleum. . . .

SUNDAY, MAY 28
. . . duster occured at 15 till 6. only lasted a 15 minute period southeast wind terific . . . Ma give the frontroom also kitchen a theour going over. Which she had been neglected yesterday. At 3 P.M. We went to the Willet Farm. Where Cliff & family had went very early A.M. at 15 min till 6 we returned home also the Warners. Before the duster occured. . . . rolled in at 8 after a chat about their Farm activities and a lot sauscasum along with all of it ha.

TUESDAY, MAY 30
Southwest wind local duster A.M. . . .

WEDNESDAY, MAY 31
. . . all House was quiet empty and lonesome. The Warners had moved to their happy home at 6:45 A.M. a little while after dinner they came back Cliff left for Syracuse 15 till one to have some part fixed he returned 3:30 . . . While Ma got old Roan she wore a blister on her Heal, and o how sore and painfull it broke amedietly after it has rose O O O she cleaned 4 rooms free from dust she sloped hogs morn & eve. . . .

THURSDAY, JUNE 1

. . . Cliff & Pop went to town it was to awful wet to work they returned home at 5:30 . . . it rained hard at 5:30. Cliff & Thelma stayed till it was all over with at 7 they hit the trail for home & learned that they hadn't got as much rain as we did. Well another incedent occured, during the rain period. Mas Featherbed also 2 comforters and spread where very badly soiled by the effects from the leakage of the Roof. Brick poarch on the west side of the house took a tumble

FRIDAY, JUNE 2

. . . 6:40 we started on our way got the Warners and started on our way to the Show Dodge City[8] . . . Pop & Cliff didn't see the Show Tomcated around. . . . We returned home at 11:10. and only had 4: hours & 30 min. sleep Ma ironed and cleaned up Pops clothes took a bath played hookie no dinner to get. She just eat a snak. I baked a batch very good Bread had it all ready 11:30 aired & dried our Bedding to mend the runs that occured yesterday during the rain storm.

SATURDAY, JUNE 3

South terific wind local dust occured at 9 A.M. camed at 6. P.M. . . . We rolled out at 4:15 breakfasted at 4:45. Was on our way 5:15 to the Warners in the Hoopy & O how I did freeze one mile north Pop lended me his Jacket blanketlined. And O Was it ever comfortable & Pop sat & froze ha. The poor fellow. I had so much activities to tend to & forgot to comfort myself. And what adventures we had ha. We returned mostly sunset Pop got old Roan milked eat a snack dolled up & away to the dance we went 8. returned at 11. And o how sleepy we where from the efects of the good show Dodge City from the night before. Thelma and I was snoozing on the Bed when sudden we heard a nock on the Door. It was Olin & family. Ma snoozed a period of 1/2 hour while Thelma was preparing the Spuds for dinner I was lying on the little ones Bed. While the howling wind was raging. I snatched 3 1/2 hour periods of sleep. . . . on our way home We sat under the shady Tree south of the Mailbox for a bit of relaxation. Pats thought it was grand. We picked up all wood, which we found lying on the Road back. Going back to some adventures that day. Sudenly Patsy seen the Hydron starting to run ha. The little ones chouted for joy. They started right in making mud Pies ha. What a grand time they had.

SUNDAY, JUNE 4

Terific [wind] at 7 A.M. . . . dust didn't come in the House much. . . .
We rolled out at 7:30 ha. Leo Danials was abroadcasting Pop just the
same in the Hay all that time ha. Where breakfasting at 8 Ma finished
dishes at 10:30. Some note to do things in such way. At 8 Pop fixed
the hitch on the hoopie at 11 a.m. he started after his Tractor . . . He
cerveced the Tractor and changed Oil He dressed up at 15 min. till 5
he left for the Ball Game while Ma rit her dairy also read Truestories.
. . . And back to Mas usual acetivities. she shined all her floors cleaned
up. And started dinner, While The men where chating about all events
which had taken place. . . . One of our Hens crossed the chilly devide.
so while making a fire in the Cookstove she was creamated. Goodbye
old Hen.

MONDAY, JUNE 5

Southwest terific wind A.M. and mournfull. Howling all over . . . It certenly was blue Monday. Ma completed churning at 4.P.M. her head was
mostly upside down. She tried to seprate at 1: P.M. seprator wouldn't
work It took 6 hours to complete her Bread. And back to churning.
she churned over 1 1/3 period Sunday let all sat & went to the good
old Hay. Lux Play was Wonderfull Ma listened no interference . . .

TUESDAY, JUNE 6

. . . We rolled out at 4:15 had breakfast at 5. Pop went to the field
north and planted. Came in for dinner at 12 noon started with the
puddler and Oneway at 1 P.M. to the 40 ackers. . . . I patched some
garments while listing in on the radio. Ma Milked also seprated A.M.
and cleaned up the two rooms also Bedroom. While dinnering right
in the midst Thelma & family arived with her Bread ready to put in
the Oven & Bake it was exelent. She then made her family some dinner. I only had fried second hand Spuds & cheese Dumplings she
thought they where grand, so did Patsy. But Leroy didn't like them.
At 4:30 Ma went to the pasture to milk the Cow so the Warners could
take 1/2 gal milk. Also gave them 19 Eggs that's all I had Thelma played
the Piano, also the Fonograph. . . . Ma buisy swating flies. Door was full
of Flies so the misses spend a lotta time swatting them. . . .

WEDNESDAY, JUNE 7

. . . Ma give the House a theour going over washed the lampglobes.
Flies are very thick on door are taking advantage of me. I put in

1 hour swating them. . . . a blister had risen on my lip when I came out of the Hay. my head was going around and around. after making two trips to milk. The efects of so early milking soured the Milk. I picked all tin cans out of the orcherd south, so Pop could puddle it. at 9 A.M. I changed the battery in the Radio so I could hear my usual plays. I got the job done fine with just like new. Cant hear one Mans family cause the static wont let yourself think. . . .

THURSDAY, JUNE 8

a duster at 6:45 was generel but not a long lasting one. . . . We rolled out at 4:30 breakfasted at 5 Po milked also seprated took that much off Mas hands ha. Po washed his feet shaved dressed up at 6:20 we was on our way to town. returned at 9:20 . . . Pop went right to fixen and cervesing the Tractor took it to the field east on 60 ackers . . . Came in for chow at 6:45 just barly got in after duster had struck. . . . Flies are thick on the screen door sting me and crawl on me dont take no mercy while I'm writing the Dairy. I grab the swot and hit them ever so often. We got a Card from Verna saying she's fine & happy . . .

FRIDAY, JUNE 9

. . . A terific generel dustorm it raged on till 8 P.M. at this time some stars could be seen wind raged on most all night. had camed some next morning . . . Pop was on early. his way to Town at 5:15 to have one of the sweeps welted which he broke yesterday on the Lister. He returned at 9 & still got in 3 hours of work A.M. . . . He came in early for supper on account dust storm 7 didn't eat cause dust was to thick waited for 1/2 hour in the mean time he looked over the latest papers . . . Had to go to Bed with all doars & windows closed Pop thought it was to hot. Went to Bed naked ha. . . .

SATURDAY, JUNE 10

Northwest wind early later A.M. it camed some was a little dusty. . . . We rolled out at 3:15. The earliest record this summer so far we had breakfast 20 min till 4. at 4 Pop went to the field planted north . . . Warners called over noon to get gas 1/2 gal Milk and 20 Eggs Thelma fixed Patsys pink silk dress. They took dinner with us. Leroy was so sleepy he went to the Davenport & sleeped till noon. . . . Ma milked old Roan & seprated. made some cornstarch chocolate Pudding for Pops menue for supper later give the House & theour going over after the duster I milked old Roan and sloped the Hogs. The black Mother Cat found her kittens to-day. I heared some cats screaming & fighting. The old Tom had layed two of them to rest and poor mother only has one left.

SUNDAY, JUNE 11

Southwest terific wind local duster A.M. . . . Pop rolled out 3:30 went to work till 8 A.M. came home & eat his breakfast Ma was eating so he joined in. That was the second breakfast there was to get 8:15 after chow he watered the hogs and fead the Jersy went to the field and loaded his Puddler or dammer which he had torn all to pieces. Brought it home on the Hoopie Mabye that's what breaking the Sabath does. . . . At 9 A.M. Pop shaved cleaned up dolled up and drove around to see how Wheat is progressing. . . . At 3.P.M. He went to church to the Ballgame. And very natural Had to stay through all the crash & rain down pour also some hail. He returned home at 6. . . . Mas todays activities also happings of the day has to go down to. She snoozed till 7 A.M. in piecefull slumber while Pop was out disking with his big heavy overcoat on ha. While he was on a spree, she had to work in her old House. Also milk seprate and turn the Cows out. AM. 11. She churned made the completion over 1/2 hour period. . . .

MONDAY, JUNE 12

. . . Mournfull Southeast . . . Ma made a good batch Bread. Had it completed for dinner. P.M. She did a big Washing. Thelma & the kids called after their groceries, which Pop bought for them and 2 gals Coloil to and 1 qt milk. And back to the washing. I washed all featherbed slips also ironing board pad. And a big lotta beside Thelma did a 2 weeks washing to-day.

TUESDAY, JUNE 13

. . . Mr. Foster the Medicine man called at 15 till 2 P.M. Sold Ma handcleaner Horseradish toteled to 50 cts also gave me & Pop a drink of wild cherry.

THURSDAY, JUNE 15

a Local duster occured 3. PM. . . . P.M. it was murky and mornfull wind. The howling of the winds sounded all over the House. . . . Pop rolled out at 4:10. Ma remained in slumber While he was doing all service work. at 5 she awoke very exitenly came to the kitchen in her gown lighting the stove. When Pop entered for chow he seen none grabed up the milk bucket, and went to milk he paused for a moment. took it like a man Saying whell its real early to . . . eat enyhow. We then got through breakfast at 5:15. At 5:15 he was on his way to the Doer Quarter running the Puddler also the Oneway. . . . Windcharger is just buzzing like sixty. Ma made a Rhubarb cake cleaned the Cupboard. yesterday she washed the Doilies for the cupboard. and churned early A.M. made the completion over a 20 min period. Wind is so strong the House just gives ever now & then This seems very uncomfortable. . . .

SATURDAY, JUNE 17

Southwest terific wind at 8 dust occured at 10 kept on increasing at 4 P.M. It was mostly the worst. It kept mostly on till dusk. . . . today 103 degrees . . . Wind raged mostly all Nite along camed toards 4 next morn. Pop rolled out at 3. and worked till 6 all eat at the same time AM. Ma had rolled out at 3:30 Worked in chiffs to-day The men worked on the Combine all A.M. . . . Ma had went after the cows almost sunset to get milked so the Warners could take 1/2 gal milk home. She jumped through two draws had old Roan & the Calf drove through one they turned up their heads and away they went to old Jersy way south by the dam. So old Ma came home almost dusk all scratched up tired & worn out sick headache and not being able to go to the dance. Pop went, she was very glad to roll in and rest after enduring all these adventures to day P.M. . . .

SUNDAY, JUNE 18

. . . terific wind dust blowed for a while at 9 A.M. It camed down. So the rest of the day, it was beautiful . . . In the night we had a terif. duster. We rolled out at 6:15 Pop included. It was just one of them things. The day after the Nite before. Pop had gone to the dance and returned at 2 A.M. With Car Fender all bunged up. This incident happened while pushing another Car . . . Pop dear went to Syracuse to see if he could get the Radiator for the Combine fixed. No he couldn't. . . . We returned home at 6:15 P.M. . . . He eat a cold supper to make work easy. He milked old Jersy & feed while Mo milked old Roan. . . .

MONDAY, JUNE 19

. . . Just one puff of dust while we where dinnering at 12:15 . . . We rolled out 4:15. Got through with breakfast at 5. Mo milked old Roan, while Pop pumped Jersy & feed the calf. . . . Pop didn't get started before 6 AM. on his way to Dodge City. Henry eat at Dodge returned home at 4 P.M. . . . 4:30 they went to cutting Wheat at 6:45 they came in from the field at 7:45 they suppered. . . . Mo worked so steady & kept on going so fast that she was all tired out at 4:30 with the back-ache. She had the House to go over after such terific duster seprated churned . . . baked Bread. . . . It was blue Monday when all things go wrong. Her ears bobbing up & down P.M. . . . she was all faged out. . . .

TUESDAY, JUNE 20
. . . it was dusty & murky A.M. We rolled out 4:15 breakfasted at 5:25. Men went to the field at 6 but only started in cutting 8:30. Brought a Truck load of Wheat in at 9. A.M. . . . Mo made three Pies A.M. one Plumb & two cherries She cleaned up the House washed lampglobes. Also rit her dairy. . . . At 6 A.M. Thelma apeared on the scene & helped. Ma wash her breakfast dishes. Next she carried 1 pail of slop to the Hogs. . . .

WEDNESDAY, JUNE 21
. . . terific general duststorm occured at 2:30 P.M. It was so dark for a 1/2 hour, that we had to lite a lamp. . . . Cliff stayed all Night eat breakfast so Ma had four men including Pop. They cut another load wheat. . . . It rained enough so the men couldn't work for severel hours. . . .

SATURDAY, JUNE 24
. . . Terific duster P.M. Mens work. We rolled out about 5:15 Had breakfast at 6. Pete took the hoopie to the field, to fix on the combine. Henry went to Bishops to get his Truck Cliff went with him. He halled a load Wheat to Kendall in Bishops Truck. . . .

SUNDAY, JUNE 25
. . . Ma rolled out at 7. Cause this is the good old Sabath. So one dont need to rise so early. Pete & Henry had the milking and choars all done. . . . Pop & Pete went to the field after chow to fix on the Combine Came in brought it as far as south of the House Wanted to take it to Trussels. But weather wasn't favorable In the After noon they made two rounds. . . . brought in the machine. P.M. after finishing up for this year 1939. . . . While Ma was washing dishes to-day A.M. With House all full of dust Charlie Roberts & Cliff apeared. It was very

much embarsing to have things so untidy. They came after Bread milk & Coloil. for once in a long time Pop did the seprating ha ha.

WEDNESDAY, JUNE 28
. . . At 2 P.M. We started to Holly. I got my teeth after having them relined I churned while Pop was breakfasting. Henry bought me some ice cream. Bought Tobacco both kinds matches and tobacco for Pete. We had returned at 6. . . .

THURSDAY, JUNE 29
. . . Terific duster 7 A.M. lasted a 15. minute period. . . . Flies where terific to-day I put up the daisy fly killers to get some of them cant keep them down swating. Are to thick. Ma had a terific spell with her ears again this day. . . .

FRIDAY, JUNE 30
Last June day. Goodbye old June month. A beautifull day. . . . An Indian Doctor called at 3 P.M. Stayed for almost one hour He treats the people with Hurbs. . . .

SATURDAY, JULY 1
The most beautifull duster you ever saw It was just in rools & so very gray. rolling clowds. . . . Pop milked while Ma started churning. While Henry devoured his breakfast she finished churning. At 9:15. Pop took some gas down to Trussels with the hoopie. And run the Combine while Pete went to Town to Celebrate after 11:30. . . . Pop returned from Trussels from work at 7:15. he was needed at Combine for some help A.M. . . . Ma baked two Butterscotch Pies. Gave Thelma one. She seprated made Bread, and gave Thelma one loaf. Later she washed Windows. And Lampglobes. Ma took her bath at almost dusk, while dust, & wind was ragging. PM. She had scrubed both floures.

MONDAY, JULY 3
. . . Pop worked on the 160 ackers to list P.M. he moved to the old 80 ackers No duststorm now for two days how nice.

TUESDAY, JULY 4
. . . Duster 9. A.M. . . .

THURSDAY, JULY 6

Southwest wind also dusty P.M. . . . A very hot day 109 degrees today. . . . Pop snoozed 2/3 hour also read a little while it was so 189 terriable hot. . . . Pop suppered at 7 so he could roll in real early after milking Jersy. Ma sloped the Hogs also seprated tonite. She washed 1939 Lampglobes. And straightened up the house. . . . AM. she washed severel garments. Seprated AM. Cause the Cow had rolled around in menure. She had to have a while to dry Pop couldn't milk her. We retired with the chickens. Went to roost by the moonlight. Was no need in liting a lamp. . . . At 10 AM. Leroy was asleep out on the hoopie while he'd played there got tired and fell asleep cliff carried him in. He then finished his nap on the Davenport over a period of two hours. got up for dinner with a smilling face. hadn't eat a bite since breakfast. played & contended all day long while he was visating with Grandma. . . .

FRIDAY, JULY 7

. . . We rolled out 4:30 Breakfasted at 5 and Pop soon went to Trussels fixed on combine returned home at 9 A.M. over noon hour period he made 6 rounds for Pete. He got home at 2:15 P.M. We dinnered at 11:30 So he got an early start. He radiod also libertied during some of his leisure time. He helped me dig around the Trees also carried about 12 buckets water to them. . . . Mo worked over one 1/2 hours period to get the trees taken Care of also does away with the junk in the comode drawer. . . . A.M. The Government distributing Grasshopper poison, stoped to get some water for their outfit . . .

SATURDAY, JULY 8

. . . 7 P.M. A black duster occured . . . The Warners called at 7 A.M. just as Pete got through with breakfast. he was here for dinner, also Warners family. Cliff got the cows with the Car he milked in the midst of the duststorm they left. I gave her 10 Eggs 1 gal milk and some Butter. Thelma baked some exelent pies one raisen, & two Plumb Pies. Mo Baked some good Bread had it completed at 11 A.M. Flies where so terific stung one out and in doors. I kicked like a horse. While seprating and filling fly killers. Well Mo had her hole afternoon clowded over no sunshine to get ahold of. At 7:45 she boo-hooded around till she fell asleep along with all she couldn't hardly hear a thing all sounds where so dull And ears where driving her nuts while they where throbbing tremendously. Thelma was felling tuff babies where cross all A.M. And all things went wrong. P.M. children where good. Patsy slept 1 1/2 hours in the soft Rocker Leroy never took a nap. . . .

MONDAY, JULY 10

. . . Pop rolled out at 4:15 Ma came out of the Hay at 4:30 We breakfasted at 5. where alone. Soon Cliff apeared alone & at 7 Pete apeared on the scene. So Ma had to get another breakfast. In the meanwhile Pop had gone to the field in the hoopie. They all puttered around till 8 A.M. Henry & Pete went to the field north of Ault to combine returned at 11:45 for chow at 1 P.M. They took the Truck to the Wheatfield. Cliff was here for dinner, & went to the field 12:45 Men came in for chow with a Truck load Wheat. containg 60 bu. Going back to breakfast When Pete entered at 7 He smiled and said When a man comes in this late for chow without eny trouble. He ought to be fired ha . . . I churned the old Cream early . . . It'l do for frying. Ma made 3 cherry Pies from the white ones She was angry When opening this can, she spied that they where not seeded She had to seed them. She made a good batch Bread. . . . She gave the House a theour going over. While yesterday she had such blue and uncontrolable spell. She couldn't do a bit of her housework just cook wash dishes & swept and cleaned herself up. To day was a beautifull day for Radio wasn't a bit static till 3. P.M. Mo listened to all her epesode she usualy does. . . . The Anouncer for Lux was a scream. No advertising all he did was to sing songs Apraising Lux flakes also soap. . . . I certenly did get a chance to enjoy a clean House for once and it stayed for a while to. . . .

TUESDAY, JULY 11

. . . We rolled out 4:45. Very lazy, in a week day for a change. . . . Pete & Henry where doing some tinker work, while Ma churned. . . . They started to the field at 7 after being detained by Mr. Ault wanting to know where his Hogs where. . . . Pop read the Mail for 1 1/2 hours trying to relax. From all abuse and hard nocks running the Combine . . . This P.M. Was to dusty to wash. . . . I certenly enjoyed a clean house for 2 days, for once in a long period of time. I'm still on the job filling fly killers also seprating.

WEDNESDAY, JULY 12

. . . today warmer 103 degrees. . . . Mo hurried around & went to town with Pop at 9. A.M. He paitently awaited for me. Toots called before leaving also Mr Jourey. He hawled 1 pickup full of Wheat for us charging 3 cts a bu. for hawling. Got 52 cts a bu for it.[9] . . . Ma didn't wash A.M. cause she went to Syracuse. P.M. To much dust to do a good job. At 8:30 We rolled in Pop thought it was to hot to sleep & decided to wake for the fore part of the night. I was so tired didn't mind sweating, slept through all of it. I got weighed to-day had gained 6 lbs. Now weigh 150 lbs.

THURSDAY, JULY 13
. . . today 104 degrees . . . We rolled out 15 till 5. Breakfasted at 5:30. Made more progress even if I felt as though I was just half there. . . . Mo has swet more to day as she has in a long time. It seemed so hot she just cizeled and fried. . . .

SATURDAY, JULY 15
. . . Southwest wind terific dust occured at 5 A.M. And kept on increasing. Raged through all the day. Camed considerable at sunset. But still blowed on Murky and hazy sky all A.M. . . . We started at 2:15. returned home at 6:45. The kids bought some steak so we all had a steaksupper gravy salad. & Bananas for desert. A very intresting supper kids left for home at 8:45. And Henry went to the dance at 9 and returned at 10 just as I retired. Ma writ the direy & rolled in at 10 min. till 10. . . . I rolled out 3:30 started the fire, put on the washwater on went back to bed & slept for 1/2 hour started to wash 5:30 and finished 9 A.M. And such a dirty & greasy combine clothes, and o such mas of it. I used way more fuel as I usualy do. For just our own washing. It was so dusty that the clothes I hung out was a terriable looking site. . . .

SUNDAY, JULY 16
Southwest wind at 6:15 it increased 2 hours later it was terific also a local duster. P.M. A terific duster camed 6 P.M. . . . today 100 degrees. . . . Pop rolled out at 5 Ma 6:15 got buisy, rinsed and hung up her clothes leminating the Overalls & dark Shirts. Pop was making his breakfast when I came in from hanging out my clothes 7. Spose he had a hollow belly ha. He fried some eggs and Bacon. Ma fried herself some Spuds no Eggs. Pop enterained him self by running the Radio all A.M. also read Papers. No Work till noon. Warners apeared on the scene at 20 min. till 12. . . . They got the Cows put on the stockrack. loaded old Roan and her calf in the Truck at 5:30 P.M. Henry & the

little Warners started on their way to the Willet Farm. Cliff Ma & Thelma followed in the Car.

MONDAY, JULY 17

And at 3.P.M. sky clowed over again. In 20 min. A black duster occured. It laster 2/3 on an hour. . . . Thunder kept on increasing at 15 till 6 a big rainstorm occured. . . . Murkry had fell from 105 degrees to 82 at 3 P.M. at 7 P.M. it had fell to 63 degrees terific wind cont. mud 1/4 inch water fall. terific wind tore the west window out with frame on well house. . . . Ma rolled out at 4:15 And started to churn. She completed it over 3/3 of an hour period of time. Remained in slumber 15 min. longer When churning was completed at 5 she got breakfast. . . . Henry didn't eat much dinner to-day & said Its to hot to eat. . . . Ma cleaned all rooms in the house limanating Vernas Bedroom also cleaned the cellersteps. Only enjoyed the Clean House 1 hour till that incident occured. Such storm that the West window in the Wellhouse frame & all was torn out. In all the storm I made 2 boxes of lye into soap with the old olie we couldn't eat also the butter from the fresh Cow that we couldn't eat. Ma was so sick to-day while getting the drown mouse out of the soap grease she gaged & gaged. and had to take two doces of Mountainhurb Liniment to get back to normal. Poor old Jersy has almost bawled her eyes out on account lonyless. . . . this was one day that Ma didn't get to enjoy her cleanhouse just 1 1/2 hours. She was making starch to starch her clothes when the duster occured. She was so tired she was more then to glad to roll in.

TUESDAY, JULY 18

. . . Pop rolle[d] out at 5, And Ma slept till 5:45. She certenly did enjoy it. Was so deep in slumber, and not knowing it was time to get up It was so nice & cool. Henry had milked turned out the chickens & was reading papers. We breakfasted at 5:10 he radioed a while. . . . Ma mixed her Bread at 8 and made the completion at 15 till 11 A.M. Aunts are just thick in the House, and out on the Poarch. . . .

THURSDAY, JULY 20

. . . In the night dust had blowed considerable House was all dusty when we rolled out. . . . today 102 . . . Pop rolled out at 4:15. Went up north and puddled came in for chow at 6:20. Ma had rolled out 4:30. . . . We started to Syracuse 7. A.M. & returned at 20 min. after 11. Kids stayed for chow Henry & Cliff cut 20 bu. Wheat made 2 rounds on Louis Lameyers field came in from work almost sunset. The Warners went home at sunset. . . . I was all exausted from the afects of hurring after taking my bath. And hurring around to get the work done up I certenly felt tough from the strane. Run around bare-footed while washing dishes also Seprator. Not carring whether Cliff was present. . . .

FRIDAY, JULY 21

Northwest early durster continence of about 3 hours. . . . today much cooler 95 degrees. . . . Ma rolled out at 4. started in churning made the completion over a 15 minute period. Pop slept till it was all done. He rolled out at 4:30 I cleaned up the House before getting breakfast. We eat at 5:15 Cliff apeared at 6:30. They fixed on the Strawrack for the Combine. Till almost 10 A.M. They started cutting. . . . worked till 7 . . . Ma had missed out on the dairy yesterday so she had to write down for yesterday, also to-days. She had to go through the same old routeene as usual after enduring a duster, and not getting it cleaned up. . . . Going back to churning this A.M. it was so warm at 4 A.M. when I rolled out I took the churne out of doars to protect it some from being so soft. Howling wind most of the day

SATURDAY, JULY 22

a local duster occured about dusk not lasting long very cool & comfortable. . . . it was dusty at 5 P.M. We had a duster from the southeast . . . We rolled out 4:30 I didn't get breakfast right after I got out of Bed. Did other little ods & ends. Pop had all done at 7 ready to start to the field when Cliff apeared. They only cut 50 bu. all A.M. on Lameyers field, so at 12 noon they pulled the outfit in . . . Ma did little cleaning and straiting out but no dusting. She felt so tuff she couldn't get much done. her head hurted and some more ear trouble to gether half unbalanced. Lampglobes she washed which was very necessary. Hens where very disobident this day again smashed two Eggs and 8 of them left. They have been very good for severel days. . . .

SUNDAY, JULY 23

. . . terific wind local dust PM late before rain occured. Po rolled out at 5. when 15 till 6 rolled around he caled me out of my slumber. Wanting to know whether he should seprate the morning milk first to keep it sweet to make ice cream . . . 10 A.M. Henry had the cream all made . . . Ma was cleaning the floors the Warners apeared . . . After Chow the Warners went to Olins to help him cut Wheat . . .

MONDAY, JULY 24

Southwest terific wind local dust. . . . We were very much slowpokes after enduring such nice cool night tryed to make it last just as long as possible. . . . Henry went to work at his drills and stayed with it till 10:30 He went to inspect the rain fall on his land which he works. . . . At 1:30 P.M. he hooked up to the one way & went to the Doerr quarter to work retur- at 5 P.M. When a duster had occured & admedietly it was so dark that we had the Lamp lit for 1 1/2 hours till it cleared up and the sunset clear. It rained almost one inch. The draw just roared & frogs croaked all the harder Ma did some mendining some of her dresses while listning to the Radio. . . . Ma hasn't felt nearly as bad to-day. But her Ears are a fright. She got another shock as usual by getting out of seprating ha. Secont day in succession and fourth one on Record since Jersy has been fresh. . . .

WEDNESDAY, JULY 26

. . . No dust now for the second day in sucession. . . . Mas to-days work was clean house washed Lampglobes sewed & patched some also washed her Head. and washed severel garments also including Couple dish towls also handtowls. Flying Aunts just piled on both doors west also east. Old Hens not to buisy only layed 8 Eggs & not broke eny either

THURSDAY, JULY 27

. . . [Pop] drained the storage Tank, beings a sparrow had fallen in & drownd. This incident was enough to loose your appetide ha. Such incident occured 4 weeks ago & o it was enough to get sick. I certenly did feel tuff It took mostly all AM To bring me out of it. I took an asprin to do away with all misery. . . .

FRIDAY, JULY 28

. . . Henry rolled out at 4:15. Ma didn't wake up till 4:45 she was told by the Mr He couldn't stand no fried Eggs on account the dope that he used to treat the grain with made him think of rotten Eggs so he could go them. . . . Seemed sorta nice no dirty filty towls nor a dirty Husband to look at with a weeks groth stuble on ha. Ma sorta rejoiced over his apearence I was all faged out. Not feeling like taking my bath

just washed my feet. . . . Mr Barns called selling cherries 5 cts a lb.
I bought 20 lbs. of then.

SATURDAY, JULY 28
. . . we started to Syracuse at 11. AM. Thelma went to see Dr Grisom
while Ma & the little Warners awaited in the Car We returned home
at 20 min till 5. Thelma was sick. Henry & Mary took her home at
5:20 on our way home we stoped at Iva Klossen and returned home
at sunset. Henry started to the dance at 9 . . . Going back to some
thing that one apreaciates. No dirty man nor clothes to look at no
hard work was done at our ranch to-day. The Mr was all dressed up
and didn't do a bit dirty work. So putting it this way, shall I say. The
Mrs. Certenly enjoyed this day ever min. of it. Even if she had to do
her Saturdays work take her bath and wash the seprator. She certenly
did enjoy all this was not even tired when Night Came along. She got
up in the Night and churned She was out 75 min. sleep over all. Butter
was not to soft. The dasher almost went haywire she just got the
Butter completed before it came apart ha.

SUNDAY, JULY 30
. . . At 10 A.M. Henry went to Kendall bought a piece of ice also a
big Watermellon it was lusious. In the meanwhile Mo had cleaned
herself up cleaned Vernas Bedroom at 12 noon we drove to the Warners for dinner. Going back to breaking the Sabath he beat the rug
before leaving for Kendall. We retired before dusk not lighiting no
Lamp before retiring. Henry went to Slumbering just as he hit the
Bed. While Mo strained the Milk and washed straining rag also the
Milk Bucket.

MONDAY, JULY 31
Southwest wind terific all day local duster continued till 6 P.M. . . .
Thelma meet Iva Klossen on the Road driving Mrs. Klossen over
here on her trip back after delivering the Gas. I aired the Bedding.
that's about all I did to day. Just entertained our Company. Washed
some underthings the seprator and cleaned up the House. Thelma &
I seeded the cherries and cooked some soup also sauce out of them.

TUESDAY AUGUST 1
Well I'm beginning in on this dairy with the beginning of another new
month. With good cheer & lots of Courege to start this hotest

mounth out right. . . . We rolled out at 5:10. Mrs. Klossen stayed all Nite with us. . . . We did up the mornings work at 9 A.M. We all went to Klossens . . . from there at 10 A.M. Went to the Semetary . . . We returned home 15 till 12. after 5 hours of relaxazation the men made seprate stawls for the Mother hogs preparing them for the adition they where adding to the hog family at the Dyck Ranch they got their work completed and made 2 hog troughs out of a oil bbl. . . . During the mens leisure time 5 hours of it they where comenting on the hot weather. . . . Going back to our adventures to-day. We exploered the Ebenfluer Church after looking over all graves and chating about all the dead which where resting beneath the sod. We went inside the church & o the dust 1/4 inch thick all over flours steps benches also chairs. And was it ever a sad affair. . . . While visiting at Adolph Klossens The Rawleighman was there he had four flavors of the Nectar drinks. He treated us all to just as much as each one wanted. Iva had ice cubes enough for all the drinks to be very cold, and delicus. . . .

WEDNESDAY, AUGUST 2

. . . little puffs of dust ever little bit . . . Ma felt very tuff to-day with out the pain in her right ankle. . . . washed lampglobes washed and ironed my dress the Sunday go meeting ones also ironed the lawn ones. I got up about 3. this morning and churned, while it was cool. I churned over a period of 2/3 of an hour. It wasn't to soft. . . . This day nine baby pigs came to make their future home with Mrs. Mother Hog. At the Henry Dyck ranch.

THURSDAY, AUGUST 3

. . . A duster occured just blowed for about 20 min period . . . The Warners apeared on the scene, at 7 & was all dolled up ready to go to Dr Karbers sale. Thelma drove down to Eldas to see if she'd beak my Bread The Rogers where going to so I sat it on the table and thought it'd go to waste. But it hadn't risen out of Pan I baked it at 4 And it was just fine no damage had been done for it. Henry said O Ma your Bread is good ha.ha. At 9. AM. We all started to the Sale Things sold very good We all enjoyed ourselves had a fine time. Where sory when it was time to go home. We returned home at 4 P.M. . . . I bought two Cones Vanila ice cream Cliff bought the kids one Buns & Weinies where very good. Henry & Cliff bought some for lunch also for dinner. They certenly where louises [luscious]. The Rawleigh Man was at the sale. Was very jenerous treating people to his drinks. He offered

me one. And did the little ones ever enjoy it. And certenly did drink
a lot of it

FRIDAY, AUGUST 4

. . . It was a very fine piecefull August day very enjoyable. One felt
contented after enduring such pleasure the day before to day. . . . O for
Ma this was the day after the enjoyable day before she had all her
breakfast dishes setting supper ones to from being out entertaining our
company. She certenly washed dishes including Seprator 2/3 on an
hour. P.M. she did a big washing all washes hand towels also lotta
sheets pillow cases which added that much more to our household
while our visitors where with us. She started at 1 P.M. washed over
a three hours period. But when the wash was completed old Ma
couldn't find no place to relax, was so tired and sick from the effects
of it she drug herself to Bed not knowing how to comfort herself.
And in the night the Mr let the gate open & old Jersy got in the Barn
and foundered herself[10] . . .

SATURDAY, AUGUST 5

Southwest terific wind. . . . And ever little bit a puff of dust rolled
along it continued all day and camed at dusk. . . . We rolled out at
4:30. Henry kept the ball arolling very quickly he wanted to seprate,
before the milk got cold, so the calf wouldn't refuse to drink not being
use to skimed milk. We robbed him on account making ice cream
tonite . . . 5:30 Henry was on his way north rod weeding on the Widows ground . . . came in for chow at 6 but he supered on icecream
and crackers. We made one freezer it was very rich was made with
one can of Iga milk it was served with cake which Zelda had baked
also crackers where served. . . . Well going back to the evenings enjoyment. We chated & had lots of fun. Elmer Dyck and wife left at 10
the Warners 15 min. Later. We rolled in at 10:20. All where full of
cream and I think Ma had to much to suit her stomache.

SUNDAY, AUGUST 6

. . . A terific duster at 4:30. Not lasting over 1/4 on an hower. . . .
Henry rolled out about 5 and cooked his breakfast after he had the
cow pumped. Was reading Papers at 7 when Ma took a notion to roll
out. She tended to her activities about the seprated milk & Cream also
water Hens. . . . She mixed a lousious freezer of ice cream which
mostly consisted of 1/2 cream. To do away with 2/3 of an hour she

washed the seprator also cleaned up the mess which was setting from last Nites social gathering. Another hour was spend cleaning up dusty flours and bathing also combing her hair. . . . We eat the good ice cream in a jiffy At 1:20. . . .

MONDAY, AUGUST 7

. . . Northwest wooly day a local duster occured at 9. A.M. has contributed raging on till dust camed at 6 PM. But wind wisteled raging on. . . . Henry got started to the field at 6. . . . came in at 3:30. To dusty he read the Liberty Magazine . . . Henry carried 18 buckets to the tree close by the well house over his noon period. And also dug around most of the Trees I caried the hose from tree to tree eregated all A.M. And most all P.M. And gave all the Trees a good soaking. The ones that where near by the house. I took the old wooden Tub, and filled it so I hadn't so many steps to make. P.M. and sewed at some slips while waiting on the tub to fill up also writ the dairy while waiting. Patched made some starch also starched the clothes which had been left over from last washday. . . . All AM static was a nucence. Still I could haar the Unity Insperation Henry & Gerome on their 2 15 min period also the 7 usual plays each day [11] . . .

TUESDAY, AUGUST 8

. . . a very nice cool day to go through. Which made one feel fresh and clean. And not sticky from swet ha. . . . before chow Pop dug the silt away from the southside which had piled up in terific wind. . . . The men fixed up the panels for the female hog awaiting for the hog family. . . . The Warner family arived at 8:30. Stayed for dinner and left for home at 5. P.M. Ma didn't do much just got some chow swept the House washed severel garments also sprinkled them down. . . . The flies are to much confusing to do much of a job writing. Just a few are in doors to pester me. . . . After all activities where done for to-day Ma read a story by the name Kept Husband in the True Story magazine. . . .

WEDNESDAY, AUGUST 9

. . . dust occured ever little bit an all day . . . Wind ragged on till in the Night We rolled out at 6 Pop did all choaring before chow. He never seprated I wanted the milk to clabber for cheese also cheese dumplins. So there was no seprator to wash. Something a missing. . . . A.M. Ma cleaned all rooms also did some dusting P.M. She washed lampglobes She also churned early AM. Made the completion over a

12 min. period. Butter was very nice to take care of cause it was so nice and cool. At the close of the day she cleaned up junk, also burned some. Such endurence of howling wind wore me out to a good for nothing. . . . her cut finger continued painfull and a headache occured P.M. at 4. And a continous throbbing in her ears. This week end completes the 8th week since I havent wore eny socks cause my shoes where to small to wear cotton ones which where patched cause I didn't have eny silks to wear for everday. . . .

THURSDAY, AUGUST 10
. . . Mos working activities wasn't to inthurastic [enthusiastic] to-day. A.M. She sewed a little washed her Head. P.M. She ironed and did a little washing. . . . Wayne and little kidies called to-day AM. Brought the hoist back. Was very much disoluisened about the rain. Dust conditions and no prospects for crops. . . . Tonite, while Henry was dry — his face. Sneered at me and said, I'm going to buy some handtowls Saturday when I go to Town. These old cheese cloths, are so thin, they wont dry ha. So old Ma preceeded to have a handtowl worth while for him the next morning ha. One that was serviceable, thick one, that'd bring him satisfaction. This was a lonesome and quiet day only Wayne called and just talked a minute or two.

FRIDAY, AUGUST 11
. . . Wind came up went to the southwest and blowed by sprts also a little dust of whirlwinds rolled along. . . . Mo had a tuff day of it. Had a headache. Also got exausted from the heat she didn't do hardly enything excepting cook clean house and tended to her Chickens Her sore cut finger from efects of the grader certenly was painfull. We seen the most beautifullest pink clowds to day and red sun set. Redish big clowds mostly looked like mountains where very beautiful.

SATURDAY, AUGUST 12
. . . Cliff and little ones had arived at 6:15. They ground feed till mostly 8 A.M. he drained the oil out of the tractor and did some other work. They left for home at 9. And we left for town . . . Henry got me some icecream in Syracuse. . . . Henry voted for the highschool building Mo couldnt cause she had sat on a wet spot where Chet Carrol had spilled some Pop on the blanket It was soaked all through her underthings also dress. The men who would have seen her with the wet dress laughed and said. She must have wet her dress ha. . . . Ma certenly went through a terriable day in town. She was so sick. O my she

couldn't find the Car to sit down & relax. And got all the sicker. She couldn't stand up nor find a seat. All she did, was to walk & look for the Car. Hope I dont need to go through such cession again. Pop left for the dance after a chat with his wife. And after their return home from Syracuse. Going back to some of the things I bought to-day. Two little foot stools 30 cts a piece one black one the other blue. Henry was so glad and said I always have wanted one of those. This morning while I was taking my bath, Po was drying himself on the extra thick hand towl. The tan one with the brown strips in it. He smiled and said, O boy this is quiet a contrast this towl being so thick. And the other one as thin as cheese cloth ha. I cant wipe my ears very well with this one. But it's just like I like it. This A.M. While Henry had finished seprating he looked up and seen old Jersy in the driveway of the barn, heping herself to the feed. Pop set the Cream down and run. I spose, he had failed to shut the gate. That was reason for this incident. O O O such howling wind out. Henry returned home from the dance at 15 min till one Sun. morn. . . . Mo rolled in at 11 and a while after retiring she still heard the howling wind. . . .

MONDAY, AUGUST 14

. . . Well Cliffs Sow at last added the adition, to the Warners Hog family. She had 8 babies. Another incident happened. A red half grown pullet fell in the Tank and drowned While Ma was writing the dairy she moved the chair acidently, had her toe in the way it was cut by the glide, under the chair. And o how it did hurt.

THURSDAY, AUGUST 17

. . . Pop was very happy to day after the final effects of rodweeding August 16. Wed. 1939. . . . Ma is on a Hootowl chiff its her churn day she rolled out 20 min till 3. Churned over a 15 min period butter came quicker as it has for a 3 week period. After Completing her butter, she wrote a letter to Ervin, one to Verna, & her two days left over dairy. Which had been neglected. She did all this being in her Night gown. she went back to bed at 4:45 but didn't sleep she warmed up some she had got so chilly writing letters also the dairy with the windows and door. open She rolled out at 5:10 ang got buisy again at work. . . .

FRIDAY, AUGUST 18

To day we started to feed the calf seprated milk in the morning. . . . Pop seprated and went up north to cut weedse also dugout some more dirt. Started in on the Wellhouse at 10 A.M. And realy got into a dirty mess. Dirty as a negro. . . . Po did some more digging P.M. and at 5 he returned to the House to Liberty some more where he had left off. . . . Ma did all her Saturdays work while another another hookie day is staring her in the face Cause Pop is going to Town to settle up his insurence also Taxes. and is going to Holly to get his tooth out. Thats is his plans. for once I scrubed all the rooms and did a lotta Saturdays work.

SATURDAY, AUGUST 19
. . . The Warners arived at 20 min till 10. We all went to gether started to Holly at 1 P.M. Took in the Rodieo Henry had his tooth pulled we returned back to Syracuse at mostly 6. at 7:15 We returned home. . . . While the little babe Warners, had both fallen asleep at 9 they drove home Pop drove to the dance hall, Ma writ her dairy and rolled in at 10:30. Going back to our enjoyments to-day. Thelma & the little Warners rode on the Fariswheel. two different times once on the little train and twice on the Mary goround Leroy once on a horse next time in a little car. Patsy once on a horse & once in a little Car. . . . Henry returned from the dance at 1:30. . . .

MONDAY, AUGUST 21
. . . Pop went to the north field & rodweeded 40 ackers. he drove the tractor down to section 14 it hadn't got eny rain was no moisture and crop looked tuff. So P.M. 6:30 He drove the Tractor home & refused to harrow on 14. . . . Mo cleaned and shined the three rooms limanating her Bedroom and washed lampglobes including her every day acitivatis which are her wifely dutities. . . . Henrys tooth hurted a great deal, after enduring a long day on the tractor he certenly felt the efects of the days work. I started a letter to Verna for passtime while Pop was reading his paper.

TUESDAY, AUGUST 22
dusty morning . . . dust diseapered at 10 A.M. . . . Pop shaved early A.M. To enjoy his lay off day with a clean smooth face. Henry spent most of the day reading rocking himself not much Radio weather to much static and early lectricity. P.M. He sat out on the poarch a while, while he had taken a chaw. He had to devour it. He made a hog trough for the piggies to eat grain out of. Ma wrote a letter to sister Lizzie Made some cornstarch pudding cleaned House after the duster. Which

she did yesterday, but didn't enjoy a clean house very long. She sewed some. Wrote some neglected dairy, wattered one tree cleaned the seprator all up nice. and destroyed some junk. This A.M. She hoot owled another morning churned two batches butter the first batch. She completed over a period of 20 min. The second one for cooking she completed it. over a 20 min. period. It certenly was nice & firm the spred butter. Not so cold churning the first. But the cold wave occured at the second. she was very glad to crawl back in Bed & cover up. and sleep two more hours 10 till 3. . . . This was a beautifull afternoon was very enjoyable. All the Cameness after the storm A.M. Such piece & quiet and contment. . . .

WEDNESDAY, AUGUST [23]
. . . Pop started to Syracuse at 8:30 A.M. To tend to some buisness. . . . He returned home at 6:30 after the Warners had went home. We enjoyed some of Thelmas stories which she'd heard to-day at the farm bearu. . . . Ma had the house to herself she was listning to Dr Malone story. She washed all windows in the house, while listning to all the episodes she so much enjoyes. And does this ever time when she's home all alone playing hooky. She didn't get no dinner just eat a snack . . . Even the water in the fosset was so cool realy tasted very good. All these cool days in august changed the coarse of each day. . . . She listened to more epesodes as she has all this week and part of last week. I even included David Harem. . . . Henry was quiet a spectical to day going to town with his overalls & shirt which was soiled some.

THURSDAY, AUGUST 24
. . . Terific wind . . . very hot for a change 104 degrees. . . . P.M. I cleaned up the flours scrubed & dusted them after the dust camed. And enjoyed it 1 1/2 days for once ha. I was on a hootowl chift to-day 3 A.M. And rolled back into slumber and enjoyed it after I had got cooled off some. While churning. The butter was nice and firm. . . . Well the War summery has kept the radio very buisy. . . . Pop almost got entagnising about me today listning to so meny epesodes, when he was in the mood to hear all the War summerys. Little Warners turned on the hose wattered a tree & run all the water out of the tank so I had to carry water in from out doors.

FRIDAY, AUGUST 25
. . . We rolled out at 5. Had all choars completed before chow had breakfast at almost 6. Henry went a puddering at the drills and let

me have the pleasure listning to the Unity Insperation. Warners called at 8:15. . . . At 11:30 the men relaxed in the rockers with each on . . . a footstool. . . . Pop listened in on the War sumery over a period of 60 min all tole. . . . Today was buggy day. One in the bed pestern Pop. And one under Mos underthings crawling around. And o did she get gittery from the thought of it. . . . Henry stroled around the land that use to be our peach orchard. before this country went haywire. . . .

SATURDAY, AUGUST 26
. . . Pop rolled out at 5:15 Had all choars completed at 6 when Mo rolled out. He was sitting at the Radio listening at the War summery We had breakfast at 6:30. I never heard the Unity Insperation. Pop took in the News & listened to it mostly till 11:15. . . . Then the War summery was broadcasted . . . We started to Syracuse after 11 returned at Dusk. The Warners called right after. And at 10 they went to the dance. Pop also & returned at 12:15 Mo rolled in at 10:30. After writing her dairy. . . . Pops jaw still is swolen & is hurting yet. Its a week ago to day since he had it pulled. I hootoweled at 15 till 1 to day. and completed my task after loosing one hour of sleep. The butter was much softer as it was the last churning. Atmosphere wasn't very cool yet

SUNDAY, AUGUST 27
. . . We had breakfast at 7 Henry listened to the War summerys before seprating and feeding the Calf. Ma Caught two Rhode Island red roosters with the hook. Pop cut off their heads scalded them also picked the feathers off. I completed them ready to eat. . . . P.M. Henry snoosed a little while and got to sweating cause it was to hot to sleep long. He then got up dressed and drove to the ballgame at the Comunity Hall at 15 min. till 3. . . . Henry came home telling the sad shocking news about Mr Oren Jourys death. So that changed the hole coarse of the day. . . .

SUNDAY, AUGUST 28
. . . Pop seprated after chow at 7 he was filling up his car with gas ready to go to Cliff picked him up and drove to Syracuse to have his suit cleaned for the furnerel of Mr Jourey. The men returned at 12 Just when I was listening in on Mary Marlines program. . . . Ma baked 2 fresh Apple Pies also some custerd for Pops supper. She cleaned up the house which she'd neglected A.M. Pop while being up town he bought 1 bu. big very nice Peaches. Pete called after supper to hear the War sumery stayed till 9:30 . . .

. . . got ready and started to the furnerel at 1 P.M. We drove out to the Cemetary at Ulyses returned home at almost sunset. There was a big crowd at Mr Joureys Furnerel not very many at the Cemetary just about 10 cars. . . . This is the first day that Po wore a tie also his tie clasp for a long time. So this was another bath day, also shave day. . . . Henry bought 2 bu. Peaches to day also 2 bu. yesterday. We roamed around in Ulyses boutht 4 doz lids for Kerr Jars one big mouth the 2 doz small. Pop drank bear Cliff Patsy and Leroy a bottle pop. And the two mos, could look on ha.

WEDNESDAY, AUGUST 30

. . . wind terific for a spell a little dusty . . . Very hot for a long time in the evening. . . . after all choars where completed and soon we started in skinning Peaches and canning them. We just lunched Pop at 12:30 & Ma at 1 PM. while Life can be beautifull. She eat her snack at the Radio. Henry skined & scaulded them all while Mo carried Jars cleaned them. Took the seeds out and put them in the Boiler to process one boiler was completed A.M. The 2 boilers where processed P.M. 11 qts where canned open kettle 5 1/2 gals. and 1 qt after it was all done. Pop tore down some of his tractor & Ma baked a peach cobbler. She hoot owled at one after churning 2/3 on an hour 15 to two she rolled back in Bed. She made Bread it was completed over a four hour period.

THURSDAY, AUGUST 31

. . . very hot about 104 degrees. . . . We rolled out at 5:15 seems as if we get more lazier as time goes on & days get shorter. Well this is the last day of August Henry started to Syracuse at 8 A.M. And returned at 5:15 He went to Holly to have his tooth examined & bought 1 bu Tomatoes for 1:15 cts a bu. also 2 doz of lids for small mouth jars. He got the Sept. True story . . . It was a nice quiet day. No dust to entaganize ones mood. I just eat a snack for my dinner. I added the Epesode of Betty & Bob to the rest of the story which I've listened to constently every day when I wasn't absent. I hadnt listened to this epesode for some time to come. . . . The Warners called at 9:15 Thelma went to Bishops to the Sewing Circle returned at 6. . . . The Warners left at sunset Pop & Cliff went to inspect the Moisture. Pete called at 6 P.M. To hear the War sumery soon went away. . . . Ma scrubed the pantry kitchen also toilet she did some patching also did some other ods & ends. Leroy tried to run the storage tank dry he turned on the hose & watered one tree ha. . . .

FRIDAY, SEPTEMBER I

. . . At noon wind got terific also dusty camed about 6 P.M. . . . Pop ground at some valves for the tractor fixed a tire at 7:30 he started my washer. . . . P.M. he helped me skin over 1/2 bu. Peaches started at 4 and completed them at 7. . . . Going back to washing Mo had a great great big one completed it all 11:30. & Pop empted up the water. . . . 7:15 We went to the Weinie roast and returned at 9:15. . . . After all the crowd had left Cliff Adolph & Henry had a chat about the blowing soil. . . . Mo rolled out 20 min till 1. And churned 15 till two. It had not cooled down very much. While she sat in the moonlight churning she wasn't very much in the mood. But thinking it must be done. So it put her in good spirits so she kept on churning by the moonlight & went back to bed at 10 min till one. And after all she enjoyed her slumber much more the later part of the night. as the forepart. Well going back, to the Peaches. We coal packed them on the Cookstove. as We did all the other 3 1/2 bu. . . .

SATURDAY, SEPTEMBER 2

. . . We rolled out at 5. Pop listened to the War summery before choaring. I cleaned & swept the house before chow. We hat breakfast at 6:15. The Warners apeared on the scene at 8:15 and listened to the play Doctor Hilda which lasts 1/2 hour. It wasn't interruped by the War summery. Even the Unity Insperation was [12] . . .

SUNDAY, SEPTEMBER 3

Sky looked hazy and murky to-day Northeast terific wind all A.M. . . . She broke the sabath scrubed all flours and dusted. . . . And the most descouring thing of it all I couldn't enjoy the clean House just about 2 hours till it was all full of dust again. . . . In the evening while Pete & Mr Ault had called to listen to the events of the day which had been broadcasted at short entervalls she snoozed on the Davenport and didn't even hear the final of Mr Rosevelts speech to sleepy to keep her eyes open.[13]

TUESDAY, SEPTEMBER 5

Terific duster Southwest terific wind dust occured at 9 A.M. . . . Sky murky till 4 P.M. It let up. Wind still blowing at 6 P.M. . . . it was churning day she completed it over a period of 28 min. She stayed up and finished the kids letters which where supposed to go on their way to-day. We got a letter from Verna to day telling some jokes one about Hitler another about a pregent dog. ha. This day was a tagnising one o the dust how it did come in . . . She had the sniffels some & had a change with her ears. She couldn't hear well most of the day and all sounds where so dull she was very uncomfortable . . . Was very tired after enduring such duster including all terific wind. I was all faged out from the efects of water hogs also hens. . . .

WEDNESDAY, SEPTEMBER 6
Southwest wind . . . Was a little dusty . . . We rolled out at 5 Static was so terific that Pop refused to listen in what had happened over seas. . . . Ma cleaned house after enduring the terific duster yesterday. The house certenly was full of it. . . . Ma spend part of day sewing . . . P.M. She ironed a two 1/2 hour period of time. . . . writ her dairy and called it a day. She was so hard hearing from the efects of her ears. Couldn't hear nothing from a distance off. Ear drums where pulling down like weights. . . . While Pop & Mr Cobb where out in the car the battery blowed up in the radio. I went to tell him, but didn't make him move a bit, kept on chating. I changed it. And it went right off, so I then could hear Lindas first Love. Henry was very much confused to day while I wanted to listen if Unity insperation was on the air intagnising and left the house

THURSDAY, SEPTEMBER 7
. . . quiet till dusk a northwest terific dustorm bolled and raged in to the night . . . I tended to the Hens before sunrise while Henry was choaring I writ some dairy which I'd neglected. I was so far away from all thoughts Couldn't hear nothing from a distance off yet, ears where still pluged up as they continued all day in such state. Ma sewed some and fixed up the Coushions also made two coushion slips . . . Late P.M. she washed lamp globes and cleaned up in the basement one hour period of time.

SUNDAY, SEPTEMBER 10
. . . Henry killed the brown speckeled Mail hens O how I did hate to see them get done away with. They where so beautifull but to mean to keep for souveniers. My Henhouse visits each morning are not very much interesting to see the flock of chickens since their dismissels. It was almost to sad to eat these chickens cause I just loved

their apearence, cause they where so beautifull We had a pan of gravy some sliced tomatoes noodle soup & sour plumbs for desert. A very fine dinner even if I say it myself. . . . We went Arow hunting.[14] We and Warners. Mo sat in the Car and read the fore part of the story Women in White. While the rest where out in the sand hunting arrow-heads. . . . It was a very beautifull to day no dust no wind. So I certenly enjoyed every 5 minutes of it. and called it a very well & piecefull day. Where sory when one like this one is spend. Even after all if its windy or dusty. I'm trying to make the best of each day. . . .

MONDAY, SEPTEMBER 11
Southwest wind terific most of the fore noon . . . At PM wind & dust had camed. Not terific dust just spells . . . At 7 we had a terific dust-storm which ragged into the night. I rolled out at 5 & Po at 5:25. I had started to churn had churned for a period of 2/3 of an hour Henry finished it. He choared milked before chow & seprated after break-fast. . . . He again took in the news period when Unity morning in-spretation was on, so this has been now the 5th morning. . . . He was in the Rocker all P.M. Till 4 during this time he read a book about War. Listened to some news about War. . . . He choared eat at 6. and rolled in at 8 Mo had slept 1/2 hour in the inviting rocker after her & Pop chated about the terriable War. . . . This duster certenly put the House in fine shape. It certenly was a site to clean up . . .

TUESDAY, SEPTEMBER 12
. . . O boy it was very dusty to-day at times. . . . And o my the house was full of Dust this morning after the duststorm. . . . At 8:30 the Warners apeared on the scene. She sewed at Leroys suit. The men started to Syracuse at almost 10 after the Tomatoes. . . . They returned 4:30 and drove home at 5:20. . . . Thelma & I never cooked just lunched I never did a bit a work. Just what I have to do each day and limnating the noon day meals work. ha . . . Leroy was in an unplesent frame of mind. went to sleep in the inviding rocker, and awoke in a sort a unsetteled mood He wouldn't eat eny dinner. All he'd eat was gingersnaps and tomatoes. He wanted to go to town with the men and later wanted to go up stairs to get Ervins toys ha. . . .

WEDNESDAY, SEPTEMBER 13
Southwest terific wind A.M. Some dust P.M. It was terific duster terific till almost sunset. . . . Mos ears are almost back to normal tonite. She can understand the radio which she couldn't A.M. From a distence

off. She got up at 15 min till 1 churned. She completed it in a 15 min period. And a little after two she went back to Bed. She washed the furniture cleaned the oilstove give the house a good sweeping. And washed the Lampglobes. O say this house was certenly a site. . . .

THURSDAY, SEPTEMBER 14

Southwest terific duststorm early A.M. About 10 A.M. It had let up so it wasn't very hazy at 12 noon it took a new hold & continued till almost sunset it camed. . . . Ma got the operunity to listen to Unity Insperation at 7 at Topeka ha. Pop got beat out of the news ha. I certenly did enjoy it for once after missing out 9 days while Pops presence where in the House. He went to the Comunity Hall to work at 8:30 And returned at 12:15. We had some chow consisting of Eggs & cheese Also Eggs again for supper. Beingens Ma was buisy canning Tomatoes that's why she didn't make enymore dinner. Henry helped me skin some Tomatoes He brought the Jars up the wood in the House and brought the Tomatoes up. Also lifted the Jars out of the Boiler for me. We caned 13 big Jars. And 14 qts two of the large cans where mostly juice . . . Cold packed them on the cookstove. . . .

FRIDAY, SEPTEMBER 15

. . . Wind kept increasing ever little bit. A duster blowed over about ever hour. . . . Henry worked on the drills one hour A.M. 2/3 of an hour P.M. The rest of the day he libertied Couldn't radio much on account lectricity while the dust storm was ragging. . . . Mo cleaned good many things to day had cleaned the House all up & didn't enjoy it very long. till it was all full of dust again . . .

SATURDAY, SEPTEMBER 16

. . . Henry seprated after starting the washer. Next he listened to part of the news & I had got in on about 6 minutes of Unity insperation. Next he jumped in the Car & drove out inspecting the moisture on the different fields, where he's farming and I had to go on washing all alone. I finished up at 10 A.M. . . . Took my bath & got ready to start to Syracuse at 11:20 A.M. . . . We returned at almost 5 P.M. . . . Po didn't go to the dance tonight. This is now the second Saturday. . . .

SUNDAY, SEPTEMBER 17

. . . We rolled out at 6:15 had breakfast at 7 and seprating was done before Leo Odanials came on the air. I was washing dishes at 9. When the Warners called Henry & Cliff soon dissapeared and later about 11:30 we learned that they had been arrowhead hunting instead harrowing Had been to Kendall and got the Mail. . . . After the dishes where washed we started to Elmer & Zelda Mo stayed and visited with her also Leroy. & played with Rogers boys while the rest went arrowhunting to bare creek. But didn't find eny, soon came back. . . . We returned home at almost sunset . . . I had some disy spells to-day. And A.M. right before rolling out I was very sick to my stomache. Felt very much better later at P.M. I couldn't hear at all about 4 P.M. I got so I could hear much better. . . . I was so blue to-day I just lost my sence of balance. Cause so much trips where made the Mr. Not being consertive enough.

MONDAY, SEPTEMBER 18
. . . o so beautifull. No wind nor dust to entagnize a fellow. Clear all the way around Not a clowd in the sky. So piecefull and so much contment. . . . Ma ironed a big lotta clothes all the curtains. They certainly looked nice, even if I say it myself. She did enjoy to iron, this nice day. She washed her head and did some washing. Did other ods & ends. And retired at 7:25 and called it a day. Was so tired and Pop retired at 7:25 Wouldn't let Ma stay up and put up the curtains. Wanted me to get my amount of sleep cause to-morrow get ready ready to start East to Hutch. . . .

TUESDAY, SEPTEMBER 19
We rolled out at 20 min. Till 5. Henry choared before eating. We had breakfast at 5:30. And all soon was started to work. Ma felt so tuff couldn't get started to iron A.M. She washed the seprator cleaned up the dust in most all of the House. P.M. She ironed her clothes pressed her red dress also the Black one packed her suitcase did some mending and hunted up all things that she wanted to take with her. . . . Henry shaved dolled up and went to Syracuse to get his suit Had to wash and clean up the Car, for our trip back to Hutch. He returned from Syracuse at 3 PM. bought a big Watermellon. And old Ma was ironing and trying to clean up the flours. And didn't have much time to eat the mellon on account being so buisy. And didn't get the dairy wrote she just joged it down temperly, and wrote it after our return. We retired 7:15 Henry couldn't stay awake he dreaded to think about stering the old jitney buze [car] all the way to East Central Kansas. . . .

. . . we didn't get started till 6. Had planed on starting to Hutch at 5. But still got there to at 1. P.M. In the mean on the way up we eat our lunch which we had taken consisted of apples plumbs and ginger snaps with us so that was our lunch. Had 1/2 gal. jar full of water to drink. After getting to Hutch Pop found Verna very soon in the Agriculture building.[15] While Ma was looking at the pretty kitchens cakes & baked stough [stuff]. Verna & myself walked around looked at animals and all things which they had on display at the fair. Flowers quilts rugs all sorts quilts Cushions and varies other things stock of all description. . . .

SUNDAY, SEPTEMBER 24
. . . Mo rolled out 8:15 Verna & Patty soon rolled out Pop 30 min. later. . . . At 8 A.M. Cliff & Thelma also Leroy called. . . . Verna washed A.M. Sewed curled Patsys hair Thelma. And give Patsy a manicure. She ironed 5 uniforms and lotta other clothes. . . . Cliff drove to Wayne Rogers to call of their visit. Cause Verna came home. They wanted to visit with her. . . .

MONDAY, SEPTEMBER 25
Duststorm Northeast terific wind early A.M. Continued till almost 9 A.M. Let up some had camed completly at noon. . . . at 5 a terific duster occured. . . . Mo & Verna rolled out at 4:10. Henry at 4:30. . . . So at 6:20 We where on our way to Garden. . . . visited a little at Vernas epartment. Then drove her to her new Rose Beauty shop to get her experience . . . We returned home at 11:15 A.M. . . . my work for P.M. Today was shine flours clean dust in both rooms scrubed. Washed some windows. . . . Tonite she writ her neglected dairy for severel days. . . . This was a very plesant P.M. Cool comfortable and very piecefull It was very much of a contrast. A.M. Such terific duster

THURSDAY, SEPTEMBER 28
Southwest breeze all day till almost dusk. Wind turned to the northwest and o how the dust did roll and terific wind kept on ragging . . . Mas activities where just the same as she has to do every day. Including washed Lampglobes which she does not do every day. Static was thretning all day. as time went on. It kept increasing. This Nite as the wind was ragging. and all things where covered with dust. We two old people both with long faces while thunder was crashing And lightning was increasing, as time went on. Ma was writing her dairy, and Pop

was reading the todays mail and all things where so intagnizing. Such change in the Coarse of the day. Havent had no dust Sat Sun. Mon Tues Wed. So we for once at least could see a clean house for severel days. And enjoy it. It brought piece in ones home contment and satisfaction. So this old evening is a misserable one, also intagnizing. Pop cant radio nor be contended this eve. . . .

FRIDAY, SEPTEMBER 29

. . . The Warners called at 9:45 Where here for dinner. Thelma sewed on Leroys suit. Ironed a dress for me, also the green apron while she had her gas iron agoing. Well back to the dust. I cleaned all bath rooms before washing the dishes. Cleaned some things before breakfast House was a looking site such duster as we hadn't had for a while. I almost lost all my strength just to see it after dawn had came. . . . I mostly hookied all day Just went through the same old routeen which I go through each day including cleaned the 2 flours free from dust. . . .

SATURDAY, SEPTEMBER 30

. . . at 10:45 we started on our way to Lakin to take in the New Courthouse Dedacation.[16] Got all wore and tired out waiting for the progrem to come to a close. And have some dinner. It was almost 1 PM. When we started back to Kendall. All of us ocupents where out of sorts all where hungry. Leroy went to sleep in the meantime . . . Thelma and the little ones came home with us. We made some coffee and lunched . . . We read till almost nine and retired. I got the gigers so I just had to quit and lye down. Po stayed home he didn't go to the dance. This is now the fourth day that my ears have been back to normal.

SUNDAY, OCTOBER 1

Well this is the beginning of a new month. It certenly came in like a Lion. With a terific duststorm from southwest started in about 8 A.M. Seemed as if it had let up around 1 P.M. But not Wind turned to the Southeast and ragged in to the night . . . Lectricity ragged all day while dust was in full blast. . . . We both read in the evening. Cause the old radio stood still on account lectricity. Well this Octobers first day went out like a Lion. not only come in like one early with terific dust.

MONDAY, OCTOBER 2

Southwest terific duster started in early . . . A Howling wind all day . . . Dust camed at dusk wind at 8 PM. . . .

TUESDAY, OCTOBER 3

. . . Mo being not very enthuesastic She washed 12 hankies some dresses & aprons and three shirts. . . . She cleaned dust after the two terific dusters. In the evening she sewed some & called it a day. . . . Well again today two pullets fall into the Tank Pop came to ones rescue. The little baby pig took a notion, to go to some other place beside staying on in this big old world. Mo took a notion to seprate for a change. . . .

WEDNESDAY, OCTOBER 4

Southwest terific duster occured at 9:15 ragged all day long P.M. The wind turned to the northwest. Camed at 4 P.M. . . . The Warners called at 8:35. A.M. . . . Thelma baked Leroys Birthday cake And took his picture with his cake It was an angle food with 5 Candles also pink triming. I gave him 2 dimes, had forgot to buy him something. After she had baked his Cake she patched overhawls and hemed one fancy dish towl. Ma sorta played hooky. Cooked three meals swept the hole house & seprated. Tending to the chickens was included After supper she sewed for about 3 hours. . . . Both ears quit roaring for a while today. It's the first time in 2 years since May. The right one has been back to Normal most of the time for the last 3 days.

SUNDAY, OCTOBER 7

. . . southwest terific duster at 11:15 A.M. camed some after ragging a few hours. And took a fresh hold. And continued till dusk. . . . at 20 min. till one we started on our way to Garden to get Verna. We got home at 5. P.M. . . . The Warners where here when we returned. . . . Henry went to the dance at 6 and returned home at 1:30. the next morning. Patty stayed all Nite with Verna. We got a Card from Verna also a letter from Ervin. He's very happy. . . .

SUNDAY, OCTOBER 8

. . . Henry rolled out at daylight milked choared and drove out to the field to look at his crop returned at 7:30. . . . We seprated & Mo churned completed it over a period of 10 min. She & Verna dressed two roosters. One Buff one & the other was black. . . . The Warners called at 9:30 A.M. Pat had stayed for breakfast also last Nite for supper They all where here for dinner and left at 5 Mr Cob Nada & Della where here to see if Verna would come & work for her Tuesday and all the rest of the week. They only stayed I spose a period of one hour. . . . Henry was just clowning all day along. . . .

MONDAY, OCTOBER 9

Northwest terific duster early occured at 6 Oclock A.M. And ragged on till 4:45 P.M. . . . Ma rolled out at 4:45. Went to the wash house & started the fire Had started to wash at 6:15. Pop & Verna rolled out about 1/2 hour later. . . . At 4:45 P.M. We started on our way to take Verna to Syracuse to Cobs. To help with hair dressing. We returned at 6:10. . . . Going back to our washing activities. We finished up at 9 A.M. Couldn't hang none of it up cause it was to dusty. Verna hung up her Uniforms on chairs & some other necesities and mostly had to iron them wet. Ma only ironed one dress wet. . . . We left our clothes set in a tub and jar till the next day to dry them. Was to cold to hang them out so late about sunset. Ma had a very bad cold yesterday all day also to-day. It took a many a handkerchief to keep her nose wiped. We never seprated this day. And it was a long long day. The way it seemed. . . .

TUESDAY, OCTOBER 10

. . . it was a very beautifull all day long no kinda interference. This day was very much enjoyable and apricate. . . . I hung up all the close which was left over from yesterday, which wasn't dried in the House. I'm still sneezing Coughing. And added some more discomfort to my terriable injuries. Cut her hand and a poke between her thumb and first finger on her right hand makes it unhandy to do the work, with all aches. and pains. . . . Pop got to freezing wearing his shorts and had me to get out his long under to put on. Its a wander, he didn't want the blanket ha . . .

WEDNESDAY, OCTOBER 11

. . . Warners called on their way up to Waynes to a card game I felt so tuff I wouldn't go I had to lye down. I ironed all P.M. Had washed some A.M. And baked 2 Grape pies & 8 Cream puffs 2 where filled with whipped cream and 6 with cream pie filling. I was so broke up all day on account loozing my good pink silk slip which Thelma had gave I had it hanging on the line. Coalmens old big mother hog jumped up and tore it all to pieces. And was I ever tore up about the lost of this slip I almost bawled. . . .

THURSDAY, OCTOBER 12

. . . A very quiet piecefull day which was very well spend with the greatest Comfort and contentment . . . Pop & Cliff took me to the Hall to help the Wimen quilt on Eldas quilt. . . . Well going back to the most apriceated faul day. And all trees are undressed certenly makes it seem beautifull.

FRIDAY, OCTOBER 13

. . . A Local duster occured at 8 A.M. and camed at 10 A.M. didn't last . . . Henry didn't acomplish nothing to-day just choared and seprated. At 9 Cliff Pop & Leroy went to town and returned at 5:30 P.M. Mo just played hooky. Churned made a snack for dinner didn't cook cause no men where present O what fun. Just Thelma & Ma. She just swept the House And made the Bed. ha. . . . Today P.M. While Mo was on her way to get some fuel. on the east wall lay a bull snake a small one. She killed it. Was the first one this 1939.

SATURDAY, OCTOBER 14

. . . southwind. Now & then a puff of dust occured. . . . Ma was so sleepy couldn't wake up. Sudenly she heard Pop Calling get up its late. We huried around and had breakfast 6:30. Men soon started to the field. Cliff & Thelma apeared on the scene also Elmer. Men had a lotta trouble all day long. . . . They cut feed with the Header. . . . Pats stayed all night. She went along to Syracuse with us when we went after Verna after a 6 day period of work in the Cobb beauty Shop. We started on our way 15 till 7. And returned 9. Henry decided he'd rather go to Bed, as to the dance. Cause he was so sleepy. Patsy Verna & I eat a dish of breakfast food before retiring. . . . Mas poor blue flowered bowl which she treasured more then enything Stuck to a crock, and while lifting up the crock. It let loose, and hit the flour in 4 pieces she balled about it.

MONDAY, OCTOBER 16

. . . A duster occured, which only lasted about 2 hours, and let up. . . . the men cut feed on the north field. . . . Leroy came along with Cliff & stayed all day also for dinner. . . . Leroy went to see the men to-day at the field all alone. A.M. All Ma did to-day. Churn washed Lampglobes and tended to the chicken. Verna & myself wrote a letter to Ervin. Mo discovered the pig which drowned in the tank Sun. She wasent aware of it before.

WEDNESDAY, OCTOBER 18

. . . Verna & Ma washed started at 1 P.M. finished up at 4. The machine run out of gas. And stoped. We couldn't get it started, so Ma had to wash over alls 2 blankets underwear also Pops shirts by hand. And Verna did all the wringing by hand, Washing wasn't to big either. Ma seprated, washed some glass doars and Lampglobes. . . .

SATURDAY, OCTOBER 21

. . . We got a sad letter from Ervin to day, saying about his Nees having to be operated on if he ever wants them to get well.

SUNDAY, OCTOBER 22

. . . Has been very beautifull, now for severel days. A beautifull Autum. Verna rolled out at 5:5. Ma & Pop 15 minutes later. She started in packing. . . . 8:8 AM. We where on our way to the train It was 25 min. Late left 9:25. Only Verna alone in one coach. With 2 conducters ha. . . . Mr Bishop called tonite, while Pop was suppering. and told us about the furnerel of Mrs. Freece was to be held to-morrow on Monday instead Tuesday. . . .

MONDAY, OCTOBER 23

. . . We eat dinner and got hastly to be ready to start to Mrs. Freeces furnerel at 2:30 P.M. . . . We drove out to the Cemetary. . . . Going back to the furnerel. She had the most flowers I ever seened. About 30 boquets & Reethes. And o such big crowd. Mrs. Bradoc put a boquet on James grave and wathered them. She layed herself over his Tumbstone and cried, with a broken heart. . . . after pop had retired. Ma balled and shed enough tears to float a battleship. All was so lonesome and all emptness after Vernas departure, made me so lonly and hearing all about Ervins knees in such condition. I couldn't keep from crying. She churned after the letter was rit which was, caturated with tears.

TUESDAY, OCTOBER 24

. . . We went to Carl Griswolds also Max Gums Birthday party at 7 had a card party. Run three tables. At 11:30 We all had dinner consisted of Coffee and Cake. One burned sugar and one white one. Both where birthday Cakes. We returned home at 12:30. Henry was asleep when he hit the Bed. ha. Took Ma longer to undress & get ready for Bed. . . . The sad defate of the little black Kitty who was diseased, had been sleeping with the pigs. When I tried to feed her, she couldn't see the milk I had to put her nose in the milk. today the hogs tore the poor Critter in pieces. Leaving the ribes and bones lay. O O.

THURSDAY, OCTOBER 26

... Dust occured at 9 A.M. A little at noon it got started from new. ... Dust continued all P.M. At dusk it had let up. ...

FRIDAY, OCTOBER 27

Northwest terific duststorm occured early A.M. About 8:30 And kept on ragging till 1 P.M. ... Extremly howling wind all A.M. ... Ma made three cherry Pies A.M. Ironed Pops white shirt washed lampglobes and cleaned up Pantry and the rest of the rooms liminating Vernas Bedroom. I had got all ready to go to the Holloween party and missed Elda she must have came while I was dressing. At 7:30 we started to the Box supper and came home at 10:40. ... Raymond Harrington bought my Pie. We also had coffee to go with it. Henry didn't buy no Pie. Cause he didn't feel like eating, was sick. ...

SUNDAY, OCTOBER 29

Northwest wind dust occured about 8. A.M. Soon it sprinkeled just enough to settle the dust . . . Henry went to Adolph Klassen at 10:15 A.M. And returned 3:20. PM. And never eat eny dinner. He saw on my face that I had balled & was very blue. Just refused to eat. Went to work at his hoopie [truck], and stayed there till sunset. . . .

MONDAY, OCTOBER 30

... Po seprated for me to day for a change. All I had to do to it was to wash it ha. ... I cleaned up all rooms dusted them, and scrubed them. Did a little patching. We had supper at 5:15, and drove down to the Warners and returned home at 9:20. I took the Pumpkin to the little ones for a jackie lantern. Thelma carved the nose & eyes also mouth in it. lit the kandel and o how they did spend their evening with Laughter . . .

TUESDAY, OCTOBER 31

... Ma had broke the Worlds record she thought cause it was her first time, that she had milked old Jersy. Pop was even surprized to learn about it. She went up north of the tamerecks to get old Jersy And just filled up her slippers with silt had to sit down, to empty them up in the mean time so she could keep on walking. Thelma apeared on the scene 1:45 to Bake Patsys birthday cake. It was a very beautifull one an Anglefood all trimed up of the very best. Thelma gave her a ring for her birthday. We baked six Cups of Egg custard from the yolks . . . O boy my feet ache so after my long journey bringing home the cows, had to take off her shoes to relax her feet she didn't know where to put them for comfort. . . . Well this is holloween night & radio has been puting on goast stories and was broadcasting lota laughter about Witches Hoblin & Goblins and Gosts.

WEDNESDAY, NOVEMBER I

Well this is the beginning of a new month and a new day. Is very beautifull quiet and piece. The most beautifull red clowds in the west makes this day very much apriacative and enjoyable. Was something new to look at. . . . Ma ironed P.M. cleaned House A.M. darned some socks and washed Lampglobes. . . . Ma made some coffee Cake Bread and two storie biscuits. Wasn't not so good. Bread was fine . . . We haven't seen none of the Warner faces, for two days. . . .

THURSDAY, NOVEMBER 3

. . . At 1:15 We where one our way to Carl Griswolds to quilt. . . . We returned home sunset. While Ma was away she had a pan of two storie buiscits in the Oven. Pop made up a red hot fire and burned them all black. Where beyond eating. Verna got a letter from her exames from Topeka. Kansas State Board Cosmetology. Going back to A.M. I patched the yellow blanket. And put it on the Bed to comfort Pop so he can sleep warm, & give him real satisfaction which hes been long-ing for, for severel days since Mr Winter man called real gruff. . . .

FRIDAY, NOVEMBER 4

It white frosted early A.M. . . . O boy it certenly made an extremely change, and got down to 10 above it didn't seem so cold as all that . . . Pop Zelda & the Warners played a couple game of cards. to cold to work to-day Pop said. . . . Old Ma didn't do much of enything. She sweep the House. Got dinner and tended to her Hens to keep them alaying . . . after loading the grain A.M. Henry was in a very unplesent frame of mind. Being exausted from the effects of driving Bishops cattle out of our field A.M. Also had to fuss around with them yester-day A.M. So tonite he let out a yell saying Mo, yoll halfto help me out of Bed in the morning I'll be so stiff from all running and exerction.

I got rumatics in my left leg to Nite not being able to hold it still for pains and continued all Nite. . . .

SUNDAY, NOVEMBER 5
. . . all the household broke the Sabath. Henry fenced . . . fixed on the Lister a while. . . . And Mo went the limit. Made 4 Pumpkin Pies A.M. Cleaned up the hole House did all the dusting also scrubing. At 12:45 we had dinner Later she churned washed all lamp globes Cupboard doors one window. Later she sewed some. Next she dressed a Buff rooster for tomorrows Menue. . . . wrote the dairy and called it a day. . . . While Henry was getting the Car ready to go he smashed the old yellow & red slop bucket. he had filled the Car with water. When I discovered it and called his tention to it. He out of sorts denigned it. But was good natured while straightening it back to normel. While driving the Tractor into the driveway he crushed another bucket all to smitereen. ha. That makes two for today He seems to be on the job to-day. Doing away with buckets. It certenly make them get less ha. Thelma called at 11 A.M. With Olin in the Car sitting beside her, wanting some Butter. I gave her two Pumpkin Pies, beings I had baked four. There where more ocupents in her House hold, to feed them two.

MONDAY, NOVEMBER 6
. . . a very inviting day to live through being cheerfull bringing piece & Contment. . . . Pop went to the field at 8:15. drove the tractor to the north field and listed while sowing Wheat. . . . Mas today acativi-ties cleaned up patched & sowed a little and washed some She sep-rated A.M. The cow came in late P.M. So she correled her, and didn't need to get her. Next she milked her. . . . Later in the day she pared 1 gal Pars cooked the cranberries, to put through the Colender, for sauce for to-morrow, for Thelmas Birthday. . . .

TUESDAY, NOVEMBER 7
. . . Weather has been lovely 7 days no dust. . . . Pops work to-day. . . . he planted Wheat . . . We soon left for Warners and took her some cranberries and her birthday Cake which Ma had baked P.M. For her It was supposed to be a white one. But it looked some what yellow. Cause she used butter instead Lard, to make it white. I also baked two cups full of Egg custard from the yolks. And one cranberry Pie Which I didn't get for Witches Night . . . Today Cliff had a boar fight They

where all exited and scared out about the exitement. This was Olins
Mail hog who tried to get Cliff by the pantleg.

WEDNESDAY, NOVEMBER 8
. . . howling wind occured which made one feel very lonesome &
forlorn. A Puff of dust from south & southwest which made the
south murky for a 20 minute period but wind kept on till mostly
4 P.M. . . . Pop dear soon drove to the east field listed and planted
Wheat east of the field . . . Ma patched P.M. Churned A.M. Cleaned
up the House. And had the stomache acke most of the day. She drank
painrelief soda and mountain hurb to get relief. Went up north to get
a basket of wood to get some fresh air while she climed. 30 lister
furrows. A.M. She cleaned the sut out of the cook stove & say it was
a mess Looked like an Engineeer, when she had completed the job.
The melting Coal, certenly did choak it up. . . . Rolled in at 8 while
Henry dear has his face in a truestory. She had reached slumber land
when he came to Bed.

THURSDAY, NOVEMBER 9
. . . Dusty which we haven't experrinced for a week. Excepting yesterday had a little which lasted a period of one hour. . . . Ma spend
another misserable day. With Belly ache back ache and ears not felt to
good. She drank painrelief and liniment to relieve the pains. Had the
trots most of the day. She cleaned House oilstove & the Heatrola. . . .
The Cow came in at 4. So I correled her & saved the trip going after
her. While going to the Barn to feed old Jersy & milk her. The 7
shoats where all nesteled closely together, and mostly scared the wits
out of me being almost dark, not being able to see very good. I had
to seprate this A.M. Milk had soured on account, it being very warm
for it. Got myself ready to go to the sewing circle. But didn't get no
chance to go. Pop wanted to finish up there & no one gave me a lift
ha. And so old Ma didn't care to much, stayed home & finished up
fixing up some underthings ha. . . .

SATURDAY, NOVEMBER 11
. . . It was to beautiful words couldn't began to express the aprecation
and piece we endured to-day. . . . Henry put on his Overcoat & over
Shoes started to the field rather early. Felt rather comfortable on the
tractor, while it was very very cold. With murkry down to 20. It
seemed very comfortable for the first time. Sleeping between the

Blanket up till now It wasn't cold enough, to be sleeping in between the Blanket. . . . We where very cold at the dance cause fire was out & doors open about 75 coupels where present music was very beautifull We returned Home at 6 and started to the dance at 8 and returned at 11:15 There was a big crowd. . . .

FRIDAY, NOVEMBER 17

. . . my embarsing moment occured A.M. While I was washing my teeth. My most importent epesode, was on the air. In the mean while I tuned in on the radio Leaving the teeth on the table While listning to this play I heard a wrap at the door. When I went to answer it At first I rushed and yanked my apron off From the bewilderment, I haden't missed them. Had been so much engrossed in the epesode. Till the caller looked up and said, Say Mrs. where is your Husband. . . .

SATURDAY, NOVEMBER 18

. . . We got a card from Verna from Topeka, and a very nice letter from Ervin from Dexter. While he still is on the section Gandy Hoppers, they call them.[17] Mas saturdays work to-day was oiling all flours scrubbing them dusting. Going up north to the timber. & carried home a big Basket wood which she prepared for Kindling. Later in the day she cleaned up rugs and ods & ends which needed it. She had churned A.M. Henry took a bath after the Gangbusters where off the air. Dolled up & went to the dance, While Ma rit some of her dairy which she had messed up . . . And Henry dear went to Bed at one the next morn. . . . I certenly had a difficult night acked and pains all night long. And froze so much that my back had ice in it, the way it felt. To hardwork for the old hag ha.

SUNDAY, NOVEMBER 19

. . . Well this was the day after the night before the dance. Cliff and Thelma drove up at 10:30. Men broke the sabath and I dont mean maby. To start this day off. first we rolled out at 8. Had breakfast at 8:45. Next the old cow was milked, and chickens got their water and crops. after a while of constration the men where at working at the Truck. . . . Ma had seprated. A.M. She had dusted and cleaned up the House. . . . The little Warners where very quarrelsome to-day The sandman Came to Leroy while Patsy was reading a story to him. She was ofended cause he wouldn't stay awake & listen to her story ha. . . .

MONDAY, NOVEMBER 20

Northwest breeze brought us a very fine and a plesent day Which was very much apracative. Not a clowd in the sky. And o was it ever beautiful to endure such wonderfull day in old dusty Kansas. . . . Thelma arived at 10 A.M. Cliff at 10:45. Men both got ready to thrash. They thrashed three shocks. . . . Ma didn't . . . do much to-day. Seprated washed all lamp globes and doors. The Aladin she had to scour. On account being tourched last night with all that smoke. . . . Leroy took a notion to-day going at the Combine, till he was all greased up. His poor Ma had to put Coloil on them to get it off. He brought his dog with him to play . . .

WEDNESDAY, NOVEMBER 22

. . . This wonderfull days indurence was well spent & enjoyed very much in old dusty Kansas. Seems as if we're living in another world. . . . 7:30 Henry had went to the field. They thrashed . . . This has been a very trying week on hand towls just see how much dirt they could stand from the effects of thrashing dirty feed ha. It'l cost lotta elbo grease

THURSDAY, NOVEMBER 23

Thansgiving This day changed the coarse of this week. Mostly all night long the wind blowd from the North. At 7 A.M. It got higher at 8:30 The dust started in raging after a while it got terific at 9:30. It had camed some. Dust had completely camed. . . . Well alone to-day. all alone just us two had dinner But didn't have no turkey. . . . We didn't even have a chickenroast. . . . Ma listened to so many epesodes, cause they where so good most of them gave thanks for this day. All was very good. I didn't acomplish much washed some also cleaned up the House after the duster. Our Menue this great day was left over scraps from yesterday squash and spuds with the jackets ha. Late P.M. I went to the timber up north after a great big basket of timber. And picked up some junk. After supper I certenly made the time usefull. Sewed up the rug scrubbed both rooms cleaned up the middle Bedroom. And cleaned up more ods & ends. And dusted.

SATURDAY, NOVEMBER 25

Well this is the dawn of a new cold & clowdy day. Even if it was cold it certenly was a wonderfull one. And apricative with piece & contment. No wind much and no dust. . . . Cliff Pa & Ma went to town.

Dolled up in his best and started to Syracuse at 10:20 returned home at 2:30. Early for once on Saturdays. Cliff Warner & family had apeared at 8:45. She and the little Warners stayed home during our absence. Thelma embroaried at her pillow Cases for the Baziear. Little ones played with their domanoes & decaroated them all up with paper dolls and flowers. Had a beautifull flower garden made where Leroy was put through Matriona [matrimony] ha ha ha. . . . We got a very encouriging letter from Ervin & one from Verna having the blues. Poor kid. I was so sick last night, after Pop had went to the dance. I drank painrelief severel doces, and 2 doces soda. To get a relief from pains. It let up some at 11:15. So I rolled in. Read all evening. Sewed a little wanted to sew more, but was to sick. . . .

SUNDAY, NOVEMBER 26

. . . We rolled out at 7. It was the day after the night before Henry got home at midnight from the dance. Henry had a time getting old Jersy home she had went to Waynes right after she was milked. . . . And being very considerate he brought all the milk, also seperator in to be washed. All Ma did was to clean up the two rooms and make the Bed. . . . We eat dinner at 11 and went to Warners. . . . I brought 13 1/2 gals jar home from the Warners to can meat. . . .

MONDAY, NOVEMBER 27

. . . We rolled out much latter to-day. as we usualy have up till now on week day. Henry decided this morning early A.M. Wind was to harsh to go out of doars and get chilled through A.M. . . . Pops work P.M. He went out and dug some postholes. . . . Late P.M. He drove down to Adolph Klossen to see about buying a Hog. . . . Well we've now endured, three days of windy weather in cucession Cant yet, become acustumed to it. such a change. It hurts our emotions. Our soul is willing, but the flesh is week. The beautifull spring weather which we've endured a period of 15 days. Its something which I'll never forget. I can still hear the echoes of it. And smell the sweet fragrents. Will always see its sweet apearence. And the sweet memories linger on. Its almost Comperhensief [incomprehensible] that such beautifull weather ever ever existed, in the Kans. Dustbowl. The past four years. . . .

TUESDAY, NOVEMBER 28

. . . Well this was another day that Pop dear, didn't have enough will power to get out of the House and get started to work He libertied

A.M. P.M. He looked over the mail and swept out and cleaned up the Basement. P.M. He put the new wick in the Aladin Lamp. Ma shined the bowl and globe all up. So now its bran new and serves the same purpose. . . . Ma scrubed the house and dusted all furniture. P.M. She baked 4 Pumpkin Pies and filled up all lamps. . . .

THURSDAY, NOVEMBER 30
. . . Men worked Did some sodering A.M. P.M. Pitteled with the Car. . . . Mo cut a big rip in her thumb, & O how it did sting. It caused me lotta mental anguish ha. After this thumb was cut. . . . The little Warners where in a very unplesent frame of mind. When all things went wrong and no one wanted to come their way. Thelma felt very tuff with her terriable. Cold. Well this brings this month to a close with a misty chilly day. It rolls into the past and never to return again now only one more month in the year of 1939.

FRIDAY, DECEMBER 1
. . . Pos work to-day. Had dinner at 1 P.M. After Pop returned home after being out on a hog hunt He found a 400 lber. At Mr Cobs. . . . Mas work was just a very little. She washed all Lampglobes cleaned up in these two rooms. P.M. Pop seprated, and being very generous he brought in the seprator, also all the milk. And forget the rod for the discs, which he forgets 7 times out of one dozen. . . .

SATURDAY, DECEMBER 2
. . . Pop choared before chow. Dolled up shaved. And on his way to Syracuse at 8 . . . returned at 6:15 P.M. was a period of 10 hours. And O boy was it ever quiet. Ma had a hookie day. She eat a snack at 2 P.M. After she had made the completion of her saturdays work. . . . Pop came home from the dance at [ ] and Ma retired at she recopied some dairy which she had jogged down last June while so buisy in harvest, and a number of interruptions. To make it imposibale to get it rit.

SUNDAY, DECEMBER 4
. . . Got the water on the Cook stove to scald the Hog. the men killed him at 9:15. So we had liver for dinner ha. They cut him up some. at 2:30 P.M. The Warners left. Took some tenderloin along with them a sholder & some liver. . . . All Ma did to day was to Cut out a garment clean up the house & washed all Lampglobes. And be the messenger. boy ha. . . .

TUESDAY, DECEMBER 5

. . . made much progress Pop ground up the Lard and cleaned the Head & feet. At 10 A.M. Ma started in rendering Lard & completed it at 6:30 P.M. . . . The Warners called at dusk. Cliff eat some cranklins the little ones eat fresh ribs and apples. . . . Saturday Thelma helped Cliff top Maze & sprained her wrist. Going back to the lard. We got four gals. 2/3. . . .

THURSDAY, DECEMBER 7

. . . Henry fixed up the Henhouse windows. Set up the Stove. Ma was making Liver sausage. We eat 15 min till 12. At one P.M. Ma started to wash. And completed it at 4:15. She hadn't washed with the Machine for 5 weeks. Just washed a little by hand. And o boy did the Machine go aflying also wringer It almost did the work its self. I certenly can feel it to, on my self. . . . And did I ever have a batch of it. Washed all sweaters and fleece lined Jackets on the place. . . .

FRIDAY, DECEMBER 8

. . . This day was very much apricative for all the living. No wind no dust. And O how Wonderfull. . . .

SATURDAY, DECEMBER 9

. . . Henry cleaned the Henhouse A.M. And hawled fresh straw in it. . . . P.M. He put the ladder in the Truck & crawled through the window. He nailed up the Window and did away with that bird den. So now the Birds wont be a twitteren up there and fite, with each other early after the down of the day. In the mean while, while he was up over head. He brought the dolls down, and the little toys, which belonges to the little ones which they use to play with In their baby days. Later P.M. he took the box off the Truck. And swept the Bedroom, which he filled with dust, while opening the upstairs door. Well to-day was Saturday, and we where home all day, also in the evening. And beings it was Saturday. I had a great deal of work to-do. Went up north to the timber twice, and brought home two big baskets full. Pop seprated this A.M. This is one day we was all alone, with no iterference, nor no one interrupting. . . . Ma started a letter to Ervin. In the meanwhile I got such gitters couldn't write no longer. We got a letter from Verna to-day. And the poor girl is very blue.

TUESDAY, DECEMBER 12

. . . A terific duster in the night. . . . It was dusty today a little while. Wind camed considerable at 3 P.M. . . . We certenly did do some baking. Old fashioned shugar cookies. And next Thelma baked a batch of oatmeal cookies. Both batches where good . . . Leroy was all smiles to-day when he spied the little traveling wagon, which Ervin use to play in his little boy hood days. The little Warners xmas arived to day. . . . Back to the duster in the night. O boy the yard, certenly has been damaged by the duster. Its apearence is all ruined dust is laying in waves & domes. Mo with a bad ache to-day, and a big blister on her lips. And a crip she was to-day. And how, did she look. . . .

WEDNESDAY, DECEMBER 13
Very beautiful It was such quiet day. I dont believe a leaf moved on the trees . . . Mas working activities, was Give the House a going over free it from dust. Washed some windows. Lampglobes shined the caster cups. And scrubed the Toilet. A.M. she ironed scrubed the kitchen & Pantry & baked bread to-day. . . .

FRIDAY, DECEMBER 15
. . . We got a letter from Verna saying. She has a chance to get another job. In McPherson. . . . Wayne Rogers called 11:15 AM. to collect for the xmas Tree. As he entered the House. Seen I was getting dinner, and said. Got dinner ready. I says no I'm sory. You'l halfto wait another 2/3 hours for it. ha. Both Pop Wayne and I Had us a laugh. . . .

MONDAY, DECEMBER 18
. . . Well this new day sorta came in like a Lion. Howling wind occured at 4 A.M. At 7:15 Dust started arolling a little later all was terific . . . It ragged on till 2:15 P.M. Dust had Camed also wind not a bit bad. . . .

THURSDAY, DECEMBER 21
. . . We received a very nice letter from Verna, from her knew place. In McPherson. Well all I did to-day was cook dinner for all the well workers five of them. Churn Baked a batch of Cookies Carried in three Baskets of wood from the trees. And one from the Timber. Later I ironed Pops big shirt. He eat supper at 5:15. Later I had a spell with rhumetism in the right shank. . . .

SATURDAY, DECEMBER 23
. . . The ground was blanketed with 8 inches of Snow. . . . Pops Work. He was the messengerboy to-day for once. He worked on a Tire and tuned to his out door activities. The bluish Jersey. Was the prowd Mother of her baby Calf. at 9 A.M. Today. . . . The Warners apeared

at 1:45 P.M. Car stopped so they got hung up and stayed all Nite. Had to walk in from the hill east of our house. Pops work. He skooped paths, to the Barn, east Henhouse, Granary. Toilet and Grage. The kids slept on the flour retired at 8 Thelma & Cliff in Vernas Bed. . . .

SUNDAY, DECEMBER 24

Whell this day is Xmas Eve. . . . This was a very buisy day. Hunting up the gifts, and wrapping them. . . . The Warners got started home at 9 A.M. Got stauled east of the draw. But managed to get loose again. It took them a period of 2/3 hour to get home. Found her plants froze but 2 and a dead Hen. . . . Henry dear, started to Kendall at 1. P.M. Retur- home after a period of 3 1/3 hour. He fixed a tire. And changed one. Cause it was to slick to travel through the Snow, with the one being worn so much. It was a very hard task to get there & back. We seprated. Ma made Bread. . . . She gave the two rooms a theour going over. And the rest of the House, a lick and a promise and called it a day. It certenly was a mess. . . . We had a underwear party around here to night, after our return from the Xmas Tree. Po was warming his feet & Ma while she was, taking the powder off her face. We returned home at 9:15. . . .

MONDAY, DECEMBER 25

And this is Xmas day. . . . Snow flurries falling all day. . . . Ice cycles on the Buildings. Trees where all covered with Ice and grass Thistels. Weeds. All was so beautifull Stayed on all day. . . . So grown was blanketed with 5 inches of Snow. No wind to cause drifts. Continued till in the night. . . . Well we didn't get to go to the Xmas dinner. Ma made one gal. Fruit Salad. We spend a nice cheerfull day at home. Had all kinds enjoyment over the Radio. . . .

TUESDAY, DECEMBER 26

. . . The ice trees and Xmas had falling off early A.M. Execpting the Evergreen Tree is covered with snow. His limbs are almost dragging the Ground. . . . Snow Fluries fell mildely, and full of moisture A.M. . . . Well I preceeded to have the spare Bedroom cleaned to stay, for a period of severel weeks. While snow is so deep on the Ground. And will continue to stay for a period of time. I certenly enjoyed doing this. And enjoyed ever minute of efforts and energy it took, to put into it. I also cleaned up every speck of dust in the House. Not en-cluding the Basement. Just the Steps. And did away with consider-able junk. . . .

FRIDAY, DECEMBER 29

... At 12:15 We and Cliff eat dinner. At 1:30. He started on his way home. I send the 1/2 Anglefood Cake and Jello, which was left over from xmas Bread and other articles. Also their little gifts, which they never had got Xmas day. . . . Henry motered to Kendall at 3 P.M. To mail the Letters, to the kids. Also got the mail. . . . I never did a bit of work out of doars to-day. Its now one hole week, since the Overshoes. Where one of the most use Its now the 4th day. That I didn't venture out. Except when nature called me out. Yes now for two days ago. It was sweep snow at the Joneses. Instead dust ha. . . . The Roadgrader came by and opened the road by our place. . . .

SATURDAY, DECEMBER 30

... After all choars where completed. Pop says, whell now I'm thowing out the Pipes if they bust. So there it went. Where uncorked in the Basement. Fosset was froze to pieces in the kitchen And how the water did pour out. So Henry took a bucket in the Basement and dustpan. Skooped out the Water. ha. So he had some of his time occupied. . . . Ma got out to day atended to the Hens Carried in some Coal. AM. She washed some under things and socks.

SUNDAY, DECEMBER 31

Well this is the last day of this eventfull year of 1939. . . . Well again It was Sun. And the sabath was broken. By both ocupents. Pop skooped snow away on the east side of the House. So he could put the chains on the Car. . . . At 2 P.M. He started to Kendall after the Mail. Returned home at 4:30. . . . Well I had made the Completion of the Bread over a four hour period. Raisen Bread and Coffee Cake one hour later was completed at 4. P.M. . . . Ma Certenly had a sick spell for a period of some time. Drank Painrelief to bring her out of it. Pop is enjoying himself in a truestory. . . . Henry snoozed in the Rocker a while. So at 15 min till 9. We rolled in.

6. BLIZZARDS, RAIN, AND BOUNTY

1940

MONDAY, JANUARY 1

. . . We rolled out at 15 min. Till 7 Had breakfast at 7:45. Pop seprated next he drove down the road torads Wayne. But road hadn't been driven yesterday. So he turned back home. On his way he met Olin Warner, saying Him & Cliff where going to butcher the old big Stag. So at 9:45 We started to the Warners. They killed him about 1: P.M. We returned home at 4:30 and o did we have a time east of the Hall. We almost got hung up finally he got a new start, and the old Car pulled us home. Olin gave us the Hog head. The didn't get it scawled it was very heard to clean and no one, wanted to bother with it. So we have it ha. Pop skinned it. that was the easiest way. . . . We certenly had a good time today. . . .

TUESDAY, JANUARY 2

. . . Pop finished milking at 8 So we had breakfast at that time. . . . He took a shave dolled up in his gray Trousers. at 10:15. He had started to Syracuse. We sold our first Cream since we milked all 3 Jouries [Jerseys] which toteled to 2.20 . . . And sold our first Eggs since last April Excepting those two dozen to Elda for the Anglefood Cake & 1/2 doz to Wayne last May. Sold 7 dozen which toteled to 82 cts. . . . He returned home at 4 P.M. . . . while Pop was away I didnt do much at all. Just clean up the two rooms fill all the lamps, cleane them and finished write Lizzies letter answering on the xmas gift. . . .

WEDNESDAY, JANUARY 3

Trees beautiful . . . Trees grass, and all bushes full of ice. Everthing was hanging full of icecyles. All out doars and porch steps where all icy so one just went sliding along. . . . After breakfast was over Pop seprated. A.M. He read most of AM. P.M. He cleaned the Barn. Skooped some more real paths smoked the meat. And sowed up the Head of the Warners Hogs. Its now ready to make up. . . . Ma felt so tuff all A.M. She just couldnt get no ware. P.M. She got buisy cleaned up pantry shelves. Swept & dust all four rooms. limanating the south Bedroom. She also took a bath, and washed all lampglobes. Cleaned up little things which had been neglected, for some time. . . . After supper Mo patched most of the evening.

THURSDAY, JANUARY 4
Snow fleuries occured at 4 P.M. . . . All looked like Christmas. So very beautiful. Cant be put into words. . . . Snow hasen't thowed a bit for three days. Henhouse almost broke down, with such heavy snow. . . . Mas the messenger boy. While Ma was giving the House a theour cleaning. Darning Socks. And did some washing. P.M. She banked 4 Pumpkin Pies. Which should have been made for xmas. But on account of being Snowbound and no one could Come she put it off. We gave Cliff one to night while he Called at almost dusk. After Tobacco & Vicks. Mas Gums where so painfull to day. She had to take her lower teeth out to let the cancer soars heal up the time being. . . .

FRIDAY, JANUARY 5
Southeast terific blizzard continued all day. . . . Snow was very full of moisture. It Snowed about 3 inches in the Night. . . . Pop was the Messenger boy. He carried water to the Cows and choared Ma never did a bit of work out. The only time she seen the out doars when Nature Called her out. Way down to the Jonses. She had to sweep the rain & Snow out. It was very slushy out there. . . . Ma spent the [day] Patching and cleaning up the two living rooms. She finished cooking part of the Hoghead. It was so big. filled three kettles full. Henry spend most of P.M. reading the Country Jentleman Leroy felt so proud of his Cap. Put the goggles down & said He was keeping the dust, out of his Eyes. next summer in the duration of the dust-storms ha ha. . . .

SATURDAY, JANUARY 6
. . . Had light snowfluries to day AM. over a period of 3 hours. About 2 inches fell during that period Last evening, in the night. About 5 inches snow fell. And O what a lot was on the Ground. . . . Ice all

continued the live long day. . . . Henry skooped some paths cut some kindlen wood lit some paper. Tried to thow out the frozen pipes, but wouldn't budge. The lantern has been burning 2 weeks under the storage tank. Pop passified himself Truestoring. Rode the Leather chair. . . . Ma spent the forenoon cleaning & scouring. P.M. Patched & sewed. Pop looked up at me, and said, well Ma. To Morrow you wont need to sew. Its Sunday ha ha. . . . Not much radoing going on Cause we're saving the Battry. Its almost two weeks, since the Wind charger blowed up. Mail didn't Come to-day. . . . Last night I got very cold in Bed. While Pop ran away with most all covers. Left me with just one thin blanket as thin, as a slice of ham. During this terific zero night ha ha.

SUNDAY, JANUARY 7

. . . Very cold with murkry 7 below zero at 7 A.M. . . . Pop had more activities to atend to to-day as usual. He carried so much water to the stock. Was the messenger boy. Ma didn't go out to atend to eny work. Cause it was so very cold. Pop torched all the pipes till he got them thowed out. It was froze right on the bottem on the Cement. . . . We all broke the Sabath. Ma baked Bread. . . . She realy give the kitchen and living room, a theour going over. Scared [scoured] & cleaned all lamps, and globes. Pop is passifing himself. Reading Truestories, which he has comented on so much. ha, ha. He rides the Leather chair while reading. . . . The duration of all this day was spent with a terriable back it continued all the while. I was on my feet & working. I was so cold wore my jacket most all day, to keep warm. Was an icecicle all day long.

MONDAY, JANUARY 8

. . . Mo passed the day rummeging through papers, trying to find the Liturture for the wind charger. And sewed some. . . . Well the yellow Jersy was wanting to make a special call to see her gentleman friend. But old Grandma tried to amuze her. Its 17 days ago since she went through the same preceeger. ha. Old mr pipe decided to freeze up last night. We run out enough water, to do us all day. It never did thow all day. . . .

TUESDAY, JANUARY 9

. . . after chow Pop put another battry in the radio. The one blowed up, while Ma was listning to the Guiding Light. Tonite after the Windcharger went to charging Pop passified himself, with the radio. He truestoried Libertied. P.M. was the messegener boy. He fed & watered Hens. . . . Pop listened to Rosevelt speech which laster over a period of 2/3 on an hour. Ma washed some. Churned got butter in a 3 minute period. She rugged most all day. To keep off her feet. She had a spell with her Ears. And o such backache.

. . . Going back to some activities Ma cleaned living room kitchen Pantry also Bedroom. The rest of P.M. She raged and sewed.[1] After supper she washed some and called it a day. . . . A.M. She caned up 8 cans mince Made two Mince Pies. Cleaned up, some ods & ends. . . . Well for a bit of passifying this P.M. Henry popped some corn & we certenly did fill up on wind ha ha.

. . . Northwest terific howling wind whisteled and doors banged northwest terific blizzard. Snow was drifting all A.M. Pops paths all blowed full, which he skooped yesterday. . . . Pop went to work. Cleaned out the barn. Puttered around some at the Car. And lurned that the Battry in the car was all froze to pieces. Was not a very good one, after all. Patched the flat front Tire. . . . Ma ramsacked her bedding fixed up some of them. She completed the one which, she had started in 1938. A brown one. She ruged some & gave the House a theour going over. Washed all Lamp globes. After supper she patched and ruged some more. This is now the second day, that the water pipes hasn't froze. This is now the sixth day that we've had no visiters, No mail now for a hole week. None going & none coming . . .

. . . After all choars where done Henry adventured to Bishop It felt as if he was turned out of prison. After all this long friendly chat. He returned home 10 min. till 1. . . . He took the Tractor drove around by the Mail box to open it Then set it back on its place. . . . At 4 P.M. he looked up & seen a man, with Cliffs telescope hoofing it through the Snow. Stayed and chated over a period of 1/2 hour. It was the first Humen Mo'd seen for seven days. . . . Haden't seen hide nor hair, of enyone during this seven day period. Both of us felt as if we where an imprisoment ha. . . . Reopened the letters, which where stale in the Mail box for one hole week. and added some more to them. . . . The burn on my finger, has been very sore to-day which broke while atending to the washing activities. Henry whiteled down my teeth they'd been making big canker sores, again.

SATURDAY, JANUARY 13

Northwest terific Howling blisserd . . . Banks now 6 ft high on places. Windows are all snowed up. Cant hardly see out. . . . Pop completed the Choars over 1/2 hour period. . . . Next he hunted up, more True-stores & Libertyes, which he hadn't all looked over. In the mean while Pop snoozed a while, while he had been libertying. . . . Ma did the Saturdays work. Then she sewed, patched and rit, some back dairy after supper. This is Saturday no mail yet. It's the 4th mail since we've lost out. . . . Static banged like thunder on radio. as the evening passed on, it got worse. Storm must be aproaching, close by. . . .

SUNDAY, JANUARY 14

. . . For passifing Henry Truestoried. . . . Cause I felt so tuff, all A.M. Took most all that time to get the House tidied up. I read stories, added some more to the stale letters. Next I shirked the rest of the day ha. Eggs where our menue all meals, of this day. With raisen bread to go with it. And Prunes for desert. We both snoozed on a in the Rocker & Pop near the Radio. We rolled in at 9. Listened to part of Orsen Wells play.

MONDAY, JANUARY 15

. . . Where breakfasting when the clock hand pointed on 15. min till 8. Pop had all choares completed, was truestoring. House was quiet. At once breaking the silence. Looked up & said. I hear a Tractor. went out and spied Mr. Bishop, and Ruths bow. they had got hung up right straight west of the House. Skooped their way out. all three rode the Mr Jonnie Dear three miles of here. It was east & north. There they reached the Mans car Mr Edison drove on to Kendall. Got a bu. Mail, Also the Xmas box which was behind time. . . . They returned home at 3 P.M. The tractor was pulling the Car north from here. Verna was with them. Ma certenly got a shock. . . . Pop was on vacation after being an imprisoment ha. He certenly was happy to have Pete stay all night so he really could chat. . . .

TUESDAY, JANUARY 16

. . . This day the mail was brought out. I send off the stale letter off to Ervin to-day, which had been rit for 11 days. Send with it the papers

for his Car. Today Verna did all dishwashing also seprator. Mo wiped
them all. The rest of the day she shirked. . . .

WEDNESDAY, JANUARY 17
Northeast terific Snowblizzard . . . Snow which fell about one inch at
Bedtime murkry was mostly, up to zero. . . . Ma to day washed cushins
and some underthings. Ironed. A.M. Sewed up some rugs which was
torn up, from usage. Verna pressed & ripped up her gray suit. After
supper she wrote a letter to Ervin. Sewed buttons on some under-
garment and patched some. . . .

THURSDAY, JANUARY 18
Northwest blizzard all day till 3 pm. . . . Pop skooped out the menure
& cleaned up the Barn P.M. A.M. he puttered some For passifing he
still had some papers to look over. All pipes froze up. So we filled up
severel buckets and washtub, to keep from carring in water, from up
in the storage tank. Verna & I cleaned the Cabinet Cupboard. Verna
cleaned the two rooms & Pantry. And Ma scrubbed the kitchen The
rest of this day. I shirked. . . . such complacations to endure.

SATURDAY, JANUARY 20
. . . Ma shirked to-day Verna did most of all what was done. Later she
had to water the chickens got coloil & had to see that someway the
celler had to have some atention after the efects of all the zero
weather. The Apples froze Cabbage all 3 bottles of the Vanilla extracta
blowed up. Some fruit jars where froze but not broke. Battry water
blowed up the jar. . . .

SUNDAY, JANUARY 21
. . . The County opened the road to-day 2 P.M. came in from the
south. They got hung up, with the Grader had to do a lotta backing.
And the County Truck had to skoop his way out. . . . Seeing the Road
Grader coming by our place C[h]anged the Coarse of the day. Also
seeing a lite drive by seemed as if we where in a different part of the
world. Pop still had carried in water to-day. With pipes all froze up.
Even if it was Sunday Ma baked a big batch of very nice Bread to-day
even if I say it myself. Had a lamp in the Basement all day to thow up
the frost which did the damage. . . .

MONDAY, JANUARY 22
. . . Pop & Verna had went to the Warners at 11: AM. from there,
went to Kendall got the Mail . . . returned at 2 P.M. In the mean while

the Warners had called, all as happy as a lark. Ma being home all alone all this time had to be overseer while the Windmill was pumping water. The plug pooped out, and she had to make a plug for it. Next the Wellhouse tank cloged up, wouldn't carry the water away so she had to shut off the Mill. Atend to the Hens also be the messenger boy. House not much was done. Just churned & wrote a card to Ervin. & smeared, around with the Cream. . . . 11:45 Mr. Bishop & Dan Edisen got his Car out, where he stuck it, last evening at 8. Came walking in Car was about 1/2 mile north. Well seeing all these faces, which we hadn't seen for some time, changed the Coarse of the day. . . .

WEDNESDAY, JANUARY 24
. . . Ma spent the day working at her Bedding. and went through the same old routeen of the housework. . . . she froze terriable Ma spend most the evening with a horibal backache. . . . Well we're still rejoicing over the wonderfull duration while dust is not in progress. Cant be put into words. . . .

THURSDAY, JANUARY 25
. . . Pop rolled out at 6. Ma 15 min. Later. When he looked at the themoyther and spied that murkry was so far below zero. And said O I cant milk before 8 I'll have my breakfast before milking. At 9:45, He had all completed. Hoofed to Bishops & at 10:30. They had returned with the Hogs loaded our 3 & cliffs 7 shoats at 11:20. They where on their way to Garden, with the Hogs. Returned home at 10 min. Til 5 P.M. telling all the sad news what they had realized out of the Hogs. Bishops Male $5. Big female a little bit over $6. Ours & Cliffs 2 dollars a piece. . . . Elmer & Zelda called at 3 P.M. Wanting some Maze to feed their Hens stayed a period of 1 1/2 hours I gave them the groceries, that Pete got from the relief.[2] Well that changed the Coarse of the day to some other faces. Which I hadn't seen & chated with for a longtime. . . .

FRIDAY, JANUARY 26
. . . Cliff came after his big sum of hog money. Was very much disoluisened about the little dough, he had got for them. Ma spend the day patching washed some cleaned up the 2 rooms and washed all lampglobes and filled all them with oil. Another day with a lotta backache head ache and hangnails. To make the day mostly a drudgry. Go-

ing through the same proceger, wearing a jacket, and overshoes, most of the day. to keep warm. still freezing. as each day passes on. . . .

SATURDAY, JANUARY 27

. . . This day change the Coarse of the cold winter for some time This day greeted us with temp of 8 above. And o boy today murkry rose to 38 degrees. And at dusk it had dipped to 32. How wonderfull & apricative. It thowed so much that the Snow was all slush. Icecles all had fallen off the ruffs and snow was all gone of the ruffs. . . . We drove around by Kendall to mail a Card & bought a box of groceries. On our trip up. First we drove in Huffmans grown next a long distence on our land, then mostly on the road close to the ditch the last mile, some distence some place else. Driving over lister riges, and O O O Just giggling and bouncing around till again, at dusk we reached our destenation. And my what a relief and What a dreary old day Ma endured with the Backache the live long day. . . .

SUNDAY, JANUARY 28

. . . At 8 we got the wash boiler on to scauld the Hog. Old Mother hog. They got her all dressed by 12:45. And had some Liver for supper. . . . The Warners Called at 10 A.M. Well it was Sunday and the Sabath, was broken. Thelma baked a jellyrole in the hot Cookstove, while Verna ironed. She had washed A.M. Got her clothes ready to go, back to Hutch. . . .

MONDAY, JANUARY 29

. . . Well this day the outdoars was all slush to walk in. O such mess to dray around in. Snow certenly had thawed with a great deal ground sticking out away from under the Snow. . . . she Was very lazy shirked most of the day cause she had such backache All she did besides what had to be atended to patch some socks. . . .

TUESDAY, JANUARY 30

. . . Pop had to be on his way early to get Verna to the Train, on her way to McPherson. She took the Buss at Hutch had to wait 1 1/2 hours. She took the fast train to Hutch. Pop returned home at 12:15. . . . Ma give the two rooms a theour going over. And o it certenly look nice. Was very untidy before I started in. I also scrubbed the kitchen . . .

WEDNESDAY, JANUARY 31

. . . We rolled out at 7:15. Had breakfast at 8. Next Pop cleaned out the Barn. and went right at grinding lard. We rendered 4 1/2 gals lard had it competed at 3:15. In the mean while in the Oven we had 14 1/2 gal jars Meat prossing later we processed 7 1/2 gals Meat in the Boiler and rendered 8 gals lard on the back of the stove completed the meat at 8. And Lard P.M. In the mean while we listened to the Radio. Ma stired some butter, with a spoon while the meat was prosessing and that while she also washed all lampglobes & filled them, and cooked part of the Hoghead. . . . O boy this kitchen was steamed up water run down on the walls. And o it was hot. Made one swet I'm so glad that this smear is again put up for this season. . . . Ma was very tired this eve. It was 10:30 when we got all the Lard completed and rolled in

THURSDAY FEBRUARY I

This February comes in like a Lion. . . . 2 P.M. Snowflurries started falling and continued into the night sometime. Ground was blanketed with about 4 inches of Snow. . . . It seemed so funny to-day after the ground was blanketed with Snow. It made one think of Xmas & New Year when we first got the Snow. Recalled old memories only not quiet so cold. Our Water pipes are all corked up. We haven't had them fixed through during the continnation of the 6 day period of Normal weather. Well Ma had lots of ods & ends to clean up of scraps of Lard & cranklins to put away and finish up the Liversausage. Some of Pops work. He cleaned out the Barn Cut Kindling Carried all the Caned Meat & Lard into the Celler finished the letter which I had started a day ago. . . .

FRIDAY, FEBRUARY 2

Ground Hog day comes & greets us with Snowflurries, most of the day. . . . Henry shaved after choars where done Next he got ready to go to town at 9:15 The Warners apeared & at 10 they started to Syracuse & signed up to take out the reabelation [rehabilitation] Leroy stayed home with Ma.[3] They brought him a little Garage & Car, for staying home . . . returned home at 3:15. Warners started for home at 3:45 Well Ma finally got all mess cleaned up & sausage made and cleaned the two rooms all over and washed all Lampglobes. The well was froze up this morning so Henry couldn't pump no water. . . . Ma left the evening pass by. Didn't do nothing, but listen to the Radio . . . felt cold and rather moodie couldn't get intrested. . . .

SATURDAY, FEBRUARY 3

. . . Henry hung around A.M. Rode the Rockenchairs. When he got
tired of one. He tried another ha . . . Ma made Bread baked a raisen-
pork Cake was good wrote a letter to Verna at her newplace. Watkins
Beautyshop at McPherson Kansas. Well it was Saturday and very
natural she had to go to the same old Routeen, she does every Saturday. The cut in her hand. and all diffuculties in her ears and head,
made her week & and the evening wasn't very much enjoyable. Was a
drugedry instead. . . .

SUNDAY, FEBRUARY 4

. . . We motered to Waynes Rogers took the kettle home. They were
not home, so we decided to go to Olin Warners. . . . We returned
home almost dusk. . . . On our way up we started to drive east
of Bishops. the road didn't look favoriable. We then drove back to
Bishops to get some infermation. He told us to drive through their
Pasture where they had broke the road. till we got to the road which
went south. The Stanton County road was wonderfull. But o o o the
mile souut to Bishop east and the Hamilton road. I had such backache
on the way up also a while after we got to Warners. Took 1/2 hour of
relaxation, for me to get back to normal. . . . O O O Doc Brinkley
certenly is making a talk Certenly is cinical at present and in an unplesent frame of mind. Is very radical[4]

FRIDAY, FEBRUARY 9

. . . Made a great deal of progrees. Henry skooped the ice and dirt out
of the Wellhouse cleaned up the Washer at 10:30. Started in washing
and finished up at 3 P.M. O such a lot. Ma washed a great deal of
bedding. Henry got a snack for us to eat at 1. P.M. at 4:30. The Warners called and stayed till 9:30. Going back to some of todays events.
Slipping in and out of overshoes 1 1/2 doz times, made Mas legs side
and ankles ache, so she was half sick when it was time to roll in. She
had the yard all mucked up with tracks back and fourth to the House
& clothesline. The evening was spend playing Cards. And a great deal
rejoyicing while Joe Luis & the [ ] where fighting. Wasn't a fair
fight[5] . . .

SATURDAY, FEBRUARY 10

. . . Before rolling out wind was blowing terriable. So all the starch
was out of the Clothes. Which I had left out on the line. Cause my
poorself couldn't hardly navigate most of the frost was out and one

sheet on the ground all dirty. . . . Started on our way [to Syracuse] at
10 A.M. started for home at 3 P.M. Got stranded almost three miles
of here and never did get the Car out, walked torads Bishop when
they came along one hour later. They drove around by the Hall. Almost got hung up. Pop pushed, & Mr Bishop drove So one mile east
of here we got out of the Car & walked home one mile. At dusk we
reached out destenation. And o how nice it seemed when we got
through with all this puddling in the Snow & mud Pulling the overshoes out of the mud. O how nice when it was all over with. We
walked about 1/4 mile in our pasture. So there it wasn't such job. not
so much of a job on our Carkus ha. Was very funny when we had it
behind us safe back home in our dungin. . . . Ma almost got Caught,
this A.M. washing her self in her slip, and Coming her hair. While
Van Trussel apeared on the scene ha. She hurried and got her dress
back on, when she seened him out in the yard ha. Its 8:30 P.M. At
present. And Pop is listning in on some policitions. He enjoyed it very
much He's very happy with laughter. . . .

SUNDAY, FEBRUARY 11
. . . Pop milked with Lantern at 6 we had breakfast eat. He was on his
way hoofing it to the Car. At 7:30 he Came home with the Car. Van
Trussel called at 8 & had started home. But looked back & seen that
Henry was coming. He then turned around & came back after his
Cream Cans. The two men chated a while. Vans Dog came along with
him & stayed all day. Henry tried to drive his Cows to visit Wayn Male
cow. But they wouldn't budge. So he left them in the stalkfield. . . .
And o say the radio was kept buisy most all day long. We had dinner
right on twelve & at one we listened to the Truestory. Ma felt so good
for nothing she couldn't stay awake snoozed in the Rocker. Pop had
a nap in his usual rocker. She was so glad after she got her untidy house
cleaned up. O it certenly was in a mess. When she got through moping
and dusting. She had such backache. She did a good deal of reading.
Till her eyes stuck out & couldn't hold them open. She had most all
the white clothes on the line, eversince Friday. when the Highwinds
came up some of it blowed down on the ground. And a puff of dust,
on the garden patch where the cilt was pilled up whirled up just as the
wind Came up also a pile where we turn around the Corner. . . .

MONDAY, FEBRUARY 12
. . . Henry finished choaring at 9 Had seprated at 9:15. started in stiring paint and painted the Ceiling in kitchen completed it at 2:30 P.M.

And almost finished all of the Pantry excepting the spots where the plaster had fallen off. . . . Ma went through the same old routeene which she goes through everday. And added to it. She gave the Bedroom a theour cleaning & filled all Lamps cleaned all globes. Sewed & worked at the Bedding a rolled in at [   ] Going back to some happings of the day. The paint certenly got in our eyes as the day passed on. Made one weak & fell tough. . . . . Well a surprize came to me AM. While looking out south. The grader was grading the road quiet a shock to see them get buisy . . .

TUESDAY, FEBRUARY 13
. . . Mud is getting less every day. But the roads are terriable bad. The Mailman came along 5 PM. he was stranded in the draw . . . The Snowbanks are stil there yet. . . . Ma didn't make much progress today A.M. . . . Henry finished painting the pantry and two walles in the kitchen. Blue. . . . Ma worked on the Bedding activities and cleaned some dust she felt so very good fornothing . . . the Trussel dog left us, after visiting with us for a period of three days. . . . Mr Rob said during the period, while gave the weatherforcast. There wouldn't be enough wind to stir up a duststorm ha. It was funny to hear him say something about a duster. Cause its been so long since dusters occured in this fecnity [vicinity]. . . .

WEDNESDAY, FEBRUARY 14
. . . Pop went right to fixing the pipes the elbow was broke in the Basement by the frost. fixed the pipe under the Storage tank. And worked in the well house. Cleaned out the dust over head. . . . Then he fixed on the starter. and O was he ever dirty & sented up with the fumes of gas. ha. Ma gave the two living rooms a theour going over had mostly completed this work. Washed the lamp globes door glasses. And ironed a big ironing. at sunset she went after 3 gals battery water. After spending the evening with wonderfull programs in connection with valentine day. Where weary from efects of a hard days work. . . .

THURSDAY, FEBRUARY 15
. . . The same old routene each day for Ma to go through early. she spent the day before she knew it, it was gone. She washed some comfetor material got three big crockery containers with Snow to melt for battry water . . . After supper she wrote a letter to Ervin & hemed some seprator towls. the longer she sewed, the worse her back

got. . . . Some bonehead Ma pulled while having a kettle setting on the stove, which had, had greasy pork cooked in. She put the dishrag in it, and thought it was the one with water. And o when she felt the dish rag it was grease & o o o how! stiff it was. Next in the evening she sat a hot stuepot on the Lenoleum. And o boy it was glued there. A knife had to be used to get it loose. And how she had to scratch, to get the varnish & stick off the stuewpot.

FRIDAY, FEBRUARY 16

. . . No letter from Ervin and Vernas not to encourageing. Makes Mas spirits very low this day seems as if she cant keep her mind ocupied. . . .

SUNDAY, FEBRUARY 18

. . . At 11 AM. We started on our way. We had dinner at 1:30. Thelma had baked a sour cream cake and some muffins with 5 minute icing on cake & muffins. Where both very good The cake was suposed to be Mas birthday cake. Was all covered with cocoanut, & Candies. She gave us each a Muffin and 1/4 of the Cake. That was very nice of her. . . . We returned home at 5 on our way home east 1 mile of the church we got into a rut & slide side ways, backed around for a while and finaly got through came home south & east of the Church on our way home going up we drove north one mile and east O boy how Pop did curse the fumes just rolled up into the air ha ha. . . . Ma with the rumatism she tried to start in on some letters, to the dear ones in the far away lands. . . .

MONDAY, FEBRUARY 19

. . . after we had eat. A great deal of progrees was made He opened up the Can of paint, which he had bought. It was yellow instead of light brown. Was very angry ha. Got buisy and got started to varnish Ma cleaned up the walls and woodwork and furnite. He varnished some after having got the two walls painted to match it. He got all the windows 4 doars and some mop board varnished. Later he had to cut some wood. . . . never made no fire to cook supper set it out cold. So that was only one hot meal for Henry dear to day. And that was break-fast. Cakes & cranklins ha. We also had the muffins & Cake for desert, which Thelma gave us. . . . At A.M. Before Ma got started to sand-papering. She shined the flours scrubed the kitchen and cleaned all lampglobes. . . .

TUESDAY, FEBRUARY 20

. . . We rolled out somewhat earlier to day 6. Had breakfast at 6:30. got buisy and started in cleaning more woodworks and some furniture. And Pop dear Varnished more woodwork in here & all the furniture Limanating the chairs At 10 A.M. . . . This home seems like a hum drum. Being in such untidy condition while we're cleaning . . . Pop painted the slats on the ceiling. In the mean while Ma made some Butter in a bowl stired it. she cared up some battry water. And how she spend the evening finishing up the letters, which she'd started. . . .

THURSDAY, FEBRUARY 22

Well this day is Washingtons Birthday all programs on the air where very good & most all of them where conected with Washington. . . . The Warners apeared at 9:15. AM. And 9:45 the Men started on their way to Sale at Coolige. . . . The men returned home at 4:30. And these are some of todays events. No men to get dinner for. Just Thelma myself & Leroy. I fried a pan of Eggs. I shirked most of the day. . . . Well I had to atend to all those little erends which I don't do every day. when Henry dear is present. Thelma did a lotta sewing to day & Leroy couldn't passify himself. Was in an unplesent frame of mind at the begining of the day. Mostly at the close of the day I did a little washing. Well the Chickens certenly had a treat to-day. After being pendup 60 days they got the pleasure of the outdoar world. instead. Where very happy. . . . Mrs. Bishop called this morning and said. O boy your kitchen is beautifull. I bet you've been apainting. . . . We got a nice letter from Verna to day saying She's much happier and making real good. . . .

FRIDAY, FEBRUARY 23

. . . Pop painted the ceiling in the Basement started AM. . . . Took the fosset off of the storage tank and the boards off the Henhouse and finished the ceiling. Next he varnished the 4 kitchen chiars and the chiffener in the middle Bedroom. fixed the door on the Basement. Eat his supper at 6. Dolled up in his dresssuit, warmed up his Shoes & socks & said, O boy! that feels good ha. Next sat in the Rocker and warmed hisself while the Radio was going in full blast. With static like no, bodys buisness Ma cleaned up the furniture for varnishing cleaned lamps And took her bath, and washed somethings. She had the Rhumatisum like nobodys buisness. Sewed some. P.M. We started to the Hall No lights just flashlights A big crowd was present Pop got out

of sorts on account the lights where not in working order, and said.
Ma lets go home alright she answered. And away to the Car we went.

So our roundtrip was only a period of 1/2 hour ha. After our return
he sat with his feet way up on the top of the heater. And said now my
feet are very nice and warm. So at 9 we both rolled in. And that was
the final end of the good of Friday.

SATURDAY, FEBRUARY 24

. . . Cliff apeared at 9:15 went to Syracuse to see the doctor about
Thelmas condition. . . . At 2:30 We motered to the kids to see how
Thelma was. returned home at 5:15. At 6 Henry had finished supper
soon left to the dance dolled up in his dress suit. Was very sweet &
considerate. And spend a happy evening, while he was home. Was
very plesent returned home at one in the morn. Ma wouldn't go to
the dance cause she wasn't worth, a shot to blow her up on ha. She
rit the dairy read some & start a letter to the kids. And o she had a
tuff time. Added to all a terriable backache. . . . While we where at the
kids she champooed Patsys hair & put it on rags. And o boy, she
hadn't did this for a period of a number of years, and o boy she was
out of practice and o boy how good for nothing she was ha. . . .

SUNDAY, FEBRUARY 25

. . . Well this was the day after the Night before We rolled out 15 min.
Till 8. But made quick progress had breakfast at 8:30. Next we seprated the milk which had been saved for 3 days. Ma cleaned up the
House. Eat our dinner at almost one Listened to the Truestory. And
at 2:30. We motered to the kids to see how Thelma, was getting
along. . . .

MONDAY, FEBRUARY 26

. . . Was just like the springtime. . . . the remander of the Snow went
off to-day. . . . Henry went puttern around at the Lister and other
work Shaved got ready to go to the Meeting. We had dinner at
10 min. Till 12. He soon returned home at 2:15. And said Ma Get
ready to go to the kids Thelma is awful sick. So that changed the
Coarse of the day. . . . When we got to the Warners. Mrs. James was
there. At 4 they loaded her in the Car & took her to the Hospital.
Returned home from the Hospital at 6:15. Saying the little Newcomer
had arived it was a girl Thelma was felling fine.[6] . . . Ma was right in
the midst of baking Pies butterscotch hadn't got the frosting on them

just started to whip the frosting. In all this shock, she forgot to put eny flavor in the Pie filling.

TUESDAY, FEBRUARY 27
. . . We went to the Hospital to see Thelma, she's real fine . . . Ma bought Thelma a Housecoat for one dollar . . .

WEDNESDAY, FEBRUARY 28
. . . Cliff apeared at 10 AM. And 11 they started to Syracuse after Thelma and returned home 4:15.[7] Ma had dinner ready at 4. They eat ther dinner & supper combine at 5:30 Cliff and Leroy started for home. Pop & Ma really cleaned the hole house. He helped me cary all the bedding on the Line to air which belongs to the southwest room. P.M. She ironed somethings & 4 sheets and some gowns. And the hardest garment to iron was Pos white Shirt. Later I washed the door glasses & lampglobes. So that way the day was spend & never seemed lonesome. But rather long. . . .

THURSDAY, FEBRUARY 29
. . . East and west and southeast a local duster continued till about 3 P.M. after duster occured the sky was very hazy and Murky blowed through our pasture. . . . The wind howling seemed to sad for one to put into words. . . . We rolled out at 6 After a long night was spent with dreams & nightmares. . . . Cliff & the kidies apeared at 4:20 And went home at 5:30. . . . Ma planed on washing but couldn't on account of the dust coming from the East. She went through the daily routene to-day. And added washing all windows to it. and scrubbed the celler steps. . . . This Nitation with a duster changed the hole coarse of the season. After piece has occured and stayed with us for 80 days. It seemed to complicate things for us . . . Well this first duster seemed to make us low in spirits. . . .

FRIDAY, MARCH 1
Well the beginning of a New Month & a new day. It came in like a Lion & hopes it goes out like a Lamb. . . . Highwinds soon was terific at 8 and 9 AM. The dust had occured at about 11 AM. It started in sprinkling. It stoped soon & another terific duster occured that we couldn't see enything. Sky was overcast & wind banged & ragged static was as harsh as thunder . . . Snow was very full of moisture big Snowfluries lighting & thunder kept on snowing in the night . . . Ma

had finished the big washing, as far as she could dust was blowing 40 miles an hour at 11:15, she had to put it water & left it stand over night. . . . Work to day was only choars start the Machine empty the water & eat ha . . .

SATURDAY, MARCH 2
. . . Henry milked before chow choared & drove the two young Cows to see their jentleman friend The yellow one specialy . . . The little Warners & their dadie took dinner with us. Zelda & Elmer apeared at 2 P.M. To see Thelma all Where very happy. . . . He brought the Cows home with the Car. They didn't give only 2 gals milk, after their chace ha. . . . Old Ma had to go through the daily routine to day Cleaning dust after the storm. . . .

SUNDAY, MARCH 3
. . . she got ready and went along with the folks when they drove Thelma back to her destanation after being with us a period of five days. Was in the Hospital Monday till Wednesday. Was taken there Monday 4 P.M. and came to our place Wed. 4 P.M. . . . And now this night the House is all empty lonely. One sees all the vacency breaks ones heart. And old Ma Can't live these day to the fullest till she makes an adjustment tears are more plentefull as work to-day. outch outch Ma certenly has a batch of rhumetis. . . .

MONDAY, MARCH 4
. . . to-day I stayed with Thelma cooked her some potato soup & cleaned up things while the men where tomcaten around & stick in the mud. ha ha. ha. . . .

TUESDAY, MARCH 5
. . . Pop started the fire for one in the washstove at 9 Ma was washing completed it at 12. Had the starch clothes to hang out. . . . She had severel spreads 2 blankets quilt one sheet. Some clothes for us. & all of Thelmas clothes. P.M. she sprinkled the clothes down swept the House twice washed lamp globes got coloil filled the lamps. and did some other ods & ends. . . .

WEDNESDAY, MARCH 6
. . . At 10 A.M. The biggest Snowflurries fell. Till the ground was white. Where very full of moisture. Later in the day It had all thowed,

and ground was very muddy. . . . Pop started to Kendall at 9 AM. . . .
Returned home at 12:15. Said he had to clean off the windshield
10 times on his way home. Drove home in the blizzard. . . . Pop
Liberties slept in the Rocker severel times. Nuted a while to stay
awake. . . . Ma ironed one hour AM. Eat her dinner and ironed till
5:45. She did all of the Warners and did part of ours. In the mean
while she had such backache almost croaked also rhumetis. after completing this big days ironing. . . .

MONDAY, MARCH 11
. . . This was a longlonesome day for Ma. She worked on some bedding. . . . She cleaned lampglobes & cleaned the kitchen & living
room. After supper she did some sewing. She wanted to milk. When
she looked inside the Barn Bishops gentleman Cow was there. She
ventered back to the house such a scare. And so, Ma never pumped
the Cows. Old jentle man Bishop has visited the Dyck Ranch part of
Sat. Sun. & Monday ha. . . .

TUESDAY, MARCH 12
. . . North east snowblizzard continued most all day. . . . Snow fall was
about 3 inches all tole. . . . Ma had a sleepy spell & how she did sleep
stayed in the Hay till 15 min. Till 7. ha. ha. Pop had gone out to milk.
But he didn't halfto wait on breakfast. How he did laugh & kid me
that I had stayed in slumber so long. . . . P.M. He varnished the sewing
machine also painted the ironparts varnished the rockers all the
woodparts. The 5 upholstered chairs and the feet on the davenport.
About 2/3 hour period snoozing with his pipe in his mouth. . . . Static
was a mess all day. But as the day passed on it got so terific. We could
scarcely hear We the People & was they ever good. So while Fiber
Megee was on he couldn't stay awake ha. Henry said to-day when I
reminded him about the varnishing the rockers. O boy now I know
I'll got to roost after supper. Cause I cant sit in the rocker. But the
easy one only had the rockers varnished so he could rock rock as
much as he pleased ha. He also put the lats on the Windows in the
livingroom, and varnished them. The Bishop Jentleman is still calling
on the Dyck ranch. . . .

THURSDAY, MARCH 14
. . . Pop rolled out at 6:15. And old Ma was such a sleepy head stayed
and snoozed till 15 min. till 7 O and was it grand she certenly enjoyed

this moment in bed asleep. how piecefull and enjoyable it was while Pop was pumping the cows ha. He got cakes for breakfast and at 7. He dolled up at 9 A.M. He started on his way to the John dear tractor show. returned home at 5:15 P.M. . . . Ma did some odd jobs to-day while being alone part of the day she patched and cleaned up the Lampbowls & o the flat slim one certenly looks like a blooming rose with the new wick having the red edges on the wick makes it looks very dreesy. she did a little washing It was a long day with lots of pep and acomplishment this day was well spent she had the radio running most of the day. It certenly was wonderfull. . . . Well the Bishop Male is still contended with the Cow family at the Dyck Ranch. . . .

SATURDAY, MARCH 16

. . . We started to Garden at 11 A.M. returned home at 4 P.M. . . . On our way up to Garden we got a Card from Verna, also a letter from Ervin saying, he was to sick to work, had been so fortenite [fortunate] to work some over time & made over hundred smackers a month & this sick period enterfeered with his extra hours. Pop had a flat on our way up severel miles east of Kendall. And O how he did Curs. That the fumes rooled up into the air ha. . . .

SUNDAY, MARCH 17

. . . a little dust whirled across the yard at the Warners. . . . Doars are going rattle debang the kitchen one is real loose. . . . Well here rolles in the good old Sabath. And very natural it was our sleepy day. 15 min. till 7 when we came out of the Hay ha. . . . Listened to the Truestory at 1:30. We started on our way to the kids. Where all very happy and in very good spirits. where painting their living room ivory. We rolled in the Hay at 8:30. Henry boy was very sleepy. Ma a bit chilly wore her sweater to be comfortable while writing her Dairy. & started a letter to the beloved ones far away. . . .

MONDAY, MARCH 18

. . . Had breakfast at 6:45 Pop had choared and 7:15 he had left for Kendall to have his breakbands put on and fixed the stiring wheel. . . . So this mostly was another long shirk day. No dinner to get. . . . Well Mas working activities didn't amount to much. She washed lamp-globes & cleaned out the lampbowls put a new wick in one. give the kitchen & livingroom a going over. Sewed some & wrote at the kids letters. And wrapped up their Easter gifts. P.M. She washed most of the starch clothes for the Warners & a few blouses & one sweater.

and some other things. She has raised a blister on her heal on the wrightfoot & is she glad that its now night. All the todays activities are over with. She's very tired and aches a great deal. O was she ever mad tonite when she saw the kettle with 23 Eggs on the feeder while shutting the trap doar. An old Hen flew up at the kettle. Down it went and o o o all where broke but 3 most of them where cracked. & 6 of them where crushed. And did the Hens ever have a feast ha. ha. So Ma had to wash the straw and mess of the ones that where cracked. . . . Ma found the Sons of the Pioneers, to day at 6:30. And was she ever tickeled. They sing so beautifull.

WEDNESDAY, MARCH 20
. . . 7:45 Elmer Dyck apeared they fixed up things to get started thrash-ing at 9 Van Trussel apeared they started up the Tractor & got 1/2 stack thrashed. quit at 4 after having finished up one stack and pulled Pops Tractor into the driveway, in the Barn. . . . They came to the House for dinner. . . . after they had eat their dinner. They sat around the Table had a social chat for 1 1/2 hours. . . . Ma give the House a going over A.M. P.M. She ironed had the headache when she rolled out and again P.M. She took two asprins. A.M. While listning to her epesodes she sewed at her nightgown & patched some washclothes. . . .

THURSDAY, MARCH 21
. . . We rolled out at 6. Had breakfast at 6:30. After choars where done. Pop tore his tractor down. At 12:15 We had dinner and he went right to work on it at 1:30 Ma & Po started to James to the sewing circle He went on to Kendall to ship the Cream to Garden. . . . He came after me at almost 6 when I had been at the Warners for a period of one hour. We got a letter from Verna saying she was almost in an unplesent frame of mind, the day she rit it. Well these where some of todays happings. The cream can, had not been wired to the lid. And while Pop was driving around the Corner east of here stargazing around. & over turned the poor Can, and some of the Cream spilled out & o o o such mess. Did Mo & Po ever clean & scrape. To get the Can & Car both cleaned up. So it detained us almost 2/3 on an hour. & old Ma got there real late. And still got in on a real bit of quilting. . . . Well to-day she didn't need to cook for men just pop & herself. . . . Am she had broken the big blister on her heel had to tape it up with Cotton. O O it did hurt. At first I couldn't stand to have no shoe, on that foot. Well there was a big bunch of Wimen, at the sew-ing Circle . . .

SATURDAY, MARCH 23

. . . O it seemed so cold. All grass weeds trees posts was iced over and O it looked very beautiful. But not so comfortable to live through. . . .

SUNDAY, MARCH 24

. . . Well this is Easter Sunday. We rolles out at 5:30. Pop wouldnt let me sleep. Made to much noise to stay in slumber. Wanted his fried chicken steak. . . . Pop had a chat with Mr Lameyer . . . after he had finished up listning in on some Easter sermans. So Ma had her own way while she give the house a theour going over. He would make no remarks, while looking on. Our dinner was real late cause our Company didn't arrive till 12:20 & 12:30. . . . After dinner was all over with. And wimen where washing the dishes. The 3 men where having a heated argument about years gone by. Cliff & Henry O boy & was it amusing. At 2 P.M. Dishes where all put away And all five where intrested in a Card game. At 4:45 they were all through while the little ones where rejoicing over their Easter Eggs. . . . Well this was Easter Sunday. So we all tried to enjoy it. Our dinner consisted of Mashed spuds Cellery roast Beef Lettuce Carrots gravy. Fruit Salad & Brown Cake. . . . Well we all had a fine time. . . .

MONDAY, MARCH 25

. . . Very dusty in the yard. Bishops and Recters fields blowed like sixty . . . Sky was clear to-day Till it got murky after the effects of the dust blowing. Wind ragged into the night. when I retired at 9 it was in full blast. . . .

WEDNESDAY, MARCH 27

. . . had a duster for about one hours period of time. . . . today was house cleaning Washed the glass doars. Lampglobes cupboard doars. And cleaned the Cupboard. she did some sewing while listning to some of her usual epesodes. she had enough rhumatics, that she couldn't sit still, for some time. this continued for some time, after retiring.

THURSDAY, MARCH 28

. . . We got a letter from Verna to day saying she made $8 this week. As I got up this morning with a headache and half out of sorts. I worked all day, but never made much progress. Went through the daily routeen and beside it. Had to clean the lamps and fill them. . . .

SUNDAY, MARCH 31

. . . Well here goes good old March. Which did us so much justice, brought so much piece, and satisfaction Well Henry went to work before breakfast on the tractor. . . . Men way down in grease breaking the Sabath. Cliff grinding vales. P.M. After the dishes where done. We listened to the Truestory. I want a devorce at 1 P.M. 2:30 P.M. We listened to Grand Hotell. Thelma baked a sour cream cake 2 Loafs she decorated them up fine with powered sugar icing. . . . Leroy found a nest of 5 Eggs, & how proud he was.

MONDAY, APRIL 1

. . . At 10:30, It started in getting dusty. . . . Wind ragged on till at almost dusk it camed some. At 10 P.M. We had a terific duster . . . Mo started to Wash at 7:30. At 11:15 the machine went haywire so I didn't get the quilt & blanket washed. And didn't get the Over alls wrung through the ringer. She let them set in Water and hung them out at almost dusk. The dust was to bad to hang eny of them out after 11 AM. We had a very big wash the two families. Would have been 2 weeks tomorrow since she washed. . . . The wind was so strong to-day. That it pulled the east screen on the front room, right off its hinges. . . .

TUESDAY, APRIL 2

. . . At 7:15 P.M. A duster occured and just lasted over a period of 2/3 of an hour. Today severel times when the clowds floated around over the top. A big duster would occur. And with it some lectricity. . . . Well some of todays activities. House cleaning and ironing Pops trousers and O boy I had them to mostly wash over. I almost spend 2/3 of an hour ironing them. A shirt added to all of this work. . . . Well tonite while Pop was lighting the lamps. Down went the Lampglobe in all sorts of pieces. ha. And this he said. I must not have got it on right. . . .

WEDNESDAY, APRIL 3

. . . A little dust wurled along severel times to-day. . . .

THURSDAY, APRIL 4

. . . Van Trussel & Elmer Dyck apeared about 9. At 10 they had all set & started in thrashing. They thrashed at the stack and the they mostly finished up but broke something 5 P.M. & elevated the grain in Elmers pickup unloaded, the grain, and called it quits. Just had a very little which they hadn't got thrashed. Pop eat supper before milking. Was so tired he couldn't hardly navagate. Ma was mostly in the same condition. . . . Ma had so meny errends to make to day. While setting the Hens She had to go all over the House being away for two days. With the dusters. Had to clean lamps & fill them. And not much embetion to atend to all activities. Ervins birthday was to-day. he's 28 years of age. . . .

SUNDAY, APRIL 7
. . . At 7 AM. it sprinkeled on & off. And a duster as soon as the dampness quit. The dust started ragging. P.M. 4 it had let up. . . . Pop rolled out at 6. Ma 6:15. Soon had breakfast. While I was listning to Revern Brown. I washed dishes. And scrubbed two rooms. At 11:10 AM. The Warners apeared. She brought 1/2 Spice Cake. It certenly was good. Pop fixed one hinge on the door and did some more puttering. Got mad at the wind & quit. Came to the House & rode the rocker. Radioed some. & Libertied. . . . We listened in on Doc Brinkly . . .

TUESDAY, APRIL 9
Wind in all directions . . . A little dust rolled over the southeast of Bishops ground and through our pasture . . .

WEDNESDAY, APRIL 10
Northeast highwinds. Local duster occured mostly noon. . . . 3 P.M. started in sprinkling. kept on increasing, as the day passed on. At 6:30. Water was standing, everwhere. . . . Adolph Klossen Apeared. So the three men drove around to see about the blowing soil ha Adolph drove home, in the full rain at almost 6. Henry made him a slicker, put on his overshoes choared & milked. Next he put on dry duds his new trousers & dry shoes. . . . Mas activities to-day. She cleaned up & swept in the Basement While listing, to her epesodes. She ruged some sewed a little. . . .

TUESDAY, APRIL 11
. . . Green trees all froze in the forenoon. Tipical blizzard most of the day. . . . Pop went a tomcatten around. Beings it was to cold to give his tractor the second coat of paint ha. . . . Well beings it was to dissagreeable for Ma to bee a cleaning out in the Yard. She stayed

indoors. For some passtime she made one pr. Bloomers. Patched
while listning to her epesodes. . . . this is the night all damage was
done on the tractor froze the block

FRIDAY, APRIL 12
. . . Pop went to look at his tractor and found his Block froze up.
Which he had forgot to drain. O was he sick. Took all the joy out of
this beautifull day. It certenly changed the Coarse of the week. . . .

SUNDAY, APRIL 14
. . . some dust part of AM rolled across the ground & a little in
the yard. . . .

MONDAY, APRIL 15
Terific generel duster at 2 AM. From northwest. It had let up at 4.
But o how, our house looked. The door had opened in the night.
And my poor milk, how it looked. Well it blowed locely at 8 A.M.
But later near noon. It had camed. . . . Wind raged in to the night. . . .
Well after the duster she had to go through the same old routene as
usual, after a duster. O how dusty everthing was. . . . The House
certenly was untidy from the efects of the duster. . . . Sunday P.M. She
cleaned part of the yard And lifted to hard. And in the night she
couldn't get much sleep. on account of the Rhumatics. Was so warm
so we didn't need no fire. Nor a blanket. Lots of saurcasum cumalated
at this ranch by the Mr. ha.

TUESDAY, APRIL 16
. . . At 2 P.M. A terific duster occured and increased till 5 P.M. . . .
Snow in the night & drifted on banks. Wind ragged into the night . . .
Pop pumped up tires. And at 8:15. He had got ready to start to the
North widows field. . . . Drove in with the Tractor at 4 P.M. Walked
up to the Car, drove it home & called it a day. Beings the dust was
raggind, couldn't see your way. . . . He was so black from dust & Eyes
wher sore. . . . O boy. the windows where black on the north & east
from big raindrops on the outside. Our faces looked like negroes.
Coated with dust. We rolled in at 8 Henry was all fagged out, from
the dust effects. Put all thoughts & consetration aside & called it a
day. Put his mind at ease. Mo slept between the blanket & he on it.
So our Bed was devided into halves. ha. Each had our seperate
stauls ha. . . .

WEDNESDAY, APRIL 17
Northeast tipecal Snowblizzard from about 6 AM. til 7:30 A.M. . . .
This rain & Snow changed the hole coarse of the week. This northeast
duster. Was very damaging to the north wall. With the rain seeping
through, the windows. Well this day was very strangeous [strenuous],
one. With all the Housecleaning activities. To much reaching, and
exersion for Mas, Rhumatics at this present time. Not only arms. Fingers & hands included. & headache eversince she rolled out, to-day.
She put on her long thicker bloomers, to warm herself up a bit. She
shirked dinner. Cooked her Coffee on the heater & eat a snack. Made
a dozen trips to the Henhouse. To see how her newly setting Hens,
where progreesing . . .

SATURDAY, APRIL 20
. . . This was Saturday. And old Ma had to go through, the Saturdays
routeen. Couldn't make much progress. Cause to much rumetism.
She patched some underwear, while listning to the Kans. Roundup.
And the Lincoln Highway. . . . She baked some dried Apple Pies and
Biscuts for dinner. So we had a change in Menue, to day. Churned
in the churn for once. Churned just 2 minutes. . . . Very fidegty &
worn out.

MONDAY, APRIL 22
Northwest highwinds. With terific duststorm. Which occured at
9 AM. . . . Blowed into the night. So this was a grim and a very
gloomy, very chilly day. . . . After choars were done. Hitched the
Traylor on the Car. to get the new Calf. it had just arived. Said it was
the biggest one, he had ever seen. So slick Couldn't handle it. Came
home & left it out in the pasture. . . . Had to do three days of writing
on the dairy. Which was neglected on account all intrusens. She
patched some underwear. P.M. And feed the Calf. Cleaned & packed
the Eggs. And didn't acomplish much this day. Left the dust alone.
Cause all was blowing. . . .

WEDNESDAY, APRIL 24
. . . dust occured about 8 A.M. So the sky, was all murkry. Couldn't
see to Bishops from dust effects. . . . Pop was all ready to start to the
filld at 6:30. Onewayed on the Piffenger quarter. At 8:30 He came
after his overshoes sweatter Jacket and another pr. Overalls. Ma had
to help him into his overcoat ha. I bet he felt like a stuffed toad. . . .

Mo didn't acomplish enything, which was noticable. Not to enthuastic this day. with the tooth ache in her gums & Couldn't hear to good. All kinda dificulties occured. since I rolled into Bed, and out again. . . . Had to make severel arends. after the Cows. Milked old Grandma. & atended to her every day, activities. And called it a day. No dusting was done. Cause no use. Dustblowed over all Late P.M. she decided to wash lampglobes & filled them. . . .

THURSDAY, APRIL 25
. . . sprinkeled, a wee bit. duster, from the northeast. Wind blowed into the night. . . . Well this was an eventfull day. A.M. Mo went through the same routeen, after the duster. . . . She's more full of peep & vitality for once this day. Didn't have so many pains with her tooth. But cant hear much at all. . . .

SATURDAY APRIL 27
Southeast terific duster. . . . Ma didn't do much to day. Only swept the House. Was no need, in dusting. Picked up & put things up. Baked a Rhubarb shortcake. Washed some. Scoured the oilstove. She was so good for nothing. Just puttered some. Set the black striped Hen on the west end. Was so disgusted the black Hen which hatched two days over time mashed 2 chicks. And that didn't start, the day off just right. Drove my desire away for things which I had planed on doing. . . .

SUNDAY, APRIL 28
Northwest terific duster occured at 20 min. Till 5 P.M. This was a terriable black one, & very pretty to see it, occuring, in the southwest It ragged into the night. O was it terriable. Worst one, so far in 1940 . . . Almost had to have a light during duster. . . . I never milked old grandma. Pete was here, & milked her for me. Pop seprated. And at 9 They drove to Adolph Mr Brothers went with them, to see Mr Cobb. Looked at the blowing soil stayed till 10:15. Mean while Thelma & family, apeared. . . . all was going fine. Till Henry & Cliff, had one of their tandrums. They Couldn't get out of their nasty unplesent state of mind. Henry with entagnisum, went to burning Weeds. Thelma had cried in the mean, while. And at 15 min. Till one. They drove home. . . . O my how did Mo feel she couldn't see nothing but clowds. . . . after looking at the dust rage, got tired and turned in at 7. . . . Ma was very chilly. In the duration of the duster.

MONDAY, APRIL 29

. . . A duster occured from the northeast. . . . The duster camed at 5:30. . . . Pop seprated and at 6:30. He had gone to the field disked southeast quarter, on 14 Early he finished on 14 section southwest quarter Came in for dinner at 12:10. & worked east 160 on 14. Came in at 20 min. till 4. Just ahead of the duster. . . . Mas same old Routeen. After such terriable duster. She cleaned all A.M. & P.M. she listened to the Kansas Roundup. . . . I was getting ready to wash and, up sprang some dust so I camed down. I had made an effort, for the second time. But got out of the notion, when I seen a little dust, whirling. . . .

TUESDAY, APRIL 30

. . . a local duster occured at 6 AM. kept on till almost noon It camed some at. At 12:45 a black one occured. It soon blowed over [   ]. At 1:45 another black one occured. It blowed about 2/3 of an hour. At 20 min. Till 4. The fourth one occured. And continued till almost 6. Pop had came in from the field the third time on account of the black dusters. It got dark ever time one of these occured. But not so dark. So had to light the Lamp. Sprinkeled 2 different times. Was real chilly to. I made a fire. The 4th time he came home. He said now I'm home to stay it was then 4:20 P.M. . . . He drove home 4 different times, on account, of the duststorms . . . We where all tired out & all out of sorts, from the dust efects. . . .

THURSDAY, MAY 2

. . . Henry drove to the field at 6:10. On [section] 24 and one wayed. . . . Had a great deal of grief, with the tractor P.M. . . . Pop took Ma to Trussels to quilt, for the sewing circle. . . . Well this was the duration, of the most wonderfull day spent, for a long time. All Ma acomplished to day. Was to atend to her every day activities. . . .

FRIDAY, MAY 3

. . . All P.M. it was murky from dust effects. Couldn't see no distence. Local duster occured at 10. A.M. . . . The red heifer, had a important date, with Bishops Jentleman Friend. AM. Ma gave the House a theour going over. And didn't get a chance, to enjoy it. At dusk it was all dusty again. And such mess. Cleaned Lampglobes & ironed P.M. Sewed up her bonnet, while listning to the Kansas roundup. When the day had passed on. Ankels all joints arms And the sore on her left ankle. Which she taped up a few days ago. This sore has become a problem. all so painfull. The hole she poked in her finger, on the right hand, with the fork. So all these pains played her out. . . . She churned in the big churn for the first time this year. . . .

SATURDAY, MAY 4

. . . We drove around south, & meet the Mail man. Got a letter from Ervin . . . Hes very happy & has started going to dances. Has the foundation made, for his Garage. Well We returned home from town at 6:30. . . . Pete had called and left, a note on the Table. Gave us an invetation, to the suprize party for Zelda. They played Cards. Had Cake & Coffee for desert. Anglefood & Devilsfood. All had a good-time. Was 12:30 when we came home and rolled in in a giffy. . . . Today was the first day, for the mocking birds being back, from their winters vacation and did they ever sing & where very amusing.

SUNDAY, MAY 5

Northeast & north Local duster occured early A.M. . . . Wind Camed, some after noon. So at almost sunset. It started to roll again. Wind real brisk at dusk. Wind howled into the night . . .

MONDAY, MAY 6

Northeast high winds early AM. And a local duster occured at 6. kept on encreasing till 8. And was terific by 11 AM. At one P.M. It had camed. And was very plesent till 7 P.M. A duster. . . . A duster occured at 9. With howling terific wind & ragged into night. . . . Well Ma had to go through the usual routeen, as she does. After a duster. She washed a little. AM. And made some Soap. From the Joursey cows fresh milk. Patched some P.M. And wrote the two kids each a card. . . .

TUESDAY, MAY 7

. . . A cold wave with duster at about 9:30 A.M. Let up some after one hours period. But wind continued real brisk. . . . I had so many arrends to make. Washed a little and puttered at some activities. She made her soap from the new milk from old Grandma. Got about 8 chicks to-day & 10 yesterday. She went after the cows for the first time, this summer.

WEDNESDAY, MAY 8

. . . Lightning in the night. 1/4 inch rain. It was sprinkling heavy yet, when we rolled out at 5:10. . . . The rain was so wonderfull, &

changed, the Coarse of the day. Alls where happy. . . . at 12 we where on our way to Garden & got 75 Leghorns chicks 34 White Winddots which where 4 weeks old, price 12 cts a piece. Legorns just hatched 8 cts a piece . . . And all of us enjoyed this day. With a new lease on life Was cool so we had to wear a wrap all A.M. during the day it warmed up. In the evening at milking time a wrap was very comfortable. And another comforter on the Bed was also comfortable through all the night. I drank in, a lot of the fresh air. No dust how nice

THURSDAY, MAY 9

. . . So many things happened to day. Found a Lamb. And a lizzard under one of the tubs, in the damp ground. Mo spade it in to. And o was she ever sick. Well Ma had a very buisy day. Had so many errands to make after the Chickens. She found 10 eggs out in the granary. and also 10 out on the Barn and 24 in the Henhouse. The house was very muddy. So she had to scrub. And dust cause yesterday she shirked from work. Only did, what had to be done. Washed Lampglobes late P.M. She's so tired, from all steps & again had, lota rhumatis. Pop had to pen up the Hogs three times today. The old hehog. wouldn't stay there jumped out, & stayed roaming around. So he had to nail both Henhouses up, so he can't get in, and eat the chicks.

FRIDAY, MAY 10

. . . It was so very beautiful & seemed just like Spring. No dust at all. So quiet, & piecefull it was, to live through the day. . . . Well this was the day, to feed the chicks, where 36 hours old. And did she have some erends to make. AM. Their behaviour was good. P.M. The Hens was slautering them one after another got 3 all dead. And had started on the 4th one. I hobeled the black Hen, & pend the red one completly up. So she couldn't get ahold of them killed 3 she whirled them around by the bills, till they crocked. So when it got chilly at 5. They where all scatterd all over both Henhouses. And did I have me a time, for a while getting them all boxed up . . .

SATURDAY, MAY 11

Southeast & southwest wind. Northeast by the Comunity Hall, it was real murky, from the efects of dust blowing. Bishops field, did the blowing just a little silt north of here blowed. . . .

SUNDAY, MAY 12

. . . A real nice day to celebrate Mothers day. We awoke at 4:45. Chatted a while & Pop said, I'm going to sleep awhile yet. Both went back to slumber for a while. He rolled out at 5:30. Mo stayed in the Hay till he had all the milking done. She rolled out at 6. And had breakfast at 6:30. . . . the Warner family called. Where here for dinner. . . .

MONDAY, MAY 13

. . . A black duster occured. Very slowly and when it struck it was so dark I had to light the Lamp. Was so dark & terific With howling & whistling wind. . . . Rained a shower & was sprinkling at dusk. North windows where all plastered with mud. So one couldn't hardly, see out. Till it started in raining. Then it washed most mud off. It burned the top of the trees black. And o the storm, was terriable broke the fence east of the House & upset the mens toilet. . . . Mo washed her head early AM. And after the duster occured. She couldn't hear from the efects, of the dust. . . .

WEDNESDAY, MAY 15

. . . Local duster most of the day . . . Mas work, for this day, She Certenly had a mess of it. After the duster Monday P.M. Didn't get it all cleaned up yesterday. . . . So she gave the House a theour going over. Cleaned the Cellersteps and washed lampglobes. Later, she cut out her slip, while she was resting. . . . Certenly enjoyed my nice clean House, with the new oil cloth on the Table. The old one lasted just one year.

THURSDAY, MAY 16

Southeast & southwind. And no duster to pester us, for one day . . . Pop got started to the field at 6:15 rodweeded on the Batten ground. Would have finished if it hadn't got so dark thundered and lightened. was home at 4:30. P.M. Only had 1 1/2 round to make till he'd had finished on that ground. . . . One little chick had kicked off this morning. Ma presed pops suit cleaned it, also her dress black one. And ironed some more. She dug out Vernas Bedroom. Cleaned up the rugs. And o it, looked nice. AM. she churned, about 1/2 hour till the completion was made. And lotta more errands to make. Her legs are so very tired, and played out. With severel hang nails so very painfull, it certenly played her out. Mail Mr. Bishop came to our pasture today. To doctor the Black Jersy cow.

SATURDAY, MAY 18

. . . When we got through with breakfast. Pop put on his rubber boots and fenced, till 10. feet hurted very much from the torcher of rubber-boots. At 10 he decided to go to Syracuse . . . Meanwhile the Warners apeared & men Pop & Cliff drove to Syracuse. returned home at 5:30. . . . Thelma patched fixed patys dress cut out Leroys shirt, out of Vernas Uniform & made her red dress, all ready to put on. Ma baked a brown Cake. Thelma iced, half of it. She shirked most of the day. Wrote the kids each a card. And atended to her every day activities. She got 3 chicks 2 they smashed. And got 26 chicks, from two settings. It certenly is muddy, and hasn't made much progress drying. . . . Pop went to the dance at 9 & Ma rolled in at 9:30. She felt so very tuff. With all confusments . . .

SUNDAY, MAY 19

. . . Ma never milked the old grandma this A.M. she had so much to atend to. . . . Pop build a chicken pen for the chicks AM. Ma had so many dishes to wash, stacked up from the day before She worked till almost 10:45. Till she'd completed all. At 11 We drove to Kendall, after the Mail. . . . This day old Grandma & Mr Mail Bishop. Certainly had a Important date. ha. . . . I set the last Hen for this season in 1940.

MONDAY, MAY 20

. . . Had a general duster. didn't last just 2/3 of an hour. Another small one blowed over. . . . Ma started the fire in the Washhouse & got on the water. Pop started in cranking the moter continued for almost 3 hours. Soon took it up to Elexander was out soon returned only was gone 2/3 of an hour. So at 10 AM. Ma started in washing. Some of the overalls & Pops dress pants endured some of the dust. Had to wash them over. . . .

THURSDAY, MAY 23

. . . This morning Mas ears where mostly normel again. But at noon all was gone again. Rushing & not being able to hear well at all. Tonite worse as they've ever been. . . .

FRIDAY, MAY 24

. . . A duster passed over not lasting long . . . We rolled out at 4:15 for once again. And the day brought many working hours. . . . Pop got to the Batten field at 5:30. . . . is listing. . . . Mas work today. Am she baked a burned sugar cake. Iced half of it with powdered sugar. She did a great deal cleaning. . . .

SATURDAY, MAY 25
. . . Ma made Biscuits for dinner to-day Iced the rest of the burned sugar Cake & made part of another One apple Pie. dried. She really gave things a cleaning to-day. But didn't get all the windows washed. Cause she fooled away so much time, trying to get the wick in the oilstove. Wouldn't budge. it slipped cogs. But just the same, she got the oilstove all scoured up. Had the toothache and lotta pains in back & all over. But still, had a lotta will power along with all of it but o after the day was finished. Then the worst had came to stand after retiring. A evening at home, for once. Pop never had no desire to go to the dance. Well another difficulty she went through to-day while moping the flour. A tin Can had been opened, & put into the mop bucket. With lid upward. And while putting the moprag into it. It wedged into her little finger, cutting a gash in it. And ! did it bleed & hurt ha. Tuff luck was the duration of Saturday. . . .

TUESDAY, MAY 28
. . . Well Mas everdays activities is about all she did. . . . Finished up the dear ones letters. Cleaned & packed 12 doz Eggs. . . . and mostly had to heard the Hog. And was that ever a job. Was afraid he'd nab the chicks, which where running loose. Has one crip chick to nurse. Which they had down Sunday trying to tear him apart. . . . And in the evening the chicks had a fit, wouldn't go to roost by them selves. So she had to run them down throwed a sack over them so she could catch them. One was hanging on the role of wire ready to dye by inches Bishops Papa Cow has visited this ranch for 3 days this time. . . .

THURSDAY, MAY 30
. . . At dusk a duster occured. Just a mild one didn't last to long Came with a cold wave. . . .

FRIDAY, MAY 31
And here goes old May out for this year And never more to return With A beautiful day quiet. Not much clowds, nor hardly eny static in the evening. Radio gave very good reception for once. . . . Ma iced her burnt sugar cake A.M. Ironed P.M. And made lotta errands atend-

ing to the chickens. One hen hatched 12 chicks mashed one. Cooped up some Hens which, was wanting to set. . . .

SATURDAY, JUNE 1

Well here is a new month, and a new day. And the first day of June. When Romance starts to bloom. To make a successfull mariage. . . . We started on our way to Syracuse, on our way home, stoped a while at Kendall . . . Pop went to the dance and Mo hit the Hay at 10:45. O was it ever inviting, the good old Bed ha. . . . Well Ma got a good braining to-day from the mother hen, while taking care of the chicks. She's so vicious that brute. . . . Seen a lotta Army boys, where 1200 of them in Town they reminded me of Ervin, while having his CCC Clothes on. Town was just jamed full Trafic was almost block at times. . . .

SUNDAY, JUNE 2

. . . Pop had been up had all choars completed, & had finished eating breakfast. Had gotten it his self. Fried Eggs & meat. ha Some fun. And old Ma stayed in the Hay, till 7. Henry dear soon went to work at his Lister stayed there till noon. Eat at 12 & listened to Cantennburg War News 1:10 P.M. He went back & put on some rubber tires on his Lister. Mean while Ma was in sweet slumber And Po certenly did break the Sabbath. After 4 P.M. He build another chickenpen, For the latest hen who had hatched. . . . Pop eat supper, before choaring. Him & Pete chated read the war news and radioed to get the latest. . . .

MONDAY, JUNE 3

. . . Well Pop looks rather cool with his new blue rayon underwear on. & no socks which he took off Wednesday. Well to day its so warm, & was the first day that I rose the north & south window had to rid the dirt out of the cills. The doar has answered the purpose up till now. Excepting the Bedroom window window has been opened up for some time. A Big Bullsnake was crawling under the clothes line. Thelma spied it & killed the criter. . . . This is the first day the baby chicks didn't get any of their hot water, to hover around. Was to warm. . . .

TUESDAY, JUNE 4

. . . Ma was good for nothing to-day so she only did what needed to be done. Finished the kids letters, and send them off. This was a terriable day to content with. Cause the Black Hen slauttered some little chicks. . . . For once Ma scrubed the toilet. After a long wait.

WEDNESDAY, JUNE 5
Southwest wind mostly terific. Local dust most of the day. . . . Ma was realy good for nothing this day. After dinner she got so sick to her stomache, she took a doce of soda. Didn't do a bit of good. She had layed down & taken a nap. And felt just as bad as ever, when she awoke and after, taking her doce of soda, Later she took an asprin, & then she felt some better and some of her disnesses [diziness] left her.[8] This was certenly a grim day. Such a terific wind & a local duster. O such day, when one feels so tuff.

THURSDAY, JUNE 6
3 local dusters 3 dusters P.M. 4th before rain . . . Well some of to-days hapings. Another chick slaughtered. It seems like Hitlerism. This week Hens slaughter chickens as Hitler slaughters the poor young men. It was so cruel . . . Ma felt very tuff this day. She took a nap & came out of some of it. . . .

FRIDAY, JUNE 7
. . . Cliff apeared after 15 gals. Gas A.M. P.M. he came after the Rod weeder and brought his family. Leroy was very much concerned, about the Bullsnake they had in their granary. Well to-day one chick was trampeled down and all the brothers & sister, helped tar him apart. This day Ma felt good so she did get something done. Cleaned up things, which needed it. Beings it was a very plesent day. Decided to air the Bedding. And did some washing. Made some soap, from the spoiled cream. Bread was rather slow rising, But still got it completed for dinner. And o did homade Bread taste good for once. Hadn't baked for 6 weeks at least. . . .

SATURDAY, JUNE 8
Southwest west wind, and a duster after 1/4 inch of rain. Before 2 dusters occured before the rain. . . . Terific wind at times. Was so dark Couldn't hardly see. . . .

SUNDAY, JUNE 9
. . . Pop rolled out before Ma. She came out of the Hay 6:15. Never milked all day cause she was dizzy & week. Henry choared before breakfast. After chow he really did break the Sabath. Worked on the

rims bend rods, & dug up around the Trees. At 1 P.M. He had made the completion. At 2 P.M. We all motered to Syracuse. The Warners had called AM. Stayed for dinner. While we where in Syracuse. We bought some chocolate icecreams & Candy. . . . We drove around by the Wheat, to see how it looked. After our return trip, Thelma washed the dinner dishes, which we had left set while going to Syracuse. . . .

MONDAY, JUNE 10
. . . Pop rolled out 4:15, Ma 4:45. He milked & at 5:30 He eat breakfast and then he atended to all the chickens. While Ma never eat a bite just had cooked Pops breakfast. When she got her dizzy sick spell & had to lye down. He drove to Cliffs at 8:15. Thelma went to town with us, while we went to see the doctor We got back home at 15 min till 2. . . .

WEDNESDAY, JUNE 12
. . . Thelma came at 8 AM. Today as I was to week yet, and hadn't done the dishes & seprater. I wiped them. She ironed one apron 3 shirts for Pop Mas dress. and Leroys trousers, while Cliff fixed on the Mag.

THURSDAY, JUNE 13
. . . Ma wrote to the kids each a card to-day. got dinner put the cream in the can. Washed the Seprator & dishes. . . . She washed 6 or 7 pieces P.M. Slept & shirked after attending to the chicks. She milked for the first time, last night & this morning. Is feeling much better this day.

FRIDAY, JUNE 14
. . . I shirked slept & layed around most of the day. Read two stories. Shining Star & falling Star.

SATURDAY, JUNE 15
. . . We never came out of the Hay so early this day. Pop did all milking alone and atending to the chicks. Eat breakfast at 5:30. & drove to the field at almost 6. He rodweeded on the ground next to the old 80. . . . came in from the field at almost 7 hurried and dolled up took his bath. . . . At 7:30 He was on his way. Bishops called stayed a few minutes, to see how I was. Well this June month, of blooming romance, is half gone. . . . I Just got the 3 meals made Biscuits for dinner slept and shirked most all day. Elda called to see me. Had heard I was sick. . . . Pop also looked in at the Kendall dance. . . .

SUNDAY, JUNE 16

Well this is Fathers day. Gets a pr. Of socks 5 handkerchiefs & a card from each one of the girls. Hankies from Ma. Socks from Thelma. This was a very plesent day. Was specially dedacated to all the Father I spose. . . . Pop came out of the Hay at almost 6. . . . He soon after breakfast went to the next to the 80 ackers & rodweeded. finished at 6. Broke the Sabath. I didn't. Just slept and did up the days routeen just what had to be done. At 4 P.M. We went to Kendall & got us a hired Girl. Ireleen Shindler. Came home at 5. Soon after the Warners called. & Stayed till sunset. . . .

THURSDAY, JUNE 20

Southwest wind & somewhat dusty in the hills on our way home from Kendall. . . .

FRIDAY, JUNE 21

. . . Some of to days events. Warners called at 8:30 AM. . . . Thelma had cleaned and shined the flours. Worked on her block, for the sewing circle. Later P.M. she made Patsys orange dress. trimed in white & orcard [orchid] tape . . . Ma still shirked to-day. But she having the scar[e], about the santape [centipede] crawling on the pantry flour. She tried to kill him, but he got away in a big hurry. . . .

SATURDAY, JUNE 22

Southwest terific wind A.M. And dusty P.M. It camed was very quiet. . . . at 1:15 We started on our way to town. Got the Parity payment 2.41 cts. . . . Pop went to the Community Hall dance tonight 9:20. Returned home at 2 in the morning, but never went to bed. Ma had rolled in at 10:15. . . . He bought a new pr. Overalls and a pr Gloves. He put on the newones & went to milk. Decided to look eluring. So he'd enjoy milking. Being all dressed up in new clothes.

SUNDAY, JUNE 23

. . . This day is very grim with all this wind and dust. Is very sad with all this howling & whistling wind. Makes the sunday seem so mornfull. Pop came home from the dance. Pete came with him. The two never sat in the Car. Just stood on their two feet and chated about the terriable War. Ma came out of the Hay at 5:15. Just as she heard Henry put on the water to seprate. He had just got through milking. The duration of such night. I noticed that he never had came to Bed . . .

Work for this sabath. Pop again broke it, Cause he's so far behind with all. . . . I slept 3 period of this day. Was very sleepy. . . .

TUESDAY, JUNE 25

. . . Patsy broke the news about getting Vernas letter, saying she was coming home & take over Nadas shop if it still was for rent. Thelma apeared at 2:15. Was going to Kendall. So I went to. And what kinda boner I had pulled. Never wore a belt. And the letter which I had rit to Ervin. I had addressed to Kendall Kans. Mrs Ross called my tention. And was I glad I was there to fix it up. . . . One of the Leghorn chicks took a tumble in the tank. And this hapened to be the last tumble. No rescue for her. . . .

WEDNESDAY, JUNE 26

. . . Cliff went to Henry when the yellow Jersy cow got sick. Which, they Called pickels. She died amedetly. Must have been poisioned. . . . Pop started to town in the Car. Took the Cream & Shiped it . . . Henry returned home at 9:15. Brought 1 pt ice cream it was melted . . . And o what a night it was she had lyen down on the bed. just fell asleep and he come home. After supper He hunted for a repair book so it was past 10. When he turned in. Such a night it was All Ma did today. Was just atended to her every day activities. And adeded to it. Washed her head AM. Starched 6 garments & poured the Cream in the Can. & Wrote a card to Verna at McPherson. The rest of the day she shirked and slept some. Flies are very thick on the door. & going over some of the days hapnings. The Warners had a furnerel at their house, Cause Pickels met her doom. And this news about the cow & the Card from Verna, saying that Nada had sold her shop. And now she'd not come home at this time. So all this Cast a shadow over all our joys. & this particular day. Brought nothing to our life. Just sorrows. And Cause Pop was away, so late in the night. Made it very complicated. . . . Well this certenly is bug night & I dont mean maby.

THURSDAY, JUNE 27

. . . The doors have both been full of flies all day long. Way worse in the evening. Mo mostly shirked all day. Its very hot. And flies stung her all AM. While she was doing up the morning activities. All during that period. She got such sting. Her legs itched and hurted a long time. From the efects of it. And swet so much, while she rit the dairy. Swet drops kept leaking off of her face. & blotted it all up. She put on

her thin dress, so she wasn't so hot. This is a very pesosmestic day.
Cant do nothing, but swat flies, cause they sting so terriable. And the
swet streaming down your brow that you cant see nor hardly hear ha.
I didn't feel to good to-day. . . . Well we certenly got aquainter with
the tempture being in the neighborhood of 100 degrees & over yesterday & today.

FRIDAY, JUNE 28
Northeast terific wind in the night . . . Dusty with all doars & windows open. . . . I didn't do much to-day. Just washed the Eggs and
packed them & washed a few, pieces Ever day activities. Shirked. at
11:30 I eat a snack & went to sleep at the radio while the Kansas
round up sang their beautifull songs. Didn't hardly hear enything to-
day. On account the static just on KOA stations. . . . Henry brought
a hired man home at dusk.

SATURDAY, JUNE 29
Southwest wind. . . . a little dusty. . . .

MONDAY, JULY 1
. . . dusty most of the day and high winds Pop rolled out at 4:30. Verna
rolled out before Ma she didn't wake up. We had breakfast at 5:30.
After choars where completed. The hired man went to the field on
the Batten ground & Rodweeded. Came in for dinner at 12. Went
back to the same field P.M. . . . Henry Cliff & Mr Bishop drove
to Dodge & Liberal after combine repairs.[9] The men got home
after dark. . . .

THURSDAY, JULY 4
Southeast wind dusty all P.M. . . . A very nice fourth all afternoon.
Pop rolled out at 4:30. Ma 5. Had breakfast at 5:30. Henry went to
work at the Combine. Cliff apeared and helped them. Pop decided to
dry up the yellow Jersy.

FRIDAY, JULY 5
. . . A.M. it was dusty. . . . A great deal later, Pop rolled out for a
change Po 5. Ma 5:30. We choared and had breakfast at 6:15. Pop
drove to Syracuse after some parts for the Combine returned home
at 9:30. Cliff & the little one apeared at 8:30 where here for dinner.
He worked on the Combine & the hired man Mr. Hayner worked

on 24 . . . Another event, Ruth Bishop run over a Hen killed her. We drest here soon & had noodlesoup. . . .

SATURDAY, JULY 6

. . . So this day we never rolled out very early Henry 5. Ma 5:30. and Verna soon came out of the Hay but the hired man stayed in the Hay till breakfast was anounced. Was 6 when we eat hired man helped Henry on the Combine till 9:30 he drove to the field. Meanwhile Mr Brothers had called and said they had got a big rain. Couldn't get across the Creek mostly 3 miles north. Cliff apeared about 10 AM. Helped on the Combine. . . . Pop took a bath Had supper at 6:30 The hired man took his bath while Pop milked. Never washed no supper dishes at almost 8 we started on our way to Syracuse. . . . Ma in our Car sound asleep we where parked nearly the bolding [bowling] alley. During this sleeping period. Pop & hired man Mr. Hayner where drinking bear . . . On our way home from all this excitement Verna was sick had to take an asprin. Ma was sleepy. Returned home at. 11. The men had stoped at Kendall . . . And 11:10. They motered to the Hall dance. to get in on a good time. And going back to some more of town enjoyments. The men got us a pt. Ice cream. & a package of gum. And Spose the men got to bed about 2 or three the next morning Sun. And this winds up another chapter of so much more bunk. As I so call it. The family dairy. . . .

SUNDAY, JULY 7

. . . Flies stung where very thick, on the door & flying aunt day. . . . the new hired man Meyers had apeared . . .

MONDAY, JULY 8

. . . This bunch was sorta lazy rolling out of the Hay. Henry rolled out at about 5. Ma 5:15. . . . Meyers went to work on the truck Mr Hayner worked on the ground straight east of the Hall. . . . Henry went to the field & looked at Cliffs Wheat, and said it was ripe enough to cut. . . . After supper was served the 2 hired men went in the livingroom & both ocupied a rocker. Juniour tunned in the Radio didn't know how to tune it in. It wouldn't budge. . . . Verna washed her head, & Ma shirked, cause she felt very tuff didn't do nothing. Later in the day she cut my hair. . . . Della Cob & family apeared & coaxed Verna to take over her beautyshop.

TUESDAY, JULY 9

. . . at 2:30. All set on their journey to the Warners. Cut 2 swaths around the field. Got home at almost dusk for supper. And soon after Chow Pop milked the Cows. Men sat out on the poarch cooling their Carcuses, while Mrs. Petty & Ma where doing the dishes. . . . Della called, got Verna & brought Mrs Petty to work for us. So this is the first day that we worked together. And had lots of fun.

WEDNESDAY, JULY 10

. . . The men started to Cliffs at 6. So Mrs. Petty & Ma where all alone. . . . The men came in rather early. We didn't have our supper all completed. So they had to wait a while. on supper. At 7 it was all completed. Pete called after supper. While the men where all spradled on the poarch chatted till 9:15 Mrs. Petty & I had rolled in so the men had some chatting to do. Us 2 wimen had chatted a while after supper. . . .

THURSDAY, JULY 11

Southeast terrific wind & dust most all day. . . . Men drove to the Warner field to Combine. So Mrs. Petty & Ma where all alone we just eat a cold snack for our dinner all three days while the men cut at Cliffs place. . . . A duster in the night. So Mrs. Pedty had a lotta dust to clear up. Ma cleaned up the Bedroom. She scrubed the kitchen & pantry and shined all the flours. The men returned home after dusk. . . . Ma had an embarsing moment to day. While going down in the Basement, after some thing There was Jounner, putting on his socks. O how I felt. Pop had told me, he was up, and washing. I certenly did excuse myself ha ha. . . .

FRIDAY, JULY 12

. . . Today 102 . . . Men started to Cliffs field at 6. And finished up right after dinner. They came to our field & cut 2 swaths around the field old 80. . . .

SATURDAY, JULY 13

. . . Went to the field rather early. Henry came home at 10 AM. With the first load. Got 3 loads wheat this day. Had dinner at 12 noon Relaxed one hour & went back to cutting again. Came in a little early had supper. . . . She cleared the table off while the 3 men all took their baths. She had taken hers A.M. We had dinner at 12 noon. Poor

Junniour was to sick to hardly eat a bite. Was so ill. Just hung his head. Was 6:15 when we started on our way to Syracuse. The 3 men all got hair cuts & the 2 a shave. Pop had shaved AM. Got Verna. And got started to the dance. Got there at 11 And the dance ended 1:30. . . . Verna dance 3 sets with Jouniour home sweet home. 2 dances with Jack Goodspeed.[10]

SUNDAY, JULY 14

. . . A duster occured came very slowly. But didn't last just a few minutes. The clowds chaced it away. . . . Junier left on a trip and never showed up Junior was Pops Combine man.

MONDAY, JULY 15

. . . We rolled out at 4:30. Henry choared & had breakfast at 5:30. Went to the field at 6:30. Cutting straight east Cliffs hired man worked on the Doerr quarter with Cliffs tractor Got that patch finished up about 2:30. And drove home a load of Wheat. Cliff Jack Goodspeed Mr. Hayner. All 3 where here for dinner. So Ma had 3 men. For dinner. Cliff was fixing something.

TUESDAY, JULY 16

. . . today it was 100 & o how hot AM. Cause it was somewhat quiet. . . . Pop rolled out at before 4 and got a load of Wheat before breakfast. Ma rolled out at 4 and went to work . . . We got 10 loads Wheat ha . . . Came in before sunset so we had supper rather early. While suppering Junior Meyers & Glen Clark came Junior certenly did apoliage for not coming back Sunday, to work. . . . Mo was so good for nothing she took severel naps. . . .

WEDNESDAY, JULY 17

. . . Pop brought in 3 Loads Wheat. . . . Today somewhat we where slowpokes slept till almost 5. . . . Men went to 24 and cut Wheat. . . . men came in from the field before sunset. And old Ma was a slowpoke She never got home from town till 6:15 So the men had to wait on supper. Was 7:20 till they got something to eat. . . . Cliff Thelma the kidies & Mo motered to town, after the cherries. Thelma & I each got 2 lugs. at 5 1/2 cts a lb. Sold 7 1/2 doz Eggs. at 10 cts a doz. toteled to 75 cts. Bought it out in groceries Peaches fresh Tomatoes Loaf Bread 6 cts Bananas 17 cts at Maricals. . . .

... To start the day off he puttered and choared Went to the field at 6:30 Cut on the Battenground. P.M. Pop came home & got the Oneway to do some work in the draw so they could cut the Wheat there. Tonight they came in much later for supper. They eat at 8: ... Mo pitted & caned 11 qts cherries. She didn't feel to good AM and washed out some underthings & towls Today we had our first chicken fry. ...

FRIDAY, JULY 19

... O it was hot. With the temp 102. ... The men left at 6:15 on the Batten ground where they cut all day ... Mo caned another 11 qts cherries & o was she ever glad when it was all completed. After supper while the men where away, She did little ods & ends. Which had been neglected. ...

SATURDAY, JULY 20

... Today 105 degrees ... a terific duster came with a Cool wave. Not lasting very long. but 1/2 hour later the murkry had drooped to 82 degrees. ... Was very nice & cool to sleep. ... and did I shout for joy over the cool comfortable weather. ... Men brought the combine home, from east of the Hall. Drove by the House & elevated the Wheat in the truck south of the House. ... wind up our Wheat this years harvest. Hurrah with joy they shouted. So our wheat had came to the final end. And how glad. ... At 5:30 All Bath had been taken, All dressed up. Supper had been served. & On our way to town to take our man home. & brought Verna back. So at 9 we all 3 motered to the dance. And retired allmost 2. The next morning. Jack danced Homesweet home with Verna. ha

TUESDAY, JULY 23

... Then men went to the field at 7. Brought in on Load Wheat AM. Jack unloaded it in for dinner at 12:15. Went back to the same field & cut wheat at one. ... And at 6. sunset they finished up the wheat harvest for this year, And, o, how they rejoiced. Knowing that they need not work the next day. The Warners & Jack, where here for dinner also Supper. ... The little Warners had them selves a playhouse out of tamarics on the north side Leroy was breaking up logs. out of tamaracs. ... Ma & Leroy went on the Barn & got a nest of 5 Mean while Leroy played with the little kitties in the granary. . . . no cows where milked to night.

WEDNESDAY, JULY 24
. . . Today 106 hot & quiet. Flies thick on the door, also stung like no ones buisness . . . Pop certenly did shirt [shirk], and celebrate. Drank 2 bottles of bear on ice ha ha . . .

THURSDAY, JULY 25
. . . today temp 106. . . . Men celebrated this day. Cause the harvest was over for this year ha. Choars where done & we had finished breakfast a bit after 6. Pop soon drove to the field the 60 ackers & curlered. . . . Mo write her left over dairy. Which had been neglected during the short harvest period. A.M. She cleaned up some ods & ends. cleaned up the pantry shelves cleaned the oilstove. And gatherd up the bedding for the bunk bed out on the poarch. Which we prepared for the period of hot weather. For last night it was a scoarcher, all through the night. . . .

FRIDAY, JULY 26
. . . this was the day that Jack Goodspeed reached the parting of the way. & the, sorrows which they all had to face. With sobs they departed. The Warners & Jack. Leroy hadn't yet cheered up, while sitting in his inviting chair. Where he always goes to sleep. Also heals the wounds, after getting bruised and where he goes to sob. As he gazed up at us. He rocked rocked rocked And as these thoughts where still on his mind after he'd fallen into slumber, with big tears in his eyes. The poor little wounded guy.

MONDAY, JULY 29
. . . Ma found a nest of Eggs on the Haymow. Sewed up her bonnet. Wrote a letter to Ervin & shirked the rest of the day. Beings it was a blue Monday. And, so very complecated. A Very nervous & a very straneous day for Ma. First the house swormed with flies. All so untidy. After she had it tidied up a bit. Her ankle pained so terriable. Was all swollen. So she was very stiff legged all day. Did very much greasing & messaging. With Sloans Bakers linement also mentholatum. After all this had been taken Care of. Another spell occured with her ears. Not so terriable as they have been sometimes.

WEDNESDAY, JULY 31

. . . Well this ends up the July month for this year of 1940. & I must
say it was a very hot month to. . . . The men emptied up my washwater, & that was very generous of them. Hank & Cliff. This is the
first time Mo washed with the machine, since she had a clapse [col-
lapse]. And o did she had a termendous washing 6 Bedsheets. And
about 15 washclots & also that meny towls Was all faged out and after
I went to Bed. I didn't know how to lye, to comfort myself.

THURSDAY, AUGUST 1

. . . This was a very bum day for old Ma. Took a snooze in the easy
rocker. While her ears where of the worse. At 5:30, Made a considerable change. So she could hear for the time being. Pop brought me
some more medicine. For building up my system.

SUNDAY, AUGUST 4

Well this day commences with a different view point after the nice big
rain. We all fell refreshed & in much better spirits . . . Ma broke the
Sabath today canning apricots she caned 4 qts of them.

MONDAY, AUGUST 5

. . . Thelma & Ma fixed up the apricots. She did the canning. & Ma
helped prepare them. Got 9 qts & 5 yesterday from 1 bu. I felt very
good to-day. Excepting being hard hearing most of the day. . . .

WEDNESDAY, AUGUST 7

. . . The wind sounds very mornfull makes one feel sad. Pop arose
much earlier as Ma. She stayed put cause she was sick & very dizy.
Had endured a very tuff night. . . . When she was getting breakfast
she was so dizy & sick. & couldn't eat. Drank a cup of Coffee. After
taking an asprin she felt much better. & eat a dish of Wheaties. . . .
Well at 5 a cold wave, from the northeast whistling and high winds
occured & local dust from the Bishop field occured. I soon rolled in
was 7:30. Pop shut all doars & windows and followed me. . . . Well
she shirked most of the day on account being so ill. Took 3 asprins all
tole and layed around & slept awhile to prevent vomiting o she felt so
tuff. A Badger or coyote swiped our game hen and all chicks Just
leaving one so lonely. 2 others where eat by some crither. Which
Henry found.

THURSDAY, AUGUST 8

. . . Where greeted in the night with good news mostly 2 inches of rain. The roof leeked had a pan to catch the water. And Basement & the celler was almost flooded. O such mess. . . . Ma had a tuff time to day that's why she shirked good for nothing she was all P.M. . . .

FRIDAY, AUGUST 9

. . . At 5 when Ma came out of hay, [Pop] was driving Cows in. . . . He puttered around at the radio, it wouldn't start and make a sound. smeared a lotta battry acid on the flour. Ma soaked it with soda. . . . Well this was a dismall day with a radio no music & epesodes to listen to. Was very lonely

SATURDAY, AUGUST 10

. . . At 11:20. AM. We was on our way with the radio to Garden. It had the condencer burned out Cost 2:30 some cents. We returned to Syracuse at almost 5 . . . We returned home at 9. Verna rolled in at 11. & Pop went to the dance & Ma rit some dairy. So it was 11:30 when she retired. . . . Henry didn't stay at the dance, very long. Returned home before 12. I just had fallen asleep.

MONDAY, AUGUST 12

. . . Its now been 4 days since I couldn't hear very well. But the ears are not roaring. But sounds are all so dull. Well this is a much more cheerfull day Having the radio. To bring fun & frolic into the day. . . . A pan of 36 Eggs where setting under the stove. Someone came along, & gave them a kick & o o o. Only where about 10 of them left. The rest of them where all cracked & some of them poured out. Such a mess to clean up ha ha.

WEDNESDAY, AUGUST 14

. . . Wind sings different tunes all day along. . . . While I was resting, with the coolbreeze blowing over me for relaxation I rit the dairy & Cat sitting in front of the Door looking in. For her food. AM. she made 2 glasses Apricot Jelly 1 1/2 cherry jelly. while she heat the dishwater. Also dressed a chicken for dinner and washed her cupboard doilies. And severel more pieces. While she had some starch left from yesterday . . .

THURSDAY, AUGUST 15

. . . We took our baths got ready at 8:15 we drove to the James Party. They pined numbers on our back. Telling what we should ask say or do. Played games & had music & all joined hands. . . . Today was a straneous day for Ma. Hunt hunt for things. And getting all things ready for the party. Baking a cake. Wrapping all those things. It was 10:30. When we returned home from the farewell party. & O did she ever get gifts. . . .

FRIDAY, AUGUST 16

. . . Well Mas Ears are on a blink to day again. Lost their hearing last nite at the James Party. And to day her head is on a bum. . . . To day is another flying aunt day. Ma dressed a big wopper of a chicken for dinner. P.M. She patched & washed Lampglobes her housework activities added to it. . . .

SUNDAY, AUGUST 18

. . . At 7 Henry & Elmer started to Kendall after the refragrator came back at they unloaded it.[11] And Elmer went home. Verna & Henry unscrewed it. Soon Cliff apeared. He helped get the thing in the house Had to take the Kitchen doar off. to get it in. Moved the Cabinet in the Pantry to make it convient. Cause it was so wide. . . .

TUESDAY, AUGUST 20

. . . Pop puttered at something before he choared & had breakfast at 5:45. Soon went to see if he could get Pete to clean out his Wheat. So Pete soon apeared on the scene. . . . And as the Basement was all torn up including the Bed. Ma had to prepare a place for Pete to sleep She felt rather tuff to-day. Her head hurted and was sick, so she had to take an asprin to keep going. Cause she had 3 to cook for to-day instead 2. The old Red Hen took her last ride today. Seems queer. Tonite to see Henry sit at the table & read the paper instead being parked in the rocker. . . .

WEDNESDAY, AUGUST 21

. . . Mo forgot to get up 10 till 5 So she had to rush breakfast. Because of staying in the Hay so long. . . . Before Henry went to the field Him & Thelma started the Fredgrator. . . . Pete came home for supper at 6:15. So him & old Ma had a real chat. poured his heart out . . . The Warners called Thelma helped me wash the dishes Seprator she washed. Helped dress two chickens Ma churned. Completed it in 30 minute period. Later Thelma baked 3 Pumpkin Pies She had brought some pumpkin also a qt Can of stringbeans. . . .

FRIDAY, AUGUST 23

. . . Pop rolled out before 5. I slumbered, till 5:10. Had to hurry with breakfast. Cows had came home. . . . Pop soon went to fixing on the straw rack. Mean while Cliff & family apeared. . . . While Thelma was present she washed the seprator I helped her with the dishes. She cleaned up Vernas Bedroom including dusting. We dressed three chickens for dinner. . . . Later PM. I cleaned up & packed the Eggs. And washed some. . . . Went dragging along with the backache burned my finger on the fridger burner. Washed lampglobes before sunset and called it a day.

MONDAY, AUGUST 26

. . . At 15 till 7. Henry & Verna where on their way to Syracuse Returned at 10:15. . . . We rolled in at 7:15. And next a car drove in. It was Joe Wofels bringing Verna home. She quit on account the pay.

TUESDAY, AUGUST 27

. . . We rolled out at 10 till 5. Verna soon came out of the Hay choared first. . . . Verna & Ma hurried around & got the dishes & seprator washed. And atend to the chickens at 7:30 We got to the Warners. Verna stayed there for dinner. Po & Ma came back home. . . . Henry fixed up sepered pens for the Mother Hogs to add an addition to the Hog family. He also worked on the drills P.M. . . . Going back to some events at Warners. We took our Car, drove to the field & looked over their watermellon Pumpkin Squash & Cantelope patch.[12] . . .

WEDNESDAY, AUGUST 28

. . . We drove to the Warners . . . Verna & Ma did a good sized washing. Made the Completion 10:15. While we where at Warners. . . . Got some Rhubarb String beans & cucumbers. She gave us some of all these vegetables. one half squash, a small pumpkin. And some Beats. Verna & Ma returned home at 3. . . . We had a lots fun while we where eating a snack. Ma & Verna. . . .

THURSDAY, AUGUST 29

. . . Verna did a big ironing while Ma shirked most of the day. She made some beat pickles cucumber pickels. And prepared a small Pumpkin to cook. Wrote a letter to Ervin. Nursed her soar finger, which she cut 2 days ago, on the tin Breadbox. It hurt to bad, to put into words. Well a muddy house at present, instead of dust Its just sweep out mud ha ha.

FRIDAY, AUGUST 30

. . . water standing in all holes & ditches. But o how nice since it rained one inch & about 1/2 at one this morning. We had water standing by the radio. East door also around the table before all windows where closed. Henry had to down the basement, get his Coat, Shut the Car windows, which he had all left open ha. Hard for him to roll out of Bed, and get dressed, for such occasion. ha ha. So this changed the Coarse of the week. With this good rain & lots of Mud. . . .

SATURDAY, AUGUST 31

. . . This day & this day winds up old August. . . . One mother Hog, Added 8 babs to the Hog family. . . . Henry puttered at the drills most of the day. . . . P.M. A while him & Verna where sitting out by the Car. Verna sat on the fender. The two had a very nice chat. He soon took his bath. . . . & soon went to the dance. . . . Verna backed one pumpkin Pie. & Ma made a plain Cake for Rhubarb short cake. Verna did all the Saturdays work & Mo just cleaned up her Bed room. As Verna was very blue, tonite & Pop was tired. So while they had inter-mission. The two wanted to go home. Pop had taken a nap in the Car while the dance was in cession. Verna & Pop listened to the Barn dance tonight.

MONDAY, SEPTEMBER 2

. . . 3:30. P.M. A duster occured, but not lasting very long. Wind camed considerable, after a period, of 2 hours. . . . This was Leroy Warners, first day at School. At about reasess. He said to his sister Patsy. Say, Is it about time to eat. Said. O say, I love school. The Warners called P.M. After school was dismissed. . . . A Lady who owns the Buty Shop Mary Ruth at Lakin. Was wanting Verna to work for her. So she excepted the job. For 1/2 of the Buisness they take it. This day the Fredeger, scared us stiff. When the flame was red, & the sut flew around. The third Mother hog, added 10 Little Babes, to her family. And mashed 3 after, they were one day old. . . .

THURSDAY, SEPTEMBER 5

. . . At 4:45 a southeast small duster. . . . Henry started to sow Wheat on the 60 ackers at almost 9 A.M. at noon. He had moved 2 miles east. Sowed 50 ackers P.M. . . . Ma had a tradgic dream all night along. Couldn't sleep near, all night. Nor slept well. On account. all the sor-rows & heartbreaks, which occured. And saddened, the hole coarse of the day. It was all over shadowed. And mist was so heavy. We couldn't see no sunchine all the rest of the day. Nothing but burdens, which where, much to heavy, to bear . . .

FRIDAY, SEPTEMBER 6
. . . Ma shirked. excepting her every days duties. Ma & Verna drove to the Warners. Thelma & the kidies, where here. But had driven another road. So we didn't meet them. Cliff was taking his bath. They had gotten their Wheat loan. And was planing on going, to Lakin. And their little ones, here. So Ma & Verna, drove to Syracuse, without Thelma. And got along, fine. No difculties at all. . . . The most, disgusting boner. Ma pulled to-day. Was to go to town, & let her 8 doz of Eggs set at home. . . .

SATURDAY, SEPTEMBER 7
. . . Ma rolled out just day break. Henry had gotten up, & had atended to some of his activities, while sowing Wheat. . . . We drove to Elmer Dycks, to see if Pete Dyck, would work for us. . . . 7:15. P.M. Us & Pete had eat supper. At 8:30. We where on our way to the dance. We returned home at 1 in the morning. All eat a snack before retiring. All three had a hollow belly ha. After retiring, Ma went through the awflest dream, it awakened her. And could not sleep enymore.

MONDAY, SEPTEMBER 9
. . . Henry started to the field, a little after 6. Sowed on the 160 north of the old one. . . . Mas Work today. Was Canning 11 qts Dill Pickels 4 qts sweetpickles. Washed some. Wrote a card to Ervin. And her every day activities. . . . Well this is the beginning, of a new week, and a new day. But all overshadowed. With all emptiness, stirring me in the face. Lonely & grim feelings, every where she can see. And goes. But just the same. All work stirring her in the face. She puts her noes to the grindstone & continued to keep it there all day. Didn't, sleep much just dreamed.

TUESDAY, SEPTEMBER 10
. . . Well here comes Mas bunk. She washed some windows. Finished the Card, to Ervin, at Dexter. And a letter to Verna at Lakin. At her knew place, in Mary Ruths Beautyshop. She also got a hit with her hammer, raised a blood blister. And o how painfull, for a short period. . . . This is now the 5th day. Since my head, has been in an

uproar. And had, a time to hear from a distence off. Today for once flies where sorta a pest, just crawled & where a botheration. Well this was one night which, I certenly slept well, & didn't dream, and have nightmares.

THURSDAY, SEPTEMBER 12

Well this was the duration, of a very beautifull day. Not a clowd in the sky. . . . And now back to rejoicing, over the Completion, of Wheat sowing for the year of 1940. Sept. 12. At 6:45, P.M. Was very happy at 7 while eating his supper. Talked very Causel. And looked over the todays mail. Rolled in at 8 and called it a day. . . .

SATURDAY, SEPTEMBER 12

. . . Henry really celebrated a great bit of the day. Painted the Drills part of them AM. & a little finish, he put on them P.M. And the rest of the day, he libertied. . . . He radioed after supper some. And turned in at 8. Well this was a day for work. Ma had her nose to the grindstone. Added to all the Saturdays work she had to iron. Which she couldn't do yesterday. She killed 3 roosters for Sunday. One black one, & the rest was a white one.

SUNDAY, SEPTEMBER 15

. . . Thelma & little ones apeared. So Verna & I went along with them. Took dinner with them. Some time P.M. Just as they where on the east, Poarch. Heard a rattle Snake. No man was present, at that time. They where so scared. Rushed to the Telephone & foned up Rexroads.[13] To kill the Snake. In just a little bit. They apeared. Just then, Henry Dyck, drove up. So these two men, soon had the Snake murdered.

MONDAY, SEPTEMBER 16

. . . Had about 2/3 inch of rain. Around 4 AM. Lots lightning & Thunder. . . . In the night Henry had quiet, a job. When the rain occured. Had to get up. And close all windows & doors. And Ma got rained on. On account of the leaking roof. It aroused her slumber. Had to push the Bed, next to the wall. To protect it. She was very chilly, With these wet clothes next to her skin. Was just, on one side. . . . Ma baked 4 Pumpkin Pies. Give the middle Bedroom a theour cleaning Washed some underthings & washed Lampglobes. Her ears where of the very worst. Which have been raising cane. Now for 2 weeks last Thursday. During this period She only had 3 days of normal conditions. . . .

TUESDAY, SEPTEMBER 17

. . . Going back to some hapings of the day . . . Ma had to Iron some & churned. And late P.M. She washed her head & packed her clothes. . . . She helped Henry clean up the Car. Washed the windows scoured the bumpers, & cleaned the Wheels, also the Hubs. Well it seems to me, as if the 3 stags are having a quaker meeting. House is all silent, Cause I know, they're there. I can see their presence.

WEDNESDAY, SEPTEMBER 18

. . . We eat breakfast about 5:30. Got ready & started to Halsstead.[14]

SUNDAY, SEPTEMBER 22

. . . Going back to some of the forenoons events. Ma & Vernas blues. Sunday was all over shadowed. by us AM. While we where all alone. One balled harder then the other. And did we pour our souls, out, to each other. . . .

MONDAY, SEPTEMBER 23

. . . Henry & Verna started on their way 7. Stoped at Cliff & took him, along. He took 3 baskets of Cantalopes, & got 25 cts a doz. Also took their Cream. Henry took 5 1/2 Eggs. price 14 cts. And toteled to 76 cts. At about 10:45, Thelma apeared on the scene. So her & I had dinner alone. . . . Ma give the 3 rooms a theour going over. And washed some. . . .

TUESDAY, SEPTEMBER 24

. . . Henry rolled out at 4:30. Went to the field & scattered hopper poison. Ma was eating her breakfast, when he returned. She had rolled out at 5. Stove was empty. No Caresene in it. So she had to go to the bbl. To get some to get breakfast. And after vacaning for a period of 4 days. Was out of practice, And didn't pay to much atenttion, run the Can over. Such boner, and waste this was due to her neglect. . . . Well this is Mas dab of Work for this day. She spent most of the day writing letters, Was to nervous, to do much. She finally churned, & cleaned up the Pantry shelves. And fixed up some ods & ends. Which had been left undone. And later, washed lampglobes. . . . Ma eat so many cantelopes & watermellons. And the results, Was to spend some time, visiting the Joneses ha ha. . . .

WEDNESDAY, SEPTEMBER 25

. . . at 8:40. We started to the Warners, & on our way to Garden Was
9:30 When we started from the Warners. To get our Windcharger
fixed, & the kids Maytag . . . We started on our way home about 5.
And at Lakin, Verna was buisy, so we waited till 6. To have our chat
out with her, at this time. It was 6:15. . . . Got to Warners. . . . We
took supper with them. . . . Meanwhile the little ones, had gone to the
Hay. After a enjoyable time seeing all the purties, which they had
gotten from Garden. . . . It was then 8:40. We started on our way
home. And then yet. Was for the worst to come. Both doors on the
big Henhouse had blown shut. A great number of Hens where scattered all over. We chewed them and drove a number, of them to their
roost. But severel of them, wouldn't obey. So they were left out. And
north, a Cyote eat a layen Hen. And another one, in the feed. Had
been caught. After this excitement. We both eat a snack & rolled in at
9:45. And called it a day. . . . This day, was very erratating for Ma. . . .

THURSDAY, SEPTEMBER 26

. . . Well Ma is again on the job, dressing chicken. She dressed two.
One for dinner tomorrow, & one for supper. A.M. She washed out,
some things Silks & cottens. Cleaned up some & washed Lampglobes. And my ears had a very bad behiveour today roared so terriable. and I was very nervous. While listning to the Radio AM. She
did some mending. The static was a nuicence AM. And got much
worse P.M. . . . Ma had a very tuff night after retiring. She soon awoke
and couldn't make sleep come to her eyes. Lay awake 3 hours. And
then dreamed a terriable dream.

MONDAY, SEPTEMBER 30

. . . Well this was the first day, after daylight savingtime, has gone off.
So I had to do a lotta hunting, to find all the epesodes, to which I've
been listning to. Was all alone, all day. And a very straneous day for
old Ma she dressed 2 chickens And did just what had to be done.
Late P.M. She washed the doars & lampglobes. And rit a letter to
Ervin. O boy, and was the programs on the air ever muddeled up.
Where very hard to find. . . .

TUESDAY, OCTOBER 1

. . . Mr Charlie Miller, had called to see about cutting feed. . . . [Henry]
went after his Bindertwine & some groceries Got home at almost
dusk Mr Miller brought his outfit. . . .

WEDNESDAY, OCTOBER 2

. . . he shocked feed & at 9:30 He got the Cows & milked Shocked more feed. Charlie Miller & his man cut feed up north. Sedan & cane finished up at 2. P.M.[15] They where here for dinner. . . .

THURSDAY, OCTOBER 3

. . . Dusty & sky was over cast most all . . . The howling wind was a nuicence. . . . Ma had got ready to go to the Sewing circle. So at 12:30. We started on our way. Nona Bishop & Nina called at 11:15. To take me. I couldn't go. I had just started dinner. They brought me home at 4:15. . . . Us wimen finished up the apricue [applique] quilt. I was there 3 2/3 hour. . . . My ears have been alright now for 6 days. And how much it was apricated. . . .

SATURDAY, OCTOBER 5

. . . got a letter from Ervin saying Vote for Rosevelt. Why Wilt with Wilkie ha ha.[16] . . . Pop finished shocking feed. Before taking his bath. Shaved & got ready to drive to Syracuse Went to see Doc Grisom about my enfected finger. Well he lanced it & o. Couldn't freeze it cause it was swollen, so big & would take effect. charged 1 1/2 dollars, for this call. We got back home at dusk . . . We drove to the kids Verna had came so far with Hazel Anderson. So from there we drove to the dance. . . . We got home from the dance at 11:30, after midnight. All eat a snack before retiring.

SUNDAY, OCTOBER 6

. . . Well we stayed home all day. Pop & Verna snuized a while Henry on the flour. Verna on the Davenport & Ma some in the rocker. Mas finger came along real good. But very painfull from exercison. Had to aply one third alchoal & 2/3 water, added to it. Give it 5 aplications a day. . . .

MONDAY, OCTOBER 7

. . . Ma never did no house activities. Just gathered Eggs & watered the Hens. Eat. ha. And nursed her finger severel times to-day. red papers, writ her dairy. Which hadn't been done since three days have passed. And once, each day. She has to dress the soar finger. This was the duration, of a most wonderfull and also a beautifull day. Radio Was very plain & clear with no static till P.M. . . . Well Egg production is getting rather slim. 11 today. And the last 3 days only 8 & 9. So its no more to sell nor no Cream. Just buy most of the butter. . . .

TUESDAY, OCTOBER 8

. . . Well all Ma did, this day. Was churn nurse her painfull finger rit the dairy. Shirked. Red, & radioed. She finally got Ervins letter wrote & send off. Was a choar for her. . . . We drove to Syracuse at 4 P.M. To get Mas finger lanced, once more. It had came to a head ready, for relief. Has been very painfull most of the day. Well after all the abuse & torcher. Almost at Kendall. It felt relieved quiet hurting. So I went to Bed. And how did I sleep & it was a enjoyable night after all hard knocks . . .

WEDNESDAY, OCTOBER 9

. . . At 12:45, Thelma & Ma drove to Lakin, to get Verna. And couldn't get back eny sooner. We also got Thelmas mail on our way home. . . . On our way home. We drove through a Hurrican. Thistels piled up severel feet high in the road. Mas ears took another spell with dull sounds. and not in a normel condition.

SUNDAY, OCTOBER 13

. . . Pop rolled out around 6. Had all choares completed. Ma had stayed in slumberland, till almost 7. So Henry fried some chicken fried steak, & made gravy. So our breakfast was lucious. Soon he washed up the dishes. Took the fried roast to the Warners, and took dinner with them. . . . Pete called at dusk. So we all drove to Elmer Dyck. Pop & Pete chated in the Car long after Ma & Verna hit the Hay. . . .

MONDAY, OCTOBER 14

. . . Highwinds & duster which made the sky murky & very chilly to This was the beginning, of a new week also day. So this brought, the green season to a close. For the year of 1940. . . . trees green bushes are all full of ice on the inside, & brown on the outside. So all has suffered . . . About 2:35. We drove to the Warners. . . . They had went to Kendall after Coal. In the meanwhile Ma eat a muskmellon & Verna eat some beans. While Pop chated, with the working men. Before they got home, Ma sat out in the warm car & red a story of Just one While the House had grown chilly. Ma out in the Car, where it was the warmest she read a story. While Verna, was in the house reading. Soon the warners came home, & started a fire. . . . Got home after dusk

TUESDAY, OCTOBER 15

Clear & cold this morning. . . . And mr Jackfrost visited at our house in the night. . . . So this is the day after Jack Frost gave us a punishment to harsh for us to stand up, under the strain. Punished us, till we let our branches & heads hang Our green beauties have been taken. And now we've lost our apearence. . . . They moved the outfit to the field. . . . Cut on Cliffs on Sect 35. With the header came in for supper at 5:30. Henry & Pete a star border. Is just a mootcher here. While working for some one else. . . . Verna started a crochet rug at P.M. She cleaned up the Clothes closet AM. P.M. She started crocheting a rug. And Mas ears & head is howling at the worse. Cant hear today. She's still nursing her sore finger. Which was lanced. Its gash was healed shut this morning.

WEDNESDAY, OCTOBER 16
. . . Well last night & the night before frost. Have shriveled up the trees & other green branches & twigs. So this morning all looked sorta brown & weather beaten. After getting the once over. By Mr. Jack Frost. ha. . . . Men went to the field at 7 Cut for Cliff on 35 All 3 came in for dinner at almost 12. . . . Cut on the same field P.M. Came in for supper at 5:45, Next they listened to a thunderstorm which was put on by Wendall Wilkie. Well this was Regestration day for all the boys & young married men.[17] . . . Ma rolled in at 6:30. Couldn't stand the noise & shouting & trampling on account her ears.

THURSDAY, OCTOBER 17
. . . They cut for Cliff on 10 AM. & PM. Moved to 14. And cut for us all three men came here for dinner. . . . Ma shirked her duties, this day. Verna ironed most of the day. She dressed a chicken for dinner. & rugged some, while the ironed het up. . . .

SATURDAY, OCTOBER 19
. . . Ma & Verna drove to Syracuse. Work Men cut on sec. 14. All day. Got in from the field before sunset. . . . We got home from Syracuse, at 10:20. Ma all wore out. And work was piled up very thick And at 3 P.M. A Argonian Car drove up with 4 ocupents. Adolph Hildebrand, & his family.[18] stayed for supper all night, & for breakfast Sun. 20th. Was, we shocked to see them. . . . Verna had most of the dusting done. when the Guests arived. Vernas Bed was occupied by Mr & Mrs Adolph Hildebrand. Us Wimen rolled in about 8. Henry & Adolph chatted a while longer. Verna slept with Ma & Pop in the Basement.

SUNDAY, OCTOBER 20

. . . We had a reunion to day. While Adolph Hildebrand & family, had come out to see us folks in Kansas Land. We all took dinner, at Edger Dycks at the big Hotell in Kendall. Eat Cafeterie style Had a variety in Menue. O boy was it ever good. And did, we all enjoy ourselves Had a watermellon party late P.M. All the nieces & Nephews also the old Dyck family. & Mr Pete Dyck, where present. We returned home almost sunset. . . .

MONDAY, OCTOBER 21

. . . Pop puttered around so long before breakfast. So I helped my-self to the meal. And let him eat when he prefreed. Verna waited up for him ha. . . . The Men soon drove to the field and cut east of the community hall. . . . Ma & Verna Cold packed 9 qts tomatoes, Verna baked bread crochated around her dresserset. And rugged a while. While Ma only radioed rit her dairy & helped some with the daily, routeen. . . . Adolph Hildebrand & family called early at 7 AM. Started back home on their trip, to Oregon. Mas Ears & Head now have roared for a hole week last Thursday with Will be 2 weeks Thursday. . . .

THURSDAY, OCTOBER 24

. . . The Men both worked on the Combine all day. Thelma & Cliff stoped on their way to Olins. She and Leroy came back, & Cliff stayed. Went to Coolige, to see what they could help there. After get-ting a fone Call. About Grandpa Warners death this morning. . . . Verna backed Bread & rugged after supper. Ma tore up rags. And sowed some. Henry is down in the back & is taking a bowl tonic. Mas ears are still, in an uproar. And today P.M. She had another sickspell, & had to take an asprin. . . .

FRIDAY, OCTOBER 25

. . . Pop is still having a pain right over his hip. Ma was to sick after supper to exzist. She was sick through the night. Had female pains. & all other ailments. Didn't vommet though.

SUNDAY, OCTOBER 27

. . . Duster mostly all day locely . . . Henry worked on the Combine some . . . Verna had baked some doughnuts Saturday Pats helped her While Ma shirked most of the day. She felt tuff & today she had another spell, of dizzyness. And Vommeted till she was as sick as a grub worm. . . . Its now 17 days since my head has howled & roared. Just about a few hours of 2 fore noons, That she Could hear some better.

MONDAY, OCTOBER 28
. . . Men chocked feed a while. About 10 AM. They Combined on the Doerr quarter. all day . . . Verna washed P.M. And, rugged, a little AM. Ma sewed up some rags & stockings, for her rug ready to go, so she could crochet ever few minutes, of her leisure time.

TUESDAY, OCTOBER 29
. . . hawled grain. Men cut on the Doerr quarter. Mr Cliff helped Pete Combine while Henry & Ma went to Minneola.[19] We left home at 7 But discovered on our way up that the breaks, on the Car wouldn't hold. . . . we drove to Syracuse & Less Danials fixed them. We, then got started on our way to Minneola 10:30. And those at home. Thelma was here, and helped Verna get dinner. While Verna, did a big ironing. . . .

FRIDAY, NOVEMBER 1
. . . Pop Pete & Cliff cut Maze for Cliff all day. Elmer & Zelda where there Elmer skooped & Zelda helped Thelma cook. We stayed for supper & got home a little past dusk. . . . Ma helped a very little with breakfast. . . . Ma was deaf & was feeling very tuff She had to face severel spell of dizyness.

TUESDAY, NOVEMBER 5
. . . Well this is the great day of Generel Election day. Pop served on the Lection Board.[20] Verna & Ma shirked their usual duties to-day. We rugged on Vernas rug. Ma tore up the rags & Verna. croched them. . . . Pete & Elmer apeared, to see how the votes where coming. . . . Pete finished up at Cliffs 10:30. He came home in his Car. Went home & up to the Schoolhouse came after us wimen, at almost 4 to vote. Our roundtrip to vote & back was a period of less then one hour. . . . Pop came home way in the night, almost 12. . . .

WEDNESDAY, NOVEMBER 6
. . . Henry & Pete got the outfit home from Cliffs & cut on the patch 2 miles east. Never cut A.M. Just got the outfit set up ready to go. P.M. They cut all day. With good luck. Elmer hawled in 6 Loads maze. And shocked feel till late noon. . . .

THURSDAY, NOVEMBER 7

... Men where Combining on the Johnson 160 all day & finished Cutting. apeared early to hawl the grain 6 loads Maze. ...

SATURDAY, NOVEMBER 9

... At 7 AM. We started on our way to Minneola. Never took a snack with us. & had so wait so long till our tern came. So many patients where present . . . Was dusk when we returned home. ...

SUNDAY, NOVEMBER 10

... at 12:20. While dinnering a duster occured, about a 20 minute period. Next a short period it rained, so the surface was very slick. At 1:30 P.M. snowflurried fell in full blast. ... At 4 P.M. the 3 inches of Snowfall was drifting on piles. It was blizzering, for 3 hours or more in succession. Well this certenly was a shock for all of us. ... Verna worked some on her apquie quilt. Thelma had the Blues. ... Pop had worn his rayons, up till now & had to put on his long underwear. And Bed still had only had a Bedsheat on it till now. So Ma had to dress it, with its warm blanket. And o such comfort

MONDAY, NOVEMBER 11

... P.M. Verna & Ma rugged. We completed the rug, which I started 2 weeks ago Sunday. Ears are not to good. Cant hear very good atall. They're raising up a howl, ever time I stoop, and lift, they're so awful bad. ...

TUESDAY, NOVEMBER 12

... This Morning the fosset wasn't froze up. Yesterday it was froze up. With out giving it a thought, We never had no water drained out So Pop had to carry water out of the storage tank. ... We started to the Warners, at 10. Cliff had the water hot. At 1 PM. They had the Sow all dressed, & we had liver for dinner . . . And was it ever good. ... After supper Verna worked on her Tulip Quilt, Pop read, radioed, snoozed for a little bit. Ma all wore out. Didn't feel to good. She snoozed most of the evening. ...

WEDNESDAY, NOVEMBER 13

... Pop went to the kids & got the smallest calf home, while getting half of the dressed hog. Got back late dinner Ma had already started in eating. she was very hungry & thought Henry cood eat, when he took a notion. cause he didn't try & get home on time. Verna worked

on her appraque quilt. Made Bread. 12. & cleaned up the pantry while
it was warm. . . . Po snoozed on the davenport & Ma in the easyrocker

mostly all evening. She could hear all things over the radio. Well the
waterfosset has been frozed for 2 days.

THURSDAY, NOVEMBER 14
. . . Henry fixed up the north side of the Basement with Straw. the
Henhouse the little one, with celetex. And nailed the windows back
in it. He started to town at almost 10 AM. In the mean while he
couldn't get the Heater fixed he started to Garden at 12 noon & returned home at 8. . . . So this day was a batchler one. The Warners
came after the sausage grinder, at 12:15. while Ma was writing a
letter . . . Verna was eating a snack Thelma joined in. Soon Ma had a
snack. At 3:30 P.M. She got meat hungry. Fried a pan full & eat all she
wanted. And was it ever good. . . . Ma apricated this day very much,
Cause she could hear. And ears where back to normal. Well Pop was
being very funny to-day while Verna Clock wouldn't run he gave it a
hit & kick, & O boy the glass just flew.

FRIDAY, NOVEMBER 15
. . . We where breakfasting at 5:30. At 7. We all where ready. And
started on our way to get a treatment. At Minnola, and o it was
10:30. We missed out on our turn, cause we didn't regester. We didn't
get worked on till 2:30 O was there ever a big crowd in the yard
awaiting. . . . Returned home at sunset And both of us Wimen certenly did feel buggered up. after what we'd been through.

SATURDAY, NOVEMBER 16
. . . All the members of this Household seemed to be rather sleepy.
All snoozed one in each rocker, & Verna on the Davenport. She soon
retired, Ma had slept on the floor for a while. Mean while the Barn-
dance was on & was it ever wonderfull. Was 9 when we retired. And
o, did Ma & Verna feel tough today. Verna shined the floor. Baked
Bread. Ma didn't do enything she shirked all her duties. But her ears
acted Wonderfull. Back to Normal.

MONDAY, NOVEMBER 18
. . . Well Pop rolled out about 5. And soon started a fire in the Wellhouse after breakfast at 7 Started to Crank the machine, but she
wouldn't budge. So he had to work the motor over. At 10:15 AM.

It went off. So Verna started in washing. She finished up about 1:15.
Ma helped some but didn't do hardly eny hanging out. Henry fixed
the Windcharger & did some more puttering around A.M. After the
washer was completed, he ground up Mr Hog meat & Lard.

TUESDAY, NOVEMBER 19

Well today it was gloomy all day. Sky was overcast & windy. Got so
dark P.M. One couldn't hardly see nothing. . . . Ma didn't feel to good.
Verna wasn't feeling very well. Well this was a loaf day AM. Pop went
tomcaten to see Olin Warner. To see about the Elotment came home
late noon. Ma had started to eat she had boiled some Eggs for herself,
also Verna. When Pop apeared on the scene. After dinner was over.
He drove to Kendall & returned about 4:20. Mean while Verna ironed
all day. Included her bed room curtains, also her 2 Uniform. Beside
all the rest of ironing. Ma ironed a few pieces. P.M. She rendered lard,
but never got it all completed. She also tore up rags & sewed a lot of
them up. . . .

WEDNESDAY, NOVEMBER 20

. . . Pop was the messenger boy. Cut a batch of Kindlyn wood Carried
in new straw, for his hogs to bed in. Today Ma ragged all day. . . .
Verna Baked a nice Batch of Doughnuts P.M. & completed her long
rug at about 4 P.M. & worked on her aplique quilt. Well Pop passified
himself listing to the news & more news ha. A great bit of the day was
spend that way ha.

THURSDAY, NOVEMBER 21

. . . Pop rolled out at 6, Ma 6:20. We had breakfast at 7. while Pop was
listening in on the news. After the choars where completed this AM.
He read & listened to more news. And added to this. Listened to a
Football. . . . Verna writ a letter, while Ma rit her 4 day dairy. She
didn't do a bit. Just wipe dishes. And shirked all her duties. . . . A cold
got a hold of Ma to-day, & did it ever treat her tough. She ached all
over including her head. She's been able to hear now for 8 days in
sucession, including this one. . . .

FRIDAY, NOVEMBER 22

. . . We rolled out at 6:15. Had breakfast at 7. Pop & Verna soon
started to town, while Ma stayed at home. And nursed her sore nose
& wounded head head & stomache She took asprins, to help herself

on legs. Took 3 naps during the 5 hour period. While they where away to Town. They returned home at 1:15. . . .

SATURDAY, NOVEMBER 23
. . . Henry drove down to see Pete chatted for severel hours. & returned home at sunset. Meanwhile Verna had baked a 2 Egg sour cream chocolate cake. With white icing. She gave the 3 rooms a going over. Ma completed the Lard & Cracklins. Got good 3 gals lard. & did a few little things and most of the time she shirks her duties. The Radio was so Wonderfull. Pop & Ma stayed up till 10. . . .

SUNDAY, NOVEMBER 24
. . . The Warners called and took dinner with us. . . . Thelma sewed up her comfortor top & Verna embroaried. . . . The little ones cut up papers wrote made colored Bills. And Leroy Cut out Cars. also read funnies, after the mail came home. Well this is one day Pop was obident, But clung to the rocker very close. So he wouldn't loose it. Cause he's very found of it. Well our little kities all both meet their doom the last two days. Spose they lived in the Hen House, or with the Hogs to much. Couldn't take it.

TUESDAY, NOVEMBER 26
. . . After supper Verna started in on Thelmas xmas rug. Mas rug growed considerable P.M. She washed some dresses & socks while Verna fixed some Cranberry sauce. A change in menue for supper, we had Tomato soup. Well Mas nose still needs nursing, is very sore & Ears are still behaving themselves. . . .

WEDNESDAY, NOVEMBER 27
. . . Henry choared after breakfast. & shaved. In the forenoon he went hunting for his Pigs, which he thought were missing. Also ask Elda & Wayne over for a card game, Thanksgiving. He shaved cleaned, & dressed up. So we had an early dinner, at 12:15. He was on his way to Syracuse & bought a batch of Candy Nuts Popcorn & celery . . . Returned home at sunset. Meanwhile Verna had baked Cliffs Birthday Cake. Who now is 35 years of age. 2 Pumpkin Pies dressed a chicken. Scrubed kitchen & Pantry. Also did all the dusting. While Ma was rugging & ragging. All she did was what she had to do. And included Baking Bread Was real good completion was made at 8. She had stayed home, while Verna & Pop went to Warners, To ask them over

for a Thanskiving feast in the evening. Radio was so Wonderfull we couldn't get to Bed. Stayed up till 10. . . .

THURSDAY, NOVEMBER 28

. . . Well Po & Ma plunged out of the hay earlier, as usual. So the old Hen could get into the oven & Bake, to get nice & Tender for dinner. . . . We eat our lonely & good Thanskiving dinner all by ourselves, Cause all whom we asked over, had already been invited out Our dinner consisted of Pumpin Pie dressing Cramberry sauce Cellery & baked chicken Mashed Potatoes, & gravy. And was it good. Verna had made some brownfudge & Popcorn So at 4:30 Thelma & kidies came for supper while Cliff went home & choared. Wayne Rogers & family also Elmer & Wife where present. Enjoy the evening with card games Popcornballs Candy. At 10 Cake & Coffee was served. We rolled in at 11. The Warners where the last ones to leave so we couldn't expect much sleep. On account of our trip to Minneola for the next day.

FRIDAY, NOVEMBER 29

And here came the day Saturday so we rolled out at 20 min. Till 4. To get started early on our way to Minneola at 7 AM. To get our treatments. . . . A lotta patients where waiting for a treatments, some in the House & some in the House. So we had severel hours to wait. . . . we all went to the Comity meeting. At the Hall Verna & Ma out in the Car snoozing. The Board men where having their usualy meeting. was 10:30 when we rolled in.

MONDAY, DECEMBER 2

. . . Pop completed the choars at 7:30. He got ready & hawled 3 Loads feed. And put the Antifreeze in the tractors tires. Verna died the blue sheet for Thelmas rug. Just when we where right in the midst of it. Here they came to sow up their blue cloth, for their chairs. And o did we ever made a get away, with her Xmas rug, to keep it a secret. So Ma went to work on her own rug & Verna got buisy at her embroadrywork. . . . Verna went home with them, & said, Now you, Ma & Po can go Honeymooning ha ha. . . .

WEDNESDAY, DECEMBER 4

. . . We suppered & at 5:30. We started to Warners stayed till 10:10. We spend the evening, playing cards. The kids had baked filled Cook-

ies, also made toffy. Had a very splendid time. . . . Mas work to-day.
She gave the 2 rooms agoing over scrubbed the Pantry & kitchen.

Well quiet a shocking sprized Ma got. When she found 2 young pullets Eggs in the north Henhouse. After those Pullets have been in
such condition. 6 Eggs all tole.

THURSDAY, DECEMBER 5
. . . Ma rugged a little, and made some cream soap. Washed a few
pieces & Pops heavy underwear, & o my, how I felt, from the effects
of it. We all took our baths P.M.

FRIDAY, DECEMBER 6
. . . At 10 We got to Minneola & had to wait for our treatments, till
2 P.M. We started on our way home. Henry Verna Elda & Donald,
eat their snack around 12 Ma eat her snack after she was through with
her treatment. Elda had taken a cherry Pie & cheese sandwiches. We
took some ham sandwiches & one Apple Pie, & some Apples & a jug
of water. We stopped at Montezuma bought some Tobacco . . . Verna
hurt very bad after her treatment & Ma spend the evening looking at
the Xmas Catalogue. Cause she had a great deal of hurts, from the
effects of the treatment. So she shirked all her duties. Pop snoozed
by the Radio before rolling in.

SUNDAY, DECEMBER 8
. . . The Warners called . . . They played Cards till 3:30 P.M. & Warners
went home. While the little ones cut out paper dolls eat a Apple &
played hidinggo seek. . . . Ma & the little Warners, took a strole and
hunted for Eggs. And while we where looking in the Barn. The littel
ones, spied the dead kitties which where lying on the manger. Little
ones, felt very sory over the dead ones. . . .

MONDAY, DECEMBER 9
. . . Henry drove to the field 15. min. Till 8. He hawled 6 Loads feed
to-day. He really worked to day. He really worked. this day. . . . Well
this day sorta seemed like blue Monday. No pep for Ma. She just
shirked most all her duties. Just did, what had to be done. She sewed
Pats dishtowls & croched some on Thelmas Xmas rug. She didn't feel
to good. either. Well its now 3 days since the Hens are laying. We have
enough Eggs to eat, & Cook with. And dear Pop Can have 2 ever
meal ha. No more one Egg at a meal. . . .

WEDNESDAY, DECEMBER 11

. . . Pop had a load of feed to unload, and hawled in 4 loads. Cliff Warner apeared . . . So him & Pop went to Kendall he got the Xmas parcell & the mail. So they had plenty of passifing the rest of the day. Verna ironed till 3 P.M. Ma never did a bit of it. She washed lamp-globes. & washed 4 pr. Socks, & 3 flour sacks. had 3 dizzy spells. P.M. And her ears went haywire. And pressure occured in her wright ear. So she couldn't hear to well. She ragged after supper. Verna passified herself making Potholders. Bonnet girls[21] Some more, about the days ironing. Verna had the Pantry Bedroom & frontroom Curtains to iron. And this day was also Mas Asprin day. . . .

THURSDAY, DECEMBER 12

. . . Pop had went out to choar. . . . Next he scooped a path through the Snow, to the Jonses & Henhouse. Cut some kindling. He true-storied to passify himself & libertied. While Verna and Ma came to the Completion of Thelmas Xmas blue rug was about 11:15. After supper we came to the completion of Mas oblong rug which she mostly made all her self. . . . we both laughed after it was all completion was made. Egg production 15 today. While Henry had gathered them, & said, Ma if you can guess, how many Eggs the Hens layed this day, I'll give you a quarter. I guess 12. He then spoke up & said, o no, you're to far off ha. . . .

FRIDAY, DECEMBER 13

very very Cold. Well this was the coldest day, we've endured for sev-erel weeks. The blanket of Snow was disturbed by the heavy freeze. The Snow sifted around, all foot tracks where filled after a short time. . . . Well this was an eventfull day. AM. Verna Coverd the foot-stools with Velvet, also the Rocker. Pop helped her nail the stools up & took the strips off. P.M. we baked a double batch old fashion sugar cookies. Some where filled & some of them with raisins. All sorts of the Cutters where used. . . . After we eat Verna worked at her dressen plate quilt.[22] Ma put the procter on her brown comforter. & cut out some pieces for her quilt, which she's patching up. And Pop true-storied, libertyed, & some more of todays events. While Pop was right in the midst eating Cookies He looked up & said. O Ma these certenly are good. Why don't you bake cookies oftner ha. And some more of Mas daily duties, she didn't shirk. Atending to her Laying Hens, so they'd pep up with their Egg production. . . .

SUNDAY, DECEMBER 15

... AM. All the members of the family read some. P.M. Verna & Ma broke the Sabbath. Part of AM. Much entagnisum took place while Pop was trying to fill the the Lantern, for the storage tank. Globe wouldn't stay put. Pop took it, set it on the floor very harsh. O how did he fume Mo held her breath, for fear, it would break. So Ma helped him & Pop said it takes the hole family to fill the Lantern ha. Also while he was trying to put battry water, in the Battery, The tester had froze fast in the jar of ice. So Ma had to grab it with her fingers while Pop breaking the ice. All was fine, & he got the battry all filled up, without eny more Curse words. Well about breaking the Sabbath by Ma & Verna, She sewed up some pieces & cut out some for her dressing plate quilt. And Ma started a very very long rag crochet rug ha. ...

MONDAY, DECEMBER 16

... It was 1:30. When we got started to Syracuse. We finished doing our Xmas shopping, Send off the Cards. ... Ma bought Ervins shirt. a gown. for Verna. Send off the Belt for Pop. And the dress for Thelma. Also bought the nuts & Candy for Xmas some Bananas Cranberries, & Pineapple. ... Late P.M. Ruth Bishop called & gave us an invetation to the Moving picture Show tonight at the Schoolhouse. Ma wrote a letter to Ervin. While Verna wrapped us the Xmas packages to go to Oregon to Ervin Vernas sent one to Ervin, & the one Po & Ma send to him. We got our Xmas from Ervin, to-day. ... What a spell Pop had putting the new generator on the Gas Lantern. And o, It wouldn't budge, hardly, make a bit of light. So he got saurcastic, & turned it out a flying shook it Took a Coloil lamp, & went to reading, as if nothing had happened, ha ha. ...

TUESDAY, DECEMBER 17

... Well this was an unfortnute day. When Pop awoke it was 6 & o o o We had planed on rolling out at 5 or before. Ma didn't sleep sound, she feared she wouldn't wake up in time. Cause the first time it was 12. ... We started down the road to Wayne Rogers to get Elda & Donald to go to Minnola, & take our treatments. Ma made the lunch while Verna fried the Eggs. In all the rush, she forgot a drinking cup. And the lunch turned over & the Apples, & cookies fell out, on the flour ha ha. And back to our trip down there. ... as it was not a very early buisy day. No Car was present. So we got our treatments right off the bat. ... So then 2 more Cars drove up, & at 11:15, We started on our way home. Returned home 2:20. ...

WEDNESDAY, DECEMBER 18

. . . Mas Spirits where all wounded to-day. So tonight when she heard. Eddies Canters. Song. I don't want no Xmas present, Just let me keep what I have. Was Wonderfull. . . . Well the members of the family had hit the Hay Verna 8:15 Pop 9:30. After the news cast was completed. Ma stayed up & worked on her quilt, & ragged 1/2 hour. Was 10:10. When she hit the Hay. . . .

FRIDAY, DECEMBER 20

. . . Grieswold stopped on their way from Town. & told [Verna] that Mary Homes wanted her help, at the Beautyparlor.²³ Verna turned in at 8:15. Henry 15 min. Till 9. & Ma at 10. She certenly enjoyed to work at her longrug, while all, in piecefull slumber. ha. After rolling in she had taken the heavy comforter off the Bed. And she almost got to Chilly her own fault ha ha

SATURDAY, DECEMBER 21

. . . Pop choared before we eat. . . . He had to fix & pump up a tire before starting. So it was 15 Min. Till 8. When they started on their way. So they had a time finding Christie, to see if Verna could stay with her, these 4 days. Well this was a piecefull & quiet day for Ma she was at home all day, by herself and certenly did enjoy it. No Intrusion . . . So Ma wrapped up her two packages, & send them off. . . . Also wrote a letter to Lizzie on the Xmas card she send to her. . . . Well she was the messenger boy. And had to atend to the Hens. & Carry in the Eggs. Even if there only where 8 of them ha. So most of the day was taken up. And all her daily duties. So she didn't have much Leisure left. . . . And being all alone to do the work. No one to lend a helping hand to help do Saturdays work. Dusting was limnated also scrubbing. Cause its so very muddy. She'l do it the next day. . . . This day seemed rather long. No dinner to get. . . .

SUNDAY, DECEMBER 22

. . . Ma cleaned & dusted her house. After she had her dishes washed. She went to see the Jonses, & heard Henry's voice in the barnyard. She walked torrad him, & thought, I bet he found a nest of Eggs which she dreamed. And all at once it occured to her. I bet there are twin Calves. And really when she encountered him & there was the Cow with 2 little ones. One Heifer & one Steer. This was quiet a surprize for us all. . . . going back to some incedent which happened to me very early this morning at 2. I had an urgent call. I hurried out of Bed & by the Heatrola stood the foot stool. I stumbled over it & skinned my leg. & after I got back to Bed. I had a good laugh & Henry lay awake & wanted to know, what all had happened to me while he heard me laugh ha. About all we listened to tonight was War News. & more news. . . .

THURSDAY, DECEMBER 24

. . . [Pop] went right out to [c]hoar. Is now breaking in the two twin calves. One drinkes fine. He took a shave and dolled all up. . . . at 2:10 we started on our way to Syracuse after Verna. And returned home at 7. Was a little after 8 when we was all ready to start to the Xmas Tree. & returned home from the Hall at 10 P.M. The Warners came along home with us. The little ones drove in our Car with us. And got their Xmas treats. Also the Turky & the Roaster to cook it in. Was so large thelma had to cut off one wing also the Legs. So she could get it in the Roaster. . . . Well Henrys rejoicing since the twin Babes, drink by them selves.

WEDNESDAY, DECEMBER 25

. . . Henry rolled out at 6:30. Ma & Verna 20 min. Till 7. Ma listened to the Unity Program, & was it ever good. Henry milked & choared before chow. Was through 7:30. And had breakfast 7:45. We tried to get started to the Warners before very late. But didn't make much progress. Cause we had our Xmas to unwrap from Ervin. . . . Verna never unwrapped none of her gifts till this morning. We all hit the Hay at 11. . . .

TUESDAY, DECEMBER 26

. . . Verna shined up the House & read. Ma washed Lampglobes for once, again, which hadn't been for severel days. She also worked some on her quilt. & rugged a little while, after all the Household had retired. They've been, very sleepy ever since the Holidays, & rolled in early Ma hit the Straw at 10. . . . Early AM. Verna & Pop devoured part of their treats. . . .

FRIDAY, DECEMBER 27

. . . Ma washed Pops Underwear some socks & some under garments & aprons. To passify herself the remainder of the day she rit some neglected dairy, & ragged. At 7 P.M. Pop was passifying himself listining to the Gangbusters. Well now for a 7 week period, Ma has coughed & sneezed. And yesterday she got a new Cold & added to this. A blister under her nose & a hurt in her head. And her left ear has raized cane, now for 2 days, ever time, she stooped. Later in the day, she took an asprin to hear up these pains. The house was lonely Verna not being here. Henry hit the Hay at 15 Min. Till 8. And Ma was intrested in cutting out blocks. & stayed up till 9:10. . . .

SATURDAY, DECEMBER 28

. . . Had to fix & clean up the Cream Seprater. Had stood Idle for a period of almost 3 months. So this was the most eventfull day during a period of almost 3 months. We got 1/2 gals Cream. O how Wonderfull. And that means a starting of a little Cream check. And added to this, Hens finally produced 19 Eggs. So that'l be the beginning of a little income. Tonite, while Henry went to Kendall after Verna Ma was to lazy, to get ready & go along. She stayed home & o how she did enjoy herself, listning in on such beautifull music, also such Wonderfull sacred Songs. She was so lazy, just spend the evening radoing. . . .

SUNDAY, DECEMBER 29

. . . Well this Sunday the Sabath wasn't broken. Listened to War news & Sermans. Had dinner at 12:15. And at 1:30 Henry motered down to see Pete. Verna & Ma passified them self with a firesidechat. & devouring some chocolate fudge, which she made today A.M. He returned at 4:20. P.M. . . . The President made a speech from the Diplematic reception room, right from the Whitehouse.[24] Continued 3/3 of an hour. . . .

TUESDAY, DECEMBER 31

. . . The Warners where here 2:30. P.M. & brought the little ones to stay allnight. Verna Made some date Pudding. 2 Pumpkin Pies. Some Cream colored divenety. also dressed 2 cocks P.M. After supper she pieced quilts. Ma made some Bread. & picked the feathers off the biggest rooster She had such pains on her blistered nose. And the left ear was throbbing so terriable. so when the night came along she was to tired to hardly stand up. & efects from coufing. Her sore nose, kept her from sleeping well at all. Henry rolled in at 9:45. And said. I'm sleepy & wont stay up, to see the old year die. & the rebirth of 1941. . . .

7. THE END OF AN ERA

1941

WEDNESDAY, JANUARY 1

New Month & a new day Came in with new spirits new pep & new courage. We had a little get together at our House a New Year dinner. Thelma & family. Elmer & wife. Also Pete Dyck. Took dinner with us the first day of the year 1941. . . . The wimen chatted Cliff fixed something on his Car. Pop & Pete Where out for a chat to themselves Later they listened to the Ball game. The little ones played with paper dolls. Leroy loaded up Coal in his little traylor. And made this catterpiller pull a big piece of Coal. After supper, after dishes where all washed & put away. Zelda & Verna, where ingrossed in a cincear chat. Mean while Henry was milking. Elmer & Pete radioed Later, they all listened to the News, also comediens. We where all not in to plesent a mood, from the happings of the day. . . .

THURSDAY, JANUARY 2

And here is another new day. With a new spirit of the 2th day of the Year of 1941. . . . Henry cleaned at the Basement most of the day & sorted a great deal of papers & other trash. He is planning on butchering soon, so he has to have the store room clean, so he can butcher. . . . Us Wimen all joined in cleaning up junk. . . . Verna cut, & sewed up some pieces on her Dimondfield. Ma at her waves of the world she sewed up one big block & cut out some. . . .

FRIDAY, JANUARY 3

. . . Well Ma & Verna worked on their quilts to-day. Verna on her Dimondfield. And Ma made a block, for her knew dimond quilt. The first one she made. Its now the second day after the New Year ushered in. And she's made something each day, to show up. . . . Notice. A big Steercalf was born to day. The Mother is the very yellow Jersy. Pop thought he got a good joke on us. She gave a half bu. 1/2 full of milk. At the first milking. Well Pop knew all after noon the Cow, had found her calf. Hadent told us. Till Ma seen the bu. of Milk ha. . . .

SUNDAY, JANUARY 5

No Sabath broke. . . . Henry had completed all the milking at 7. When Ma came out of the Hay. And amedetly he asked for breakfast. While Ma was rather slow, getting some chow. So it was almost 15 mi. Till 8. When we breakfasted. Wo and soon the saurcasum fumed around this room. When Henry seen, the cut scraps which where lying on his dress coat. Which he had left there last night after his return home from Syracuse. And not long after this event had taken place. And there was the milk which hadnt been strained. So some more intagnisum was spred. And so all this, created some disturbenes this day. And It mostly clowed over this day. It was a black day. And so after all. It was a make believe Sunday. . . .

TUESDAY, JANUARY 7

This is a chilly dawn its Vernas Birthday. . . . A great event full day, also part of it was intagnising. . . . Three guys selling books, also pamplets on religeon. One came in the House. turned his Fonograph on & played a religous reccord. While the Biblestory was being broad casted on the air. & o, if that wasn't nervie. Taking our rights away from us, in our own house. While we where listning in on this epesode He was very entagnizing. Well Ma sorta shirked her daily duties. Didn't acomplish much. Just baked the first batch of very good Bread . . . And to-day Mas deaf again. After a long period of being back to normal, thats excepting her left ear has had a lott a preshure most every day. Henry lost another babey pig by the cyotes, I spose. Thats now 7 that are gone out of the bunch . . .

WEDNESDAY, JANUARY 8

. . . Pa & Ma breakfasted at 6:20. Thats the earliest Ma came out of the Hay for 3 weeks. Henry eat before he choared. He seprated started the fire in the Wellhouse & butchered Hogs. Pete Zelda & Elmer called at 8:15. About 12:30 They had the second one dressed. Pete Elmer & wife left for home at 3:35. They took dinner with us. We had some fresh liver for our Menue at noon. . . . Mas Ears caused

lotta confusion to-day. She couldn't hear. . . . Ma has a painfull sore
on her right arm. Looks like a boil. Henry took a needle, & opened it.

THURSDAY, JANUARY 9
. . . Had breakfast 7:30. When the choars where completed & he had
the Washer started. Henry then took a joy ride to the Warners, after
the bone knife. Returned home 11 A.M. The washer had quit so Ma
got a chance to listen in on the Topeka staff & o it was wonderfull. Machine It hadn't quit purcelating very long till Henry returned
home. So it was 12:30. When the washing was completed. We washed
2 blankets, the blue quilt, & all the jackets that was on the place.
And had a real big washing. And poor Po, had to wear rags, while he
was getting his good clothes cleaned up ha. . . . Pop cut up some of
the Hog. . . .

FRIDAY, JANUARY 10
. . . Well we sevrated this day for the last day. ever other day. We have
started in seprating twice a day. Its to much mess to save the milk
over. Well we hurried around got the cream ready. Eggs where all
ready to go yesterday also baths where taken. It was almost 8:30.
When we started on our way. Cream test was 42 price 26 toteled to
$1.74 cts. Eggs 17 cts a doz Toteled to 2.55. We got a very nice letter
to-day from Ervin saying, he still has his New Car in Ugene getting it
worked on a little. And never been to the dance for 2 weeks. Neither
seen the Blond. But is going to see her this coming Satur. He also
said. He hadn't made any reseloutions. But was going to try & do
better in this New year of 1941. . . . After dinner was completed,
and our Biblestory was over with Pop worked at his meat. grind
up a bit of Meat & Lard. And Ma stuffed 10 Cans full. . . . Well Ma
didn't acomplish much to be seen. Mostly she cut out Poems &
red. So many activities had to be atended to, after our return from
Town. Seprator had set also the dishes. Couldn't atend to them, in
such rush. . . .

SATURDAY, JANUARY 11
. . . Henry cut a pile of kindling, and ground up some more meat &
Lard. We had some chow at 12. while Pop had put the ribs on to
boil in this lard. The completion was made of rendering lard at 3:45.
Lard 11 gals. Cliff call at 8 PM. sometime & ground the Lard, from
his share of the Lard. Beings he had got 1/2. And we butchered 2
of them.

SUNDAY, JANUARY 12

. . . Henry soon drove to Pete & Elmer to take them some sausage & ribs. Was sunset when he came home & Ma had got all ready to go to the Warners to see how Thelma was. He brought Pete along so he was here for supper. and stayed all night. . . .

TUESDAY, JANUARY 14

. . . Henry cut some Kindling cleaned out the Barn. & ground up the filling for the sausage. He helped Ma stuff them. Verna fried the sausage down P.M. Later, she worked at her vanity Set. Also did some washing. Pop had a lotta rhumetism, while Ma still was nursing her boil. Pop & Verna hit the Hay at 9. Ma stayed up till 9:40 & rit her dairy, which she'd neglected for 2 days. Henry awoke while she was turning in, & said. What are you getting out this time of the night. While he was half in his sleep.

WEDNESDAY, JANUARY 15

. . . Cliff & Thelma called at 9:45. took dinner with us. The men drove to Kendall at 1:30. . . . They returned with their groceries at 3:10. The kids took their meat & went home. In the mean while Thelma piece at her quilt. Did some patching Overalls & made some pillow Cases, from some curtains. Verna worked at her Vanity set, till she had all her floss used up. Ma made Bread to-day, & Verna made some cinnamon rolls. . . .

FRIDAY, JANUARY 17

. . . very cold. . . . And the most purtiest scene of it all. Was, a string of ice cickles all along on the Henhouse. A few on the Barn, Wellhouse, house, also Barn. But the Henhouse was the prettiest of them all. . . . Verna took her bath, thought Henry was going to start to Syracuse right off the Real. He said o no, its to cold. So she shined up the House & he truestoried, also cleaned out the papers, & trash out of his buisness boxes. So at 12 we dinnered & they started to town at 1. . . . they returned home at 4. ha. ha. The road was a fright the 3 mile north of here. In the meanwhile, Ma smeared most of P.M. She cleared up the scraps of Butter, & Cream. And made 2 big batches of Soap. She had to nurse her boil. Didn't have no tape nor cotton to wrap it, so the rag came down till the boil was very sore from the abuse. Verna brought some tape & cotten. So she wraped it & taped it. And now it dont get abused no more stayed wrapped, & what a relief. . . .

SATURDAY, JANUARY 18

. . . Verna gave the two rooms a theour going over. swept her Bed-room. P.M. She sorted her ecumalated letters over, which she'd saved for severel years. & Ma cut out 46 Stamps. She also cleaned up the pantry. cleaned up the middle Bedroom good. Also made another batch of Soap. After supper she took her bath. While she didn't hurry much, Verna wanted to know, what she was doing. ha.ha. . . . Her ears have howled now for severel days. But not eny interference in her hearing. When Pop spied Mas clean Bedroom, he said o it seems like home again.

SUNDAY, JANUARY 19

. . . Henry came out of the Hay I spose some past 6. He had the milking all completed. Was getting the Cream crock when I came out of the Hay. It was then 8 oclock Verna had beat me this time. Was baking cornbread. So we had some chow at 8:30. ha, Thats a Sunday for you. At 11 A.M. The Warners appeared. They took dinner with us. after dinner was served. They all 6 went up in the attic & exploured it. And o the junk they found there & in such mess. The men nailed up some holes, to keep the birds out. And the duster they brought with them even the poarch endured a duster. And they all was almost choaking, from the effects of the dust.[1] In the mean while Ma started in on a knew round rug. she sewed up some & certainly broke the sabath. Scoured the smoking stand which was all black, from burning matches & cigretts, also cleaned the black smoked Aladan lamp flue. which she almost had to scour. 3 days ago the Mantel blowed up which was all shot. & added to it the lamp was full of sut that the black sute was flying, & the results where, room was all dark. from the effects. And going back to some more included to break the Sa-bath. She put clean paper on the Pantry shelf. & to spend the rest of the day. The four get intrested in a Card game. & o did they have lots of fun & frolic. . . . Ma rit a letter to Ervin, who is enjoying the Lure of the West. . . . After Ma had started in on Ervins letter, she left it on the Piano Bench, while she washed the milk Buckets. she looked up, & spied Verna reading it. Ma quietly up & goosed her. O she did jump & yell. And how, Pop did laugh.

MONDAY, JANUARY 20

. . . never heard the Light of the world, on account of the Presidents reangation [re-inauguration]. nor Adopted daughter. . . . A.M. It sorta seemed like blue Monday for Verna & I. she also was half cracked in the head. . . .

TUESDAY, JANUARY 21
. . . In the evening. Ma read the Cappers Weeklies A.M. Verna the Unity & Bible some Po also read the story of Joseph. A.M. They where also nutting. for passifying later P.M. Ma baked some Bread, was good to. . . . Ma rugged some. She felt so terriable in her head & O my how her ears roared, & howled. this is the second day that they reacted like that. But didn't work but just a very little on my hearing. . . .

THURSDAY, JANUARY 23
. . . Verna retired very early. She got a Card, from Mary Homes to day saying. your job is open now for you enytime you can come in. The radio is very stattac to day P.M. Henry really had to listen to more news & more news. About War. Cause he wasn't in the House much. . . . And along with all this a bit intagnistic some how all things went wrong with him. Verna was blue and not very cheerfull. Ma not so bad to buisy to complain ha ha.

FRIDAY, JANUARY 24
. . . At 8:55, Henry & Verna started to town. . . . And this was a very sad endurance, to-day. House was all lonesome & Empty. just all by myself. Ma rugged after she had the two rooms all gone over. She eat her snack at almost 1 P.M. Henry returned home from town 15 min. Till 3. He certenly radioed all the while he wasn't choaring. & after supper He eat his dinner at almost 3, & supper at 7. And hit the straw at 9. Ma at 9:15 she rit her dairy after he retired. . . . Verna stayed up town, on her job with Mary Homes.

SATURDAY, JANUARY 25
. . . Had breakfast at almost 8. Ma got to hear the Unity Program. . . . Henry stacked up some shingels A.M. Also P.M. about 2 hours all tole. The rest of the day He truestoried & read papers. We got a Card from Ervin said. He almost got the Flue. And a letter from Grandpa Dyck, which he rit himself. Jerman & was Po saurcastic about the dutch letter ha ha.[2] Ma baked a batch of Doughnuts A.M. scrubbed the kitchen & Pantry also washed the Lamp globes. And rugged part of the day. She felt very tuff her back ached something terriable had

such sticking in between her sholders. And o her Ears just raised cane. She couldn't hear just about half. of P.M. . . .

SUNDAY, JANUARY 26

. . . Henry had the milking & seprating all done 7:50. When Ma came out of the hay. O say its a wonder she didn't look like a pitch fork ha. We breakfasted at 9. So was almost dinner time, when Ma got the two rooms, all going over. Had dinner straight up 12. Next Henry feed the stock & went out hunting with his gun. Returned home at 3 P.M. So Ma had a very lonely day. she read Listened to Revern Brown preach his serman. Also Leo Odanials & Charlie McCarthy. . . . A day that no Soul showed up. I spose cause the roads where so terriable. Mas hears where about half there this day. Such roaring & preassure. She could only hear halfway. And her back still in a pain. & very weak. She washed a little today & while she wanted Henry to put on his clean shirt he said, o such rags its all worn out. I'm going to buy me some knew ones. So I gave him his dress shirt to put on. To heal his wounded emotions. about the rags ha ha. . . .

MONDAY, JANUARY 27

. . . A change in activites to-day. We rolled out at 5:30. And break-fasted at 6. Henry milked at 6:30. At 8 he started on his way to Ken-dall to ship the cream returned at 9:45. . . . Henry swept & cleaned up the east granary. Had to clean out his Barn, so he was out of doars most of the time. Radioed some, while reading the todays mail he was puffing his Cares away. Ma rugged after her every day activities, when taken care of. Her Ears where not so bad to-day. Roared & howled. But didn't effect her hearing much. Just a little in the evening. Her back wasn't to good today. Ma stayed up till 10:15 & tried to finish up the roundrug. But couldn't do it.

TUESDAY, JANUARY 28

. . . Henry choared at 6:45 & when they where completed. He soon went to work at his granary. Also had to clean up the Barn. Had to pre-pare some kindling wood. He wasn't in the House very much. Elmer the mailman drove into the yard, & mucked it all up. Had to have water for his car. Thats the first caller that entered onto this ranch so far this week. Henry had a passifyer after he got the mail. . . . Well Ma rugged at the round one after her days routeen was completed. . . .

THURSDAY, JANUARY 30

. . . O say old Ma has had the tooth ache. & hasn't been able to wear
her lower teeth for 5 days just when she eat. And o it didn't feel so
good. Ma cleaned herself late P.M. to get ready to go along to town
tomorrow. She also cleaned & packed the eggs. After chow Pop took
off his dirty overalls & shirt. And put on his gomeeting trousers, but
his shirt he didnt put on, just made his uper under answer the purpose, for the evening. . . .

FRIDAY, JANUARY 31

. . . We started to Town at 8:15 AM. It was misting heavy & the glass
was all steamed full on the inside. Henry couldn't hardly see. Had to
keep wiping the windshield off again & again. Road was bad one
mile north of here, & a 1/2 mile north of the correction line. After
that we could just sail along. We returned home at 25 min till 2. When
we got home the Warners where here had eat a snack. . . . After our
return trip how did I feel so bad didn't know whether, I was going or
coming. & how the old piece of tooth did ache me. . . .

SUNDAY, FEBRUARY 2

. . . At 8 the clowds cleared away and the old jentleman saw his shadow.
So now we have 6 more weeks of serious weather. . . . Henry rolled out
at 6:15 & Ma at almost 7. He came in after the bowl & water to seprate.
We breakfasted at 7:25. I hurried around & cleaned scrubed & dusted
the two rooms at 11. The Warners apeared. Thelma sewed at her dress
some We had late dinner. Next we motered down to Elmer & Zelda.
Thelma Elmer Cliff & Henry played a few games of cards. And the
little ones played with the little pups. We all had a swell time. The
roads where so rough, that we just flew around in the Car. We got
back home at almost 4:30. The kids went right for home. . . . And
while Po was milking Ma listened to One Mans family. And was it
ever good. We radioed & Ma read some also played lazy. . . .

TUESDAY, FEBRUARY 4

. . . Well going back to some events of the day. We had dinner at 5 min.
Till 12. & supper much later as usual. at 6:20. We got home at sunset
from the Warners. Ma made Bread & a brown Cake all with one fire.
But never got the Cornbread baked, cause we got home to late Henry
never got to hear all the program, of We The People. Got the choars
completed at 7:15. We the People now have a song sang about Sangta

[Sanka] Coffee. This was the first time they sang it. Uncle Walters Dog House. Gave a talk on Mariage problems. where so different & harder to content with as in the old Pioneer days. He says they have to much make up on. So a Hubby don't know what they look like. Says they get heartbroken over a heated Magazine ha ha. It was the very best program they every gave. He thinks the Wimen ought, to take care of their families. . . .

THURSDAY, FEBRUARY 6

. . . Ma started in washing at 9 A.M. she finished up 11:30. Didn't blue the big slips & sheets, left them stick in the water. Dried severel pieces in the House Henrys dress trousers, & Overalls. Aprons & towls. What she hung on the clothes line soon froze & didn't dry much. . . . Henry fixed the gas tank on the machine did some more sweeping out in the granaryes. & puttered some more. . . . P.M. She really cleaned House. Cupboard all rugs shined the little Bedroom the middle Bedroom, aired the Bedding in both Bedrooms, & atended to many other activities. So after supper she's so stiff ached and sorta froze. While she was giving the stove some draft she raised up & hit something & raised a big bump on her head and cut it. While empting the washwater, she had to use a pliers to turn the didie open & off it broke, & o, if she didnt make a reck out of the machine. O how I felt about this. Felt as if I'd ought to be spanked. . . .

FRIDAY, FEBRUARY 7

. . . Henry went to work at his granary at A.M. Also P.M. he had to sweep some more. While Ma didn't have the Broom in action. . . . Well Ma had to bluing & hang out most of the clothes which she had, washed yesterday. She cleaned up the kitchen also the frontroom & o she did ache & hat a fit in her head, had to take ansprin. Her ears where much worse 4 hours A.M. As they've been for a long time. It efected her hearing a great deal. She ironed some early A.M. She washed the east & part of the northwall. After supper she cut out her Apron, which the Warners gave her for Mothers day, severel years ago, also cut out some blocks for her dimond quilt. She had the jitters in her legs till she couldnt see straight. At 9:30 She retired & froze in bed from the efects of Rhumetism. While Henry listened to a fight and to death Valley for the second time. He hit the straw at 10. And Ma had fallen into a deep slumber ha ha.

SUNDAY, FEBRUARY 9

. . . A.M. at 10:15 the Warners called had left the little ones at Sunday school. Henry & Cliff went to get the little ones. We all broke the Sabbath. Verna sewed her Uniform. Thelma her yellow Apron trimmed in red Ricrac, also cut out her Lavender dress & sewed up part of it. This dress she trimmed it in white braid. We where all engrossed in sewing. All at once while it was 20 Min. Till one Henry spoke up & said. When do we eat ha. Ma hurried around, and got something to eat. . . . Verna had completed her Uniform. She washed & ironed. While the irons where hot Ma pressed out some pieces. We eat a snack sometime P.M. . . . Verna & Ma hit the hay at a little past 9. Henry hit it after 10. He found a meeting on some station, where they had Babtism. I had fallen into a deep slumber by the time he came to Bed.

MONDAY, FEBRUARY 10

. . . Ma didn't feel to good today she sewed up some rags. Baked some Bread not so very good. She also cut out her pink apron with green braid. got some Easter liture from Unity program. After supper she wrote a letter to Ervin, and got his Candy Valentine ready to send to him in Oregon. . . . Well to say some more about the evening, Ma had to wear her Jacket, to keep herself comfortable for the evening. The House had grown very chilly. And old Pop laughed & kidded me about it. Ma couldn't hear to well for severel hours P.M. . . .

TUESDAY, FEBRUARY 11

. . . Ma had to put the cream in the can. & washed a little. Rugged some. Cut out some blocks after supper and sewed up some rags. She was messenger boy beings Pop was buisy. Egg production 41 today. The men where reading papers radiong, house full of smoke fumes. And while Ma eat her dinner. They where in an intresting chat & puffing away. She almost choked from the smoke effects. Mas ears roared all day. both of them she couldn't hear to well. O say it certenly seemed like a different house tonight, after Pop put the New mantel & globe, & did the Aladen lamp work wonderfull such beautiful light.

WEDNESDAY, FEBRUARY 12

. . . Henry dear busted his finger on the left hand next to the littleone. & o it did bleed & pain him. Had blood all over the floor also mecurcome [mercurochrome] spilled over the washpan. & sink.[3] . . . Ma

baked some Cornbread for supper also a chocolate Cake. She patched
Henrys shirt & ragged some also croched on the long rug. Washed all
the Lampglobes & filled them all. & Mas ears howled all day long. She
couldn't hear to very well. part of the day. This was a very bleak day
with doars banging & such euccin [confusion] from the howling &
high winds. So deslent, to endure such day. This is Lincoln birthday.
We listened to play which was played in Honhor to Lincoln. Notice
today. Male Trussel & the Black Jersy completed their decision on
Lincolns Birthday. ha.[4]

THURSDAY, FEBRUARY 13
. . . At 8 The men where at Work at their Pit. At 9:30. They started in
on the celler, also on the northend of the Basement. cemented all the
edges also the floor. ha ha. What a help itl be[5] . . . Notice. The expected calf arived early A.M. Henry couldn't find it for a time. Soon
it lay behind some thistels. Ma cleaned house churned a lotta butter
she rugged some also washed severel garnements. She got some Unity
Litture. also a book. & Easter suggestions. And for the first time egg
production was the best, yet so far this season. . . .

FRIDAY, FEBRUARY 14
. . . The men went to the field at almost 8 and turned feed came in for
chow at 12 noon. P.M. They did some cement work in the Basement.
And plastered the Pantry where it had fallen off. We suppered at 5:30.
Soon after chow The Warners called and brought us a Valentine heart
filled with Cookies was beautiful also one for Verna. & us to combine. We devoured Henrys Valentine heart of chocol after supper. Ma
ragged a little and cleaned house some more. And almost played out
she had to take an asprin to keep going after she sat down to rest a
while. After supper she prepared a pumpkin, for some Pies. & washed
some glassdoars. . . .

TUESDAY, FEBRUARY 18
. . . No work was done by the men, cause Henry was sick they just
choared. Pete was the messengerboy. Ma cleaned house beat rugs. &
scrubed the pantry. Lizzie swept the little Bed room, & beat the rugs.[6]
& chroted [crocheted] during her leisure time. Ma never had her right
side of her head roar so hard. And could hear well most of the day.
She got her Valentine heart & Bible. Mailman brought it to the
House. . . . Ma was sick after supper, took some Pain relief. An asprin

P.M. on account of her head. Sister Lizzie crochet on her doily. The men listened to all the trash P.M. Pop was sick with a pain in his chest.

WEDNESDAY, FEBRUARY 19

... P.M. at mostly 4 Pop decided to go & see a doctor. When he rolled out this morning all pains where gone. He eat dinner & some squash & did he get sick. And to some more about their trip from town he & Pete returned home at 7. Got some pills to take & some white medicine. So after retiring he asked Mo to bring him some Asprins. And those are the first Asprins he ever took in his life. What a shock & surprize it was for Ma. So then we suppered at 7:20 & Pete choared all by himself. Henry always had helped him. Mo set up the seprator & Pete did all the rest. Lizzie finished up the doily P.M. some time. & next we looked at all the snapshots & old post card Album, which where saved eversince post cards came in style. ... Henry got his pain back right after dinner & felt very bad had a very yellow color in his face. Ma just atended to her every days duties & visited. Was going to iron she had sprinkled some clothes, & forgot all about it, when Pop got sicker had to shave & clean all up. ...

THURSDAY, FEBRUARY 20

... Henry was a sick man in the night. He got up & took asprins at 12 midnight. & sat up a while. Went back to bed to see if he could sleep, with his pains. Ma rolled out at almost 6. We breakfasted at 7:15, After Pete had choared all by himself We hurried around and at 15 min. Till 10 AM. We started on our way to Syracuse. They took a Urine test & a bloodtest. & some time P.M. They took an exxray. Verna phoned down to the kids and told them how he was. We stopped at the Warners on our way from town to them about Pops illeness. ... We returned home from town at 5:15. ... Some Joke tonight while Ma was ironing her bloomers. Wayne came to look on. I told him be carefull, you'll get your eyes full & how he did laugh also Elda ha. ha. ...

FRIDAY, FEBRUARY 21

... Well old Ma rolled out rather late, after sleeping all by her self which she's never did for years. She had to make the fire & take out the ashes. ... The Warners called at almost 11. They took dinner with us. Hurried & got ready to go to Syracuse. ... We brought Henry home from the Hospital. In Thelmas car. ...

SATURDAY, FEBRUARY 22

. . . Henry rolled out 6:30. . . . Henry felt pretty good. Just weak. last totato soup for dinner carrot soup for supper & drank a glass of milk for breakfast eat a little dish of Bran. Also drank orange juice but no smoking. Smoke stand stayed very nice & clean. Pete smoked in the Basement most of the time. . . .

TUESDAY, FEBRUARY 25

. . . Pop & Ma came out of the Hay at 5:30. And breakfasted at 7: Ma just washed the dishes & Lizzie wiped them. Then she put the Cream in the can. . . . We hurried and jump into our clothes, the rest we had ready to go. We started at 10. & reached Minnola at 12:15. Henry Hildebrand, & Pete Schroeder soon apeared at 15 Min. Till 3. We started on our Way home so did Lizzie & Henry to their home at Inman. . . . All I did today is taking care of the Hens was to give them water & their scraps. And Ma made a mistake & poured the hole milk in the chicken scraps & forgot to start in on the daily routeen, after her long drive to Minnola. Forgot the strain rag, & cream container, with the seprator ha. Henry send the Cream along with the mail man. He washed all the cream containers, also seprator, drank milk for his meal. And the juice of about 6 oranges. . . .

WEDNESDAY, FEBRUARY 26

. . . Pete took one car and went after his clothes & washed some clothes. Ma also washed Pops underwear & some towls, dish, also handtowls. And some how this was the duration of the very blue day. Some how Mas spirits where so low, she couldn't choak the tears back. Was all broke up. She felt so tuff was sick all day tended to her duties, she washed lamp globes, and filled them. And had to make some fresh bread, it was good. She cut out some blocks after supper. dimonds, also some for her (Wayes of the *world*). . . . Her ears have been rather muddeled up. Could hear not good at all yesterday & today. . . .

THURSDAY, FEBRUARY 27

. . . And a duration of another Bleak day for Ma & how week & nervous clowds shattered all of AM. P.M. Not so bad. She churned P.m. & washed some. Mr Bishop called to see how Pop was. And we got an air Mail letter from Ervin send off at Eugene. Was very excited & shoked over Pops condition. also thanked me for the Valentine Candy.

After supper Ma cut out the Blue aprons, with the roses in them. . . .
Pop didn't care to read much to-day, nor very much radoing. . . .

SATURDAY, MARCH 1

March came in like a Lamb. And here is Mrs. March to greet us with
the best of her ability. And we're standing on the threshold of a new
Month, and a new day. . . . Pop tried to work to day. But o boy he's
so week & looks tired & worn out. Eat milk toast for supper. . . . Well
it was Saturday. & she had to atend to her Saturdays duties. & made
one Pan of cinnamon rolls one raisen Bread, & one pan of light
Bread. While recurapating she cut out some blocks. O she did feel
good for nothing P.M. her hearing wasnt to good. & much roaring in
her head. Henry napped in the soft rocker a great bit of the day. Was
very patient this day. . . .

SUNDAY, MARCH 2

Shifting winds to day. Clowds kept going & comming, later P.M.
15 min till 3 a northwest terrific wind occured, & how it did tear
things up and rolling thistels & fodder going all directions. & howling
wind mostly continued. You couldn't see 1/4 mile during that hour
while the wind, was at the worst. Hens lost their ballence in all that
strong wind. . . . Pop snoozed in the rocker by the radio & Ma on the
Davenport, she had to cover up little. Later Pop snoozed on the Davenport. This was a bleak day for Ma. She felt so nervous & o week &
tuff. She could hear real well. . . .

WEDNESDAY, MARCH 5

. . . The men tore the rods out of the Tractor & took them to Johnson
and had them fixed. They returned at 12. Ma had eat a Snack. So they
eat their dinner by them self. P.M. They sat by the warm fire, choared
at 5:15. They suppered. And radioed some. . . . AM. Ma cleaned up
P.M. She ironed some, & baked some pumpkin Pie. She cut out, some
dimonds, also the Waves of the World. Ma was all shot to pieces
tonight, after supper, and no dishes where washed up. She never
worked in the evening at all. Took off her shoes, & snoozed a while
in the Rocker. Hit the straw at 8:10. She had gone to slumberland
when Pop retired also Pete.

THURSDAY, MARCH 6

. . . Was 6 When we all rolled out. Choared, & breakfasted at 7. We all
got ready & the Warners apeared at 9:45. At 11 We eat some Pumpkin

Pie & Coffee. . . . at 12. We got started to Syracuse & Meet the Mailman at the Bridge. Cliff made a settlement with the John Deere men.
At about 3:40 When we where all ready to start home. Pete had a spell
& decided to stay and get himself a glass of Bear. And said go on
I'm not ready I'll get another chance out. So we drove away. . . . So
for the first time since Pop has been sick he choared all alone. He
completed the choars at 8. He suppered after choaring & next he
milked & seprated. His menue to day was 2 poached Eggs for breakfast, supper & 2 slices of milk toast dinner just one slice of Bread,
toasted. . . . Some one helped himself at our coalpile fell very fast the
last day or so.

FRIDAY, MARCH 7
. . . Ma is stiff with rhumetism to day. Didn't do much more as she
had to do. Washed some & Put feet on some socks, and cut out
some blocks for her waves of the world. Well we eat our dinner breakfast & supper, without Pete, he's still selebrating. His car parked, in
our yard. . . .

SATURDAY, MARCH 8
. . . We rolled out at 15 min. Till 6. Henry milked & we breakfasted at
7:20 Work. Henry went a few hours A.M. And worked at the tractor
had to rest some & drink a glass of milk. He was so week couldn't
stand it. We dinnered at 11:45. He worked a while on the tractor at
2:30. Cliff & family called so he never worked. Rested the rest of the
day. . . . Verna came home with Van Trussel at 11 oclock. . . .

SUNDAY, MARCH 9
. . . murky & soon a Local duster occured. . . . dust & wind had camed
at 5 P.M. . . . The prodic [prodigal] apeared. early A.M. Pete Unruh
brought him down. He took his suit cases, car, & drove home. Was
smilling when he looked in, & said. How are all of the Dycks.

MONDAY, MARCH 10
. . . Pop rolled out at 5:30. Ma at almost 15. Min. till 6. Verna at 7. But
Henry wouldn't eat. Pops diet Just drank a cup of hot water some
soda. And later drank the juice of 2 oranges. And the rest of the day.
He drank milk twice Him & Verna started to town at almost 7:30. &
got home straight up noon. . . .

. . . Well it was rather comforting, this day, to see no dust blow. . . .
7:15 Pop & Pete where at work at the tractor. Thelma & Cliff apeared
at almost 9. they completed the tractor at 10. We had dinner at 10 Min
till 12 after dinner Pete & Cliff listed on 35. They got the harrow. At
3:30 Thelma took our Car & drove to the field. Then they soon drove
home. Pete returned home, with the Tractor at 5. So Cliff apeared at
this time. wanting a generator. . . . Thelma sewed & patched some.
Hemmed some dishtowls & stamped on some patters. Pieced a little
on her quilt flower garden. She had such ache and pain in her back.
P.M. She truestoried & red some. . . . While Ma baked a jellyroll. She
gave the kidies some to go in their lunch buckets. She cleaned up
some dust & scrubed the flour. Also baked a little batch of Bread.
Was real good. & late P.M. She hemed up some things & sewed a
little. Also washed a few garments. They froze stiff, she brought them
in the House & hung them on a hanger to thow out the ice. . . .

WEDNESDAY, MARCH 12

. . . The men went out at 5 min Till 11. Returned back to the warm
house at 11:40. Was to cold to puder at something We had dinner at
11:50. At 2:45, They went to work . . . Returned back to the warm fire
for supper at 5:25. They passified by reading cataloging, & radioing.
All the newscasts where tuned in. Ma cleaned dust ironed & sewed
her gray apron She rolled out of Bed with her head in a mess. finally
she got sicker & took an asprin. But never came out of it. Her ears
where in a mess for severel hours. She couldn't hear to well. For severel days they never interfeered with her hearing . . . The longer I
write the worse I felt in my head also jaw & rhumatism in my leg &
arms PM. . . .

THURSDAY, MARCH 13

. . . The men worked on the bits & had a fire in the forge. Dinnered
at 12 noon. They looked over the todays mail & at 1:15, They got
buisy again. At 5, They came in & got their supper at 5:15. Pop is just
clowning so much of the day. . . . Baked a real nice batch of Bread.
Washed a batch of Vernas Handkerchiefs & ironed them. & made
out the order for her blue Comforter. Cliff called after his battery and
Mr Miller Pops Landlord. & another guy. He chatted a while & o my
it certenly was an embarsing moment for Ma so early A.M. And the
house was so untidy. And P.M. She had to fight backache & rhume-

tism, and the howling ear And a boner she pulled, while toasting Pops
bread scoarched it all black. & while poaching his eggs, one she stirred
out of the pan, & fell, down on the oilstove. And what a mess, she
had to clean up ha. . . .

FRIDAY, MARCH 14

Southeast terrific dust storm. A Local one High wind had occured
early A.M. And ragged throughout the day You couldn't see but a very
little distence . . . Well this day a bleak one. Was a humdrum. The
duration of such bleak one centenly got on ones constution, to live
through. Callers. This day. First Mr. Brothers, & Ike Clower. Brothers
with a saurcastic look on his face, & said to Pop Say Henry what
would do with this thing. When he put in his apearence Hoffman
grown was blowing terriable ha. And said again, what would you do.
Was all out of sorts, while he chatted to Pop. . . . Well the Men sat
around the House. & it certenly was filled with smoke fumes. Weather
was to complacited, to work. . . . Mas head was all out of balance P.M.
And it effectd her hearing some, for a little spell. She cut out some
blocks, & cut out some dimonds. But the nearer the end of the day
was along. The worse her rhumatis got. And o, she felt tuff And as all
the members of the family where fagged out, from the effects of the
wild duststorm, we all rolled in 8:15.

SATURDAY, MARCH 15

. . . It was all cleared away & how beautiful it seemed. Just like spring
after the duration of a terific duststorm. . . .

SUNDAY, MARCH 16

Northeast duster early A.M. Thistels rolled all over and everthing
went raddle debang. Dust camed about 10 AM. But the wind ragged
on till noon. . . . Well the men had almost finished seprating when Ma
rolled out of the Hay. So we breakfasted at 7:30 The closer the fore
noon had came to an end. The worse Ma felt. She took a snooze in
the rocker, & Po on the Davenport. Was 12:25 When we dinnered.
Soon Pete drove to his farm, after some laundry And at 3 P.M. We
motered to the Warners. Ma took the little ones, their blue & red
pencils which she had bought yesterday. Olin Warner & family had
called on the kids. They where intrested in a cardgame when we entered. Soon after a few games where completed. They drove all over
looked at the Wheat, the blowing fields. Hogs & what not all. So it

was sunset when we returned home. . . . after supper her ears where all muddled up so she didn't hear to well. Pete got back home for supper. . . .

MONDAY, MARCH 17

. . . Southwest terific wind & a duster most of the day it camed at about sunset. Sky was clear, after all had camed. . . . Ma sorta had a blue Monday. Hunted for her yeast cakes on & off all AM. But never found them till Pop came home. She still made Bread yet Had it completed at 6:45. Well she washed some & washed all lampglobes & filled them including the Aladenlamp. No dusting just swept everthing no use to dust when we're right in the midst of a duster ha. . . . Well this day seemed to be sorta intagnising from the head of the House Pop is still on a milk toast diet. . . . Well I'll say a little more about the intagnisum. At the dinner table this very bleak day. Both men where very entagnistic. The House stayed very clean to night. No man tore it up, nor smuttied it all up. The hard man [Pete] took advantage of his own deen [den]. So we all turned in at 8:30 Pops eyes where very sore & couldn't read. He relaxed in the rocker.

TUESDAY, MARCH 18

Southwest local duster. Sky not clowdy. Just murky from the dust efects. . . . The men drove to the Doerr 160 & burned weeds. came home at 10. & Pete took the tractor & curlered till 12:45. . . . P.M. they worked on the drill. . . . Well Ma did some mending, also cut out some dimonds. She just swept, cause it was dusty. She cleaned up some things which had been neglected. So that took up some of her time. She felt so tuff sorta had the heart burn. And while she went down celler and got her heal caught in her dress. So almost lost her balance. She swung her arm to get a grip on her self, & hurt her arm all-over again. She pulled the same boner 2 weeks ago Wednesday she had got her foot caught in some wire & when she got a hold of her grip again She hurt her arm very bad. When she almost hit the ground. With a pan of Eggs in her hand. Her head has roared & roared all day. The radio was terriable full of state A.M. early. O Ma certenly did enjoy her Unity man while she had the House to herself. And was it good. She got her beautiful comforter material 10 yrd blue also pink.

WEDNESDAY, MARCH 19

. . . very plesent seemed, as if Spring had arrived clear sky no interference. Just a whirl wind occured while Ma just had hung out her dress.

& apron. . . . Ma cleaned House washed the Doar glasses & baked 2 plumb Pies. O say the radio went bang bang on account of the weather & later she, cut out some dimonds & sewed up a few.

SATURDAY, MARCH 22

. . . Henry & Cliff took his traylor to Syracuse & sold 2 sows. Got 35 dollars for them. Also got Mas Bible storybook & o you should have seen the muddy car which the traylor caused mud balls all over it. So tonight Ma took a rag & cleaned it all off. The men returned home at 4. Pop didn't even get no kindling was so worn out from the effects of the sale also loading the hogs. . . . O say Mas to stiff tonight she can't hardly stand to write the dairy. After doing the Saturdays work. . . . last night the piece of tooth in her lower jaw axedently fell out & o o o o what a relief all pains are now gone. It felt as if it had as big a hole in it, as if it had been a hole tooth ha. It felt very fine today. Pop run off & left the Cream set & o was I bewildered. Suddenly, it occured to me. I'd send it with the Mail man cause he was due at 12:30. What a relief ha ha. Ma still has a bad cold. & stiff sholders & back. Late P.M. She was to tired to iron. And rolled in at 8 Pete took a paper to the Basement & read. Pop snitched some creamed spuds & it never did hurt him. He seened the doc today. . . .

SUNDAY, MARCH 23

. . . Pete drove home at 9 am. So we where all alone Certenly enjoyed it & was very greatfull for this chance. . . . Sunday the Sabath A.M. & Pop cleaned out the Barn. Pete motered home 9. AM. & washed. He returned at almost 6. . . .

MONDAY, MARCH 24

. . . Its very chilly to-day & takes a real fire to be comfortable. We all rolled out at 5:30. The men had completed choares at 6 Had started in breakfasting at 6:45 where there a while, while Revern Webber was on the air. Soon to finish in on the Cerman. Both occupied each a rocker and listened to the Radio till 8:30. Pop went to see if the Hens where out of grain. Soon they started in on counting up Petes time during his period of work. Took them almost one hour to get it all counted Paid him $10. today. Ma had to get her direy to get them out their tanglement. So they could get their acurate time . . . And while we where listening to the play Those We love Thelma & the kidies apeared on the scene & told us about buying a 10'20 tractor.[7] She bought some raised doughnuts. Just stayed a period of 1/2 hour. . . .

TUESDAY, MARCH 25

. . . Well Pete never did get back to-day. . . . Now for the first time for a while since Henry choared all alone. . . . Ma ironed washed some handkies, also churned and washed lampglobes. O say Ma certenly did rejoice she run into Batchlers Children, which she hadn't heard for over a years period. Couldn't hear that station. She found them on Omaha in time, to hear their Epesode. She also send off for the little booklet to Adopted daughter. . . . Mas ears certenly are in a mess to day. Much pressure on both of them P.M. & at noon she couldn't hear well at all. After supper she did some patching. Pop was very sleepy. P.M. He snoozed a while, in the comfortable rocker. . . .

THURSDAY, MARCH 27

. . . Pop build a washbench started in at 9 had the Barn cleaned at 10 he drank some milk, again P.M. He drank a cup of milk with a little Bran in it. We dinnered early 11:30 & also suppered earley at 5. . . . We had rice & spud soup for our Menue. This was Pops menue to. He drank milk for each meal also 2 slices of toast all 3 meals for breakfast he had 2 poached Eggs. And o the funniest of it all was while poured the water off of the Eggs. One slipped off into the slop bucket. & so he only had one left for his breakfast ha ha. O! he said. O! Ma almost shirked all day. She read & washed she shirked most of her daily duties.

SATURDAY, MARCH 29

. . . Ma took a turn for the worse She certenly had a sick spell ameditly after Breakfast, so Pop had to do the dishes, also seprator & the cooking the rest of the day. A very little that she eat today. Pete called almost noon. And got the balence of his pay. . . .

SUNDAY, MARCH 30

Terific wind. Northwest Duststorm about 11: AM. . . . Ma rolled out at 6:30. Pop had almost completed the choars. She got breakfast at 8 We had driven to Cliff Warners. Cause the Sabath had certenly been broken. The men took Cliffs Traylor & went to Cliff Daves after the Tractor parts for the 10/20 Got home at 12. When Ma & Thelma had been home for almost one hour. We took the kidies to Sunday school & Thelma had got them home at 12:15. And next she got dinner But Ma couldnt eat. She was so dizzy & sick as could be to her stomache. She never came out of this spell all P.M. Regardless of the asprins she'd taken. Henry took his jar of milk with him so he'd not become so week. He needed some nurishment, after loading up the heavy tractor.

TUESDAY, APRIL 1

Well this is the begnning of a knew month. And April fool. The duration of this day seems sorta like a Wolf coming in. Southeast Ferocious wind & sky overcast most of the day. P.M. With heavy thick clowds. . . . We struck rain just falling down rapidly one mile west of Doc Schlitenz. . . . We got there at 10:15. 2 Cars where ahead of us. So we had to wait with our treatments. Ma first. We started home at 2:40. . . . Well while Pop was getting all choares completed at 7 Ma listened to the Unity man for once in a long while. And was his talk good. She certenly did enjoy it. All she did to night helped get a little supper. . . . notice a little hail on our way home Minneola a heavy duster

THURSDAY, APRIL 3

. . . Pops work Just unloaded the coal. Pop rolled out 5:30. Ma at 6. She had to wait on the men. Cause they didnt make much progress. . . . Henry to Kendall after some Coal & Bread. oranges Lemons & Grapefruit. & stamps. . . . he returned at 11. Soon he got dinner all by himself. Ma felt so tuff. She'd fallen asleep in the rocker. He fixed mashed spuds & canned meat It was good. . . . Ma had got most of the supper. . . . The men hit the hay later as Ma did. She had fallen asleep. Radio wasn't very intresting she was as did [dead] as she could be She felt very tuff this day. O say we got a letter from Ervin to day saying he's going to study Airkraft. Was so funny Ma just laughed & laughed about this his letter ha ha.

FRIDAY, APRIL 4

. . . Ma wrote a letter to Mrs. JB. Klassen to-day And one to Grandpa Dyck. It was very straneous on her, cause she felt so tuff at times, she couldn't stand all that exerction. And had to rest some She helped a little with the dinner and mostly got all of the breafast. Pop did all the dishwashing, also seprator. She wipped the knives & forks at noon, also stewpots. . . . Ma & Po retired about 8. she felt very tuff in the night & was very sick to her stomache & didn't sleep abit well her ears made a change in the night so she could hear

SATURDAY, APRIL 5
Southeast terrific wind P.M. And a big duster. . . .

SUNDAY, APRIL 6
. . . Pop broke the Sabath puttered on the drill also treated some
Barley ready to sow tomorrow A.M. Verna did some washing A.M.
& ironed it P.M. She ironed Mas dress also one apron. Thelma called
at 10 she come after some oil & & invited us over to dinner We took
our roast & Jello down which we'd prepared for our dinner. Verna
went with Thelma & Pop & Mo drove in our car. And the Jello
hadn't Jelled to good. Some splashed on the doarglass. & on Mas
dress, ha ha. . . .

MONDAY, APRIL 7
. . . A terrific northwest duststorm. It camed at about 5 PM. . . . Henry
drove around to inspect his ground To see which needed working. . . .
Well this was a very straneous day. All responsibilities was put on my
shoulders also to much to do. Head & ears where howling & buzzing.
AM. Words where all mixed up for me P.M. from 4 I was deaf as a
doarnail. . . . O say this Morning everthing was so dusty one just lost
his apetite. Even the Jonses where all covered with dust ha. And
what a mess it all was. Ma went to water the chickens, after 8 days
of rest she spied the dead carcuses. & did she do away with them
fast. She creamnated them & had to get a little coal. Was chilly, and
needed some fuel. She had to wash some unmentionables and some
stockings . . .

TUESDAY, APRIL 8
. . . Henry rolled out very early before 5 cause it was our day to go to
see Doc Schlitenz We breakfasted at 6:15. Work. Henry helped Pete
to get started to the field He onewayed Weeds A.M. also PM on the
next 160 east of the Comunity Hall. At 20 min. Till 8 we started on
our way. Thelma went with us. We got to Doc at 10 A.M. & returned
home at 4:15. PM. . . . did we half to wait at Docs. There where 4 cars
ahead of us. We started on our way at 1:30. PM. Ma felt very tuff &
was as deaf as a doornail. Early AM It wasn't so bad. She had a sorta
pain in her head, after been worked on. . . . o Ma had a very dizzy
spell. This one started in her legs. after she lay a while on the Davenport she fell asleep. At 8:30 She felt very much better & her hearing
wasent half bad. . . .

WEDNESDAY, APRIL 9

. . . Pete drilled Barley in the hogpen & Pop burned Weedse along the hogfence PM. AM. He churned & cleaned up & put all the 3 nobs on the Stewpots . . . AM. Pop got hungry drank some milk, also eat an orange. He washed all yesterdays dishes early AM. excepting the yesterdays dishes Ma got breakfast today but never turned a hand at dinner. Pop got it all by himself. She sat and snoozed in the easy rocker. She felt very tuff all day. Henry certenly cleaned house to-day. Used the oil mop & took the dust off the flours. He was so tired at 4:PM & snoozed in the easy rocker for about 25 min He'd been so tired from being on his feet most all day . . .

THURSDAY, APRIL 10

Southeast terrific duststorm. Occured at 8:30 AM. & continued till 5. PM. Lectricity had let up & the sky had cleared up some but the wind ragged, into the night. . . . was mostly clowdy till this duster started in hooping her up. . . . Pete He onewayed up one mile east & north. Got in for dinner at 12 noon. & about 12:30 He got huffy cause Henry wanted him to work on 35. And Henry paid him off. Still had 10 smackers a coming. . . . So today P.M. Po & Ma are batching . . . Ma had a dizzy spell after breakfast, while she was wiping the seprator, didn't get the dishes wipped Her ears where not so good early A.M. Had improved with sounds & hearing as the day stretched forth. . . .

FRIDAY, APRIL 11

Here comes Good friday with its beautifull rareness of Spring with green living things. . . . 8 P.M. A local duster was in full progress from the southeast. . . . He choared gathered Eggs, watered the chickens. At 1:30. He started to the school meeting. returned home 15 min till 4. & worked till 5:30 Came home & choared Suppered at 6:45. Henry put the Cream in the can & Ma hit the hay at 8. She didn't hear him roll in. Some of the days work. or things which should be done. She made 2 bottles of handlotion. but not all duties, shirked most of them.

SATURDAY, APRIL 12

Dusty a Heavy dew early A.M. Wind kept on increasing at about noon Local one sorta looked murky in the northeast, also south. Wind a keeping time raddle de bang goes the east doar keep it closed. . . . Henry drove to the east field 7:40. Sowed Barley. Came in at 12 noon at 1 P.M. He went back & sowed till he just had 2 more rounds. Also curlered the field, to keep dust from blowing. He came in from the field 5:15 We suppered at 5:25 we started to Syracuse at 7:20 & re- turned home at 10:30 & rolled in after a long friendly chat with Verna. She had quiet for the night, was taking her bath & figgured on retiring. Thought it was to bad for us to come in to town. . . . We run into a dustorm & rain pouring down on our way home. The windshield was so thick with mud we couldn't see our way for a while. . . . Certenly enjoyed the Boys from the Ozarks. . . . & where they ever Wonderfull. They certenly started the day off right, while I was in not to good a spirits. And then she sheared [cheered] up. She was very weak in the legs & weak all over. . . .

SUNDAY, APRIL 13. EASTER SUNDAY.
Southwest terrific wind all day. Just a very little clowdy P.M. Sky was clowded over & no more sunshine. Murky from the dust effects. . . .

MONDAY, APRIL 14
. . . At a little after 7 Verna & Pop started to town. And returned home at almost 12. He certenly did blow himself for 13 dollars worth of clothes Stetsion hat & a tan summer suit. . . . Henry came home at 12 noon with the hired girl[8] . . .

TUESDAY, APRIL 15
. . . The hired girl had got up & started in at breakfast. Was 6:15 When we breakfasted. Had dinner 15. min. Till 12 & supper at 6. . . . Henry cleaned out the Well House and puttered on something. out in the Granary. Also fixed up the Stove & Pipes & wash machine. Ma rit a letter to Ervin today. & she got her Liberty heart pin from Those We Love. Her ears where real normal till late P.M. yesterday. So many noises in the sounds of her hearing to day. It interfeered with her hearing. . . . Henry took a snooze in the rocker. The hired girl cleaned up the Pantry shelves. Beside her daily duties. . . .

WEDNESDAY, APRIL 16
. . . Ma came out of the Hay sick as a dog. But had come out of it at 6:50 when we breakfasted The hired girl washed started in at 8:45 & had completed it at 11:25. . . . Ruth scrubbed & shined the floor. Next she cut out her slip, & after supper she sewed it up. . . . O the house is full of gas fumes which had been poured over the greasy clothes in

the Washer. & by the way. One Pillow case was pulled right in two by the wind. And Ma rolled in at 9:30. She read the story of Wildfire in a Liberty and finished it, while all members of the family had hit the hay. Her ears where a complecation severel hours of the day.

FRIDAY, APRIL 18
Shifting winds today. A dusty sprinkle in the night & ragging wind in the night. Windows got a dust bath. this special duster came in with a chilly northwest wave. . . . Ma shirked to-day. She felt much stronger. Ruth read some A.M. & crochet. Beside the daily routeen. She dusted all both of the rooms. Yesterday she scrubbed the kitchen & shined the three flours.

SATURDAY, APRIL 19
. . . Snow could have been 6 or 7 inches deep before drifting. It was a tippecal blizzard at 6 A.M. Later AM. Snow squads where falling, very rappid. but fine. And soon let up A.M. Old Saul peeped out. And P.M. He played peaceboo. & O, the Snow went off. Excepting the big banks but had sunk considerable . . . not much work was done to-day. Henry Cut Wood P.M. & stuck his car. In the Snow while driving around south of the Correl at 1. P.M. And the Car stuck there till Sunset. . . . The poor setting Hens in the Coop where packed in the Snow. Early. So Pop took them out, & put them in the Henhouse. & where happy. . . . As Pop had gone out to milk, Ma took procession of the radio. She listened to the Unity man, & was he ever good. & did she enjoy him. . . .

MONDAY, APRIL 21
. . . Cliff soon apeared at 7:30. Pop put on his old shirt & Pans. And drained the oil out of the Tractor. & O. did he look like an old man. The most oil that man ever had on himself, as long as I've known him. O. o o. And the first thing occured after chow. Ma I want some rags for the tractor. Thats an ever time occurence. When they work on the inside of the old big Horce. . . . The two went to Town. Henry dressed up in his new Stetsion Hat, his New tan suit. And o boy did he look spiffy. He had to punch a hole in his belt. It got way to big during the period of his illiniss. . . . They got home from Syracuse at 5: So at 5:30, We suppered. And by the way. Pop soon discovered that his Cows had left. They had went to Bishops. He took the Car after then. And at 6:25 He had bought them home & had gone to milk

them. O Ruth didn't get at crocheting AM. She shined all the flours & washed the Lampglobes, also baked bread. She crocheted P.M. & after chow. . . .

TUESDAY, APRIL 22
. . . We breakfasted at 6:15. Got our lunch packed up & at 7:40. We all started on our way. . . . We got to Doc Schlitenz at 10:20. They had 3 cars of patients to treat. But right at 12 we got our treatment. I was first Henry next & She treated Thelma. . . .

SATURDAY, APRIL 26
. . . Henry drove the Car to the Miller ground & burned thistils from 7 till 10:15. He returned home. We fried some Eggs eat dinner at 10:30. And at 11. We where on our way to town. And returned home at 5:30. Everthing went fine on our way home. Roads where not all slippery. Till about one mile north from home. The car slipped & skided around. . . . O say. If Pop didn't drive to every junk house Junk Barn & lot in all Syracuse where they had junked cars & irons, of all descriptions to be found. Pop was very happy today. When he had taken advantage of a bottle ha ha. Mas ears where all upside down at almost the time to retire at 8 when we hit the hay.

SUNDAY, APRIL 27
. . . Po & Ma started on their way to the Warners Just so happened, that they where not home. Was 1:50 When we returned home. Henry made out his order to send for the Window & some other articles. also planed on getting some coal. But Jones wasn't there. Ma stayed at home during this time after I once got back home safe. She had no desire to take another chance Safe at home ha. O say, while on our way to the kids the roads where so slippery Was a shoar to keep the Car from going into the ditch. And some how this seemed to be the day, when Henry felt like clowning. He offered to wash the seprator, & said. I haven't got enything to do, So I might as well do it. He also cleaned up the dinner table, while Ruth the hired girl was away.

TUESDAY, APRIL 29
. . . Well this was a day when all things went wrong. After a lotta grief & entagnisum we finaly got started on our way to Garden. Was now 8:30 Got to Garden at almost 12 noon. & was 3 a little past when we started on our way home to Syracuse & about 1 1/2 mile from here we slid in the ditch Henry stomped alotta thistels under the wheals.

unloaded the 2 socks of coal to make it pull easier. We didn't stay there very long. Soon got started on our way, to go the rest of the way. Sun was up a ways yet about 5:45. We suppered. And still Pop had to seprate by lamplight. And around supper the Frogs where croaking & having a big jubilee over the nice big rain. . . .

SUNDAY, MAY 4

. . . Henry rolled out about 6. And Ma went back to slumberland till 20 min. Till 7. She had sweet dreams. Henry had made a fire but it had went out, she had to heat the seprator water on the Oilstove. Mean while she fixed the fire. She was still barefooted during this 15 min. Period. When Pop called after the water, he kidded me cause he thought I'd just came out of the Hay ha ha He thought this, was a good joke. . . . Later she cleaned up the knew Seprator. A baby I must say. Well Henry broke the Sabath again for once P.M. He cleaned out the Barn. Him & Elmer also soldered the old Seprator. While Zelda & Ma where in the House chatting & looking at Vernas Collection of Salt & Pepper shackers. . . . later the 3 men got into a heated argurment, about the War also Linburg.[9] . . . Tonight after Ruth returned. & was Pop ever happy. They joined Ma friendly chat. Seemed as if he'd been lonely without her presence this day ha. Some how the members of the Household enjoy staying up for a change. Hit the straw at 10 min. Till 10. Ma sorta broke the Sabath she made a crock of soap out of some strong scraps.

MONDAY, MAY 5

. . . Henry put the Window in the Basement on the northside AM. P.M. He fixed the Windcharger & drove to the field to see about his Maze. Said, he thought it had all rotted. . . . Its just like a man, & I told him so . . . I started to take a look at the tempture, & there lay the themoyter all busted. Henry, had tried to fix it and put it up, on the Window I, spose he was to rough. Well Mas legs where stiff today. She made a few trips down the celler steps yesterday And o, she certenly had a bad cold today sneezed many times, & kept her buisy wipen her nose & head hurted very much. Nose was also stoped up all day long, with a hoarse voice. . . .

TUESDAY, MAY 6

. . . At about 7 Henry was skooping the dirt out of the Wellhouse. A very little later he drove the tractor to the east 160 of the Comunity Hall. He also curlered on that same ground P.M. We drove after him for dinner. Was 10 min. Till 12 when we eat. Well this seemed to be rather an eventfull day. Thelma called at 4:30 P.M. wanting to go to Elmer Dycks and exchange some Eggs. We all both went along Ruth & Ma. Zelda wasn't at home. But Elmer was and she got to trade setten Eggs after all. . . . Mas Ears where not to good for a little while P.M. She also had a hoarse voice, & had her nose aleaking, sneezed many times. . . . And P.M. about 4 Ma certenly heard the first mocken bird sing. And how wonderfull. She also Heard Ralph & Earl sing at 5 & how wonderfull it was. Also the Unity Man.

WEDNESDAY, MAY 7
. . . Ma jailed some Hens & to much brutality going on, so Ruth turned them out. And for once Egg production better 54, yesterday only 44. So this washdays Menue consists of Eggs For breakfast fried & the rest of the day boiled. . . . And Ma spend the third day sneezing, coughing, & nose all stoped up, & head all misserable.

THURSDAY, MAY 8
. . . We breakfasted at 6:15. So Henry got to listen in on Doctor Web-bers Sermon. Henry got started to the field at 15 Min. Till 7. Work he worked on the ground 2 miles east of here curlered. Came in from the field at 6:5 We dinnered 10 Min. Later as usual & suppered at 6:10. After choars were completed we went to the Warners came home. We got a letter from sister Lizzie Ma got her Shoes & where they ever high healed O my was she dissapointed. Got the bills for the Bruderstove saying that they'd send it with in 10 days. So we wrote & told them not to ship the stove. We couldn't wait for it, all that time. Thats if they didn't have it started on its way yet. . . .

FRIDAY, MAY 9
. . . At 10 min. Till 7 We where on our way close to Kendall. Stoped in at Earl Ross & got some Bananas, also one Box Graham Crackers. Next we drove to the Depot Agents House. He drove up to the De-pot & took the man with us, he sat in the back of the Car with Ruth, ha. A very good match. And next we got our freight. And on our way to Syracuse we went. Arived there, just as Verna was close to the Shop ha. She spied us & said. O say what time do you folks roll out. So next we drove to the Hardware store, & got the Window lights. So Henry & Ruth went to her folks after the Brooder. Mean while Ma stayed at the Shop & chated, with Verna. . . . Henry & Ruth set up the

Brooder, got it started off right. . . . At 10:30 Dinner was over & Pop on his way to Garden after the chicks. . . . And at 3:15 He had got home from Garden with the Bab. Chicks. So all 3 of us out there getting the chicks out of the boxes & stuck all their bills in water.[10] . . . Well old Ma did a very little to day. She aired all of the Bedding on our Bed. also helped to get the chicks to drink & started a fire in the Cookstove and fried out some fat for soap also made a fire in the Heater and gathered up the kindling.

SATURDAY, MAY 10
. . . We arose at about 5. And Pop a little earlier Was 6:15 When we started in breakfasting so Henry heard most of Doctor Webbers Sermon. He shaved & changed clothes and at about 8 him & Elmer started in to town with a load of Hogs. all they could load. & returned home at 10:15. Loaded another load, got 187 dollars for both loads. . . . Henry dolled up & after the choars where completed We started to Syracuse Got to town almost 8. Pop got Ma a red & blue flowered box of asorted chocolates for Mothers day. And a thymemoter which can hang in the Window on the outside so we don't need to go out of doars to see the tempture its very handy. . . .

SUNDAY, MAY 11
. . . Sun sorta drove the clowds away about 3: P.M. clowds where so beautifull early A.M. They just looked like the Waves on the Ocean. . . . At almost 11 the Warners apeared on the scene. With all their Mothergifts. Thelma brought a very nice white cake, which she baked while getting breakfast. Put white icing on it. Ervin send me a box of handkerchiefs White, Yellow, Pink. Verna gave me a Mothers Card also a pr of pink bloomers. Thelma a white basket of toiletries. Bathsaults perfume chacet [sachet] Toiletwater, and toilet soap. Pop a red and blue flowered box of esorted chocolate, with a big Carnation & all wraped with all the beautiful roses, you ever saw . . . Well the Sabath again was broken to day. First he hunted up the Calves & found them. Next Henry & all the Warners went to dig out a Cyote Den. But had moved it. So all work was in vane. . . .

MONDAY, MAY 12
. . . Was murky Northwest, also northeast from dusteffects, & sky never cleared up. . . .

TUESDAY, MAY 13

... at almost 5 We had a duster only lasted 20 Min. soon another one occured & lasted till almost dusk. second general duster. . . . O say, the wind came from the southwest, strong wind a terific duster lasted almost 2/3 of an hour. A cool wave developed, in the night, blowed from the west. And some how a quilted quilt to cover up with, wasn't enought to be comfortable. . . .

WEDNESDAY, MAY 14

Terific wind early from the west. Was real dusty in the roads later P.M. as the day stretched forth. . . .

THURSDAY, MAY 15

... Was 15 Min. Till 7. When he started to the Field one Mile east of here on the old 160 ackers. he worked. Curlered all day. Also burned some Weeds. He send the cream along with Elmer the Mailman. . . . Also burned some Weeds. Our land Lord & his negro shoefer apeared on the scene almost 8 A.M. went to see Henry. . . . Well Mas day was very refreshing & most enjoyable. She got to listen in on a very intresting Unity talk. Also heard Ralph & Earl sing & Was they ever wonderfull. To much static to listen in on the Dinner hour also Roundup. She got her liture from Fridays talk, also Saturdays. On what kind of seeds to Sow. . . . O say, Ma did a little bit to-day she cleaned out the Window cills, of 3 windows North kitchen south frontroom also our westbedroom & washed severel pr. Socks and the 2 blue handtowls. Ruth washed socks & handkerchiefs A.M. And tru-storied P.M. While she wasn't studying the Bible. . . .

SATURDAY, MAY 17

... Sky soon looked rather murky from the dust effects. . . . This was the awfuliest day of all times when Cliff & Thelma told us about our poor boy got his leg broke later they called & said gangerreen had set in I couldn't stand to think about it. . . .

The 1940s, by all rights, should have been better years for the Dycks than the drought-ridden thirties had been. They had spent nearly a decade buffeted by high winds and dust storms, and had suffered repeated crop failures. The tide began to turn in 1939 when Thelma and Cliff returned to farm in southwestern Kansas. In 1940 the drought began to ease. Those who had survived the dirty thirties were well placed to participate in the agricultural boom that came with World War II. The price for grain soared as demand grew at home and abroad.[1] Sadly, for this family the Great Depression really represented the calm before the storm.

Although the Dycks recovered from the economic woes of the 1930s, the next fifteen years were destined to be much more difficult than the darkest days of the depression had been.[2] Two spare items in the *Syracuse Journal* explain why May 1941 was the end of an era for the Dyck family. On May 23, a small notice appeared that read "Mr. and Mrs. Henry Dyck of Kendall were called to Eugene, Oregon, Monday evening by the critical injury of their son, Ervin, in a saw mill accident." Ervin's injuries proved fatal, and he died before his parents could reach Oregon. Mary and Henry Dyck brought him home to be buried in the cemetery on the hill above Kendall. On May 30, his obituary appeared in the *Journal*. "Funeral services were conducted for Ervin Dyck, son of Mr. and Mrs. Henry Dyck, at the Kendall church Monday afternoon, and burial was in the Kendall cemetery. . . . Mr. Dyck, 29 years old, died from complications arising from an accident in a saw mill at Eugene, Oregon. His leg was broken on May 16, and five days later he died from a blood clot." From Mary and Henry's perspective, the day on which their son was injured was indeed "the awfuliest day of all times."

It was a terribly sad situation. Just when times should have been becoming easier for the Dycks, their lives as they had previously known them were coming to an end. Their situation stood in marked contrast to what their neighbors were experiencing. While the Dycks were burying their only surviving son, the rest of the county was

suffering an embarrassment of riches. On the same page as Ervin Dyck's obituary, the local newspaper ran an article celebrating the staggeringly large wheat harvest that farmers expected that year. Their primary worry was no longer drought, but where they would find enough storage space for the wheat and enough laborers for the harvest. The crop in the field promised much, and unlike 1931, the year of the last bumper crop, there was a market for it. Prices would be high. The author waxed eloquent: "But back to the wheat fields. They are beautiful now."[3]

The crop in the fields was the least of the Dycks' concerns. They had just buried their son. What followed were years of mourning and regret. Parents who lose a child often lose each other in their grief, and that is what happened to Mary and Henry Dyck. Their marriage, and Mary's life, would never again be the same. Between 1941 and 1945, Mary Dyck experienced an extended period of grieving and deep depression. Although the 1930s had been difficult years, her diary bears the evidence that Mary Dyck often laughed at life. She reveled in the antics of her children, grandchildren, and spouse. She saw the humor in her own misfortunes. After May 1941, that was no longer the case. Mary's existence had become thoroughly grim, and she was unable to enjoy much of anything. Tears and sorrow marked her days. During this same period, Henry Dyck began to drink heavily, and distanced himself from his grieving wife. Their marriage, which had previously been a reasonably happy working partnership, was irretrievably damaged. Although Mary would live until 1955, she and Henry would never be able to recapture the love and affection they had once felt for each other.[4]

Although an important part of Mary Dyck's life had ended, her diary went on. It was, however, a much different document. It was far less the story of a farm and a family, and more the story of an individual and her troubles. Her focus initially became mourning for her son, and later for her marriage. The form of her writing, too, became different. It was not until 1942 and 1943 that Dyck began to refer to herself consistently as "I." Her use of the first person increased, and then became regular, as family problems mounted. Her writing was no longer a family chronicle; her family had been broken. The diary had become a highly personal and individual story of grief, sorrows, and anguish. Whether the diary still remained on the kitchen table, open to family scrutiny, is unknown.

Mary Dyck's diary tells the story of an individual and a family that persisted when so many others gave up in despair. They held on, while others fled to the far west. They were able to find small pleasures in their lives, in spite of what were often thoroughly depressing circumstances. Throughout the 1930s, Mary Dyck continued to believe that someday the rain, the crops, and her children would all return to southwestern Kansas. That, in the end, was her tragedy. She had been "waiting on the bounty" for nearly a decade, but it was a harvest that she would not reap. In Mary Dyck's world, bounty was not only represented by the crops in the fields, but also by the intact family, home and whole. For Mary Dyck, what came after the dust bowl was surely worse than anything those trying years had brought her.

APPENDIX

Included in this appendix are six complete diary entries, one from each of the years represented in this text. Each is drawn from a different month of the year. They are intended to provide the reader with a more complete understanding of the complexities of the text. The entries illustrate the full range of the topics Mary Dyck addressed in her diary, and show the depth with which she treated them.

THURSDAY, OCTOBER 15, 1936
South west wind at A.M. & south east wind P.M. Temp at six A.M. 42 at noon 72 at sunset 60 Ervin is Drilling Wheat. Henry hawled a load Cement to the church part of the fore-noon & the rest of it he got 100 Gals. Gas from Molses. Mrs. Freese & Mrs. Fred Rogers where here some time. P.M. Mo Fried down some Meat, Baked Bread, washed some windows & cleaned dust, the rest of the day also patched 1 pr. of Trousers for Mr. Henry. Today, Bob is making plans to get his Marriage Lisense to-morrow. ha. Its very windy to day, has been Clowdy, all after-noon. It dewed some this morning very early. Henry headed Maze in after noon. Static is very bad. Another caller apeared on the sene, while I was shining the Flour, in middle Bed-room, leaving a Calender & a post Card on the stand, saying it was Rawleigh man. ha. Mo thought it was, Mr. Henry. & Cecil here at Supper time after 2 doz Eggs. We got a letter from Verna. Today Verna got her picture's. Hens layed 19 Eggs to day. Joe came at A.M. early after Lime.

SATURDAY, DECEMBER 25, 1937
Northeast breeze Clowdyness continued to day. Whitefrosted to day early Temp 18 7 A.M. At 10 A.M. It was 35 degrees. At 6 P.M. It was 26 degrees.
    We rolled out at 6:30. And got through breakfasting at 7:15. Henry got the seprating done at 7:45. We've only feed our Calf milk once a

day since she was 10 weeks old. We went to Edgers & Gertrude at 7:20. And got home at 6:30 P.M. We got a xmas Package consisting of 7 Dishtowls for Mo very fancy a dresser scarf 1 dishcloth from Patsy a Dutch windmill souvenior for Po & Mo. Po a blacksateen Pillow fancy made. Green Grapevines wild also a munch of Mose. Verna a silk perfume silkchatet a very fancy Lunchcloth Mo also got a Purple flower with greenleaves from the kidies. And Verna got a dishcloth from Patsy.

Callers. This Morning Mr. Tolsen and Son Keith came after their Horse. Whom they had sheltered here for the Night. Saturday night after Po had finished the milking he set the Bucket down in the dark while trying to keep the fouset from freezing, he covered it up with a quilt. He backed up & over went his milk. O gee was the answer. I wish I'd let that in the Cows bag. It certenly hadene'd went to waste ha.

SUNDAY FEBRUARY 13, 1938

For a change the wind's in the northeast. We had a local duster started in at 8:30 It was clowdy so that the sunrose behind the clowds. Wind's very strong AM. Temp at 7 A.M. 35 degrees. Much chiller as it was yesterday & day before. Today it was 50 degrees. At 5:30 P.M. It was 43 degrees. Work. We where very polky getting out of bed to day we where through breakfasting at 7:50. At 8:30 Henry goes to the field to pull up some wire. And another Sabath broke. Mo bakes 2 Apple Pies while Pop out at work to these Apples are dried ones. Henry gets in from the field for dinner, at [   ] Mo also cleans up the floors and does her Saturdays work. Cause it blowed yesterday. And it hadn't did much good.

Well to day the gloomyness has left Mo for one day at least. Callers, Today at 9: A.M. Dalles Johnson was here to sell a Car to the Mr. At least he tried to. He thought it was real funny to find Henry pulling up fences on Sunday. And just the same Henry got to ride with him in his New Car. Callers P.M. Olyan Warners also Lelyen Wecter & family where to vistit Lelyan wanted to find out where he could find Henry Crouse. After 5:30 We went to get the Mail and went to see Edgers. We certenly did laugh & have a splendid time. Mo got A Olson Rug Boot we also got the Country Jentleman.

MONDAY, APRIL 3, 1939

Southeast breeze part of the day and hard wind for severel hours considerable clowdyness most of the day. clearsunrise. temp at 15 till 7 A.M. 48 degrees today 72 degrees. At 6 P.M. 60 degrees.

Thelma rolled out first we came out the hay at 15 till 7 Cliff 7:15 also children. Had got through with chow at 8 Cliff Henry & Leroy went to see their feature home returned at 10 A.M. Patsy Cut out paper dolls Thelma & Mo chated about old times Men fixed on the windmill at 3 they went to Olins to chat. also went to Bishops to get the melting spoon we dinnered 12:20 they returned from Olins at dusk suppered a little later the Warners all rolled in at 8 while Pop was pumping the Cow we rolled in at 9 Ma & Dad.

WEDNESDAY, JUNE 26, 1940
clear Northwest breeze AM. Later P.M. Northeast wind. Sky with over cast clowds but not thick. Temp AM. At 5 56 degrees. Today 98 degrees. At dusk 78 degrees. In the night it was 50 degrees.

Pop rolled out at 4. And worked on the Combine. I rolled out at 5. He choared first & had breakfast at 5:30. Never was no static on the Radio early AM. Just started in at 12 noon Henry went to the field at 6 with the Car & finished planting. Took him 2 hours to finish on the next field near the 80 ackers Cliff went to Henry when the yellow Jersy cow got sick. Which, they Called pickels. She died amedetly. Must have been poisioned. Henry got home at 20 min Till 12. Eat his dinner & shaved. Cliff apeared and at [number pasted over with reinforcement] they drove to Elmer & Zelda. Returned home at 1 PM. Next they took the Combine moter out. At 2: P.M. Elmer & Zelda apeared and took the motor to Elexander. Pop started to town in the Car. Took the Cream & Shiped it to Kansascity 1 1/2 gal. Belonged to Cliff & Thelma. Henry returned home at 9:15. Brought 1 pt ice cream it was melted he never dressed up to go to town, Made 2 trips to Syracuse on account repairs He eat his supper at 9:30. And Ma her ice cream. And o what a night it was she had lyen down on the bed. just fell asleep and he come home. After supper He hunted for a repair book so it was past 10. When he turned in. Such a night it was All Ma did to-day. Was just atended to her every day activities. And adeded to it. Washed her head AM. Starched 6 garments & poured the Cream in the Can. & Wrote a card to Verna at McPherson. The rest of the day she shirked and slept some. Flies are very thick on the door. & going over some of the days hapnings. The Warners had a furnerel at their house, Cause Pickels met her doom. And this news about the cow & the Card from Verna, saying that Nada had sold her shop. And now she'd not come home at this time. So all this Cast a shadow over all our joys. & this particular day. Brought nothing to our life. Just sorrows. And Cause Pop was away, so late in the night.

Made it very complicated. No Well this certenly is bug night & I dont mean maby.

SATURDAY, MAY 17, 1941

Southwest fresh strong wind. Sky soon looked rather murky from the dust effects. Very cool this morning. Temp had huddled to 55. Today it rose to [   ] & at dusk it had dropped down to [   ]

Henry rolled out 4:30. Us wimen 10 Min. Till 5. So Henry had completed the choars, & we breakfasted before 6. He certenly got to the field earlier, as usual.

This was the awfuliest day of all times when Cliff & Thelma told us about our poor boy got his leg broke later they called & said gangerreen had set in I couldn't stand to think about it.

shorty Macinny brought Thelma & Cliff down & they took our Car & went home Was 1:30. when Po & Ma retired. cream check today test 27 price 35 toteled 3.78.

NOTES

1. A Woman and Her World

1. Roberta Woods, comp., "Property Owners of McPherson County, Kansas, 1884" (n.p.: n.p., 1970), 82.
2. "Obituary," *Inman Review*, March 14, 1924, 1.
3. Dennis D. Engbrecht, *The Americanization of a Rural Immigrant Church: The General Conference Mennonites in Central Kansas, 1874–1939* (New York: Garland, 1990), 51.
4. "Funeral," *Inman Review*, August 25, 1905, 1.
5. David Haury, *Prairie People: A History of the Western District Conference* (Newton, Kans.: Faith and Life Press, 1981), 136, 148.
6. "Landseekers, Many Mennonites Go West," *Inman Review*, August 25, 1905, 1.
7. Kansas State Board of Agriculture, *Report of the Kansas State Board of Agriculture for the Quarter Ending June, 1911* (Topeka: Kansas State Board of Agriculture, 1911), 153.
8. Kansas State Census, vol. 177, Lamont Township, Hamilton County, 1905.
9. Kansas State Board of Agriculture, *Report of the Kansas State Board of Agriculture for the Quarter Ending December, 1905* (Topeka: Kansas State Board of Agriculture, 1906), 288, 300, 320.
10. F. L. Vandegrift, "New Mennonite Settlement in Kansas," *The Earth* 7, no. 10 (October 1910): 8.
11. Ibid.
12. U.S. Department of Commerce, Bureau of the Census, *Thirteenth Census of the United States, 1910*, Lamont Township, Hamilton County, Kansas.
13. Households were classified as Russian Mennonite if either the head of household or a spouse claimed their nationality as "Russ German," or noted that a parent was born a "Russ German," as was recorded in the 1910 census of Lamont Township.
14. Kansas State Board of Agriculture, *Report of the Kansas State Board of Agriculture for the Quarter Ending December, 1910* (Topeka: Kansas State Board of Agriculture, 1911), 21, 43. Indirect evidence for the impact of the Mennonites on crop selection is that in 1915, after the failure of the Menno com-

munity, the number of acres planted to winter wheat fell to 96, and the number of acres devoted to broomcorn fell to 1,466. Kansas State Board of Agriculture, *Report of the Kansas State Board of Agriculture for the Quarter Ending September, 1916* (Topeka: Kansas State Board of Agriculture, 1916), 20, 41.

15. File 1301, Box 55, "History of Syracuse, KS Mennonite Church," Mennonite Library and Archives, Bethel College, North Newton, Kansas. The documentation of the Menno settlement and Ebenflur Church is very slim. Evidently, the bulk of the church records burned during a house fire.

16. "In the Country, Settlers in Western Kansas Full of Hope," *Inman Review*, January 24, 1908, 1.

17. "Mennonites Dedicate," *Hamilton County Republican and Syracuse News*, May 29, 1908, 1.

18. "German Paper at Syracuse," *Hamilton County Republican and Syracuse News*, February 21, 1908, 1.

19. *Inman Review*, September 14, 1906, 6.

20. "In the Country," *Inman Review*, January 24, 1908, 1.

21. Heinrich Janzen, "Our German Neighbors, Their Aims, Intentions, and Hopes for the Future," *Hamilton County Republican and Syracuse News*, November 1, 1907, 1.

22. "In the Country," *Inman Review*, January 24, 1908, 1.

23. Janzen, "Our German Neighbors."

24. "Menno Happenings," *Hamilton County Republican and Syracuse News*, February 21, 1908, 4.

25. "A Trip to Syracuse," *Inman Review*, December 6, 1912, 5.

26. "Menno Happenings," January 22, 1909, 3.

27. "Menno Happenings," June 26, 1908, 8. A local history comments, "One year they lost a thirty bushel wheat crop in only a few days when the hot winds cooked the heads of the wheat when they were still in the milk stage." Floyd Edwards, ed., *Hamilton County, Kansas, History* (Syracuse, Kans.: Hamilton County Historical Society, 1979), 54.

28. "Menno Happenings," November 27, 1908, 3.

29. "Menno Happenings," January 22, 1909, 3.

30. Heinrich Janzen, "Janzen Writes Another," *Hamilton County Republican and Syracuse News*, December 17, 1909, 6.

31. "Menno," *Hamilton County Republican and Syracuse News*, December 2, 1910, 8.

32. "Menno Items," *Hamilton County Republican and Syracuse News*, July 7, 1911, 8.

33. "Back to Hamilton County," *Hamilton County Republican and Syracuse News*, March 20, 1914, 1.

34. "Menno Items," May 10, 1912, 3.

35. "A Trip to Syracuse," *Inman Review*, December 6, 1912, 5.

36. "Sale of Church Property Stopped," *Hamilton County Republican and Syracuse News*, January 9, 1914, 1.

37. Ibid.

38. Heinrich Janzen, "Uncle Heinrich Tells His Side," *Syracuse Journal*, February 20, 1914, 1.

39. "Paid Back the Money," *Syracuse Journal*, March 6, 1914, 1.

40. Edwards, *Hamilton County*, 54.

41. "The Mennonite Settlement," *Hamilton County Republican and Syracuse News*, February 27, 1914, 1.

42. "Back to Hamilton County," *Hamilton County Republican and Syracuse News*, March 20, 1914, 1.

43. *Hamilton County Republican and Syracuse News*, April 10, 1914, 3.

44. State of Kansas, *State Census, Hamilton County*, vol. 110, 1915.

45. Edwards, *Hamilton County*, 54.

46. "History of Syracuse, Kansas, Mennonite Church," File 1301, Box 55, Mennonite Library and Archives, Bethel College, North Newton, Kansas; "Obituary," *Syracuse Journal*, August 18, 1955, 4.

47. In 1915, the Dyck farm was slightly smaller than the average for the township, the mean farm consisting of 191 acres. State of Kansas, *State Census, Hamilton County*, vol. 110, 1915.

48. State of Kansas, *State Census, Hamilton County*, vol. 110, 1915.

49. Wheat did not become a major crop in this part of Hamilton County until 1928. Edwards, *Hamilton County*, 54.

50. Information about acreage, crops, and production drawn from State of Kansas, Statistical Rolls, Hamilton County, Lamont Township, 1918–1955, Archives Division, Kansas State Historical Society (KSHS hereafter), Topeka, Kansas. The agricultural census does not indicate exactly when the automobile and tractor were purchased, but polled farmers about their ownership of such items in 1922.

51. Hamilton County, Kansas, Transfer Records, Register of Deeds Office, Hamilton County Courthouse, Syracuse, Kansas.

52. Hamilton County, Kansas, Chattel Mortgage Records, Register of Deeds Office, Hamilton County Courthouse, Syracuse, Kansas, 1929.

53. State of Kansas, Statistical Rolls, 1926; Katherine Jellison, "Women and Technology on the Great Plains, 1910–1940," *Great Plains Quarterly* 8 (summer 1988): 146–147, 152.

54. Edwards, *Hamilton County*, 54.

55. U.S. Department of Commerce, Bureau of the Census, *15th Census of the United States: 1930 Population*, vol. 3, pt. 1; U.S. Department of Commerce, Bureau of the Census, *16th Census of the United States: 1940 Population*, vol. 2, Characteristics of the Population, pt. 3 (Washington, D.C.: United States Government Printing Office, 1943).

56. Kansas State Board of Agriculture, *Biennial Report of the State Board of Agriculture*, vols. 27, 32 (Topeka: Kansas State Printing Plant, 1931, 1941).

57. "Mennonite Settlers Gave Menno Its Name in 1906," *Syracuse Journal*, May 21, 1937, 14.

58. State of Kansas, Statistical Rolls, 1935.

59. Thelma Warner to Pamela Riney-Kehrberg, personal correspondence, fall 1988.
60. Interview with Thelma Warner, Syracuse, Kansas, June 9, 1989.
61. Ibid.
62. Ibid.
63. Ibid.
64. Hamilton County, Kansas, Chattel Mortgage Records, Register of Deeds Office, Hamilton County Courthouse, Syracuse, Kansas, 1935.
65. Dyck farm accounts, 1935, by permission of Thelma Warner and Verna Gragg, Syracuse, Kansas.
66. Several of the Dyck family's friends and neighbors also received substantial payments. For example, the Bishops, who lived just a mile down the road, received $1,781 in support from the AAA. "1937 AAA List Shows 67 Here in Thousand Dollar Class," *Syracuse Journal*, March 15, 1940, 1.
67. Dyck farm accounts, 1935.
68. In 1981, John Mack Faragher encouraged historians to take a hard look at farm women's lives, in an attempt to understand "history from the inside-out." John Mack Faragher, "History from the Inside-Out: Writing the History of Women in Rural America," *American Quarterly* 33, no. 5 (winter 1981): 535–557.
69. Judy Nolte Lensink, "Expanding the Boundaries of Criticism: The Diary as Female Autobiography," *Women's Studies* 14, no. 1 (1987): 41.
70. Judy Nolte Lensink, *'A Secret to be Burried': The Diary and Life of Emily Hawley Gillespie, 1858–1888* (Iowa City: University of Iowa Press, 1989), xxiii.
71. Tom Lewis, "'A Godlike Presence': The Impact of Radio on the 1920s and 1930s," *OAH Magazine of History*, spring 1992: 29.

2. Work, Family, and "Playing Hookie": 1936

1. The use of the term "kids" generally referred to Thelma and her husband, Cliff.
2. Dyck often referred to the Works Progress Administration project that her husband worked on as "the church," because the Ebenflur Church had previously existed at the same site. She also referred to the structure as the Community Building. It was the home of the Menno Community Club.
3. Verna often worked for the Trostles. The Trostles operated a very large farm in neighboring Stanton County, Kansas, and regularly hired laborers.
4. Mary's sister, Elizabeth Hildebrandt, lived in Hutchinson, Kansas.
5. Dyck's use of the term "maze" is not a reference to corn. It was the local name for sorghum.
6. The "Rawleigh man" was a door-to-door salesman who sold a variety of products for the home.

7. The Doerr quarter was rented land that the Dycks regularly farmed. The A. A. Doerr Mercantile Company was located in Larned, Kansas, and sold irrigation equipment.

8. When Henry spent time away from the farm in the company of male friends, Mary generally referred to this as "sowing wild oats." At some times, it is clear that this includes consumption of alcoholic beverages, which was, at that time, illegal in Kansas. Only beer with a 3.2 percent alcohol content, classified as nonintoxicating, could be sold in the state. In order to purchase alcohol, men generally traveled across the border to Holly, Colorado. Kansas would be a dry state until 1948.

9. Carl Griswold was a Lamont Township farmer. According to the 1936 agricultural census, he farmed 480 acres. For future reference, all such information is drawn from State of Kansas, Statistical Rolls, 1936 (Topeka, Kans.: KSHS).

10. Wayne Rogers was a neighbor and spent a good deal of time at the Dyck farm, working with the Dyck men. He was also a relative by marriage. His wife, Elda, was Henry's brother Pete's daughter. Rogers farmed approximately 800 acres of land in Lamont Township.

11. *Betty and Bob* was Mary Dyck's favorite radio soap opera. One of the early soap operas, this show dealt with the struggles of a not-too-happily-married couple. This is an example of the way in which she wove commentary about her daily radio listening into the fabric of her diary.

12. Pete Dyck was Henry's brother, another early settler in Hamilton County. Elmer was his son. Mary's sister Phena, who had died in 1931, had been Pete's wife. After her death, Pete and Elmer spent a great deal of time at the Dyck home, and both sometimes worked as hired men on the Dyck farm. Pete and Henry did not always get along.

13. Henry generally listened to significantly different radio programming than Mary. While she preferred soap operas, comedy, religious programming, and music, he often listened to news, political programming, and detective shows. Neither one seems to have enjoyed the other's choices. For useful studies of the radio listening habits of the era, see Herta Herzog, "What Do We Really Know about Daytime Serial Listeners," in Paul F. Lazarsfeld and Frank N. Stanton, *Radio Research 1942–1943* (New York: Essential Books, 1944; reprint ed., New York: Arno Press, 1979), and H. M. Beville Jr., *Social Stratification of the Radio Audience: A Study Made for the Princeton Radio Research Project* (New York: National Broadcasting Company, 1940).

14. Many farm families received *Capper's Farmer* or *Capper's Weekly*, both of which were published by Kansas Congressman Arthur Capper, an influential member of the farm bloc. For more information on the reading habits of farming families, see Norma J. Bruce, "Serials for the Farm Family of 80 Years Ago," *Serials Review* 21, no. 3 (1995): 1–22.

15. Family members actively followed the 1936 presidential election that pitted incumbent Franklin D. Roosevelt against Kansas governor Alfred M. Landon. Although Dyck did not make her political position completely clear, the family seems to have supported Roosevelt in the 1936 election. While western Kansas farmers were traditionally Republican, the majority supported Roosevelt in the 1936 election. This was, perhaps, a reflection of their large-scale participation in the federal farm program. Pamela Riney-Kehrberg, *Rooted in Dust: Surviving Drought and Depression in Southwestern Kansas* (Lawrence: University Press of Kansas, 1994), 117–118.

16. Where blank spots like this one occur, Dyck forgot to fill in information at the end of the day. This most often occurred with temperatures and times.

17. Dyck was sometimes depressed. This usually happened on days when she was alone at home, the dust was blowing, or a family member had recently departed for a trip away from home.

18. The Bishops lived on an adjoining farm just one mile away, and were frequent visitors to the Dyck home. Eva and Sheffee Bishop lived in a two-room soddy, but farmed a very large amount of land. The 1936 agricultural census listed them as farming 4,000 acres.

19. There is considerable evidence that Mary Dyck was more straitlaced than her husband, and generally disapproved of betting and alcohol. It was not until 1948 that Kansas finally reconsidered the issue of constitutional prohibition, more than a decade after it had ceased to exist in most of the nation. Farm residents, and particularly those in areas with low population densities, voted to continue prohibition. Farm women over the age of fifty were prohibition's strongest supporters, voting nine to one in favor of the law. Robert Smith Bader's *Prohibition in Kansas* provides a useful overview of this subject. Robert Smith Bader, *Prohibition in Kansas: A History* (Lawrence: University Press of Kansas, 1986), 251–252.

20. Dyck used euphemisms such as this one to indicate when her husband was in a bad mood.

21. Radio batteries sometimes had to do double and triple duty, being used to charge vehicles and other equipment around the farm. They were also periodically out of use when they lost power, and had to be recharged.

22. Dyck often referred to eggs as bullets.

23. When England's King Edward VIII abdicated the throne on December 11, 1936, in order to marry American divorcée Wallis Simpson, it was exciting news even in the farthest corner of southwestern Kansas. The event certainly appealed to Dyck's romantic instincts.

24. According to Thelma Warner, the process of constructing the Menno Community Building was not always smooth, and "result[ed] in some pretty bitter sessions involving several who wanted to change plans etc." Personal communication, Thelma Warner to Pamela Riney-Kehrberg, 1989.

25. Like many farm families, the Dycks relied heavily on mail order for their shopping needs. They most often used the Montgomery Wards and Sears catalogs. In fact, "cataloging," or curling up with a catalog and dreaming, was one of their favorite pastimes.

26. Being short of money, Ervin had existed on pancakes made of flour and water for much of his stay in the Southwest. Personal correspondence, Thelma Warner to Pamela Riney-Kehrberg, 1989.

27. Razzle dazzle is a card game, played with five or six players.

28. Olan Warner was Cliff Warner's brother; Ethel was Olan's wife. The couple lived in Stanton County. Grandpa Warner was Cliff and Olan's grandfather.

3. Blowing Dust and Departures: 1937

1. Broomcorn, used to make brooms, was a highly drought-resistant crop grown by many farmers in far western Kansas.

2. In the midst of the depression, Thelma and Cliff were able to own their first radio because it was given to Cliff as payment for work done on a neighbor's farm. Barter was a fairly common way of paying obligations between neighbors.

3. Among her numerous ills, Mary Dyck appears to have suffered from migraines, which she called "sick headaches."

4. Pete shared a common male assessment of the era's radio serial drama, also known as "soap operas." U.S. Department of Agriculture studies showed that farm women, far more than farm men, relied upon the radio for its entertainment value, particularly soap operas. Men and women often had markedly different assessments of the value of this entertainment. Many men actively hated these programs, and referred to them as "dishpan drama" and "washboard weepers." U.S. Department of Agriculture, *Attitudes of Rural People toward Radio Service: A Nation-Wide Survey of Farm and Small Town People*, n.p.; James Thurber, *The Beast in Me and Other Animals*, 191.

5. Henry Dyck was quite active in soil conservation efforts in Hamilton County. In 1936, the federal government inaugurated the Soil Conservation Service (SCS), which aided farmers carrying out conservation projects on their farms. Dyck participated in planning meetings, received seed loans, and cooperated with local authorities in attempts to control blowing soil.

6. Cleaning up following dust storms was an enormous chore, one that destroyed the good humor of many an area housekeeper.

7. Pete Dyck was probably responding to political developments of early 1937. In early February, President Franklin Roosevelt announced his plan

to restructure the U.S. Supreme Court. His plan, had it been enacted, would have added new justices to the Court. This was an enormously controversial idea that made many voters, as well as Congress, suspicious of the president's motives.

8. Listing a field was one way to try to control blowing soil. Farmers generally used listers to plow deep furrows perpendicular to the prevailing winds. When the wind blew, the soil would then blow into the lister furrow, rather than going into the air. The deep furrows helped to trap moisture. See R. Douglas Hurt, *The Dust Bowl: An Agricultural and Social History*, 22, 67–68.

9. Mary Dyck was dieting, and doing so by not eating supper in the evenings. She generally cooked for the family, but not for herself.

10. This was the conclusion of a three-day dust storm that had blown most of the wheat crop out of the ground, and closed highways throughout the area. "Three Day Dust Storm," *Syracuse Journal*, February 19, 1937, 1.

11. Although Mary Dyck usually noted when President Roosevelt made radio addresses, the content never impressed her enough that she wrote about it in her diary. These political speeches were far less important to her than her daily soap operas. On March 4, President Franklin D. Roosevelt appeared at the Democratic victory dinner. He spoke largely about the need to reform the Supreme Court, which was threatening to invalidate a good deal of his New Deal legislation. Samuel I. Rosenman, comp., *The Public Papers and Addresses of Franklin D. Roosevelt*, 1937 volume (New York: Macmillan), 113–121.

12. This would have been Ervin's parents' portion of his $25 check from the Civilian Conservation Corps. Mary and Henry Dyck received $20, and Ervin received $5.

13. Dyck regularly sent away to the sponsors of radio soap operas to receive booklets to accompany their daily broadcasts. She received such publications from *Today's Children*, *Mother Moran*, *Bachelor's Children*, and others.

14. One of the real problems that farmers faced was blowing dirt from neighboring fields, which could bury and destroy crops. A farmer's own efforts at controlling blowing might be destroyed by fields left untended by less conscientious neighbors.

15. From "Mother ironed" to this point is written in a different hand, probably Verna's, since she was living at home with her parents at this time.

16. Dust storms wreaked havoc on machinery of all kinds. Automobiles were often disabled by dirt clogging the engines or static electricity interfering with their electrical systems.

17. There are several reasons why Henry Dyck would have been inspecting local fields. The Soil Conservation Service required participating farmers to engage in soil conserving measures. Additionally, counties passed ordinances requiring that farmers prevent blowing in their fields. Those not

complying might have their fields listed by the county, and the expense added to their property taxes. See Hurt, *The Dust Bowl*, 75–76.

18. Previous two sentences are most likely in Verna's hand.

19. Dyck referred to the privies as "Mrs. Northwest" and sometimes "Mrs. Southwest." She also referred to them as "the Joneses." There were probably two privies, one for men, and one for women.

20. On April 16, this item appeared in the local paper. "Carl Griswold and S. Bishop of the Menno neighborhood were in Syracuse Saturday. They say the wheat is about all gone in that area." *Syracuse Journal*, April 16, 1937, 9.

21. Dyck kept the family diary up to date, even though she was in Hutchinson. This is, perhaps, the best evidence that she thought of the diary not strictly as her own, but as a record of the family and farm.

22. The Dycks lived in the mountain time zone, while the Warners lived in the central time zone.

23. Iva Klassen and her husband, Adolph, were longtime residents of Lamont Township. Adolph Klassen was the son of a Mennonite farmer who had come to the county just after the turn of the century. "Mennonite Settlers Gave Menno Its Name in 1906," *Syracuse Journal*, May 21, 1937, 14.

24. Jackrabbits became a serious problem for farming families. They ate whatever was available, often seriously damaging crops and causing increased wind erosion. Locals resorted to "rabbit drives," events where they herded the animals into a confined space and clubbed them to death.

25. Louis Lahmeyer was a Lamont Township farmer who farmed 1,325 acres in 1936. He also was a traveling harvester who regularly visited the Dyck farm. State of Kansas, Statistical Rolls, 1936 (Topeka, Kans.: KSHS); Thelma Warner to Pamela Riney-Kehrberg, personal correspondence, July 24, 1997.

26. The only "carnation," or coronation, occurring in May 1937 was that of King George VI of England, who succeeded his brother, Edward VIII, who had abdicated in December 1936. George VI was crowned on May 12, 1937.

27. Suitcase farmers were those who farmed in the county but did not live there. Generally, they arrived to plant a crop, but did not return until harvesttime. In some localities, their lack of attention to their fields caused serious damage.

28. This series of dirt storms in late May 1937 delayed the dedication of the community building. Visibility was so poor that it was impossible for Kansas governor Walter Huxman to drive out to the site. It was, in the local paper's words, "a bitter disappointment." The community rescheduled the dedication for June 17, and the governor attended. "Menno Dedication Delayed by Dust," *Syracuse Journal*, May 28, 1937, 1; "Will Be Dedicated June 17th," *Syracuse Journal*, June 11, 1937, 1.

29. The Soil Conservation Service actively promoted contour plowing, or plowing with the natural curves of the land, as a means of preventing erosion. Hurt, _The Dust Bowl_, 76–78.

30. On June 21, 1937, Ervin wrote a postcard to his parents. It was probably much like the others they received, but is apparently the only one to survive. "Dear Folks Will write you a few lines to let you know I am well and hope you are the same. We got back to camp about eight oclock Monday night. We had two flat tires coming back. The second one 6 patches came off the tube. It rained here over the weekend. And rained again Monday night We didn't work Tuesday so now we will work Saturday. If you hear from my shoes write and tell me about them if I don't come home before The camp is about the same as always. I don't know for sure when I will be home again Don't know anything more to write so will close for this time. Ervin"

31. Van Trussel was a Lamont Township farmer, who worked more than a thousand acres of land. State of Kansas, Statistical Rolls, 1937 (Topeka, Kans.: KSHS).

32. During summer 1937, the men on the farm worked in shifts, and also worked from very early in the day until very late in the evening. Days could begin as early as two or three o'clock A.M., and end as late as midnight. Listing the land to keep it from blowing, as well as completing other farm chores, became an almost around-the-clock business.

33. During the 1930s, the federal government slaughtered surplus cattle in drought areas and distributed the meat to families receiving aid under federal relief programs. Local governments were also given food to distribute.

34. It is unclear if Henry Dyck had the neighbor's permission to work his land or not. However, the district court in Haskell County had upheld the right of a farmer to enter and work a neighbor's land if soil was blowing into neighboring fields. Riney-Kehrberg, _Rooted in Dust_, 122.

35. The 1936 agricultural census lists O. G. Jury as farming 320 acres of land. His address was Polk, Missouri. As a nonresident farmer, Jury's land may have been in particularly rough condition and blowing seriously. State of Kansas, Statistical Rolls, 1936 (Topeka, Kans.: KSHS).

36. The lack of locally grown produce did not keep women from canning during the dust bowl years. Families regularly purchased both fruit and vegetables grown in other states, such as Colorado, for preservation.

37. The Dycks had regular complaints about neighbors who were not as conscientious about working their land as they were.

38. Big Bow is a small town in Stanton County, almost directly south of the Dyck farm.

39. Henry's "bu. Pipe" was a bushel pipe, or large pipe.

40. Cecil Buhrer was a neighboring Lamont Township farmer who worked 870 acres of land. State of Kansas, Statistical Rolls, 1936 (Topeka, Kans.: KSHS).

41. The Warners were leaving one part of their family to join another. Cliff's parents had already moved to Oregon, and would help them to establish themselves there.

42. Tinnitus, or a persistent ringing in the ears, was another of Mary Dyck's medical problems. Sometimes she was almost deafened by it. She also experienced acute dizziness. She may have suffered from Ménière's disease, the symptoms of which include progressive deafness, tinnitus, and dizziness.

43. Much of the radio programming reaching southwestern Kansas came from distant locations. KOA broadcast from Denver, as did KLZ.

44. President Roosevelt's speech was a "fireside chat," discussing legislation to be recommended for an extraordinary session of Congress. He asked Congress to consider agricultural legislation, land use policy, and irrigation, among other issues. Rosenman, *Public Papers*, 1937, 429–438.

45. Despite terrible conditions in 1937, some farmers in Meade County (several counties east of Hamilton County) raised at least partially successful crops. Lawrence Svobida, a Meade County farmer, raised 6,000 bushels that year, at a little over 11 bushels to the acre. Lawrence Svobida, *Farming the Dust Bowl: A First-Hand Account from Kansas* (Lawrence: University Press of Kansas, 1986), 227.

46. Dyck often referred to Ervin as her "candy eater."

47. Kafir corn (also spelled kaffir) is a variety of sorghum grown in semi-arid areas. It was quite common on farms in southwestern Kansas, and used as grain, forage, and silage.

48. The Bullocs were a neighboring farming family. They were apparently quite small farmers, because they do not appear in the agricultural census. Thelma Warner to Pamela Riney-Kehrberg, personal correspondence, July 24, 1997.

4. A Little Snow, a Little Rain, and Hope: 1938

1. Irna Phillips acted in, and wrote for, a number of serial dramas. She was one of the most prolific radio writers of her day, writing for *Today's Children*, *Woman in White*, *The Guiding Light*, and several others. Thurber, *The Beast In Me and Other Animals* (London: Hamish Hamilton, 1949), 198–199.

2. This was President Roosevelt's annual message to Congress. He spoke on a number of issues, including military preparedness, agriculture, conservation, minimum wages, and taxation. Rosenman, *Public Papers*, 1938, 1–14.

3. Although the agricultural census in the 1920s showed that the Dycks had running water in their home, it is apparent from this entry that the extension of water pipes into the home came in 1938, more than a decade later.

4. This is another reference to purchasing products advertised on radio soap operas.

5. In this way, Dyck's writing was indeed a family journal, available to all family members. They were free to consult the notebook and discover what had happened in previous years. They were also free to add to its contents, although they rarely did.

6. In 1938, with so many family members on the West Coast, cooperative neighbors such as the Bishops were absolutely essential to the completion of major tasks on the farm.

7. What Dyck calls the "StrawCarrier Canves" was probably a canvas chute that carried straw into the threshing machine. Equipment catalog illustrations show just such a device as part of the machine's self-feeder. For an example see International Harvester Company of America, *McCormick-Deering Line General Catalog No. 23*, 61.

8. Dust bowl residents often claimed that they could identify from what direction a dust storm approached by the color of the dust.

9. Henry was packing the Warner's radio to be shipped to Oregon. Mary and Henry had been using this radio for some time instead of their own.

10. Mock weddings were common community entertainments in the 1930s and 1940s. These were often "womanless weddings," put on by the town's men, dressed in female attire. See Katherine Jellison, "From the Farmhouse Parlor to the Pink Barn: The Commercialization of Weddings in the Rural Midwest," *Iowa Heritage Illustrated* 77, no. 2 (summer 1996): 54–55.

11. One of the most common ways of attempting to "dust proof" a home was to seal all windows and other cracks with masking tape. Unfortunately, it was not completely successful, and made it impossible to open windows during hot weather.

12. Products bearing pictures of Canada's Dionne quintuplets, born in 1934, were common advertising premiums during the 1930s.

13. By February, the Dycks intended to make a trip to visit family in Oregon. This would involve an enormous amount of planning, since their livestock would have to be accommodated by neighbors during their trip.

14. One of the results of repeated dust storms was that fences drifted over with dust. Tumbleweeds and other debris would be blown into the fences, and the dirt would pile up around them, often completely burying them.

15. The Dycks were going to Hutchinson to retrieve Verna from her place of work. She would help them to get ready for their trip to Oregon, and accompany them there. This would be a family vacation.

16. Before leaving for Oregon, the Dycks sold some of their chickens. Others would be taken to the neighbors for the duration of their trip.

17. The cows would be at the Bishops' farm until the end of April.

18. The animals were not the only "farm equipment" that went elsewhere during the trip. The Dycks loaned out tractors and automobiles to neighbors during the weeks they were away.

19. It has been impossible to identify precisely what Dyck called a "curler." The best guess is that this was a family name for a spring-toothed harrow, which had curled tines and turned back soil in curls as well.

20. Lye soap, while it cleaned clothes quite efficiently, was notoriously hard on the user, leaving terribly dry skin and sores on the hands of those making and using it.

21. The Dycks often acted as a savings bank for their two younger children.

22. Although the Warners maintained a base at Dexter, Oregon, Cliff and the other men in the family often migrated to different locations looking for work. They would find jobs in the lumber industry.

23. On May 27, 1938, President Roosevelt spoke at Arthurdale, West Virginia. In his speech, the president spoke in favor of his tax reform bill, which would allow for greater taxation of large corporations. Samuel I. Rosenman, comp., *The Public Papers and Addresses of Franklin D. Roosevelt*, 1938 volume (New York: Macmillan, 1941), 355–365.

24. One solution to the problem of excessive static, a broken radio, or exhausted batteries was to use the car radio.

25. Dyck was commenting on the Joe Louis/Max Schmeling fight, which actually occurred on June 23, 1938. Louis knocked out Schmeling in one round.

26. Russian thistles grew in southwestern Kansas in abundance, in spite of the drought. When green, they could be harvested and salted to feed hungry cattle. When dry, they broke loose from the ground, becoming tumbleweeds.

27. Ways of the World was a quilt pattern.

28. While Cliff Warner worked for the logging industry, Thelma did what she could to add to the family income.

29. At this time, Garden City was the second largest city in southwestern Kansas, and the closest large city to the Dyck farm. Garden City is north and east of the farm.

30. On July 12, 1938, the president was in Colorado, on his way to California. He spoke in both Pueblo and Grand Junction. Pueblo was the most likely location from which the president's speech would have been broadcast. He briefly discussed the development of the Arkansas River, and the development of national unity. Rosenman, *Public Papers*, 1938 volume (New York: Macmillan, 1941), 452–456.

31. James C. Braddock, a Lamont Township farmer, died when he was hit by lightning while sitting on his tractor. He left a wife and four children. "James C. Braddock Killed by Lightening Wednesday P.M.," *Syracuse Journal*, July 15, 1938, 1.

32. Since this move to place Mrs. Braddock on the Board of Commissioners followed so closely upon her husband's death, the neighbors probably saw this as a way to provide an income to a local widow. Mrs. Braddock filled out her husband's term, and became Hamilton County's first woman com-

missioner. "Mrs. Braddock Appointed as County Commissioner," *Syracuse Journal,* July 22, 1938, 1.

33. This would be ground that the Dycks were not farming because they had enrolled it in government programs. Under provisions of the Agricultural Adjustment Act, the government paid them to leave many acres of their land idle.

34. In this Labor Day speech, President Roosevelt suggested that a farmer/worker alliance should exist. Rosenman, *Public Papers,* 1938, 512–520.

35. Changes in farm technology limited the number of workers necessary to perform any number of tasks on the farm. Some women's historians argue that this had the effect of devaluing both women and their work. See Katherine Jellison, *Entitled to Power: Farm Women and Technology, 1913–1963* (Chapel Hill: University of North Carolina Press).

36. Although times were hard, the Dycks seemed to weather the depression far better than many of their neighbors. Their purchase of yet another vehicle, this Chevrolet, is evidence of their relative prosperity.

37. Coolidge, Kansas, is a very small town west of Syracuse, just east of the Colorado state line.

38. In order to fight a grasshopper infestation, the government distributed poison to area farmers. This sticky mixture often included molasses, bran, and powerful poisons such as arsenic.

39. Five dollars spent on medical care would have been a significant sum to a migrant family, since many families spent less than that each week on groceries.

40. These speeches would have been made at the Munich Conference (September 29–30) about the crisis over German claims to the Sudetenland, part of Czechoslovakia. In addition to Adolph Hitler, Neville Chamberlain, Britain's prime minister, spoke to the conference. The Munich Conference confirmed that Czechoslovakia would lose the Sudetenland. Interestingly, from this point onward Dyck often referred to broadcasts about foreign affairs as "war news." Officially, World War II began in September 1939, and the United States joined in December 1941.

41. This is another example of the cooperative work done in the community. After finishing work on the Dyck farm, the men then moved on to help harvest at other local farms. Farmers generally harvested broomcorn by hand, and it required a great deal of labor. Harvesting other crops would have required cooperative labor also, since individuals often did not have all of the necessary equipment on their farms. In 1936, the last year of the decade that the recorder gathered this information, the state agricultural census listed seventy-nine farms in the township, with an average of 928 acres per farm. There were, however, only forty-six tractors, twenty-one combines, and two threshing machines in the township. State of Kansas, Statistical Rolls, 1936 (Topeka, Kans.: KSHS).

42. Dyck continued to enjoy radio dramas, particularly *Betty and Bob*.

43. By the end of the month, Ervin would be starting a new job. His "entagnisum" may very well have been over losing a position.

44. Losing her teeth had accomplished for Dyck what she could not do by dieting; she had lost a significant number of pounds.

45. At this point, the Dycks were not separating their own milk and selling cream periodically in town. Instead Pete Dyck, the "milk boy," arrived each morning for three quarts. It is unclear if he was collecting the milk for a creamery in town, or for home consumption. Later, they would resume separating their milk.

46. Ministers brought religious messages and Sunday services to many farm families via the radio. The radio bridged the large distances between farm families and churches more successfully than the automobile. Jellison, *Entitled to Power*, 153–154.

47. As usual, the hens had virtually ceased egg production for the winter months.

48. As the 1930s proceeded, the number of the Dyck's friends, relations, and neighbors living in California, Washington, and Oregon increased significantly.

49. Community Christmas trees were quite common in rural areas. Residents would either contribute gifts or money to be placed in or around the tree, and distributed to the area's children.

5. Dust and Hope Deferred: 1939

1. Zelda was Elmer Dyck's new wife. They married in fall 1938.

2. The reason for her depression was Verna's departure from home to return to work.

3. Fairly regularly Dyck substituted the word "dust" for the word "dusk."

4. One of the greatest concerns of farmers was that their government payments arrive on time. When payments were late, the operating expenses of the farm might not be met.

5. Like other dust bowl counties, Hamilton County had soil drifting resolutions that required farmers to prevent their fields from blowing. Riney-Kehrberg, *Rooted in Dust*, 122.

6. Henry Dyck had found a farm for the Warners in neighboring Kearny County.

7. Since a number of streams and creeks went dry during the drought, locals regularly went to them to measure the results of substantial rainstorms.

8. *Dodge City* was one of the most popular movies of 1939. Although it was made in California, the movie premiered in Dodge City, Kansas, much to the delight of local residents.

9. Throughout the 1930s, wheat prices remained low. In 1939, the U.S. Department of Agriculture listed the price for wheat as 67.6 cents per bushel. At the elevator, most farmers received less. Although the price was less than the farmers hoped, it was a great improvement over the 1932 price, 38.2 cents per bushel. U.S. Department of Agriculture, *Agricultural Statistics 1940*, 10.

10. Animals that gorge on grain may become foundered. This is a common name for laminitis, an inflammation of the feet that causes severe lameness.

11. The *Unity Inspiration*, broadcast from Unity Village in Kansas City, was a religious program and would become one of Dyck's favorites. When a segment was particularly interesting, she wrote away for the tracts Unity Village published. The Unity broadcast often conflicted with the morning news. When Henry was in the house, his desire to listen to the news generally prevailed.

12. The already tense situation in Europe had become a crisis with the German invasion of Poland on September 1, 1939. World War II had begun.

13. President Roosevelt gave this fireside chat about the United States' position on the war. He stated, "I hope the United States will keep out of this war. I believe that it will." Rosenman, *Public Papers*, 1939, 460–464.

14. The dust storms scoured the earth bare and made it easier for people to hunt for arrowheads. Many families entertained themselves this way.

15. The Kansas State Fair was held annually in Hutchinson, Kansas.

16. The residents of Kearny County built their new courthouse with the help of Works Progress Administration funds. This was only one of many new courthouses and other public buildings the WPA funded in southwestern Kansas during the 1930s.

17. Gandy dancers, or hoppers, were laborers in railroad section gangs.

6. Blizzards, Rain, and Bounty: 1940

1. When Dyck commented that she had "raged" or "ragged," she had prepared rags for incorporation into rag rugs.

2. Getting groceries "from the relief" is a reference to commodity distribution by the county or federal government. Families received staples such as beans, peanut butter, and lard.

3. This was most likely a Farm Security Administration rehabilitation loan. The FSA granted loans to farmers whose operations could become self-sustaining, given access to cash grants. The FSA also emphasized mixed farming, rather than reliance on a single crop. Hurt, *Dust Bowl*, 95.

4. Dr. John R. Brinkley was a staple on Kansas radio. He was a medical quack who promoted the transplantation of goat glands into humans to cure impotence. In 1930 and 1932, Brinkley also ran for governor. He was

a populist of sorts, promoting free textbooks in schools, tax equalization, free health care, and highway improvement, among other causes. Kenneth S. Davis, *Kansas: A Bicentennial History* (New York: W. W. Norton, 1976), 183–185.

5. Joe Louis fought Arturo Godoy, and won in fifteen rounds.

6. This infant did not survive. The Warners would complete their family with the birth of Garry Lee in 1943 and Larry Dean in 1945.

7. Upon being released from the hospital, Thelma came to stay with the Dycks.

8. Dyck had very serious problems with vertigo throughout summer and fall 1940. At times, her diary would become very sparse, because she was unable to write for any sustained period of time. She was also unable to do her chores easily, and received help from her daughters, her husband, and hired help.

9. Liberal, Kansas, was to the south and east of the Dyck farm, and was the third largest town in southwestern Kansas after Dodge City and Garden City.

10. Jack Goodspeed was the Warners' hired man.

11. This was the Dycks' first refrigerator, powered not by electricity, but by gasoline or kerosene. It was not as efficient as the refrigerator that they would buy after installing electricity. That one would make ice, and kept the food much colder.

12. Part of the FSA program was to diversify a farm's crops. The Warners grew various types of produce for home consumption and for sale.

13. The Warners had a telephone, while the Dycks did not. Telephone service would come very late to the outlying areas of rural Hamilton County.

14. The Dycks went for a short trip to Halstead, Kansas. Mary, however, never explained why they had gone.

15. Sudan grass was a common, drought-resistant feed crop.

16. Wendell Wilkie was the Republican candidate for president in 1940.

17. In 1940, under the provisions of the Burke-Wadsworth Act, the United States began its first peacetime draft in anticipation of U.S. participation in World War II.

18. The Hildebrands were related by marriage to Mary Dyck's family. Two of her sisters had married Hildebrands.

19. The Dycks were going to Minneola, a town nearly 100 miles away, to see Dr. Schlitenz (spelling varies). Dr. Schlitenz was an unlicensed medical practitioner. According to Thelma Warner, he was a religious healer, commonly referred to as a "bone [doctor] they are like our chiropractors only much better. . . . Mother had a horrible problem for dizzyness and made her terribly sick. She went to all the M.D.s around. No one helped but his manipulations cured the problem and never came back." Thelma Warner to Pamela Riney-Kehrberg, personal correspondence, July 24, 1997.

20. In 1940, Franklin Roosevelt was elected for his third term as president.

Although Dyck does not indicate her political preference, she more than likely voted for Roosevelt.

21. This is probably a reference to the popular quilt pattern, Sunbonnet Sue.
22. This is a reference to the Dresden Plate quilt pattern.
23. Verna soon began a job at the Elite Beauty Shoppe in Syracuse, Kansas. Mrs. Mary Holmes had operated the business since summer 1938. Advertisement, *Syracuse Journal*, August 26, 1938, 6.
24. This was a fireside chat on national security, in which the president declared that the United States should be "the great arsenal of democracy." Rosenman, *Public Papers*, 1940, 633–644.

7. *The End of an Era: 1941*

1. Because the grit from dust storms was so fine, it sifted into every nook and cranny of the house. The Dyck's attic, like many others in the area, had collected a liberal coating of blown dirt. Families that did not clean their attics on a regular basis risked the collapse of ceilings into the rooms below.
2. Although Henry and Mary Dyck and their children were thoroughly Americanized, the older generation was not. In the period up to and into World War II, many German speakers were criticized for their use of their native language.
3. Mercurochrome was used to disinfect wounds.
4. The Dycks did not keep their own bulls, but bred their cows with neighbors' bulls.
5. The Dycks were embarking on a home improvement plan that would last into the 1940s. This included adding rooms to their home, enlarging the basement, and adding an electric generator.
6. Mary's sister, Lizzie Hildebrand, had come from Inman, Kansas, for a visit.
7. The McCormick-Deering company manufactured this model of tractor.
8. Bringing home a hired girl is an indication of just how poor Mary's health was in spring 1941. Neither Dyck was feeling up to the work on the farm.
9. Charles Lindbergh, a national hero because of his flying exploits in the 1920s and 1930s, became a very controversial figure in the years leading up to World War II. His participation in the America First Committee, which actively campaigned against American involvement in the war, caused enormous friction with President Roosevelt. In April 1941, he resigned his commission as a colonel in the Army Air Corps Reserve. Wayne S. Cole, *Charles A. Lindbergh and the Battle against American Intervention in World War II* (New York: Harcourt Brace Jovanovich, 1974), 131.
10. The Dycks, like many farmers, did not always raise their own chicks from eggs. Sometimes they purchased chicks by mail order.

1. Riney-Kehrberg, *Rooted in Dust*, 165–182.
2. Evidence for the relative prosperity of the 1940s is in the Chattel Mortgage Records of Hamilton County, In 1942, the family borrowed nearly $3,500, evidently for an addition and electric wiring for their home. In 1943, they repaid this debt, in full, a year before the note came due. Hamilton County, Kansas, Chattel Mortgage Records, Register of Deeds Office, Hamilton County Courthouse, Syracuse, Kansas, 1942.
3. "What to Do with the Bumper Wheat Crop a Major Problem," *Syracuse Journal*, May 30, 1941, 1.
4. See Pamela Riney-Kehrberg, "'Broke in Spirits': Death, Depression, and Endurance Through Writing," *Frontiers: A Journal of Women's Studies* 17, no. 2 (1996): 70–86.

BIBLIOGRAPHY

Newspapers

Hamilton County Republican and Syracuse News
Inman Review
Syracuse Journal

Government Documents

Hamilton County, Kansas. Chattel Mortgage Records. Register of Deeds
  Office, Hamilton County Courthouse, Syracuse, Kansas, 1929.
———. Register of Deeds Office, Hamilton County Courthouse, Syracuse,
  Kansas, 1942.
Hamilton County, Kansas. Transfer Records, Register of Deeds Office,
  Hamilton County Courthouse, Syracuse, Kansas.
Kansas State Board of Agriculture. *Biennial Report of the State Board of*
  Agriculture, vols. 27, 32. Topeka: Kansas State Printing Plant, 1931, 1941.
———. *Report of the Kansas State Board of Agriculture for the Quarter Ending*
  December, 1905. Topeka: Kansas State Board of Agriculture, 1906.
———. *Report of the Kansas State Board of Agriculture for the Quarter Ending*
  December, 1910. Topeka: Kansas State Board of Agriculture, 1911.
———. *Report of the Kansas State Board of Agriculture for the Quarter Ending*
  June, 1911. Topeka: Kansas State Board of Agriculture, 1911.
———. *Report of the Kansas State Board of Agriculture for the Quarter Ending*
  September, 1916. Topeka: Kansas State Board of Agriculture, 1916.
Kansas State Census. Vol. 177, Lamont Township, Hamilton County, 1905.
Kansas State Census. Vol. 110, Lamont Township, Hamilton County, 1915.
State of Kansas, Statistical Rolls, Hamilton County, Lamont Township,
  1918–1955, Archives Division, Kansas State Historical Society (KSHS
  hereafter), Topeka, Kansas.
U.S. Department of Agriculture. *Agricultural Statistics 1940*. Washington: United
  States Government Printing Office, 1940.

———. *Attitudes of Rural People toward Radio Service: A Nation-Wide Survey of Farm and Small Town People.* Washington, D.C.: 1946.

U.S. Department of Commerce, Bureau of the Census. *Thirteenth Census of the United States, 1910,* Lamont Township, Hamilton County, Kansas.

———. *15th Census of the United States: 1930 Population,* vol. 3, pt. 1. Washington, D.C.: United States Government Printing Office, 1932.

———. *16th Census of the United States: 1940 Population,* vol. 2, Characteristics of the Population, pt. 3. Washington, D.C.: United States Government Printing Office, 1943.

Unpublished Archival Documents

File 1301, Box 55, "History of Syracuse, KS Mennonite Church." File 1301, Box 55, Mennonite Library and Archives, Bethel College, North Newton, Kansas.

Articles and Chapters

Bruce, Norma J. "Serials for the Farm Family of 80 Years Ago." *Serials Review* 21, no. 3 (1995): 1–22.

Faragher, John Mack. "History from the Inside-Out: Writing the History of Women in Rural America." *American Quarterly* 33, no. 5 (winter 1981): 535–557.

Fink, Deborah. "Sidelines and Moral Capital: Women on Nebraska Farms in the 1930s." In Wava G. Haney and Jane B. Knowles, *Women and Farming: Changing Roles, Changing Structures,* 55–70. Boulder, Colo.: Westview Press, 1988.

Fink, Deborah, and Alicia Carriquiry. "Having Babies or Not: Household Composition and Fertility in Rural Iowa and Nebraska, 1900–1910." *Great Plains Quarterly* 12 (summer 1992): 157–168.

Flora, Cornelia Butler, and Jan L. Flora. "Structure of Agriculture and Women's Culture on the Great Plains." *Great Plains Quarterly* 8 (fall 1988): 195–205.

Haywood, C. Robert. "The Great Depression: Two Kansas Diaries." *Great Plains Quarterly* 18, no. 1 (winter 1998): 23–38.

Herzog, Herta. "What Do We Really Know about Daytime Serial Listeners." In Paul F. Lazarsfeld and Frank N. Stanton, *Radio Research 1942–1943,* 3–33, New York: Essential Books, 1944; reprint ed., New York: Arno Press, 1979.

Jellison, Katherine. "From the Farmhouse Parlor to the Pink Barn: The

Commercialization of Weddings in the Rural Midwest." *Iowa Heritage Illustrated* 77, no. 2 (summer 1996): 50–65.

———. "Women and Technology on the Great Plains, 1910–1940." *Great Plains Quarterly* 8 (summer 1988): 145–157.

Lensink, Judy Nolte. "Expanding the Boundaries of Criticism: The Diary as Female Autobiography." *Women's Studies* 14, no. 1 (1987): 39–51.

Lewis, Tom. "'A Godlike Presence': The Impact of Radio on the 1920s and 1930s." *OAH Magazine of History* (spring 1992): 26–33.

Lindgren, H. Elaine. "Ethnic Women Homesteading on the Plains of North Dakota." *Great Plains Quarterly* 9 (summer 1989): 157–173.

Pickle, Linda Schelbitzki. "Rural German-Speaking Women in Early Nebraska and Kansas: Ethnicity as a Factor in Frontier Adaptation." *Great Plains Quarterly* 9 (fall 1989): 239–251.

Rathge, Richard W. "Women's Contribution to the Family Farm." *Great Plains Quarterly* 9 (winter 1989): 36–47.

Riley, Glenda. "Women's Responses to the Challenges of Plains Living." *Great Plains Quarterly* 9 (summer 1989): 174–184.

Riney-Kehrberg, Pamela. "'Broke in Spirits': Death, Depression, and Endurance through Writing." *Frontiers: A Journal of Women's Studies* 17, no. 2 (1996): 70–86.

———. "From the Horse's Mouth: Dust Bowl Farmers and their Solutions to the Problem of Aridity." *Agricultural History* 6, no. 2 (spring 1992): 137–150.

———. "Hard Times, Hungry Years: Failure of the Poor Relief in Southwestern Kansas, 1930–1933." *Kansas History* 15, no. 3 (autumn 1992): 154–167.

———. "In God We Trusted, In Kansas We Busted . . . Again." *Agricultural History* 63, no. 2 (spring 1989): 187–201.

———. "The Limits of Community: Martha Friesen of Hamilton County, Kansas." In Wendy Hamand Venet and Lucy Eldersveld Murphy, eds., *Midwestern Women: Work, Community, and Leadership at the Crossroads*, 76–91. Bloomington: Indiana University Press, 1997.

———. "The Radio Diary of Mary Dyck, 1936–1955: The Listening Habits of a Kansas Farm Woman." *Journal of Radio Studies* 5, no. 2 (August 1998): 22–35.

———. "Separation and Sorrow: A Farm Woman's Life, 1935–1941." *Agricultural History* 67, no. 2 (spring 1993): 185–196.

———. "Women, Technology, and Rural Life: Some Recent Literature." *Technology and Culture* 38, no. 4 (October 1997): 942–953.

Schwieder, Dorothy, and Deborah Fink. "Plains Women: Rural Life in the 1930s." *Great Plains Quarterly* 8 (spring 1988): 79–88.

Vandegrift, F. L. "New Mennonite Settlement in Kansas." *The Earth* 7, no. 10 (October 1910): 8.

Arnold, Eleanor, ed. *Voices of American Homemakers.* Bloomington: Indiana University Press, 1985.

Bader, Robert Smith. *Prohibition in Kansas: A History.* Lawrence: University Press of Kansas, 1986.

Bender, Thomas. *Community and Social Change in America.* New Brunswick, N.J.: Rutgers University Press, 1978.

Beville, H. M., Jr. *Social Stratification of the Radio Audience: A Study Made for the Princeton Radio Research Project.* New York: National Broadcasting Company, 1940.

Cole, Wayne S. *Charles A. Lindbergh and the Battle against American Intervention in World War II.* New York: Harcourt Brace Jovanovich, 1974.

Davis, Kenneth S. *Kansas: A Bicentennial History.* New York: W. W. Norton, 1976.

Edwards, Floyd, ed. *Hamilton County, Kansas, History.* Syracuse, Kansas: Hamilton County Historical Society, 1979.

Engbrecht, Dennis D. *The Americanization of a Rural Immigrant Church: The General Conference Mennonites in Central Kansas, 1874–1939.* New York: Garland, 1990.

Fairbanks, Carol, and Bergine Haakenson. *Writings of Farm Women 1840–1940: An Anthology.* New York: Garland, 1990.

Fink, Deborah. *Agrarian Women: Wives and Mothers in Rural Nebraska 1880–1940.* Chapel Hill: University of North Carolina Press, 1992.

———. *Open Country, Iowa: Rural Women, Tradition, and Change.* Albany: State University of New York Press, 1986.

Haury, David. *Prairie People: A History of the Western District Conference.* Newton, Kansas: Faith and Life Press, 1981.

Hurt, R. Douglas. *The Dust Bowl: An Agricultural and Social History.* Chicago: Nelson-Hall, 1981.

International Harvester Company of America. *McCormick-Deering Line General Catalog No. 23.* Chicago: International Harvester Company, n.d.

Ise, John. *Sod and Stubble: The Story of a Kansas Farm.* Lincoln: University of Nebraska Press, 1967.

Jellison, Katherine. *Entitled to Power: Farm Women and Technology, 1913–1963.* Chapel Hill: University of North Carolina Press, 1993.

Lensink, Judy Nolte. *'A Secret to be Burried': The Diary and Life of Emily Hawley Gillespie, 1858–1888.* Iowa City: University of Iowa Press, 1989.

Low, Ann Marie. *Dust Bowl Diary.* Lincoln: University of Nebraska Press, 1984.

Neth, Mary. *Preserving the Family Farm: Women, Community and the Foundations of Agribusiness in the Midwest, 1900–1940.* Baltimore: Johns Hopkins University Press, 1995.

Riley, Glenda. *The Female Frontier: A Comparative View of Women on the Prairie and the Plains.* Lawrence: University Press of Kansas, 1988.

Riney-Kehrberg, Pamela. *Rooted in Dust: Surviving Drought and Depression in Southwestern Kansas.* Lawrence: University Press of Kansas, 1994.

Rosenman, Samuel I., comp. *The Public Papers and Addresses of Franklin D. Roosevelt.* New York: MacMillan, 1941.

Saloutos, Theodore. *The American Farmer and the New Deal.* Ames: Iowa State University Press, 1982.

Svobida, Lawrence. *An Empire of Dust* (Caxton, Idaho: Caxton Printers, 1940). Reprint edition, *Farming the Dust Bowl: A First-Hand Account from Kansas* (Lawrence: University Press of Kansas, 1986).

Thurber, James. *The Beast in Me and Other Animals.* London: Hamish Hamilton, 1949.

Wiatt, Iman C. "Diaries of Iman C. Wiatt," Kearny County Historical Society, *History of Kearny County, Kansas*, vol. 2. North Newton, Kansas: Mennonite Press, 1973.

Woods, Roberta, comp. "Property Owners of McPherson County, Kansas, 1884." (N.p.: n.p., 1970), 82.